Eastern Han (AD 25-220) Tombs in Sichuan

Xuan Chen

Archaeopress Archaeology

ARCHAEOPRESS PUBLISHING LTD
Gordon House
276 Banbury Road
Oxford OX2 7ED

www.archaeopress.com

ISBN 978 1 78491 216 1
ISBN 978 1 78491 217 8 (e-Pdf)

© Archaeopress and X Chen 2015

All rights reserved. No part of this book may be reproduced, stored in retrieval system,
or transmitted, in any form or by any means, electronic, mechanical, photocopying or otherwise,
without the prior written permission of the copyright owners.

Printed in England by Oxuniprint, Oxford
This book is available direct from Archaeopress or from our website www.archaeopress.com

Contents

List of figures ii

Preface v

Chapter 1 Introduction 1
    1. Major Burial Types in Eastern Han 4
    2. Development of Burial Form in the Han Dynasty (206 BC-AD 220) 7
    3. The Social Background 10
    4. Textual Sources 15
    5. Archaeological Discoveries 16
    6. Literature Review 20
    7. Research Approaches 21
    8. Chapter Outline 22

Chapter 2 Tomb Structure 23
    1. Archaeological Evidence 23
    2. Stone as Building Material 24
    3. Wooden Architecture as Framework of Representation 37
    4. Important Structure for Ritual and Sacrifice 43
    5. Conclusion 45

Chapter 3 Pictorial Carvings 46
    1. Pictorial Carvings in Stone and Brick Chamber Tombs:
    Communication between Sichuan and East China 46
    2. Pictorial Carvings in the Shrine 60
    3. Pictorial Carvings and Memorial in the Cliff Tomb 61
    4. Pictorial carvings and the Representation of Ritual in the Cliff Tomb 68
    5. Conclusion 73

Chapter 4 Burial Objects 75
    1. Plan of Burial Objects 75
    2. The Money Tree 75
    3. Stone Coffin 84
    4. Conclusion 95

Chapter 5 Conclusion 96

Bibliography 97

Appendix 1 Stories of Filial Sons and Eminent Men and Women Carved in the Cliff tombs in Sichuan 107

Appendix 2 Eastern Han High Officials of the Areas Outside Sichuan from the Sichuan Area 111

Appendix 3 Eastern Han Cliff Tombs Excavated in the Sichuan Area 113

List of Figures

Figure 1. Distribution of the cliff tombs in the Sichuan Basin 2
Figure 2. Distribution of the major Eastern Han tombs..2
Figure 3. Outside the tomb Zijingwan M3 in Santai 3
Figure 4. Entrance to the tomb Zijingwan M3 in Santai 3
Figure 5. Plan of the tomb Zijingwan M3 in Santai...3
Figure 6. Ceiling of the rear chamber of the tomb Zijingwan M3 in Santai...4
Figure 7. A column and a low wall at the entrance to a side chamber of the tomb Zijingwan M3
   in Santai..4
Figure 8. A crane carved in the doorway of the tomb Zijingwan M3 in Santai.......................................4
Figure 9. Stoves carved in a side chamber of the tomb Zijingwan M3 in Santai 4
Figure 10. The Zengjiabao brick chamber tomb M1 and M2 under a burial mound in Chengdu............5
Figure 11. Panoramic view of the Dahuting tomb M2 in Mixian in Henan...5
Figure 12. Panoramic view of the front chamber of the Yi'nan tomb in Shandong 5
Figure 13. An ideal plan of an Eastern Han cemetery with the *que* pillars..6
Figure 14. The Yang's family *que* pillar in Jiajiang in Sichuan 7
Figure 15. Elevation of the Mawangdui tomb in Changsha in Hunan..8
Figure 16. Elevation and plan of the Feng Ruren's tomb in Nanyang in Henan.......................................8
Figure 17. The tomb of the king of Guangling in Gaoyou in Jiangsu..9
Figure 18. The Beidongshan tomb in Xuzhou in Jiangsu...9
Figure 19. Powerful families recorded in the Huayang guo zhi. 14
Figure 20. Pottery brick relief of an Eastern Han courtyard house...18
Figure 21. Rubbings of two guards holding weapon from the Shiziwan cliff tomb in Leshan 19
Figure 22. Rubbings of two archers from the cliff tombs in Santai..19
Figure 23. Plan of the cliff tomb Tianhuishan no. 3 in Chengdu...20
Figure 24. Categories of cliff tomb structures 24
Figure 25. Major features of the cliff tombs in different areas of Sichuan. 25
Figure 26. Illustration of the façade of the cliff tomb Lijiagou M355 in Pengshan 26
Figure 27. The Qigedong cliff tombs in Changning in Sichuan 27
Figure 28. Planned cliff tombs at Qijiang in Santai 28
Figure 29. Plan of the site containing the Taliangzi cliff tombs M1-M6 in Zhongjiang 28
Figure 30. Plan of the Mahao I M1 in Leshan 31
Figure 31. The *que* pillars of Gao Yi in Ya'an in Sichuan 32
Figure 32. Plan of the Bailinpo M1 in Santai..32
Figure 33. Plan of the Shiziwan no. 1 in Leshan 33
Figure 34. Plan of the tomb Dongzipai M1 in Santai 34
Figure 35. Bottom view of the Bailinpo M1 in Santai..34
Figure 36. Plan of the Dayunao tomb no. 76 in Qingshen in Sichuan 35
Figure 37. Plan of the site of the cliff tombs M1, M2, M4 and M5 at Tongbankou 36
Figure 38. Plan of the Mahao II M99 in Leshan 36
Figure 39. The rear pillar in the Hujiawan M1 in Santai 38
Figure 40. Illustration of the entrance of the Douyafanggou M166 in Pengshan..................................39
Figure 41. A pillar with the bow-shaped icon and other auspicious images
   in the Zhaizishan M530 in Pengshan..39
Figure 42. A column in a burial chamber of the Bailinpo M1 in Santai 40
Figure 43. View of the tomb Hujiawan M1 in Santai 40
Figure 44. A ceiling in the tomb Zijingwan M3 in Santai 41
Figure 45. Paintings of the sun and moon on the ceiling of the Buqianqiu tomb
   in Luoyang in Henan..41
Figure 46. Rubbing and illustration of an Eastern Han pictorial stone illustrating funerary scene
   from Weishan in Shandong 43
Figure 47. The tomb door with inscription from the cliff tomb HM3 in Xindu in Sichuan 44
Figure 48. Panoramic view of the Dahuting tomb no. 1 in Mixian in Henan..48
Figure 49. Elevation and plan of Zengjiabao no. 2 in Chengdu in Sichuan 49
Figure 50. Rubbings of the reliefs on the rear walls of the two rear chambers of
   Zengjiabao no. 1 in Chengdu...49
Figure 51. Front side of the door of Zengjiabao no. 2 in Chengdu..50
Figure 52. Illustration of the front door of the central chamber of the Hechuan tomb in Sichuan 50
Figure 53. Plan and elevation of the Hechuan tomb in Sichuan..50
Figure 54. Rubbing of the lintel of the door of the rear chamber of the Hechuan tomb
   in Sichuan..51
Figure 55. Illustration of Fu Xi holding the sun carved on one of the door posts of the door
   to the rear chamber of the Hechuan tomb 51
Figure 56. Illustration of the carving of a squatting sheep in the niche of the front chamber of
   the Hechuan tomb 51
Figure 57. Rubbing of an immortal holding the lingzhi carved in the Hechuan tomb in Sichuan........51
Figure 58. Illustration of a flute playing figure carved in the Hechuan tomb in Sichuan.....................51
Figure 59. Rubbing of a bird holding a fish in the Hechuan tomb in Sichuan.......................................52

Figure 60. Rubbing of a flute playing figure carved in a cliff tomb in Zhongjiang in Sichuan 52
Figure 61. A bird holding a fish carved in the cliff tomb Taliangzi M3 in Zhongjiang in Sichuan 52
Figure 62. Illustration of the entrance of the cliff tomb Zhaizishan no. 535 in Pengshan 53
Figure 63. Illustration of the door of the cliff tomb Qigedong M1 in Changning in Sichuan 53
Figure 64. The scene of Jing Ke assassinating the king of Qin carved on the wall of
　　　　　the front hall of the Mahao I M1 in Leshan 54
Figure 65. Plan and elevation of the Cangshan tomb in Shandong..54
Figure 66. Carvings on the western wall of the main chamber of the Cangshan tomb
　　　　　in Shandong 55
Figure 67. Carvings on the eastern wall of the main chamber of the Cangshan tomb
　　　　　in Shandong 55
Figure 68. Rubbing of the stone engravings in the niche on the eastern wall of
　　　　　the main chamber in the Cangshan tomb in Shandong..56
Figure 69. Rubbing of the front side of the lintel of the door of the Cangshan tomb
　　　　　in Shandong 57
Figure 70. Rubbing of the back side of the lintel of the door of the Cangshan tomb
　　　　　in Shandong 57
Figure 71. Schematic drawing of the middle chamber of the Yi'nan tomb 58
Figure 72. Carriage procession on the northern wall of the middle chamber of the Yi'nan tomb.......58
Figure 73. The end of the procession and the *ji* table on the southern wall of
　　　　　the middle chamber of the Yi'nan tomb 58
Figure 74. Rubbing of the relief on a door post of the entrance to the rear chambers of
　　　　　the Yi'nan tomb in Shandong..59
Figure 75. Reconstruction of the Wu Liang shrine by Jiang Yingju and Wu Wenqi................................60
Figure 76. Pictorial carvings in the Wu Liang shrine 61
Figure 77. Carving and rubbing of the story of Yuan Gu (left) in the front hall of the cliff tomb
　　　　　Shiziwan no. 1 in Leshan. After Tang Changshou 2010: fig. 4. 62
Figure 78. Rubbing of the three stories on filial sons carved in the front hall
　　　　　of the cliff tomb Shiziwan no. 1 in Leshan..62
Figure 79. Plan of the Taliangzi M3 in Zhongjiang 65
Figure 80. A side chamber with mural paintings on the tomb occupant's family history
　　　　　in the Taliangzi M3 in Zhongjiang 65
Figure 81. Expanded diagram of the side chamber in the Taliangzi M3 in Zhongjiang 65
Figure 82. Picture no.5 in the side chamber in the Taliangzi M3 in Zhongjiang...................................66
Figure 83. Illustration of the carvings on the rear wall of the shrine of Zhu Wei in Jinxiang
　　　　　in Shandong 67
Figure 84. Illustration of the carving of the tomb occupant from the Qianliangtai tomb
　　　　　in Zhucheng in Shandong 67
Figure 85. Mural painting on a dining scene in a side chamber of the Bailinpo M1 in Santai 67
Figure 86. Rubbing of the scene on sacrifice at tomb door carved in the Yi'nan tomb
　　　　　in Shandong 68
Figure 87. Plan of the façade of the seven caves (the Qigedong cliff tombs) in Changning
　　　　　in Sichuan..69
Figure 88. Entrance to the Xiaoba II M80 in Leshan..70
Figure 89. A kissing couple carved on the tomb door lintel of the cliff tomb M550 in Pengshan 71
Figure 90. A Buddha image on the door lintel of the Mahao I M1 in Leshan.......................................71
Figure 91. Dancing foreigners carved in the Taliangzi M3 in Zhongjiang...72
Figure 92. Entrance to the coffin chamber of the Taliangzi M3 in Zhongjiang.....................................73
Figure 93. Plan of the cliff tomb Tujing no. 5 in Zhongxian in Sichuan 76
Figure 94. Money tree from the Hejiashan M2 in Mianyang in Sichuan 76
Figure 95. Bronze mold for the casting of the Han *wuzhu* coin...78
Figure 96. Bronze mould for the casting of the *wuzhu* coin from Xichang in Sichuan and
　　　　　products of the *wuzhu* coins from Xichang 79
Figure 97. Rubbing of the relief on one side of the stone coffin no. 3 from Jianyang
　　　　　in Sichuan, with the inscription of "*zhuzhu* 鑄株" 79
Figure 98. Rubbing of a pottery money tree base illustrating the scene of collecting coins
　　　　　from Yong'an in Santai 81
Figure 99. Rubbing of a pictorial tomb brick illustrating the Queen Mother of the West and
　　　　　her attendants from Xinfan in Chengdu 82
Figure 100. A money tree branch illustrating the Queen Mother of the West and
　　　　　her attendants from Gaocao in Xichang in Sichuan 82
Figure 101. A money tree trunk with the image of a Buddha from the cliff tomb Hejiashan M1
　　　　　in Mianyang..83
Figure 102. A money tree base illustrating a seated Buddha from Pengshan 83
Figure 103. The stone coffin of Wang Hui from Lushan in Sichuan 84
Figure 104. Rubbing of a coffin wall from Dayi in Sichuan 85
Figure 105. Rubbing of a coffin wall from Xinjin in Sichuan 86
Figure 106. Rubbing of a coffin from Xinjin in Sichuan...86
Figure 107. Carvings and rubbing of one side of a stone coffin from Chengdu...................................87
Figure 108. Rubbing of the relief on one end of the stone coffin of Wang Hui from Lushan
　　　　　in Sichuan..87

Figure 109. A built-in coffin in the Tiantaishan tomb in Santai 88
Figure 110. Plan of the cliff tomb HM3 in Xindu in Sichuan 89
Figure 111. A pictorial stone coffin from the cliff tomb HM3 in Xindu in Sichuan 90
Figure 112. Plan of the cliff tomb at Guitoushan in Jianyang in Sichuan 90
Figure 113. Rubbing of the relief on one side of the stone coffin no. 2 from Jianyang in Sichuan 91
Figure 114. One side of a built-in coffin in a cliff tomb in Xinjin in Sichuan 92
Figure 115. Rubbing of the relief on one side of a stone coffin from Shehong in Sichuan.
   The story on Qiu Hu's wife is on the left. The story on Ji Zha is on the right 92
Figure 116. Rubbing of the relief on one side of the stone coffin no. 5 from Xinjin in Sichuan 93
Figure 117. Rubbing of the relief on one side of the stone coffin no. 7 from Xinjin in Sichuan 93

Preface

This study concerns the factors underlying the popularity of the cliff tomb, a local burial form in the Sichuan Basin in China in the Eastern Han dynasty (AD 25-220). The development of the cliff tomb was held in a complex set of connections to the development of the burial forms, and existed through links to many other contemporary burial forms, the brick chamber tomb, the stone chamber tomb, and the princely rock-cut tomb. These connections and links formed to a large extent through the incorporation of the Sichuan area into the empire which began in the 4th century BC. It was in this context, a series of factors contributed to the formation and popularity of the cliff tombs in Sichuan. The hilly topography and the soft sandstone, easy to cut, provided the natural condition for the development of the cliff tombs. The decision to make use of this natural condition was affected by many factors rooted in the social background. The inherent nature of the cliff tomb structure was fully explored, which was then followed by a series of corresponding innovations on the pictorial carvings and the burial objects. The meaning of a continuous family embedded in the cliff tomb structure was explored, as the construction of the tomb was the result of the continuous endeavour from many generations of the family, and the physical form of the cliff tomb was a metaphor for a prosperous family. Following this intention of the tomb occupants underlying the design of the cliff tomb structure, the pictorial carvings and the burial objects in the cliff tomb were made adaptations to make the cliff tomb an embodiment of relations between different family members and different generations.

This publication is a modified version of my DPhil thesis completed at the University of Oxford in 2014. Above all, I would like to thank my supervisor Professor Dame Jessica Rawson for her tremendously hard work and patience over the years of this study, and for guiding me in my academic research. I would also like to thank Professor Helena Hamerow, Dr Peter Ditmanson, Dr Frances Wood, Dr Janet DeLaine, Dr Carol Michaelson and Dr Robert Chard for their valuable suggestions during my transfer and confirmation interviews and in the final viva.

I have received financial support at various stages during my study and writing. The Travel Grant from Merton College, the Meyerstein Awards for Archaeological Research and the Au Ping Reyes Awards allowed my fieldwork in Sichuan, Shandong and Jiangsu.

Access to important archaeological sites and textual materials has been generously given by the following: Director Tang Guangxiao from the Mianyang Museum, Director Mao Jianjun and Wu Junmei from the Santai Archaeological Institute, Director Yue Huagang from the Qingshen Archaeological Institute, Director Zhou Xiaochuan from the Yibin Archaeological Institute, Director Wu Tianwen from the Pengshan Archaeological Institute, Director Lu Genzhu from the Changning Archaeological Institute, Liang Guannan from the Chongqing China Three Gorges Museum and Director Liang Yong from the Xuzhou Art Gallery of Stone Sculpture of Han Dynasty.

My eternal thanks go to my parents-without whom this study would never have been finished.

Chapter 1
Introduction

The study is concerned with one of the two major burial forms in Eastern Han (AD 25-220) Sichuan, the cliff tomb, which is carved horizontally into the hillsides and the cliffs along the riverbanks, modelled on the dwelling for the living (figure 1 and 2).[1] Cliff tombs vary in scale from several metres to more than thirty metres in length and have various local features within the Sichuan Basin in southwest China. A cliff tomb usually contains one or more burial chambers. Some cliff tombs are furnished with carved stone coffin beds, stoves and niches and may also display architectural elements resembling timber architecture. In some cases, the walls of the cliff tombs are decorated with carved images.

For example, the cliff tomb Zijingwan 紫荊灣 M3 in Santai 三臺 in Sichuan is cut into the hillside, with a corridor, three main chambers on the central axis, and three side chambers (figure 3, 4 and 5).[2] The total length of the tomb is 17.25 metres. The width of the widest part in the tomb is 7.45 metres. Most of the ceilings of the burial chambers are carved to resemble the ceilings of timber architecture, with rafters and decorated coffers (figure 6). Several entrances to the burial chambers are carved to resemble the columns, lintels and walls of timber architecture (figure 7). In the doorways leading to the main chambers, auspicious images such as cranes and gates to the heavenly world are carved on the side walls (figure 8). Two stoves are carved out from the wall of the side chamber in the west, indicating the function of the chamber as a kitchen (figure 9). The side chamber next to the rear main chamber has a wall carved with a weapon shelf, showing that the chamber was thought of as an armoury.

The local residents call these cliff tombs *manzidong* 蠻子洞 or the aboriginal caves,[3] which used to mislead the early Western researchers in the early 20th century to attribute these tombs to the aboriginal people,[4] though as later researchers suggested and as will be shown in this chapter, they were tombs of the Han people.[5] The cave dwelling-like facilities in the cliff tombs led the local residents to believe that those caves were actually the dwellings of the aboriginal people. And some of these caves were indeed inhabited in the past few centuries by some poor people who could not afford to build their own houses. The early researchers accepted the name of the aboriginal cave mainly because the burial form of the cliff tombs is so different from the common Eastern Han burial forms known at that time, the stone or brick chamber tombs, which were popular all over the Han dynasty empire including the Sichuan Basin.

The central aim of this study is to explore the factors underlying the popularity of the cliff tombs in the Sichuan Basin. The major proposition is that such tombs played an active role in Eastern Han society in Sichuan, as there were a series of activities relevant to the tombs carried out by people, from the construction of the tombs, preparing burial objects, to undertaking the funeral and making sacrifices. On the one hand people, who were involved in these activities had expectations and intentions that shaped their tombs. On the other hand, the existing burial form shaped people's activities related to the tombs, which in return influenced people's expectations and intentions. Therefore, there was a continual dialectical relationship between tombs and people. Through examining the characteristics of the structure, the burial objects and the pictorial carvings of the cliff tomb in relation to other contemporary major burial forms, we can investigate the underlying expectations and intentions of the people who created these distinctive tombs. It is anticipated, therefore, that an understanding of the factors underlying

---

[1] The other main burial form is brick or stone chamber tomb, which will be discussed later in this chapter.
[2] For the archaeological report see Sichuan sheng wenwu kaogu yanjiuyuan, Mianyang shi bowuguan and Santai xian wenwu guanli suo 2007: 80-91.
[3] *Manzi* 蠻子 is translated as 'aboriginal' here. In the mind of the local residents, the people who used the cliff tombs as dwellings were isolated from the society with culture. As T. Torrance mentioned, 'when we first discovered the nature of these caves and brought to light their coffins and interment articles we were puzzled whether to assign them a Chinese or an aboriginal origin' (Torrance 1930-1931: 88). During his investigation of the relics in Sichuan as part of the Eastern Asiatic Expedition organized by the Pennsylvania University Museum in 1916, C. Bishop recorded that 'these caves, which are of artificial formation, are attributed by local tradition to the Man-tse, or aboriginal barbarians, and are regarded as having been excavated so as to serve as dwellings'. Bishop 1916: 112. ('Man-tse' is *manzi* 蠻子.)
[4] See records by the early Western travelers into the Sichuan Basin in the early 12th century. C. Bishop used to suggest that 'a careful examination of the caves in the region about Kiating Fu, coupled with the information which I was able to gather from various sources, suggests three points which might seem to confirm the popular tradition ascribing them to the aborigines' (Bishop 1916: 114-115) ('Kiatng Fu 嘉定府' is today's Leshan 乐山 area in Sichuan). T. Torrance, an English missionary became interested in the cliff tombs in 1908 and began to systematically collect burial objects from these tombs. In his paper published in 1930-1931, Torrance mentioned that in Sichuan, one outstanding difference compared to the general sameness of the burial customs once prevailed everywhere was the 'frequent cutting of caves in the solid rock for tombs'. The majority of the burial objects in the cliff tombs were very similar to those in the Han stone or brick chamber tombs (Torrance 1930-1931: 88). In addition, the Qin and Han coins were frequently found in the cliff tombs. Therefore it was reasonable to attribute the cliff tombs to the Han Chinese people (Torrance 1930-1931: 88). In the early 20th century, Western researchers in this area include General D'Ollone in 1907, Segalen in 1914, Bishop in 1916, and Bedford in 1936. For a general introduction to the early investigation of the cliff tombs, see Cheng 1957: 139-140.
[5] The Han people here is used in contrast with those 'aboriginal' groups of people, who lived in their own life styles for generations within a relatively isolated area, barely influenced by the assimilation of the Sichuan area into the Qin and Han empires (221 BC-AD 220).

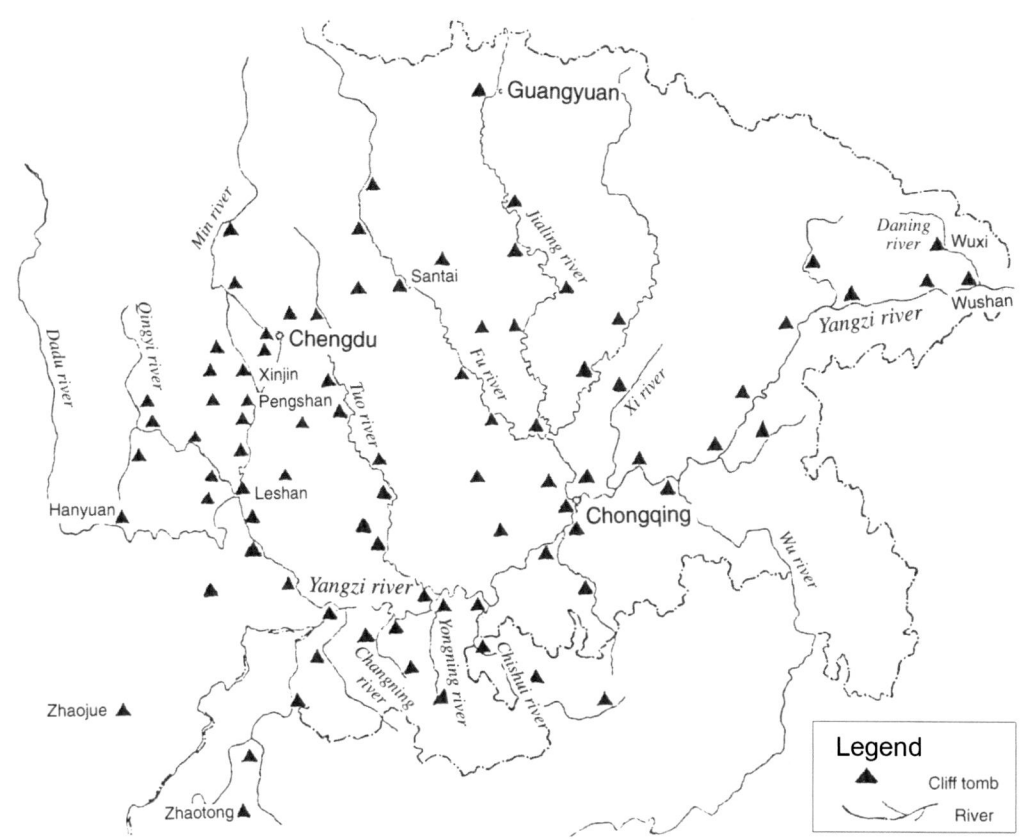

FIGURE 1. DISTRIBUTION OF THE CLIFF TOMBS IN THE SICHUAN BASIN. REDRAWN AFTER TANG 1997: FIG. 1, BY XUAN CHEN.

FIGURE 2. DISTRIBUTION OF THE MAJOR EASTERN HAN TOMBS. DRAWN BY XUAN CHEN.

the popularity of the cliff tombs will also contribute to an understanding of the role of tombs in the Eastern Han society of Sichuan.

My focus on the contrast between the cliff tomb and other major burial forms of the time situates this study within the picture of the development of the burial forms

CHAPTER 1 INTRODUCTION

FIGURE 3. OUTSIDE THE TOMB ZIJINGWAN M3 IN SANTAI. PHOTOGRAPH BY XUAN CHEN.

FIGURE 4. ENTRANCE TO THE TOMB ZIJINGWAN M3 IN SANTAI. PHOTOGRAPH BY XUAN CHEN.

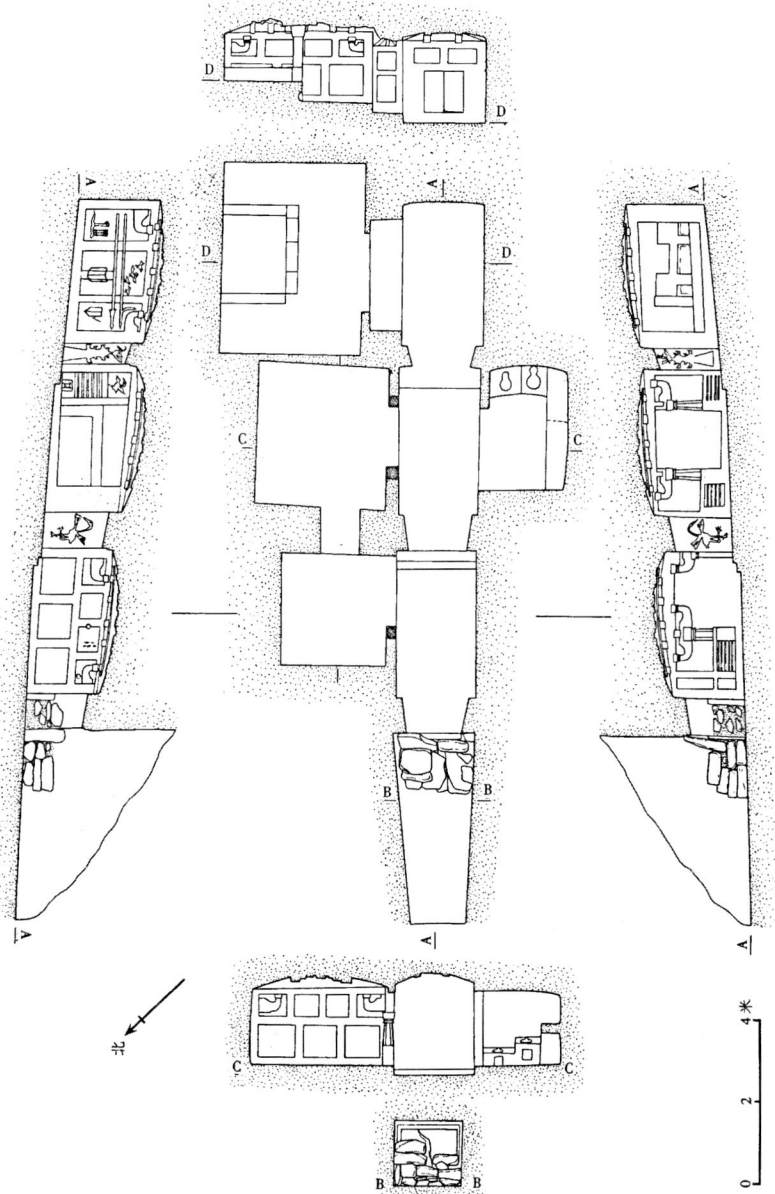

FIGURE 5. PLAN OF THE TOMB ZIJINGWAN M3 IN SANTAI. AFTER SICHUAN SHENG WENWU KAOGU YANJIUYUAN, MIANYANG SHI BOWUGUAN AND SANTAI XIAN WENWU GUANLI SUO 2007: 81, FIG. 101.

FIGURE 6. CEILING OF THE REAR CHAMBER OF THE TOMB ZIJINGWAN M3 IN SANTAI. AFTER SICHUAN SHENG WENWU KAOGU YANJIUYUAN, MIANYANG SHI BOWUGUAN AND SANTAI XIAN WENWU GUANLI SUO 2007: PL. 112.

FIGURE 8. A CRANE CARVED IN THE DOORWAY OF THE TOMB ZIJINGWAN M3 IN SANTAI. AFTER SICHUAN SHENG WENWU KAOGU YANJIUYUAN, MIANYANG SHI BOWUGUAN AND SANTAI XIAN WENWU GUANLI SUO 2007: PL. 114.

FIGURE 7. A COLUMN AND A LOW WALL AT THE ENTRANCE TO A SIDE CHAMBER OF THE TOMB ZIJINGWAN M3 IN SANTAI. PHOTOGRAPH BY XUAN CHEN.

FIGURE 9. STOVES CARVED IN A SIDE CHAMBER OF THE TOMB ZIJINGWAN M3 IN SANTAI. AFTER SICHUAN SHENG WENWU KAOGU YANJIUYUAN, MIANYANG SHI BOWUGUAN AND SANTAI XIAN WENWU GUANLI SUO 2007: PL. 111.

in the Eastern Han and the earlier period and the social background of such development. This introduction locates the cliff tomb in this larger picture of development and the relevant social background.

1. Major Burial Types in Eastern Han

In Eastern Han, the major burial types were the cliff tomb and the brick or stone chamber tomb, which were built underground or half underground, resembling dwellings, covered by a burial mound (figure 10). There are chamber tombs constructed entirely of bricks, of a combination of bricks and stone, and of stone alone, without essential differences in tomb plan. They all contain several burial chambers with walls, doors, ceilings and sometimes columns. Chamber tombs built by a combination of bricks and stone blocks usually have large stone slabs as their door panels and walls, and use bricks to construct their barrel-vaults (figure 11).[6] Tombs built entirely of stone usually have stepped

---
[6] For example, see the Dahuting 打虎亭 tomb M1 and M2 in Mixian 密縣, Henan. Henan sheng wenwu yanjiusuo 1993. Tomb M1 is located in the west and tomb no. 2 is located in the east. They housed Zhang Boya 張博雅, the grand administrator (*taishou* 太守) of Hongnong 弘農, and his wife, with burial mounds rising above the ground to the height of 10 and 7.5 metres respectively. The two tombs share similar subterranean burial structure. Both are constructed by rectangular stone slabs together

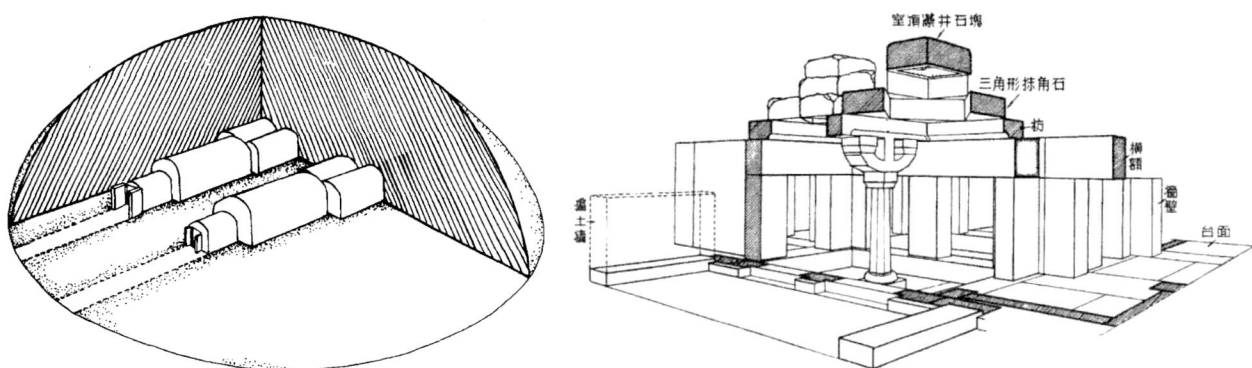

FIGURE 10. THE ZENGJIABAO BRICK CHAMBER TOMB M1 AND M2 UNDER A BURIAL MOUND IN CHENGDU. AFTER LUO ERHU 2001: 454.

FIGURE 12. PANORAMIC VIEW OF THE FRONT CHAMBER OF THE YI'NAN TOMB IN SHANDONG. AFTER ZENG ZHAOYU, JIANG BAOGENG AND LI ZHONGYI 1956: 6.

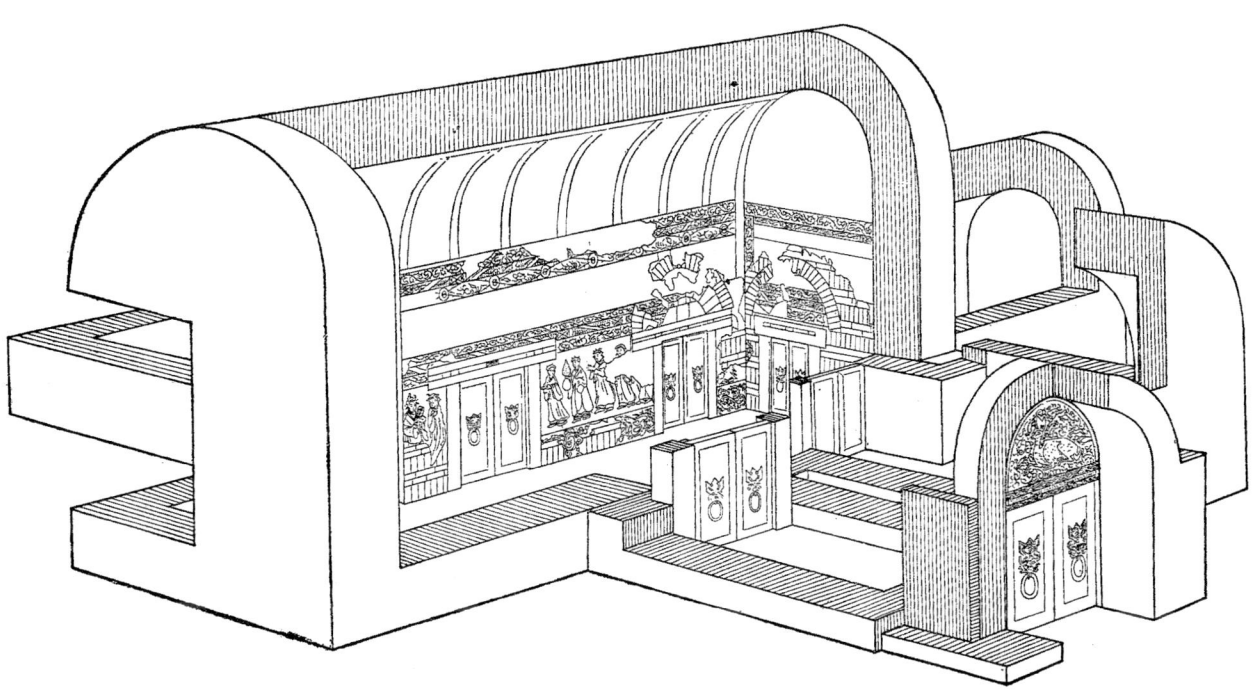

FIGURE 11. PANORAMIC VIEW OF THE DAHUTING TOMB M2 IN MIXIAN IN HENAN. AFTER HENAN SHENG WENWU YANJIUSUO 1993: FIG. 161.

roofs, which are formed by shaped stone bars and blocks (figure 12).[7] Among the areas outside Sichuan, it seems that stone-structured chamber tombs were popular in the areas rich in stone sources, especially in Shandong and northern Jiangsu in the east, where rocky hills are densely distributed. In the metropolitan areas in central China, covered by loess, in Henan and Shaanxi, where the old capitals of the Han dynasty were located, brick-structured chamber tombs were the main burial type.

with V-shaped and square bricks. The paved paths and vaulted ceilings are constructed by bricks. The floors and walls are built by square bricks and stone slabs. Tomb M1 is much larger than M2. It contains three main burial chambers, which are arranged along a north-south axis, separated by stone doors and thresholds. The three main chambers of tomb M1 measure 25.16 metres in length and 17.78 metres in width. Tomb no. 2 measures 20.48 metres in length and 18.60 metres in width.

[7] For example, see the Yi'nan 沂南 tomb in Shandong (Zeng Zhaoyu, Jiang Baogeng and Li Zhongyi 1956) and the Baiji 白集 tomb in Xuzhou 徐州, Jiangsu (Nanjing bowuyuan 1981). The Yi'nan tomb is a multi-chambered subterranean structure built on a level plane. It is 7.55 metres in width and 8.70 metres in length. The whole tomb is constructed of stone posts and lintels. The roof of the tomb is supported by the pillars together with the bracket sets in the central and front chamber. The three main chambers are laid out on a north-south axis. The Yi'nan tomb is one of the most elaborately decorated chamber tombs in the Eastern Han period known so far. The pictorial stone carvings extensively carved in the tombs contain a variety of carving styles, indicating artisans from different workshops. For detailed discussion on the different workshops for the construction of the Yi'nan tomb, see Tseng Lan-ying 2000. The Baiji tomb is a multi-chambered stone structure built on the level plane, covered under a burial mound. It contains three main chambers, which are laid out along a north-south axis in the length of 8.85 metres. The whole tomb is constructed of lintels and posts. The roofs of the main chambers are square and stepped, constructed of stone slabs. All the stone posts of the tomb are elaborated carved and decorated. Some posts still have some red paint remained when excavated. The highest central chamber reaches to a height of 3.15 metres. The widest part of the tomb is 3.90 metres.

Stone is only occasionally found in some large elaborate chamber tombs as key architectural features, such as the walls and door panels, for example in the Dahuting 打虎亭 tomb M2 in Mixian 密縣 in Henan, a tomb of a high ranking official of the Eastern Han.[8]

It is very likely that by comparison with brick, stone was a more favoured building material for chamber tombs. However, only a few regions had enough rocky mountain to use as the stone quarry for chamber tomb construction. In the areas lacking stone, people had to compromise on using bricks, the quality of which to some extent is similar to that of stone. In addition, bricks used for tomb construction were mass produced through standard moulds. Bricks were cheaper substitutes for stone and could be afforded by a wider range of people. In central China, over 10,000 small brick chamber tombs of commoners have been found. Most of them only have the space for one person inside.[9]

In Sichuan, the brick chamber tomb was also a major burial form, but not the only one. The structure of the brick chamber tomb is similar to that in central and eastern China. What is notable is that in Sichuan, chamber tombs are mostly constructed of bricks alone. So far, only a few chamber tombs have been found built with a combination of stone and bricks. Those are large elaborate chamber tombs decorated with pictorial carvings exhibiting the wealth and achievement of the tomb occupants, for example, the Yangzishan 揚子山 tomb in Chengdu 成都.[10] And only one stone-structured chamber tomb has been found in the area, one in Hechuan 合川 in Chongqing, constructed of the local red sandstone.[11]

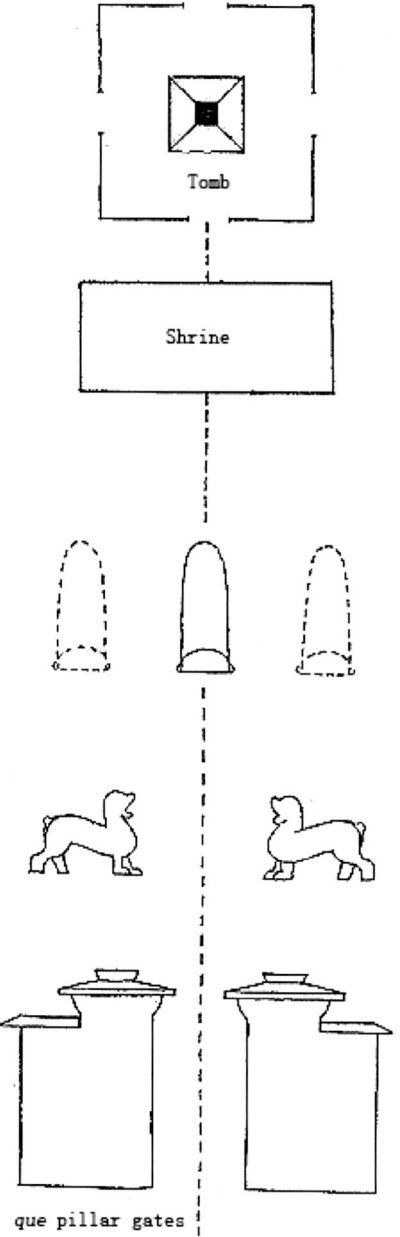

FIGURE 13. AN IDEAL PLAN OF AN EASTERN HAN CEMETERY WITH THE *QUE* PILLARS. REDRAWN AFTER WU 1995: FIG. 4.1, BY XUAN CHEN.

---

[8] Henan sheng wenwu yanjiusuo 1993: 192-205. Dahuting tomb M2 contains three main chambers and three side chambers in the south, east and north. All the doors and threshold that connect the chambers to each other are built by stone slabs. The main walls are constructed by stone slabs as well. The vaulted roofs of the chambers and the paved paths are constructed square and V-shaped bricks. The whole tomb is constructed of lintels and posts. The roofs of the main chambers are square and stepped, constructed of stone slabs.

[9] Such small brick tombs are usually found in several ten to several hundred on a planned cemetery. For example, see the Shaogou 燒溝 cemetery in Luoyang 洛陽 in Henan. Zeng Zhaoyu, Jiang Baogeng and Li Zhongyi 1956: 4-5. 445 brick tombs were found in the area of 110,000 square metres. During the Eastern Han, the cemetery expanded from east to west.

[10] Yu Haoliang 1955. The Yangzishan tomb is a multi-chambered stone and brick structure built on the level plane, covered under a burial mound. It contains three chambers, which are laid along a north-south axis in a length of 13.84 metres. The highest and widest central chamber is 3.5 metres in height and 3 metres in width. The barrel vaulted ceilings of all the three chambers are constructed of tailored small bricks. The paved floors and the upper part of the main walls are constructed of rectangular bricks. The main walls, the door lintels and posts are constructed of stone slabs and bars.

[11] Chongqing shi bowuguan tianye kaogu gongzuo xiaozu and Hechuan xian wenhuaguan tianye kaogu gongzuo xiaozu 1977. The plan of the stone chamber tomb in Hechuan is in the shape of a cross. The three main chambers are laid out along a north-south axis in a length of 12.2 metres. The largest central chamber has an east side chamber and a west side chamber. The east-west axis of the tomb is 9.1 metres in length. The central chamber, the highest chamber of the tomb is 3.6 metres in height. All the main chambers have vaulted ceilings, which are constructed by tailored stone blocks. All the walls and floors are constructed by stone slabs as well. Compared to the stone chamber tombs in Shandong and Jiangsu, which are constructed of lintels and posts, the stone chamber tomb in Hechuan is in the form of the common brick chamber tombs, though constructed of stone slabs. Inscriptions of the measurement of the stone slabs are found in the vaulted ceiling and the east wall of the front chamber: '*san wu* 三五 (three five, equals to 81 centimetres)', '*san chi jiu cun* 三尺九寸 (three *chi* nine *cun*, equals to 91 centimetres)', '*si chi er cun* 四尺二寸 (four *chi* two *cun*, equals to 97 centimetres)', '*si chi si cun* 四尺四寸 (four *chi* four *cun*, equals to 112 centimetres)' and '*si chi wu cun* (four *chi* five *cun*, equals to 103. 5 centimetres)', indicating that stone slabs were measured and tailored in advance when constructing the tomb. These inscriptions are the only measurement found in the Eastern Han chamber tombs in Sichuan.

Consequently, we need to think about why people in an area covered by sandstone hills did not utilize their local stone in chamber tomb construction like the people in central and east China. Instead of quarrying stone from the sandstone hills, they cut into the hills to create burial spaces to imitate the dwellings above ground. Many Eastern Han burial remains in Sichuan suggest that stone

Chapter 1 Introduction

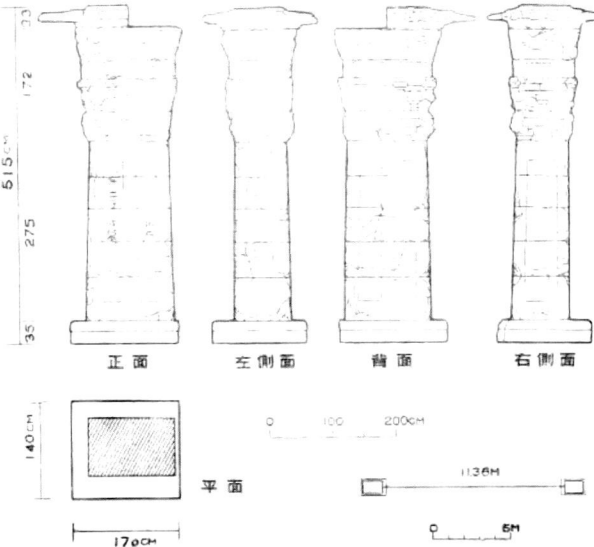

FIGURE 14. THE YANG'S FAMILY *QUE* PILLAR IN JIAJIANG IN SICHUAN. AFTER CHONGQING SHI WENHUA JU AND CHONGQING SHI BOWUGUAN 1992: 59.

2. Development of Burial Form in the Han Dynasty (206 BC-AD 220)

An examination of how the major Eastern Han burial forms developed is to some extent helpful to understanding why this particular form of the cliff tomb was adopted. The Western Han (206 BC-AD 8) was a period when the burial forms underwent two crucial changes: a change from vertical structure to horizontal structure and a change in building materials from wood to stone or brick.[14] The vertical structure refers to the tomb in the form of pit, on the bottom of which one or several wooden coffins are placed together with the burial objects (figure 15).[15] The horizontal structure refers to the tomb that is built in the similar way of building a house and contains structures used in the dwelling including doors, walls and sometimes columns and windows (figure 16).[16]

quarrying, sculpture and construction were well developed in the area. For example, the common *que* 闕 pillars made of the local sandstone in Sichuan. These stone pillars were installed in pairs above ground to mark the entrance to a cemetery (figure 13).[12] Another example, one of the *que* pillars of Yang Zong 楊宗 in Jiajiang 夾江 consists of a flat rectangular stone base, a main body formed by five rectangular stone blocks, a capital made by four stone blocks to resemble a pavilion and a stone roof on top (figure 14). All the stone blocks of the pillar gate are accurately tailored to be piled up to form a free standing column-like architecture to a height of 5.15 metres.[13] Due to the accurate calculation of the size of each stone block and the precise execution of it on stone, the pillar gate still stands stable after nearly 2000 years.

---

[12] Though no Eastern Han cemetery has survived intact, the archaeological discovery in Jiaxiang 嘉祥 in Shandong and textual records show that a common cemetery in Eastern Han consisted of a pair of *que* pillar gates, followed by a spiritual path leading to an above ground shrine, behind which one or several related tombs covered by one or several mounds were located. For the discussion of the cemetery at Jiaxiang, see Wu 1989b: 30-37. In the *Shuijing zhu* 水經注 (724), Yin Jian's 尹儉 graveyard is recorded to show a similar plan. For a standard layout of such cemetery, see Wu 1995: 191, fig. 4.1. Sometimes there are also stone guardian figures flanking the spiritual path. See Wu 1995: 191, fig. 4.3.
[13] Chongqing shi wenhua ju and Chongqing shi bowuguan 1992: 36-37, 59, figs. 13 and 14. The two pillars are arranged along an east-west axis, facing to the south. The distance between the two pillars is 8 metres. The pillars are made of the local red sandstone. The east pillar has the inscription: '漢故益州牧楊府/君諱宗字□仲墓', indicating that the tomb occupant was Yang Zong, who used to be the shepherd (牧) of the Yi Region (in Sichuan). However, according to the *Jin shi yuan* 金石苑 compiled in Southern Song (AD 1127-1279), the character '牧 (shepherd)' in the inscription should be '太守 (grand administrator)' (Chongqing shi wenhua ju and Chongqing shi bowuguan 1992: 37). According to the Gazetteer of Jiajiang (夾江縣志), Yang Zong used to be the grand administrator of the Yi Region, one of the successors of Gao Yi 高頤 (who also had a set of stone pillars remaining in Sichuan, see Chongqing shi wenhua ju and Chongqing shi bowuguan 1992: 31-33). The pillars of Yang Zong are dated to the end of the Eastern Han (AD 209-220) (Chongqing shi wenhua ju and Chongqing shi bowuguan 1992: 38).

[14] For important works discussing the two changes, see Rawson 1999: 6, Wu 1995: 126-136, Thorp 1979: 128, Huang Xiaofen 2003: 90-93 and Erickson 2010: 13. Jessica Rawson suggests that the use of princely rock-cut tombs in Western Han marked two radical departures from the standard late Zhou burial form, which was usually in the form of a vertical shaft with nested wooden coffins at the base. First, the tombs are cut into the mountain rocks rather than being built by timbers. Second, a series of linked rooms are cut on a horizontal rather than a vertical axis. Wu Hung also suggests that the princely rock-tombs are crucial to the understanding of the sudden discovery of stone as a building material and the development of horizontal tombs in Western Han. He attributes the use of stone and the use of mountain caves for burial partly to the influence of the Buddhist Indian caves, in which stone symbolized durability and eternity and the cave dwelling provided the dwelling for the afterlife. Wu Hung also suggests that the cliff tombs in Sichuan might also appear for this reason. Robert Thorp on the other hand notes that the use of brick chamber tombs in Western Han Luoyang in Henan marked two important changes in the development of burial form. First, 'the use of brick as building material marks a significant break with wood, the dominant tradition of ancient times'. Second, 'the vertical shafts of ancient times were abandoned so that tombs were no longer "open to the sky"'. The new horizontal plan 'imposed a new manner of access to the burial chamber, not from the top through the roof but rather from one end by way of a door'. Considering both the princely rock-cut tombs and brick chamber tombs, Huang Xiaofen suggests that the horizontal tomb departures from the vertical tomb since the appearance of the depictions of the doors and windows in the burial space. The construction of the corridors that link the partitioned spaces in the tomb further makes the tomb more resembling the dwelling place. When discussing the Han burial patterns, Susan Erickson summarizes that in general there were two major characteristics of Han tombs. First, 'tombs became more permanent structures, made either of durable materials like brick or stone, or by laboriously cutting directly into stone to form a pit or cave'. Second, the interiors of the Han tombs were elaborated with 'architectural elements borrowed from buildings used by the living'.
[15] For example, the Mawangdui 馬王堆 tomb no. 1 in Changsha 長沙 in Hunan. Hunan bowuguan and Zhongguo kexueyuan kaogu yanjiusuo 1973. The tomb is dated to early Western Han, attributed to the wife of Marquis Dai 軑. The box-shaped wooden chamber is placed at the bottom of the burial pit with the depth of 3.5 metres. Inside the chamber, there are four wooden coffins, one inside another. The chamber together with the coffins are all made of elaborately chiseled wooden planks in a total number of 70. The wooden planks are installed through tenon-and-mortise joints. The largest wooden plank measures 4.84 metres in length, 1.52 metres in width, 0.26 metres in depth, with the weight of 1500 kilograms. The three outer coffins are lacquered. The innermost coffin is decorated with silk on the surface. The tomb occupant is inside the innermost coffin. The burial objects are laid out in the partitioned off space between the walls of the chamber and the outer coffin.
[16] For example, the 'Feng Ruren 馮孺人' tomb in Nanyang 南陽 in Henan. Nanyang diqu wenwu dui and Nanyang bowuguan 1980. The tomb is a subterranean stone and brick structure built on the level plane. The main chambers and the entrance of the tomb are located on an east-west axis in the length of 9.5 metres. The widest part of the tomb is 6.15 metres in width. The highest burial chamber is 3.14 metres in height. The two main chambers are laid out side by side, surrounded by a gallery.

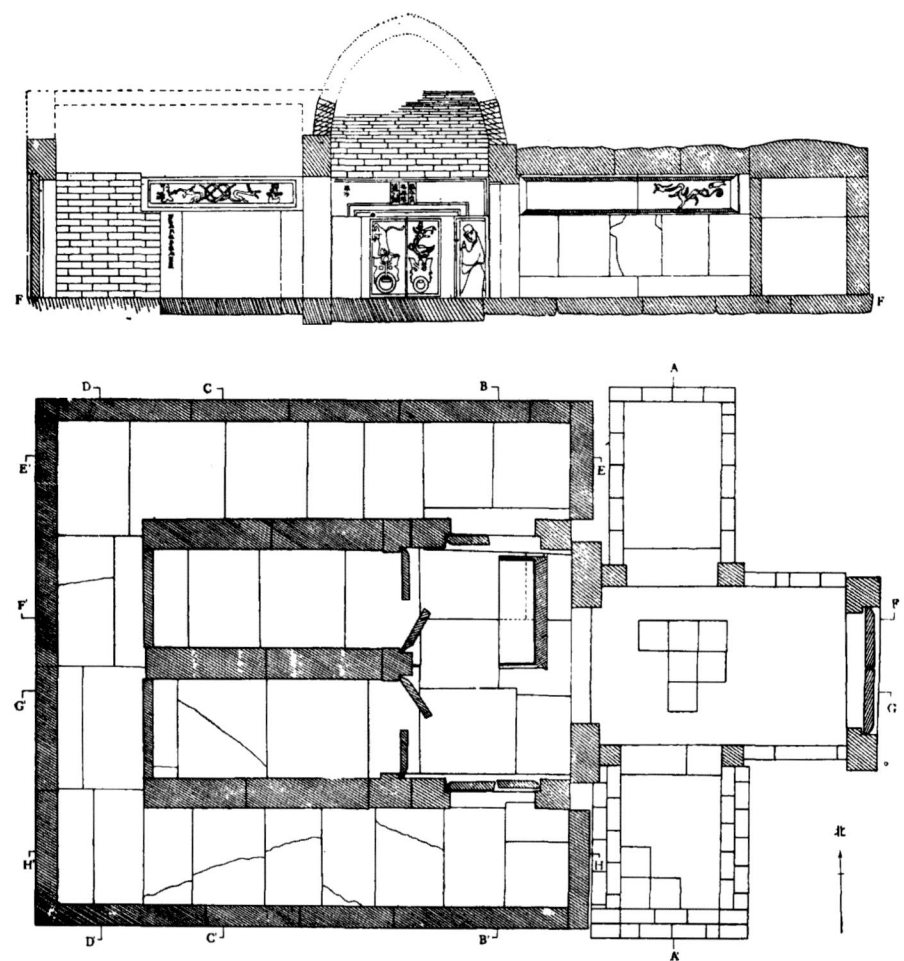

FIGURE 16. ELEVATION AND PLAN OF THE FENG RUREN'S TOMB IN NANYANG IN HENAN. AFTER NANYANG DIQU WENWU DUI AND NANYANG BOWUGUAN 1980.2: FIG. 2.

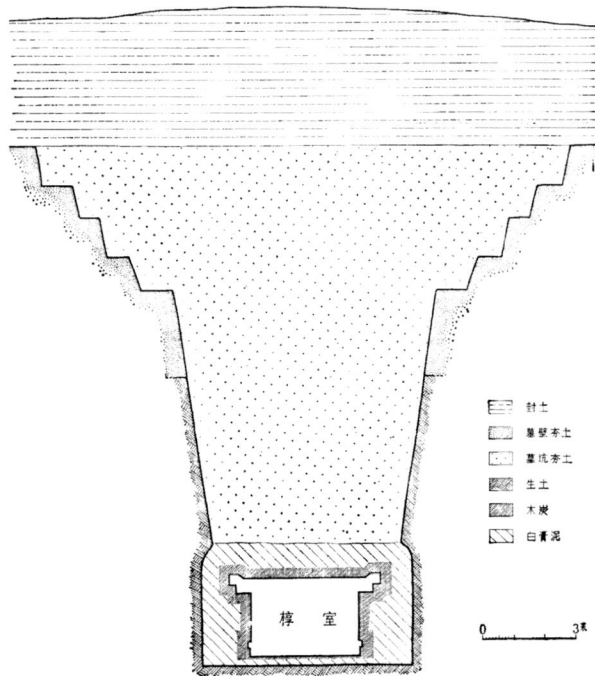

FIGURE 15. ELEVATION OF THE MAWANGDUI TOMB IN CHANGSHA IN HUNAN. AFTER HUNAN BOWUGUAN AND ZHONGGUO KEXUEYUAN KAOGU YANJIUSUO 1973: FIG. 3.

However, during the transitional period, it is difficult to say sometimes whether a tomb is horizontal-structured or vertical-structured. For example, the Shuangbaoshan 雙包山 tomb M2, dated to the Western Han, in Mianyang 綿陽 in Sichuan is constructed at the bottom of a pit in the form of an enlarged wooden coffin which occupies an area of 163 square metres.[17] The 'wooden coffin' is partitioned by wooden panels into 6 rectangular sections to form a reception hall in the front and a bedchamber in the rear, as suggested by different burial objects placed in the different sections. Door panels are placed between several of the sections, which further suggests that the tomb, though it still looks like a wooden box, was modelled on a dwelling containing a number of rooms. More transitional exmples like this one can be observed in some Western Han princes' tombs such as the Dabaotai 大葆臺 tomb in Beijing and the tomb of the king of Guangling 廣陵 in

There are also two side chamber flanking the passageway. The burial chambers are connected to each other through doors which are constituted by door posts, lintels and door panels, which are constructed by stone slabs and bars. On the door panels of the main entrance of the tomb, there are carved a pair of door rings held by the animal head appliqués.

[17] Sichuan sheng wenwu kaogu yanjiusuo and Mianyang bowuguan 2006: 34-143. The tomb is dated between 167 BC and 118 BC and is attributed to the tomb occupant with the rank that equals to a Marquis (Sichuan sheng wenwu kaogu yanjiusuo and Mianyang bowuguan 2006: 144-147).

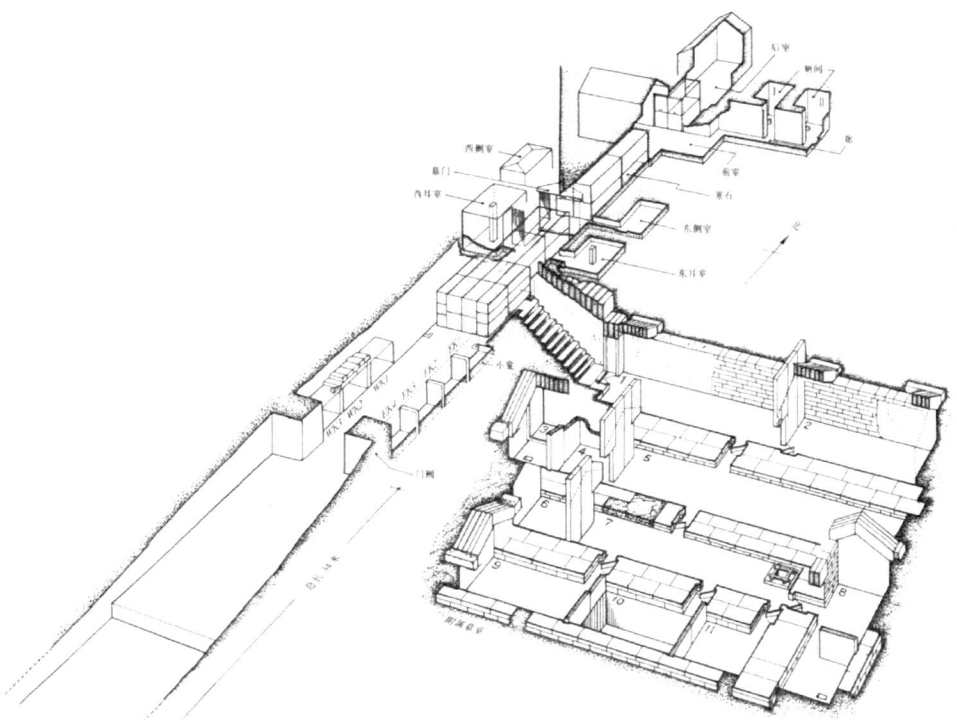

Figure 18. The Beidongshan tomb in Xuzhou in Jiangsu. After Xuzhou bowuguan and Nanjing daxue lishi xue xi kaogu zhuanye 2003: fig. 4.

Figure 17. The tomb of the king of Guangling in Gaoyou in Jiangsu. Photograph by Xuan Chen.

Gaoyou 高郵 in Jiangsu (figure 17).[18] Interestingly, tombs at this transitional stage were still made of wood. Stone or brick structured tombs only appeared when they were also built more like houses, such as the 'Feng Ruren' chamber tomb built with a combination of stone blocks and bricks in Nanyang in Henan.

By and large, the change from vertical to horizontal exhibits a process by which tombs were built more and more like houses. This process was in progress at different speeds in different areas of the empire. Finally in the Eastern Han, almost all areas had adopted the horizontal house-like burial form. In Western Han, the earliest areas began to be involved in this change are the metropolitan areas in Shaanxi and Henan, and northern Jiangsu in the east. The brick or stone chamber tomb in the metropolitan areas and the rock-cut tombs of the Western Han princes in northern Jiangsu exhibited the burial forms at the final stage of this change. Similar to the cliff tombs in Sichuan, the rock-cut tombs are also horizontally cut into the hill to form a burial space including a series of burial chambers to imitate the dwelling for the living. The major difference is that the rock-cut tombs are much larger in scale, which is largely due to the fact that the tomb occupants were the direct descendants of the founder of the empire and were allocated an area which equals to that of a commandery (*jun* 郡) to manage.[19] For example, the Beidongshan 北洞山 tomb belonging to a king of the Chu 楚 kingdom in Xuzhou 徐州 in Jiangsu is cut horizontally into the mountain rock, consisting of a 56 metres long central corridor on its axis and numerous side chambers, a rear chamber and an auxiliary hall connected to the central axis (figure 18). The grand axial plan is marked by the long central path. All the other chambers resembling the dwelling for the living are cut of the sides of the central corridor.[20]

---

[18] For the Dabaotai tomb no. 1, see Dabaotai hanmu fajue zu and Zhongguo shehui kexue yuan kaogu yanjiusuo 1989. The tomb is dated to the 1st century BC, attributed to the king of the Yan 燕 kingdom (Dabaotai hanmu fajue zu and Zhongguo shehui kexue yuan kaogu yanjiusuo 1989: 93-97). The tomb is wooden chambered, located at the bottom of a burial pit with the depth of 4.7 metres. The tomb measures 23.2 metres in length and 18 metres in width. The major structures of the tomb include the passageway, the surrounding gallery, the *ticou* 題湊 wall made of cider timbers (*huangchang* 黃腸), the front chamber, the inner gallery and the rear chamber.

[19] Such area is called a kingdom and the king had the power equals to that of a prefect (*xianling* 縣令).
[20] Xuzhou bowuguan and Nanjing daxue lishi xue xi kaogu zhuanye 2003: 6-28, 8, fig. 4. The tomb will also be discussed in Chapter 2.

In this sense, cliff tombs in Sichuan followed the development of the principal Han dynasty burial form: it is house-like, with a horizontal structure and it is constructed of stone.[21] In addition, it has a possible prototype in Western Han, though it is also possible that the development of the cliff tomb in Sichuan was not influenced by the earlier princely rock-cut tombs. As will be shown in Chapter 2 on cliff tomb structure, to some extent, the cliff tomb can be regarded as a deviation from the contemporary tombs in the central and east. Such deviation may be rooted in a specific social background during the time and the special role of Sichuan in the empire.

3. The Social Background

History

The Han Dynasty (206 BC-AD 220), traditionally divided into the Western Han (206 BC-AD 8) and the Eastern Han (AD 25-220) with a transitional period of around two decades in between, is the second empire unifying a vast area of China after the first empire of Qin, which survived less than two decades. The process of unification of the two early empires involved the establishment of a centralized governing system which took every area of the empire into the control of the central government, and the unification of culture. Some standardized cultural values of the empire were enforced on the regions. But as Mark Lewis points out, the imperial order did not eradicate the distinct regional cultures. Instead, the divisions of the regional cultures were transcended.[22] This is what happened in Sichuan as elsewhere in the empire and is well reflected from burial remains as will be elaborated in this study.

The Sichuan area was brought into the early dynasty in the late 4th century BC. In 316 BC, the State of Shu 蜀 in the Sichuan area was conquered by the State of Qin 秦, which later established the empire of Qin.[23] In the following years, the Sichuan area was strategically incorporated into the empire by the central ruling power. Before the end of the 4th century, the cultures in the Sichuan area were generally identified as the Ba 巴 and the Shu 蜀 culture, which were located closely to each other with the Shu culture in the western part of the Sichuan Basin and the Ba culture in its east. Based on archaeological evidence, the Ba and the Shu culture exhibited some different characteristics before the 6th century BC, while after the 6th century BC, it is difficult to distinguish the two cultures and the culture in the Sichuan Basin is called the Ba-Shu culture, combining the names of the two cultures.[24]

From the 6th to the 4th century BC, there are two main features of the Ba-Shu culture as reflected in burial evidence. The first feature is a boat-shaped burial form.[25] The second feature is the frequent appearance of bronze weapons of the Ba-Shu style among burial objects.[26] The body was buried in the coffin which is hollowed from a single log. The shape of the end of the coffin suggests a boat. The bronze weapons usually appear in large amounts and are of good quality, which suggests the important place of the weapon in the society of the Ba-Shu culture. There are bronze weapons with characteristic Ba-Shu features, such as the dagger-axe called *ge* 戈. Marks or signs are frequently found on the weapons, such as on the blade of the *ge*. Such marks or signs are believed to include both emblems with iconic nature and forms of writing.[27] After the Sichuan area was conquered by the Qin at the end of the 4th century BC and large populations were moved from the metropolitan area of the Qin to Sichuan, the assimilation of the Ba-Shu culture to the Qin started to be shown from burial evidence. The assimilation proceeded rapidly. One example is the rapid disappearance of the Ba-Shu signs within a century or two after Qin's conquest. Pirazzoli-t'Serstevens has a different interpretation. She suggests that the Ba-Shu signs appeared at the end of the 5th century BC, at a time when the contacts between the Sichuan area and central China increased. The Ba-Shu signs show the efforts of the Ba-Shu culture to make a cultural compromise in its competition with the metropolitan culture of the Qin and other areas in central China through imitating the seals and the writing systems while keeping some Ba-Shu features.[28] Pirazzoli-t'Serstevens further suggests that, though Ba-Shu features disappeared rapidly in the 3rd century BC after the Qin's conquest, there were still a small part of the Ba-Shu cultural elements persistent in some parts of Sichuan until the beginning of the 1st century of the Eastern Han, as reflected in the tools and cooking vessels found in the tombs in Sichuan.[29]

A major strategy of the Qin and Han empires in cultural and political unification was to move people from the areas around the central ruling power to the Sichuan area to exploit the local resources and to bring about cultural integration. There were mainly two kinds of strategic movement of people conducted by the government: 1) large scale movement of households to Sichuan; 2) dispatching powerful families who constituted threats to the ruling power to Sichuan.

The large scale movement of households to Sichuan took place in the late 4th century BC and continued for over a hundred years to the beginning of the 2nd century BC. In

---

[21] On the discussion on the important change in tomb building material from wood to stone, see Rawson 1999: 6, Wu 1995: 126-136 and Thorp 1979: 128. Chapter 2 of this book will also elaborate this question when discussing stone as the building material for the cliff tomb.
[22] Lewis 2007: 1.
[23] *Shi ji*: 207. '十四年...蜀侯來降. In the fourteenth year (316 BC), ... the lord of the Shu surrendered (to the Qin).'
[24] For the general introduction to the Ba-Shu culture from the 6th century BC to the Han, see Pirazzoli-t'Serstevens 2001 and Thote 2001.

[25] See Pirazzoli-t'Serstevens 2001: fig. 1.
[26] See Pirazzoli-t'Serstevens 2001: fig. 3.
[27] For the interpretation of the Ba-Shu signs, see Sun Hua 1987. Sun Hua suggests that the Ba-Shu signs appearing on the bronze vessels and weapons were not only decorations, but they were still not characters. When these signs appeared, the Chinese characters were already popular in the Sichuan area.
[28] Pirazzoli-t'Serstevens 2001: 45.
[29] Pirazzoli-t'Serstevens 2001: 45. The tool inventory found in the tombs in Sichuan in the 3rd century BC shows little change. As for pottery and bronze cooking vessels found in the tomb, they persisted until the 1st century AD. In this sense, Pirazzoli-t'Serstevens suggests that 'the material culture of everyday life continued to be shaped by traditional choice' no matter how the culture of elite and urban life was sinicised.

314 BC, the King Hui 惠 of the State of Qin sent around 10,000 households to strengthen his rule in Sichuan and to weaken the power of the original residents of Sichuan.[30] In the last two decades of the 3rd century BC, the First Emperor again sent large number of households from the capital area at Chang'an to Sichuan to further develop the local economy.[31] In particular, the First Emperor sent households to Linqiong 臨邛 in Sichuan, which was previously occupied by the Qiong 邛 people.[32] Some of the households were from newly conquered areas. For example, the ancestor of the well-known Zhuo 卓 family in Sichuan was moved from the old state of Zhao 趙 after the Qin's conquest; the ancestors of the Zheng 鄭 and Cheng 程 families in Sichuan were also moved by the ruler from the conquered areas in the east.[33]

Such families moved by the ruler to Sichuan included the families of powerful officials and royal relatives who constituted threats to the ruling power. Such movements took place under both the Qin and the Han. Lü Buwei's 呂不韋 family together with the families of Lü's followers were moved by the King Zheng 政 of Qin to Sichuan in the second half of the 3rd century BC.[34] In the 1st century BC, the Emperor Gao 高 and the Emperor Wen 文 decided to send Peng Yue 彭越 and King Li 厲 of Huainan 淮南, Liu Chang 劉長 who had rebelled to Sichuan. The two died, however, before being sent into exile.[35] The inscription on a stone door panel of a Han tomb in Chengdu, discovered in the 1950s, showed that the ancestor of the tomb occupant was from the family of the relatives of the empress Lü 呂, who were sent into exile to Sichuan in the beginning of the 2nd century BC.[36] The inscription on a tomb stele discovered in Pixian 郫縣 near Chengdu in Sichuan in 1966 shows that the ancestor of the tomb occupant belonged to one of the powerful families moved to Sichuan by the emperor during the Han period. The tomb stele was erected in AD 128.[37]

After two centuries of moving large numbers of people to Sichuan to exploit the local resources, the new population, including the powerful families, made great contribution to the prosperity of the local economy.[38] By the Western Han (206 BC-AD 8), the area around Chengdu in Sichuan had become an important economic centre for the whole empire. In the Western Han and the Eastern Han, lacquer, tea and textiles, three of the five valuable processed products of the empire were produced in large quantities in the area around Chengdu.[39] In addition, Chengdu was one of the most fertile breadbaskets for the empire, with its average yields of rice from farm land around ten to fifteen times higher than the average level of the empire.[40] The markets in the Chengdu city were full of goods for trade, comparable to those in the metropolitan Chang'an 長安. Chengdu city was one of the major centres for both international and domestic trade in the empire.[41]

Nylan suggests that the Sichuan area was an ideal place for exile because it is encircled by steep mountains, which formed a natural defence against the outside world. On the other hand, the weather was temperate, the soil was fertile, the rivers running through the basin encircled by the mountains were ideal for the irrigation systems and there were many natural resources such as salt, iron, silver, bamboo and timber. The ideal natural environment provided conditions for the development of economy in Sichuan. In addition, the location of Sichuan in the Yangzi River valley and the focal point of Central Asia, India, southeast China and the metropolitan area of China made it an ideal place for international and domestic trade.[42]

Expenditure on Tombs

In the Han period, lavish expenditure on tombs was prevalent among various social groups with different

---

[30] *Huayang*: 194. '周赧王元年…戎伯尚強,乃移秦民萬家實. In the first year of the king Nan of Zhou (314 BC)…the force of the Rong people was still strong, therefore 10,000 households were moved from the Qin state to populate the area.'
[31] *Huayang*: 225-226. '然秦惠文始皇克定六國輒徙其豪俠於蜀資我豐土. When the king Huiwen of Qin and the First Emperor conquered the six states, powerful people were moved from these states to populate Sichuan.'
[32] *Huayang*: 244. '臨邛縣…本有邛民,秦始皇徙上郡實之. In the Linqiong Prefecture… there used be the Qiong people, the First Emperor of Qin moved people from the Shang Commandery to populate the area.'
[33] *Shi ji*: 3277. '蜀卓氏之先趙人也用鐵致富秦破趙遷卓氏. The ancestors of the Zhuo family in Sichuan were from the Zhao state. They became wealthy through iron industry. After the Qin conquered the Zhao, the Zhuo family was forced to move.' *Shi ji*: 3278. '程鄭,山東遷虜也,亦冶鑄,賈椎髻之民,富埒卓氏,俱居臨邛. The Zheng and Cheng families were powerful households that were forced to move from Shandong. They were also in the industry of smelting and casting. As merchants, they were richer than the Zhuo family, well-known for their wealth in Linqiong.'
[34] *Shi ji*: 227. '及奪爵遷四千餘家. The noble ranking was removed and over 4000 households were moved to Sichuan.' *Shi ji*: 2513. '其與家屬徙處蜀. He and his family were moved to Sichuan.'
[35] *Han shu*: 1880. '上赦以為庶人,徙蜀青衣. The emperor demoted him to a commoner as a reduced punishment and moved him to Qingyi in Sichuan.' *Han shu*: 121. '淮南王長謀反,廢遷蜀嚴道,死雍. The king of Huainan rebelled. He was then deposed and was sent into exile in Yandao in Sichuan. He died in Yong.'
[36] For the inscription and the relevant study see Zhang Xunliao and Yuan Shuguang 1994: 107.

[37] Xie Yanxiang 1974. The stele was originally used as a door panel for the door of an Eastern Han brick chamber tomb in Sichuan. Many characters in the inscription on the stele are eroded, only several sentences in the inscription can be identified: '永初二年七月四日丁巳,故縣功曹郡掾□□孝淵卒.嗚呼!孝□先,元□關東,□秦□益,功爍縱橫.漢徙豪傑,遷□□梁,建宅處業,汶山之陽.崇響□□,□□與比功,故刊石紀,□愿所行.其辭曰:惟王孝淵,嚴重毅□,□懷慷慨'. '永初二年 (the second year of Yongchu)' indicates that the time of death of the tomb occupants Wang Xiaoyuan 王孝淵 is in AD 108. '關東 (east to the Pass)' and '漢徙豪傑 (powerful people were moved in Han)' show that the family of Wang Xiaoyuan was of the origin of east China and was forced to immigrate as part of the local powerful families in the Han dynasty. '建宅處業 (building houses and purchasing land)' and '汶山之陽 (the south of the Wen mountain)' reveal that the Wang's family finally reestablished in the south of the Wen 汶 mountain in Sichuan.
[38] For an introduction to Sichuan's prosperous economy in Han see Nylan 2001: 309-312.
[39] Nylan 2001: 310.
[40] See *Huayang*: 259 for standard yields.
[41] See Nylan 2001: 311, who quotes an example from *Huayang*: 271. The example shows that when a prefect faced the imminent execution, he negotiated with Tang Meng 唐蒙 for a delay in the date of execution so that he could visit the markets of Chengdu before he died.
[42] See Xu Zhongshu 1982: 1-6 for Chengdu as an early centre of trade. Xu Zhongshu suggests that transportation in Sichuan was not as inconvenient as traditionally regarded. During the Warring States, many bridges over the rivers and roads in the mountains had been built. The rivers on the Chengdu plain became important traffic routes for trade.

incomes all over the empire. According to the *Huayang guo zhi* 華陽國志, in Sichuan in this period, all the wealthy families built grand tombs with luxurious coffins and used sheep and pigs for sacrifice.[43] In eastern China, people with middle incomes spent most of their savings on building tombs and shrines, as reflected in many inscriptions in shrines and tombs. For example, in the shrine dedicated to An Guo 安國 in Jiaxiang 嘉祥 in Shandong, the inscription shows that in order to build the shrine for An Guo, his three brothers spent 27,000 *qian*, which equals to three to four years of income of a local governor in charge of 1000 households.[44] Such records on the costs of mortuary construction, thus exhibiting the filial piety of the family members of the deceased can be frequently found in Shandong and northern Jiangsu. Large consumption of mortuary construction, as recorded in the inscription usually forms a stark contrast to the middle or low income official background of the deceased.[45]

This phenomenon led to criticism by Huan Kuan 桓寬, a scholar of the time: 'Nowadays when parents are alive, their children do not show love and respect, but when they die, their children elevate them to very lofty positions through extravagant [spending]. Even though they have no sincere grief, they are nonetheless regarded as filial if they give [their parents] a lavish burial and spend a lot of money. Therefore, their names become prominent and their glory shines among the people. Because of this, even the commoners emulate [these practices] to the extent that they sell their houses and property to do it.'[46] This criticism points out the motivation underlying the construction of the extravagant tomb, which was to advertise the filial piety of the one who built the tombs and shrines. Filial piety had practical functions during this time. It was an important standard to be considered when recommending local officials. From the early Han, there had been a special official status, *Xiaolian* 孝廉 (filial and uncorrupt). Martin Powers further points out that the public display of filial piety through mortuary construction was effective in obtaining acknowledgement from the public, which was important to a person's political career.[47] Further benefits from such a show of filial piety included receiving prizes from the local or central government and tax reductions.

The scale of this kind of public display through mortuary construction and funerals could involve as many as several ten thousands of people. According to the biography of Chen Shi 陳寔 in the *Hou Han shu* 後漢書, 30,000 people from different areas of the country came to attend his funeral. Several hundreds funeral participants wore white mourning clothes and some stelae praising his virtues were erected in front of his tomb.[48] Such a scale of funeral was not unique in the Han period. After the famous literati Zheng Xuan 鄭玄 (AD 127-200) died, 'all those who had studied with him, from those who held the official post of governor on down, put on their mourning robes to attend the funeral, over a thousand in all.'[49] In such occasions, the funeral became an important way to maintain and establish social networks. Based on the inscriptions on the stelae for the funeral, Miranda Brown makes a thorough analysis of how different social categories were involved in such funeral occasions and she researches the ways in which funeral and related mourning activities influenced a person's political career.[50]

The function of tombs in public display and a person's political life was well exploited by the local powerful families. It is recorded in *Huayang guo zhi* that Yang Bohou 楊伯侯, from a powerful family registered in the Pi 郫 Prefecture in Sichuan, was punished by the prefect, Liu Pang 劉龐 for lavish expenditure on tomb construction.[51] This incident shows the conflict between the local governor and the local powerful family. The potential role of tomb construction in reinforcing the influence and cohesion of a powerful family, led the local governor to suppress a powerful family through inhibiting the construction of extravagant tombs.[52]

Powerful Families

Powerful families played an important role during the history of the Western Han and the Eastern Han as shown by the continuous contest for political control and wealth between the central government and the local powerful families. To some extent, the history of the Eastern Han was a history of competition between such families and the central government.[53] Liu Xiu 劉秀, the first emperor of the Eastern Han, was from a powerful family in Nanyang. These families are known as *haozu* 豪族, *haozong* 豪宗,

---

[43] *Huayang*: 225. '豪族服王侯美衣,…送葬必高墳瓦槨,祭奠而羊豕夕牲. Powerful families wore luxurious clothes like those of the imperial members,…when there was a funeral, high burial mounds were built, pottery coffins were used, sheep and pigs were used for sacrifice.'
[44] '作治連月,…賈錢兩萬七千. The construction work took several months, … cost 27,000 *qian*.' The inscription contains 490 words, recording the grief of An Guo's brothers and their lavish expenditure on the mortuary constructions. For the transcription of the whole inscription, see Li Falin 1982: 101-108.
[45] For a series of expenditure on mortuary structures as recorded in the inscriptions in Shandong in Eastern Han, see Xing Yitian 1996. For example, only the stone pillar gates on the Wu's family cemetery in Jiaxiang in Shandong cost 150,000 *qian* 錢, which equals to two years of the income of a local governor in charge of 1000 households.
[46] *Yantie lun*: 354. '今生不能致其愛敬,死以奢侈相高.雖無哀戚之心,而厚葬重幣者,則稱以為孝,顯名立於世,光榮著於俗.故黎民相慕效,至於髡屋賣業.' The translation is after Powers 1984: 148.
[47] Powers 1991: 42-43.
[48] *Hou Han shu*: 2065-2067.
[49] *Hou Han shu*: 1211. '自郡守以下嘗受業者,縗絰赴會千餘人.' The translation is after Wu 1995: 219.
[50] Brown 2007. Based on the stelae inscriptions, she discerns three kinds of important relationship between the mourner and the deceased, which are mother and son, friends or host and subordinate, and colleagues.
[51] *Huayang*: 238-239. '郫民楊伯侯奢侈,大起冢瑩,因龐為郫令,伯侯遂徙占成都. Yang Bohou in Pi had a lavish life and built extravagant tombs. After Pang became the prefect of Pi, Bohou moved to Chengdu.'
[52] The background of this incident is that the local powerful families in the Pi Prefecture became a big threat to the ruling of the local government. When the new prefect Pang came, he enforced strict laws upon these powerful families and finally Yang Bohou had to move from the Pi Prefecture to Chengdu. *Huayang*: 238-239.
[53] The focuses of the history recording the history of the Western Han (*Han shu*) and the history recording the history of the Eastern Han (*Houhan shu*) are different. There are more materials on the development of economy in the Western Han than in the Eastern Han. There are more materials on the growth of the powerful families and changes in social structures in the Eastern Han than in the Western Han. Loewe 1987: 129-136.

haoyou 豪右, *dazu* 大族 and *daxing* 大姓 in the textual sources, 'dominated the Han government and society and exercised control over the rest of the population'.[54] The powerful families are divided into six groups by Ch'ü T'ung-tsu: 1) old families: the descendants of the ruling houses of the six states overthrown by the Qin; 2) imperial relatives of the ruling family of the Han who were made kings and marquises; 3) consort families; 4) officials; 5) wealthy merchants; and 6) redressers-of-wrong (*youxia* 遊俠).[55] According to his definition, all these families had economic power in the way that they all possessed wealth and landed property, thus influencing the life chances of the rest of the population.[56] The first four groups constituted the ruling class. The association with political control made them the most prestigious groups in society. Economic power was closely related to political power. Many officials and consort families came from wealthy families. The political power also gave a family access to economic power.[57] The powerful families in Eastern Han Sichuan mainly fall into the fifth group, the wealthy merchants, whose power derived from economic power and they sometimes attempted to convert their economic power into political prestige.[58]

These powerful families were organized around a single centred family, which dominated smaller ones. The lesser families affiliated to the large family through economic or political bonds. The affiliated small families were not necessarily from the same clan with the same surnames.[59] Two elements constitute a general powerful family: 1) the possession of large areas of land for agricultural and sideline production; 2) owning private army for guarding their possessions.[60]

Such families also played an important role in the history of Sichuan, especially in the formative years of the early empires of the Qin and the Han in China. The forced movement of powerful families from other areas of China to Sichuan was one of the main strategies of the emperor to populate the area with people belonging to the mainstream culture of the empire. The forced movement of these families from their home base to a remote area, geographically cut off from the metropolitan area of the empire, was also a strategy of the emperor to reduce their threat to the central government. To some extent, the history of Sichuan's incorporation into the empires of the Qin and the Han was a history of large scale forced movements of people driven by the central government. One of the major sources of the new population in Sichuan was the powerful family. In the *Huayang guo zhi*, a transmitted text recording the local history of Sichuan, these families are referred to as *daxing* 大姓. The *daxing* families of each prefecture are mentioned in the text as an important social aspect of the area.[61] The following sections of the study will also use the term *daxing* when such families are referred to.

During most of the time of the Eastern Han, the *daxing* families served as a form of social power rather than military force. They had large numbers of affiliated peasants and servants in agricultural production and sideline industries, such as wine making and salt production. For example, the *daxing* families in the Linjiang 臨江 Prefecture in the Ba 巴 Commandery had their own wells from which salt was produced.[62] The peasants and servants were a source of the armed forces to guard the land and possessions of these families.[63] During the unrest of the transitional Wang Mang Period in the beginning of the 1st century AD, there were many individual households who looked to the *daxing* families for protection.[64] The affiliated clans and consultants assisted the *daxing* families to climb up the political ladder to come to intervene in political affairs.[65] The distribution of the *daxing* families during the Han dynasty was all over the empire. Many *daxing* families were prosperous for hundreds of years.[66]

As seen in the textual sources, there were many *daxing* families in the commanderies in Eastern Han Sichuan in the study of this book. Although in most of the cases, only the surnames of these families were mentioned. The list of the *daxing* families in Sichuan in Eastern Han or in the period close to the Eastern Han recorded in the *Huayang guo zhi* is as follows (figure 19).[67]

In early Western Han, the Emperor Wu 武 had already realized the threat of the *daxing* families to the central

---
[54] Ch'ü 1972: 160.
[55] Ch'ü 1972: 160.
[56] Ch'ü 1972: 160.
[57] Ch'ü 1972: 160-161.
[58] Ch'ü 1972: 161.
[59] Yang Liansheng 1936: 1016-1023. Yang Liansheng suggested that the so called *haozu* was not simply constituted by the same clan. Instead, it centred on a powerful clan, constituted by many individual households and people, which affiliated to the powerful clan through economic or political relations (Yang Liansheng 1936: 1017).
[60] Chen Suzhen 2010: 45-52. The large area of land was usually effectively exploited and thus became the major source of wealth of the powerful family. Chen Suzhen also mentioned many examples that in early and late Eastern Han, the affiliated households and people were organized by the powerful family as armed forces (Chen Suzhen 2010: 49-52).
[61] For example, when recording the history of the Linjiang 臨江 Prefecture, the local *daxing* families are mentioned in the following context: '臨江縣枳東四里,接朐忍.有鹽官…其豪門亦家有鹽井.又嚴,甘,文,楊,杜為大姓. The Linjiang Prefecture is located four hundred *li* to the east of Quren. The prefecutre has officials on the management of salt…Affluent families also have their own salt wells. The *daxing* families are the Yan's, the Gan's the Wen's, the Yang's and the Du's.' *Huayang*: 67.
[62] *Huayang*: 67. '臨江縣…其豪門亦家有鹽井.'
[63] See *Huayang*: 264 for example. The power families of Gao 高 and Ma 馬 in the Qi 郪 Prefecture owned personal armed forces for generations.
[64] Ch'ü 1972. 208.
[65] Chen Suzhen 2010: 52. Chen Suzhen suggests that the powerful families in Eastern Han were not military entities. Instead, they control the society through their political and economic forces. The affiliated households and people were directed by the powerful families to seize the political and economic power from the government.
[66] For examples, see the Eastern Han families of Lian Fan 廉范, Lu Xu 陸續, Cun Yin 崔駰 menioned in Yang Liansheng 1936: 1021-1023.
[67] Liu Lin notes that the names of the administrative districts of commandry and prefecture in the *Huayang guo zhi* were not names used in a certain period, such as the period around AD 347 when the *Huayang guo zhi* was written. Many commandries or prefectures were established or cancelled during the period from the Western Han to the middle of the 4th century AD. However, the author of the *Huayang guo zhi* used the names of the commandries and prefectures used during the period from the Western Han to the middle of the 4th century AD without mentioning the period when the name was used in most cases (*Huayang*: 5-6).

Commandery	Prefecture	Powerful Family (*daxing*)	Source
Ba 巴	Jiangzhou 江州	Bo 波, Song 松, Wu 毋, Xie 謝, Ran 然, Gai 蓋, Yang 楊, Bai 白, Shangguan 上官, Cheng 程, Chang 常	*Huayang*: 65
Ba 巴	Linjiang 臨江	Yan 嚴, Gan 甘, Wen 文, Yang 楊, Du 杜	*Huayang*: 67
Ba 巴	Pingdu 平都	Yin 殷, Lü 呂, Cai 蔡	*Huayang*: 69
Ba 巴	Dianjiang 墊江	Li 黎, Xia 夏, Du 杜	*Huayang*: 69
Ba 巴	Quren 朐忍	Fu 扶, Xian 先, Xu 徐	*Huayang*: 78
Ba 巴	Langzhong 閬中	Hu 狐, Ma 馬, Pu 蒲, Zhao 趙, Ren 任, Huang 黃, Yan 嚴	*Huayang*: 92-93
Shu 蜀	Chengdu 成都	Liu 劉, Du 杜, Zhang 張, Zhao 趙, Guo 郭, Yang 楊	*Huayang*: 238-239
Shu 蜀	Pi 陴	He 何, Luo 羅, Guo 郭	*Huayang*: 240
Shu 蜀	Fan 繁	Zhang 張	*Huayang*: 241
Shu 蜀	Jiangyuan 江原	Chang 常	*Huayang*: 242
Shu 蜀	Linqiong 臨邛	Chen 陳, Liu 劉	*Huayang*: 244-245
Shu 蜀	Guangdu 廣都	Zhu 朱	*Huayang*: 249
Guanghan 廣漢	Luo 雒	Tan 譚, Li 李, Guo 郭, Zhai 翟	*Huayang*: 257
Guanghan 廣漢	Mianzhu 綿竹	Qin 秦, Du 杜	*Huayang*: 259
Guanghan 廣漢	Shifang 什邡	Yang 楊	*Huayang*: 261
Guanghan 廣漢	Xindu 新都	Ma 馬, Shi 史, Ru 汝, Zheng 鄭	*Huayang*: 261
Guanghan 廣漢	Qi 郪	Wang 王, Li 李, Gao 高, Ma 馬	*Huayang*: 263
Guanghan 廣漢	Deyang 德陽	Kang 康, Gu 古, Yuan 袁	*Huayang*: 266
Qianwei 犍為	Wuyang 武陽	Yang 楊, Li 李 and other 12 families	*Huayang*: 279
Qianwei 犍為	Nan'an 南安	Neng 能, Xuan 宣, Xie 謝, Shen 審, Yang 楊, Fei 費	*Huayang*: 281-282
Qianwei 犍為	Bodao 僰道	Wu 吳, Kui 隗, Chu 楚, Shi 石, Xue 薛, Xiang 相	*Huayang*: 285-286
Qianwei 犍為	Niubing 牛鞞	Cheng 程, Han 韓	*Huayang*: 288
Qianwei 犍為	Zizhong 資中	Wang 王, Dong 董, Zhang 張, Zhao 趙	*Huayang*: 288-289
Qianwei 犍為	Jiangyang 簡陽	Wang 王, Sun 孫, Cheng 程, Zheng 鄭	*Huayang*: 290-291
Qianwei 犍為	Han'an 漢安	Cheng 程, Yao 姚, Guo 郭, Shi 石, Zhang 張, Ji 季, Li 李, Zhao 趙	*Huayang*: 292
Qianwei 犍為	Xinyue 新樂	Wei 魏, Lü 呂	*Huayang*: 295

FIGURE 19. POWERFUL FAMILIES RECORDED IN THE HUAYANG GUO ZHI.

government and forcibly moved many of them from their homeland and forbade large lineages to live together near each other. There were examples of such forced movement of such families to Sichuan in the Western Han as mentioned previously. Such policies continued until the reign of the Emperor Yuan 元 in 40 BC, when the central government became too weak to confine the growth of the *daxing* families.[68] In the Eastern Han, the central government made compromises with the growth of the *daxing* families. On the one hand, the central government allowed the existence and growth of these families and did not attempt to solve the problem of the concentration of large areas of land in the hands of a few families. On the other hand, new policies were formulated to control these families.[69]

Ch'ü T'ung-tsu suggests that the monopoly of the political power by the *daxing* families in Eastern Han came from the recommendation system of *chaju* 察舉, in which 'a relative of 2,000-picul official was given the privilege of being appointed automatically a gentleman in the court'.[70] Although in theory the recommendation system was open to all, the privilege was enjoyed almost exclusively by members of the *daxing* families.[71] In addition, though in theory 'the basic qualification for office was talent or virtue', the fact was that 'personal factors often were influential'. 'The judgment of a local official was usually based on the prevailing opinion of the locality, which was the opinion of the prominent scholar-officials. They knew only the members of the *daxing* families with whom they associated.'[72] For example, the government of the Qianwei Commandery in Sichuan often followed the suggestions from the local *daxing* in the Jiang'an Prefecture and the prevailing opinion of the locality to recommend officers and to deal with political affair.[73]

Perspectives on Death and the Afterlife

Pascal Boyer argues in his book, *Religion Explained* that religion is a practical matter and concepts in religion are developed by people at times when there is a need for them.[74] For example, when some salient event has happened, people incline to explain it in terms of the actions of some god or that someone has done things that the ancestors do not appreciate. Therefore religious concepts are exploited to understand, explain and resolve some mysterious occurrences and the unknown.

---

[68] Ch'ü 1972: 207-208.
[69] Chen Suzhen 2010: 52. In early Eastern Han, the emperor Liu Xiu attempted to control the growth of the big local families through reducing the number of the local official positions, inhibiting the owning of private armies in the local kingdoms, freeing slaves from the big families, forcing the royal relatives in the capital to go to their local kingdoms.
[70] Ch'ü 1972: 204-205.
[71] Ch'ü 1972: 205.
[72] Ch'ü 1972: 206.
[73] *Huayang*: 292. '而程,石杰立,郡常秉議論選之.'
[74] Boyer 2001: 155-191 and 232-262. Boyer has discussed the gods and spirits as supernatural agents in different societies. He also suggests that there is a contrast between theological understandings and the mundane business of representing religious agents in the practical contexts. Therefore we can see that certain inconsistencies always exist in religion. In addition, people do not just 'stipulate that there is a supernatural being somewhere who creates thunder, or that there are souls wandering about in the night', they 'actually interact with them, in the very concrete sense of giving and receiving, paying, promising, threatening, protecting, placating (Boyer 2001: 156)'.

This practical attitude towards religion helps to explain the multiple and often contradictory understandings of what would happen after death during the Han period. On one hand, people prepared to facilitate the ascension to a heavenly world.[75] On the other hand, people saw the possibility that they could continue in an afterlife that modelled on this life, instead of going to heaven.[76] Therefore, they made thorough preparation for what they would need in such cases.[77]

A general understanding of the division of the human soul into the *hun* 魂 and the *po* 魄 in the Han period could further be helpful to understand the contradiction in people's view of the world for the deceased. When a person dies, his *hun* leaves the body and ascends to heaven while his *po* remains with his body in the ground.[78] Michael Loewe makes use of this division of the soul to explain the seemingly contradictory views of heaven and the netherworld. He suggests that the tomb was prepared for the deceased for two purposes: 1) to guide the *hun* to heaven; 2) to satisfy the *po* on the ground.[79] 'The *po* was provided with the essential commodities that he might need in his continued existence with the body and with valuables that would make such an existence attractive.'[80] In this sense, 'there was no contradiction in providing for both of these contingencies for one and the same person'.[81]

In the following chapters of the book, the tomb structure, burial objects and pictorial carvings will be on certain occasions considered as providing for both the guide of the soul of the tomb occupant to heaven and a happy life after death. Consequently, the tomb itself is regarded as an ambiguous place, which is not necessarily heaven or the dwelling for the deceased.

4. Textual Sources

The major textual sources for the study are the *Shi ji* 史記 (the Records of the Historian), the *Han shu* 漢書 (the History of the Western Han), the *Hou Han shu* 後漢書 (the History of the Eastern Han) and the *Huayang guo zhi* 華陽國志 (the History of Huayang). The coverage of the four works is different. The *Shi ji*, the *Han shu* and the *Hou Han shu* were compiled in the form of the Standard History (*zhengshi* 正史).[82] The *Shi ji* was written as an overall account of human history down to the end of the 2nd century BC, the author's own time. The *Han shu* records the history of the Western Han dynasty, 'beginning with the early life of its founder, Liu Bang 劉邦 in about 210 BC, and ending with the fall of Wang Mang 王莽 in AD 23'.[83] It was mainly written and compiled by Ban Gu 班固 (AD 32-92), an author who lived in the following Eastern Han dynasty. The *Hou Han shu* describes the history of the Eastern Han dynasty, beginning with the life of its founder, Liu Xiu 劉秀 in about AD 25, and ending in AD 220. It is a composite work. The chapters on imperial annals and biographies were written by Fan Ye 范曄 (AD 398-446) based on earlier material. The treatises were written about a century earlier by Sima Biao (AD 240-306).[84] In contrast to the three Standard Histories, which records the history of the whole empire, the *Huayang guo zhi* describes the history of Sichuan and the adjacent areas in Yunnan, Guizhou, Gansu, Shaanxi and Hubei before the middle of the 4th century AD, the time of the author, Chang Qu 常璩.[85] As pointed out by Michael Loewe that there is much more information 'about political matters at the capital' than information 'about events in the provinces of the empires' in the Standard Histories,[86] the *Huayang*

---

[75] Inscriptions found on Han funerary bronze mirrors show that people craved for life as an immortal: 'If you climb Mount T'ai, you may see the immortal beings. They feed on the purest jade, they drink from the springs of manna. They yoke the scaly dragons to their carriage, they mount the floating clouds. The white tiger leads them…they ascend straight to heaven. May you receive a never ending span, long life that lasts for ten thousand years, with a fit place in office and safety for your children and grandchildren.' Loewe 1979: 200.

[76] According to a passage in the *Lun heng* 論衡 by Wang Chong 王充 (c. 27-97 AD), the ordinary people in Han thought that the dead were like the living. 'They commiserate with them, [thinking] that in their graves they are lonely, that their souls are solitary and without companions, that their tombs and mounds are closed and devoid of grain and other things. Therefore they make dummies to serve the corpses in their coffins, and fill the latter with eatables, to gratify the spirits. This customs has become so inveterate, and has gone to such lengths, that very often people will ruin their families and use up all their property for the coffins of the dead. 閔死獨葬,魂孤無副,丘墓閉藏,穀物乏постоян,故作偶人以侍屍柩,多藏食物以歆精魂,積浸流至,或破家盡業,以充死棺.' Liu Pansui 1957: 461. The translation is after Forke 1962: 369.

[77] K. Brashier (2001-2002: 160-161) notes that people in the Han could simultaneously hold inconsistent perspectives when he studies mountain inscriptions dedicated to the Spirit Lords of the mountains. Poo Mu-chou (1998: 3-5, 184) suggests that elites in the Han might practice one set of beliefs at court and another at home. On the other hand, A. Siedel (1987) revealed some coherences in Han popular religion through a certain category of burial objects, which bear similar funerary texts. Poo Mu-chou (1998: 177) further suggests that in most ancient civilizations, excluding Ancient Egypt, 'the netherworld was never a clearly conceived place', and he quotes Humphreys, who suggests that 'it is difficult in most cultures to locate the dead unambiguously in one place'. Humphreys 1993: 161.

[78] For detailed discussion on the *hun* and *po* see Yü 1987. Yü Ying-shih has traced the origin and development of the concept of *hun* and *po* in pre-Buddhist China. He suggests that by the 2nd century BC, at the latest, the division of the soul into *hun* and *po* had been widely accepted. He notes that there could be several dualities involved in the formulation of the soul in addition to the basic duality of *hun* and *po*. He suggests that the dualism can be briefly understood in the way that 'ancient Chinese generally believed that the individual human life consists of a bodily part as well as a spiritual part'. Yü 1987: 375.

[79] Loewe 1979: 11.
[80] Loewe 1979: 13.
[81] Loewe 1979: 11.

[82] For the definition of Standard History and the use of Standard History in the study of the history of Han, see Gardiner 1973: 42-52. The Standard History, or the official dynastic history, 'refers to the *Shi ji* and twenty-four other works, which in general followed its plan of construction and, perhaps more significant, were all eventually accepted as presenting the orthodox and received account of the successive periods into which Chinese history was divided'. Gardiner 1973: 42.
[83] Hulsewé: 129.
[84] Loewe: 4.
[85] *Huayang*: 1-2. '*Huayang* 華陽' is the abbreviation of '*Huashan zhi yang* 華山之陽 (the south of the Hua Mountain (in today's Shaanxi Province))'. The structure of the *Huayang guo zhi* is similar to that of the Standard Histories. It has twelve *juan* 卷, which are divided into three sections. The first section (*juan* 1 to 4) describes the history of the Liang 梁 Region, the Yi 益 Region and the Ning 寧 Region, which is similar to the administrative geography (*dili zhi* 地理志) in the Standard History. The second section (*juan* 5-9) describes the four independent regimes in Sichuan in late Western Han, late Eastern Han and the first half of the 4th century AD, and the history in the Western Jin period (AD 265-316), which is similar to the imperial annals (*ben ji* 本紀) in the Standard History. The third section describes the eminent figures from Western Han to the middle of the 4th century AD, which is similar to the biographies (*lie zhuan* 列傳) in the Standard History.
[86] Loewe 1987: 5.

guo zhi that focuses on the history of Sichuan including detailed information about some local households and individuals is especially useful to the study of the social background in which the popularity of the cliff tomb was rooted.[87]

5. Archaeological Discoveries

To study the cliff tombs in Sichuan and make comparisons with the contemporary tombs in central and eastern China, I will make extensive use of Chinese archaeological reports. The core data for this study are 289 cliff tombs in Sichuan published since the 1950s in the archaeological reports.[88] Fragmentary information on more individual cliff tombs can also be gathered from the reports of general investigation of the cliff tombs within certain areas.

Early investigation of the cliff tombs was conducted by western travelers, explorers and missionaries in the late 19th century and early 20th century. An overall investigation of the antiquities and historic sites in the area was the object of such investigations and the researchers were then impressed by the distinctive form of the cliff tombs and their wide distribution in the area.[89] After the first incorrect assumption that these tombs belonged to the 'aboriginal' people,[90] the researchers soon realized that the occupants of these tombs were not different from occupants of other types of Han tombs. The main evidence is the accumulating discoveries of the cliff burial objects mainly in the forms of various pottery vessels, figurines and models, which share the common features with the burial objects found in other Han tombs.[91] In addition, the early researchers had become interested in the stone pictorial carvings frequently found in the cliff tombs, which share some subjects with the pictorial carvings on the brick and stone in other Han tombs, though with some different local styles. The first catalogue of stone carvings in cliff tombs in Sichuan was published in 1951 in the US by Richard C. Rudolph in collaboration with Wen You.[92]

Large scale scientific excavation of the cliff tombs started in the 1940s in Pengshan 彭山 with Chinese archaeologists from the Society for Research in Chinese Architecture (*Ying zao xueshe* 營造學社).[93] In 1957, with more comprehensive archaeological evidence at hand, Cheng De-Kun pointed out that the cliff tomb and the brick chamber tomb were two major tomb types in Eastern Han Sichuan.[94] Followed by more and more scientific excavations of the cliff tombs in Sichuan together with the archaeological reports published in academic journals since the 1950s, scholars started to establish the chronology of the development of the cliff tombs and summarize their local features in different areas of Sichuan. Luo Erhu was the first one who established the chronology of the development of the cliff tombs and summarized the different types of the cliff tombs in 1988.[95] Fan Xiaoping elaborated the features of cliff tombs in different areas of Sichuan in more detail based on further archaeological discoveries 18 years after Luo Erhu's pioneering investigation.[96] In the past two decades, there have also been articles and volumes studying cliff tombs in specific areas in Sichuan. Tang Changshou studies cliff tombs in Pengshan and Leshan 樂山, two adjacent areas and discusses the similarities and differences of the cliff tomb in the two areas.[97] Susan Erickson focuses on the cliff tombs in Santai near the Qi 郪 River.[98]

---

[87] For the value of Chinese local gazetteers in historical research, see Leslie 1973: 71-74.
[88] See Appendix 3.
[89] See Torrance 1910 and 1930-1931; Ségalen 1917; Ségalen 1923; Bishop 1916; Bedford 1937; Edwards 1954. For a very early account, see Baber 1882. These early researchers were well aware of the lack of textual records of the Sichuan area in early China and attempted to explore the local history through their investigation of the local relics. For example, when examining ancient burial remains in Sichuan, T. Torrance included the cliff tombs as an important section in his paper recording his observation of the burial customs in Sichuan (Torrance 1910). When investigating stone sculptures in Shandong, Shaanxi and Sichuan in early 20th century, Victor Ségalen incorporated the cliff tombs in Sichuan into his survey (Ségalen 1917; Ségalen 1923). Their investigations of the cliff tombs were mainly carried out in the Pengshan 彭山 and Leshan 樂山 area in Sichuan. T. Torrance suggested that the cliff tomb was a local burial custom in Sichuan, the origin of which could be related to the assimilation of the Sichuan area into the Han empire from the 2nd century BC to the 2nd century AD (Torrance 1930-1931: 88-89).
[90] Ségalen 1917 and Ségalen 1923. Victor Ségalen mentioned that after E. Baber of the British Consular service, who investigated the cliff tombs in Sichuan in the 1880s and came to the conclusion that the cliff tombs belonged to the aboriginal inhabitants, the later 'European travelers, missionaries or merchants repeated from the Chinese saying that they were Man Tung, caves of the Man Tzu' (Ségalen 1917: 155).
[91] Torrance 1910: 65. As early as 1910, T. Torrance suggested that 'as a result of my investigations, covering more than a year, it is established beyond all reasonable doubt that these caves, in the Northern section at least, were tombs of the Chinese and not of the so called "Man-Tze", or aboriginal inhabitants'. His main evidence was that the content of the burial objects in the cliff tombs was similar to those in the dated Eastern Han tombs. Victor Ségalen took T. Torrance suggestion into consideration and further suggested that the artisans who made the cliff tombs might be from the same school who made the stone *que* pillars, which were typical Eastern Han tomb monuments popular in Sichuan, since both the cliff tombs and the stone *que* pillars have many similar architectural details, which were the reproduction of the wooden architecture. In addition, Ségalen suggested that the frequently found stone coffins in the cliff tombs showed that the tomb occupants were Han Chinese, since the pictorial carvings on the coffins were similar to the other Eastern Han funerary pictures (Ségalen 1917: 155-156).
[92] During the Second World War, many Chinese scholars were forced to go to west China, especially the Chengdu plain in Sichuan, where a whole field of research on the mortuary pictorial art of the Han dynasty started to attract the attention of the researcher in both China and the West. The volume (Rudolf and Wen 1951) was published in this context, through collecting rubbings of the pictorial stones and bricks from the cliff tombs and brick tombs in Sichuan and from private collections.
[93] The draft of the report, written by Chen Mingda in the 1940s was published in 2003 after editing. See Chen Mingda 2003. The original draft together with large amount of unpublished photos and sketches are conserved in the Three Gorges Museum, Chongqing. There is also a monograph based on the scattered reports of the excavation in Pengshan, published in 1991. See Nanjing bowuyuan 1991.
[94] Cheng 1957: 139-154.
[95] Luo Erhu 1988. The materials used by Luo Erhu are mainly from the reports published in academic journals by the 1980s and his personal investigation of the tombs and the available materials in the local archaeological institutes. His work becomes a major resource for the later researchers of the cliff tombs in Sichuan.
[96] Fan Xiaoping 2006: 67. The summary made by Fan Xiaoping is further elaborated in Chapter 2 of the book.
[97] Tang Changshou 1993. Most of the cliff tombs in Tang Changshou's work are not published in the form of archaeological reports. Tang's personal investigation of the local tombs is crucial to the study of the features of the cliff tombs in Pengshan and Leshan in relation to the cliff tombs in other areas in Sichuan.
[98] Erickson 2003 is the result of Erickson's field trip to Santai in Sichuan on the study of the architectural elements in the local cliff tombs. See also Erickson 2010: 24-29, which is a part of the introduction to the Han

Two types of archaeological reports are used in the study: the monograph, which usually deals with a cemetery with a large number of tombs,[99] and the journal report, which usually describes a single tomb or several tombs.[100] The journal report and the monograph follow a similar organisation.[101]

A fundamental problem with the Chinese reports on burial sites is that burial objects are divided into typologies.[102] In addition, archaeological reports are usually written according to a set pattern as noted by Lothar von Falkenhausen.[103] The assemblage of the burial objects from the same tomb are separated from their original context and reported in a fragmentary way. This means that the researcher then needs to reconstruct the content and location of the burial objects in a single tomb by reassembling fragmentary information from the division of objects into typologies. When a single tomb is reported in a journal or in a monograph, the division of objects into typologies is not so problematic.

Another problem is the information provided by the reports on individual tombs and the relationship between tombs on a cemetery site. Most of the cliff tombs have been reported after rescue excavations.[104] The rescue excavations usually took place when tomb objects were reported as being looted or when construction work of a bridge or a road uncovered a cliff tomb by chance. This means that the excavation can rarely be scientifically planned to explore the cliff tombs systematically as a single cemetery site. The ways in which the tombs are planned in a cemetery site and their internal relationships is rarely mentioned. Most of the reports choose large scale and richly decorated cliff tombs, without mentioning the lesser cliff tombs at the same cemetery sites. In addition, many of the cliff tombs have been seriously looted, so that tomb objects have been displaced from their original locations in the cliff tomb or completely removed. Furthermore, due to acid soil in the Sichuan area, few skeletons in the cliff tombs remain or have been found under a good enough condition for further analysis. This means that an important source from bodies, which is crucial to study of the burial ritual, is unavailable.

In spite of these problems, the reports of cliff tombs in Sichuan are very thorough in their descriptions of the objects and the overall features of the tomb. Moreover, the recent published volumes of the reports on cliff tombs at Santai and Zhongjiang 中江 have avoided some of these problems.[105] Both of the reports set out and separate each cliff tomb individually at the cemetery site alongside the full range of objects found therein. In effect, these reports are lists of cliff tombs and their contents. One is then able to utilise this information without first having to reconstruct the cliff tomb by sifting through various typologies. However, the two reports have problems in establishing an overview of the tombs at the cemetery sites. Only grand tombs containing architectural elements of high quality or painted reliefs have been reported. The lesser tombs at the same cemetery site are only numbered and recorded in the forms of the statistics of the cliff tombs in the area at the beginnings of the reports. This means that the information on the overview of the cemetery site and the structure of the cemetery is unavailable for research. In fact, though cliff tombs have usually been found in large numbers at particular sites, no archaeological reports so far have attempted to describe the overview of a cemetery site of cliff tombs. Such overview can only be obtained from piecing together fragmental information of individual tombs in adjacent areas reported in different journal articles.[106]

Most of the archaeological reports on the relatively richly decorated cliff tombs, or on the cliff tombs found with large amount of burial objects, attribute these cliff tombs to the local powerful families (the *haoqiang* or the *daxing*). However, these conclusions are usually simply stated in

---

tombs in the volume of the Cambridge History of China, in which the cliff tombs in Santai are her main examples when describing the cliff tomb as a local burial form in Eastern Han Sichuan.

[99] Particular extensively decorated pictorial tombs, such as the stone tomb no. 1 at Yi'nan in Shandong, are usually recorded in a monograph, rather than in a journal.

[100] The journal reports used in the book are as follows, *Kaogu* 考古, *Wenwu* 文物, *Sichuan Wenwu* 四川文物, *Kaogu yu wenwu* 考古與文物 and *Kaogu xuebao* 考古學報. These reports are written in Chinese. Most of them have an English summary at the beginning.

[101] In journal reports, the location of the tomb and the cemetery is described first, followed by the description of the structure and the size of the tomb. Then the burial objects and their location in the tomb are briefly introduced. The objects are then categorized based on typologies of material and shape. When the tomb contains pictorial carvings or mural paintings, the location and the content of the pictures are described. There is usually a conclusion section in the report, in which the date of the tomb and the social status of the tomb occupant are discussed. In monographs, location of the cemetery site is described first, followed by descriptions of large scale or richly furnished tombs selected from the site. The burial objects are then categorized according to typologies of shape and material. At the end, the date of the cemetery and the social status of the tomb occupants on the cemetery are analyzed.

[102] The typologies in these reports follow that of Oscar Montelius. Object types are defined on the basis of variations in form and subdivisions are further made. Chronology can then be established based on the pattern of occurrences of certain object types in certain periods. For discussion on Montelius's approaches to European pre-history based on typology, see Trigger 2006: 223-230.

[103] Falkenhausen 2006: 15. Falkenhausen points out that 'Chinese archaeological reports constitute a peculiar kind genre of academic writing, governed as they are by their own textual conventions and conveying their information in sometimes idiosyncratic ways.'

[104] So far, there are 289 published Eastern Han cliff tombs and 144 brick or stone tombs in Sichuan. See Appendix 3 (only cliff tombs are listed).

[105] See the authors of the reports of the cliff tombs in Santai point out that for the convenience of the researchers, they report the individual tomb one by one instead of making summary of the burial objects from all the tombs by topology (Sichuan sheng wenwu kaogu yanjiuyuan, Mianyang shi bowuguan and Santai xian wenwu guanli suo 2007: 10). The authors only make conclusions in the end of the volume of the report instead of in the end of the report on each tomb in order to exhibit the original state of the tombs to the largest extent to the researchers. Following the positive feedback on the Santai report, the report on the cliff tombs in Zhongjiang follows the same way to record the tombs (Sichuan sheng wenwu kaogu yanjiuyuan, Deyang shi wenwu kaogu yanjiusuo and Zhongjiang xian wenwu baohu guanli suo 2008: 2-5).

[106] See for example the cliff tombs in Xindu 新都 in Sichuan. Reports of groups of cliff tombs in adjacent areas at Xindu (Liu Zhiyuan 1958; Chen Yunhong, Zhang Yuxin and Wang Bo 2007; Xindu xian wenwu guanlisuo 1984; Chengdu shi wenwu kaogu yanjiusuo 2004; Sichuan sheng bowuguan 1985a) have been published over the past 50 years. The authors of these reports also realize the internal links between these cliff tombs. They often cite discoveries in earlier reports as evidence to support their periodisation of the tombs.

one or two sentences. This poses a series of questions: 1) How 'powerful' were these families, especially compared with the other elaborately decorated brick or stone chamber tombs, which are also simply concluded as tombs of the powerful families in the archaeological reports? 2) Based on what evidence, are these tombs attributed to the 'powerful families'? Simply because these tombs have elaborate decoration and many burial objects? 3) What did the members of these powerful families do for living? Were they landowners, officials, or both? These also are the questions this study will discuss when discussing the factors underlying the popularity of the cliff tombs in Sichuan in Eastern Han.

An examination of the archaeological reports will show that the evidence of the 'powerful family' background of some grand cliff tombs falls into the following three aspects as exhibited in the tombs: wealth, private armies and family organization. The following summary is based on the discussions in the archaeological reports. The chapters of this book will present discussions as to what degree were these families powerful, both politically and economically, most especially when compared with tomb occupants of some elaborate brick or stone chamber tombs.

Wealth

The wealth of the *daxing* family came primarily from agricultural and other production on the large areas of land owned by the family. Part of the wealth was used to build an ample house. The way in which a large cliff tomb was constructed to resemble an ample house will be elaborated in Chapter 2 on cliff tomb structure. An example of a cliff tomb modelled on an ample house which exhibited the wealth of the tomb occupant can be seen at Zijingwan M3 in Santai described at the beginning of this chapter. It contains many architectural features and even an armory.

Similar plans of the houses of living are found in some tomb reliefs and pottery house models in the Eastern Han tombs.[107] The Eastern Han pottery tomb relief unearthed from Chengdu in Sichuan depicts a courtyard scene with the main building, the living room in the rear, a watch tower by the encircling courtyard wall and the kitchen near the front gate (figure 20). In the living room in the rear of the courtyard, the host is seated with his guests being entertained by a pair of dancing cranes in the middle of the courtyard. The doorsteps in front of the entrance to the main building may suggest the importance of the building in the courtyard house.

The large tomb complex modelled on the large house complex further provides the stage for displaying the family wealth acquired mainly from the family's agricultural estate. The life of a wealthy landowner who managed a large scale agricultural estate is comprehensively exhibited

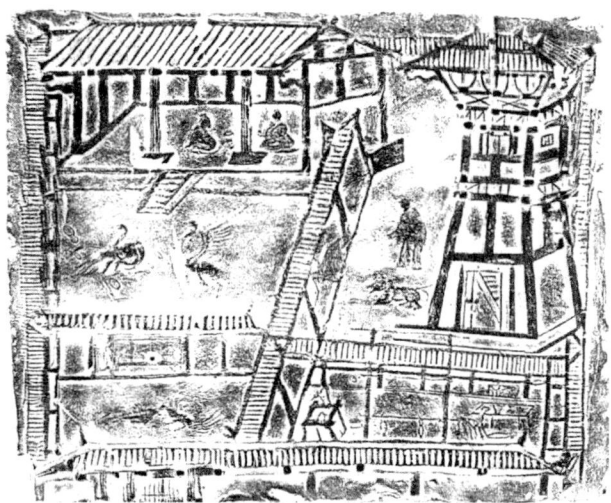

FIGURE 20. POTTERY BRICK RELIEF OF AN EASTERN HAN COURTYARD HOUSE. AFTER LIU 1983: FIG. 71.

in the cliff tomb through both the stone carving and the burial objects in the tomb.

Private Armies

Many *daxing* families in the Eastern Han had private armies to protect their possessions. Most of the members of their private armies were peasants who worked for the powerful family in ordinary times, and became soldiers when there was a need to protect the families' estates. The images of the peasant-soldiers constitute an important component part of many large cliff tombs in Sichuan in the forms of pottery figures or stone carvings. The pottery peasant-soldier excavated in the cliff tomb Baozishan 寶子山 M1 in Xinjin 新津 in Sichuan provides visual evidence for the appearance of the peasant-soldiers in Eastern Han. The three-dimensional figure stands in a height of 83 centimetres.[108] He wears a low cap, a tunic, an under garment comes to his knees and a pair of shoes opening at the toes. He carries a long spade, a tool usually used to till the soil. A sword with a ring-shaped handle and a knife are attached to his belt. The sword and the spade mark the dual responsibility of a peasant-soldier in agricultural production and in defending the estate of the *daxing* families. The arrangement of the images of the peasant-soldier in the cliff tomb may also suggest the continuing need of the large landowner for protection in his afterlife.[109] The images of the peasant-soldier also appear in the form of stone figurines and stone carvings.[110] In addition to the peasant-soldier as a part-time guard of the *daxing* family, there were also full-time private guards for these families, who are also depicted in the cliff tombs in stone carvings and in pottery figurines. In Tangliangzi 塔梁子 M3 in Zhongjiang in Sichuan, two guards are carved on either side of the entrance to the second main

---

[107] See Los Angeles County Museum of Art and China Overseas Archaeological Exhibition Corporation 1987: no. 24 for an example of an Eastern Han pottery house model which illustrates a courtyard house flanked by a pair of watch towers.

[108] Lu Deliang 1958: 34 and Rawson 2001: 305.
[109] Rawson 2001: 305.
[110] For the stone figurine of the peasant-soldier found in the cliff tomb, see Hu Xueyuan and Yang Yi 1993: 42.

FIGURE 21. RUBBINGS OF TWO GUARDS HOLDING WEAPON FROM THE SHIZIWAN CLIFF TOMB IN LESHAN. AFTER GONG TINGWAN, GONG YU AND DAI JIALING 1998: FIGS. 224-225.

FIGURE 22. RUBBINGS OF TWO ARCHERS FROM THE CLIFF TOMBS IN SANTAI. AFTER GONG TINGWAN, GONG YU AND DAI JIALING 1998: FIGS. 226-227.

chamber.[111] The right hand guard wears a long robe with a long sword attached to his belt. His robe and sword suggest his main responsibility is as a full-time guard for the tomb occupant's family. Similar guardian figures are found in the stone carvings in the cliff tombs in Leshan in Sichuan (figure 21).

In addition to the figures of guards standing still, there are relief depictions of soldiers running or marching. Many images of the archer are depicted at Santai (figure 22). There are two principal types. The archer of the first type holds a bow and an arrow in his hands. The archer of the second type places his feet on the crossbow to shoot the arrow. The archers carved in the cliff tomb Fentaizui 墳臺嘴 M1 and Huangmingyue 黃明月 M1 are shown using their full strength by placing their feet on the corssbow with their knees bending to a great extent.[112] Another archer carved in the cliff tomb Huangmingyue M1 is holding the bow in his hand, concentrating on aiming at a target.[113]

Among all the areas where the cliff tombs are found, those in the Santai area together with the adjacent Zhongjiang area contain especially large numbers of military images, which matches the records on the local *daxing* families in the *Huayang guozhi*.[114] According to the record, there were several powerful families, the Wang's, the Gao's and the Ma's, residing in the Qi area, namely today's Santai and Zhongjiang. All the *daxing* families had their own armies extending over several generations. Though no such names have been found in the large cliff tombs in Santai and Zhongjiang, the military images here suggest that they belonged to the local *daxing* families.

Family Organization

In the Qin and the Han, large families of several generations were discouraged. According to the Qin law, fathers, sons and brothers were prohibited to live in the same household.[115] The policy continued into the Western Han and the Eastern Han.[116] Ordinary households in the Western Han had three to four members.[117] In the Eastern Han, some powerful families ignored the law and had households with many family members. Exceptionally large families in Eastern Han with more than three generations sharing the family possessions are recorded in the standard history on the wealthy powerful families.[118] In such families, the number of the family numbers is large.

Coinciding with the historical record, the Eastern Han cliff tombs in Sichuan in some cases contain large numbers of tomb occupants in coffins which are placed in the multiple chambers of the tomb, modelled on a large house complex as mentioned previously. It is likely that the large family containing large numbers of family members is epitomized in the cliff tomb modelled on the house complex. For example, the cliff tomb Tianhuishan 天回山 M3 is a grand cliff tomb, which is around 30 metres in length, consisted of eight chambers, containing a total number of 14 coffins, which were distributed in different chambers (figure 23).[119]

---

[111] Sichuan sheng wenwu kaogu yanjiuyuan, Deyang shi wenwu kaogu yanjiusuo and Zhongjiang xian wenwu baohu guanli suo 2008: pl. 63.
[112] Sichuan sheng wenwu kaogu yanjiuyuan, Mianyang shi bowuguan, and Santai xian wenwu guanli suo 2007: pls. 287 and 304.
[113] Sichuan sheng wenwu kaogu yanjiuyuan, Mianyang shi bowuguan, and Santai xian wenwu guanli suo 2007: pl. 305.
[114] See *Huayang*: 263. '鄸縣…大姓…又有高,馬家,世掌部曲. In the Qi Prefecture, …the *daxing* families, …the Gao's and the Ma's had private armies for many generations.'
[115] *Shi ji*: 2232. '而令民父子兄弟同室內息者為禁. And there was the law that commoners were prohibited from living with their fathers, sons or brothers in the same household.'
[116] Lewis 2006: 87-88. As agreed by all scholars, the forms of the Han household were directly inherited from the Qin pattern in the Warring States. In the 4th century BC, during the reform of Shang Yang 商鞅 of the Qin state, household in which sons lived with their fathers were levied double taxes.
[117] Ch'ü 1972: 8.
[118] In the *Hou Han shu*, two cases of the powerful families, the Fan 樊 and the Cai 蔡 were recorded for their large size of the family, in which, three generations of the family members shared the family possessions. *Hou Han shu*: 1119; 1980. Ch'ü T'ung-tsu (1972: 9) suggests that the history's emphasis on the family size and the recording of the only two cases of the large amount of family members imply that the large families were unusual in the Eastern Han and only appeared in some powerful families.
[119] Liu Zhiyuan 1958. The Tianhuishan tomb M3 will be further discussed in Chapter 2 and 4.

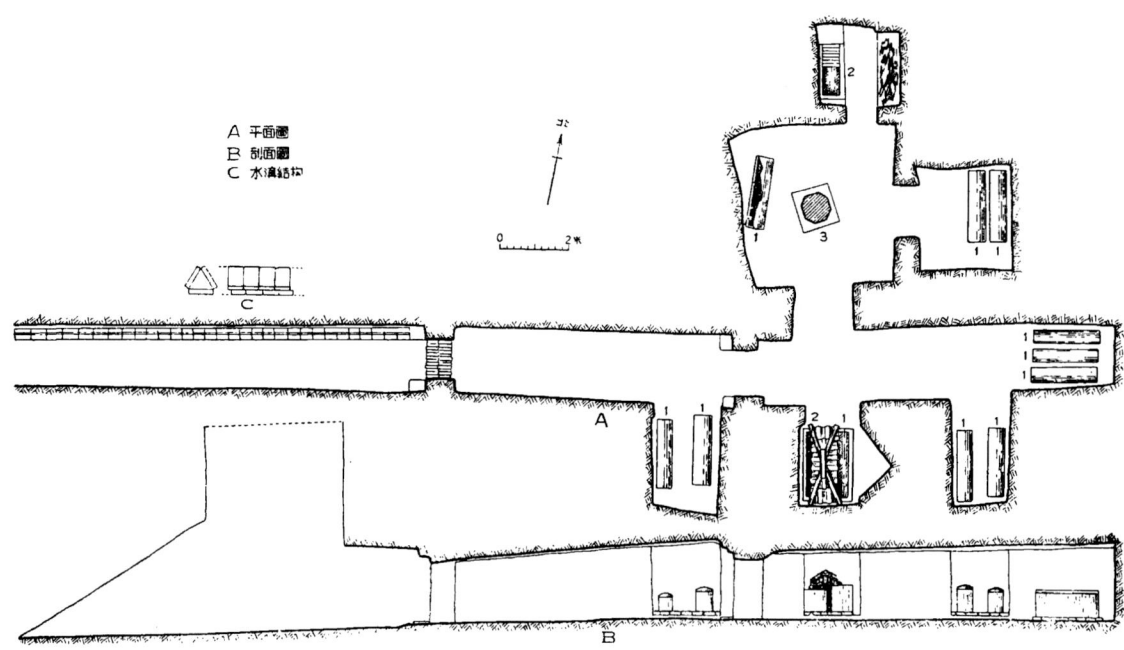

FIGURE 23. PLAN OF THE CLIFF TOMB TIANHUISHAN NO. 3 IN CHENGDU. AFTER LIU ZHIYUAN 1958: FIG. 3.

6. Literature Review

Important works that establish the foundation of my database for the study of the cliff tombs have been introduced in the previous section. However, those are mostly descriptive rather than analytical. A series of questions about the tombs have been touched upon in those works and in the relevant studies on the Han tombs. These questions include: 1) What were the identities of the cliff tomb occupants? 2) What is the origin of the cliff tombs in Sichuan? and 3) How did the cliff tombs relate to the contemporary brick and stone chamber tombs? The discussion of these questions will be crucial to explore the factors underlying the popularity of the cliff tombs in Sichuan.

On the identity of the cliff tomb occupants, most of the scholars agree that these were the Han people, the same as those of the brick or stone chamber tombs in central and eastern China.[120] In addition, the elaborately decorated cliff tombs with large numbers of burial objects belonged to the local *daxing* families, as suggested in most of the archaeological reports.[121] Wu Hung suggests that many cliff tomb occupants were the disciples of the *Wu dou mi jiao* 五斗米道, the Five Pecks of Grain, the begining of Daoism, which was popular in Eastern Han. The combined use of the three elements, the cliff tomb, the pictorial stone coffin and the money tree (the *yaoqianshu* 搖錢樹), established a distinctive religious symbolizing system. In particular, *Xiwangmu* 西王母, the Queen Mother of the West, an important figure in this religion, was widely depicted on these elements.[122] Wu Hung's suggestion provides insight into the way in which the identity of the cliff tomb occupants are studied based on burial remains, other than simply categorizing them into a social class. However, his conclusion on the religious influence oversimplifies the complicated factors underlying the popularity of the cliff tomb and the relevant objects as will be discussed in the following chapters.

With regard to the origin of the cliff tombs in Sichuan, some scholars trace the prototype of the cliff tombs to the rock-cut tombs in Persepolis in West Asia dated to the 5th century BC. Segalen was probably the first researcher who made such a suggestion,[123] which was brought up again by Chen Mingda in the 1940s and Gu Qiyi in the 1980s.[124] This suggestion will be discussed in detail in Chapter 2 on tomb structure. Luo Erhu and Fan Xiaoping doubt the western origin of the cliff tomb, mainly based on the stark contrast in scale and plan between the cliff tombs in Sichuan and the Western Asian rock-cut tombs. In 2012, Jessica Rawson again argues for the possible influence of the Western Asian rock-cut tombs on the cliff tombs in Sichuan. Her main evidence is that the pictorial scheme at the entrance to some cliff tombs in Sichuan appears to be very similar to that of the entrance to the rock-cut tomb of Darius I at Persepolis.[125] Her suggestion draws important attention to the possibility that there were various sources

---

[120] See Segalen 1917: 155, Cheng 1957: 139-140, Luo Erhu 1988: 133-134 and Fan Xiaoping 2006: 13-16.
[121] See for example, the discussions on the identity of the tomb occupants of the Tianhuishan tomb M3 in Chengdu (Liu Zhiyuan 1958.1: 102-103), the cliff tombs in Santai (Sichuan sheng wenwu kaogu yanjiuyuan, Mianyang shi bowuguan, and Santai xian wenwu guanli suo 2007: 291) and the cliff tombs in Zhongjiang (Sichuan sheng wenwu kaogu yanjiuyuan, Deyang shi wenwu kaogu yanjiusuo and Zhongjiang xian wenwu baohu guanli suo 2008: 92-95).
[122] Wu Hung 2000: 435-438. The origin and the cult of the Queen Mother of the West together with the burial objects, the money tree in the cliff tomb will be further elaborated in Chapter 3.
[123] See Segalen 1917: 156.
[124] Chen Mingda 2003b: 142-143 and Gu Qiyi 1990: 186-188.
[125] Rawson 2012: 34-35.

of information that contributed to the development of the cliff tombs in Sichuan. Without further discussing the origin of the cliff tombs in Sichuan, Ma Xiaoliang makes an important observation that the cliff tombs appeared in many different areas in the Sichuan Basin at around the same time, at the beginning of the 1st century AD, with several similar simple structures.[126]

On how the cliff tombs in Sichuan related to other contemporary burial forms, some scholars, especially those working on a general history of the development of the burial forms in the Han dynasty, regard the cliff tombs in Sichuan as being at the same stage as the stone or brick chamber tombs in the process of constructing more house-like tombs, i.e., the cliff tomb and the stone or brick tomb are in essence the same burial form.[127] In her investigation of the cliff tombs in Santai in Sichuan, Susan Erickson emphasizes that many pictorial decorations of the cliff tombs have their prototypes or counterparts in the earlier or contemporary tombs in central and east China.[128] Though focusing on the pictorial stone carvings instead of the tomb structure, Martin Powers, Xin Lixiang and Michael Nylan suggest that the stone carving style of the cliff tombs in Sichuan is very similar to that of the tombs in Nanyang in the metropolitan area, where the stone carving tradition developed earlier.[129] They suggest that there have been influences of stone carving style from the metropolitan area on the cliff tombs in Sichuan and thought that the development of the cliff tomb in Sichuan was established on the basis of borrowing both the architectural form and the stone carving style from other regions. These thoughts will be followed up in the following chapters. The reasons for such possible borrowings will be considered.

7. Research Approaches

The main factors underlying the popularity of the cliff tombs in Sichuan were in essence about the intentional and unintentional choices made by their creators. Each chapter of the book makes an analysis of the choices underlying the characteristics of specific part of the cliff tombs in relation to the contemporary brick or stone chamber tombs. These choices together constitute the preference of the cliff tomb occupants underlying the cliff tomb's design, decoration and furnishing, which are inseparable from one another. The study also considers the natural environment and the social background in which people made these choices.

They were also important factors that contributed to the popularity of the cliff tombs in Sichuan.

The choices of people for a proper burial form are embodied through the interaction between people and the material world. An important aspect of this material world is that people do not exist through their consciousness or body. Instead, as Daniel Miller suggests, they feel their existence because there is 'an exterior environment that habituates and prompts' them.[130] The exterior environment studied in this book mainly refers to the Eastern Han society in which the tombs played important roles in people's social life. In addition, the distinctive regional cultures were influenced by the imperial orders of the empire. Moreover, as Miller points out that 'every form we produce will tend to its own self-aggrandizement and interests', the tombs constructed by people also became a constituent part of an institutionalized system.[131] People had to follow certain rules or traditions in tomb construction and in funerals and sacrifices at the tombs, which had an important influence on their life. These rules and their potential influence were rooted in the already existing burial forms and the larger social background.

Certain aspects of the material world can become institutional facts in a way that is similar to playing chess, as suggested by Colin Renfrew. 'The rules of chess create the very possibility of playing chess: they are constitutive of chess in the sense that playing chess is constituted in part by acting in accord with the rules.'[132] The rules of building and using the cliff tomb also created the very possibility of its existing form: they were constitutive of the cliff tomb in the sense that building and using the cliff tomb is constituted in part by acting in accord with the rules. The study analyzes the process of the formation of these rules through reconstructing the activities involved in building the cliff tomb and in the funeral and sacrifice which took place at the cliff tomb.

Funeral and sacrifice are usually categorized as ritual, through which the burial form can be understood to embody social relations.[133] As will be discussed in the third chapter on the pictorial carvings in the cliff tomb, the decoration for ritual purpose was exploited as 'a tool for good government' and 'rituals were a regulating mechanism ensuring the smooth and efficient running of society'.[134] The study also considers the other activities

---

[126] Ma Xiaoliang 2012: 87-88. Ma Xiaoliang divides the areas found with early cliff tombs into six sections: 1) the Qijiang 綦江 area; 2) the Xindu 新都 area; 3) the Pengshan area; 4) the Leshan area; 5) the southern Sichuan Basin; 6) the areas around the Three Gorges, especially Zhongxian 忠縣.
[127] Huang Xiaofen 2003: 147 and Erickson 2010: 24-29.
[128] Erickson 2003: 409-437. Many of her interpretations of the pictorial carvings in the cliff tombs in Santai are based on the similar carvings in the brick and stone chamber tombs in Henan, especially in the Nanyang area.
[129] Powers 1991: 110-123; 1987; Xin Lixiang 2000: 353-358; Nylan 2001: 321-324. Powers, Xin Lixiang and Nylan suggest that there were different styles of stone carvings in early China and divide the styles into provincial styles and metropolitan styles based on stone carvings found in the stone tombs and cliff tombs. The provincial styles and metropolitan styles have many variations in different regions.
[130] Miller 2005: 5. He suggests that though we are unaware of the existence of the objects, they are powerful in the way that 'they can determine our expectations by setting the scene and ensuring normative behavior, without being open to challenge' and 'they determine what takes place to the extent that we are unconscious of their capacity to do so'.
[131] Miller 2005: 9.
[132] Renfrew 2005: 25.
[133] Morris 1992: 1-2. Ian Morris points out that 'a burial is part of a funeral, and a funeral is part of a set of rituals by which the living deal with death'. Ritual, to some extent, creates social structure, in the way that 'we interpret ritual as a model of the world through the prism of our own experiences, and interpret our own experiences through the prism of ritual as a model for the world'. 'It was through ceremonies such as funerals that Greeks and Romans constructed and debated the meanings of their worlds.'
[134] See Dramer 2002: 123, 107. Her argument is based on the case studies on the decorated stone chamber tombs in Shandong and Henan in Eastern Han.

related to the tombs, especially tomb construction, as equally important to ritual in studying the social relations embodied in the cliff tomb. Colin Renfrew suggests that the active social role of monuments is rooted in its construction process. Through gathering labour from a certain area and putting endeavour into the same project, a coherent large community was formed.[135] In addition, the impressive material presence of the monument in the area can become the centre of the community for public activities, such as feasting and sacrifice.[136] As will be discussed in the second chapter, the construction of the cliff tomb was a project carried out by a family over many generations. The monumental aspect of the cliff tomb will be studied through its building material, building process and structure.

8. Chapter Outline

The first chapter situates the cliff tombs in Sichuan in the development of the various burial forms in the Han period and in the social background in which large consumption on tombs was prevalent. It proposes the main question of the study: what factors contributed to the popularity of the cliff tombs in Sichuan. The following three chapters make analysis of the characteristics of the cliff tomb structure, the burial objects and the pictorial carvings in relation to the contemporary brick or stone chamber tombs in both Sichuan and east China. The reasons for the choices made by people for these characteristics are examined. The second chapter analyzes the characteristics of the cliff tomb structure. It discusses the geological condition for cliff tomb construction, the local tradition and the potential influence from the outside. Through reconstructing the tomb construction process, it reveals the active role of the cliff tomb in the local society. Moreover, through examining the features of the major architectural elements in the tomb, it reveals the preference and intention of the tomb occupants underlying the design of the cliff tomb structure, which are crucial to the discussion on the reasons for the popularity of the cliff tombs. The third chapter examines the characteristics of the main decorated sections in the cliff tomb. The functions of these decorated sections in funeral and sacrifice are revealed. Moreover, the pictorial scheme in the cliff tomb is interpreted in relation to the reasons for the popularity of the cliff tombs in Sichuan. The fourth chapter studies the burial objects with local features in the cliff tomb, the money tree and the pictorial stone. It discusses how these objects were designed and arranged in the tomb and reconstructs the social relations embodied in these objects. The final chapter points out that the tomb structure, the pictorial carvings and the burial objects are inseparable from each other and were designed out of the same needs of the tomb occupants, which were also the main factors contributing to the popularity of the cliff tombs in Sichuan.

---

[135] Renfrew 2001: 109. His case studies are mainly on pre-historical stone monuments, such as Stonehenge and Avebury. He points out that the construction of these monuments 'certainly implies some pooling together of labour of a number of the smaller, earlier territories'.
[136] Renfrew 2001: 108-111.

Chapter 2
Tomb Structure

The chapter aims to reveal the preference of the tomb occupants underlying the design of the cliff tomb structure. Cliff tomb structures were widely used in the Sichuan area, though they vary in scale and quality, they share many common characteristics. In this chapter, I will look what are the main characteristics of the cliff tomb structure and why these characteristics were chosen by the local people.

1. Archaeological Evidence

Researchers have long been interested in the diverse arrangement of the burial chambers in the cliff tombs. So far, Luo Erhu has made the most comprehensive summary of the forms of the cliff tombs into six large categories, which further fall into 24 subdivisions (figure 24).[1] The six categories are mainly based on the number of the burial chambers on the central axis of the tomb. Category I are single chamber cliff tombs. Category II are cliff tombs with two chambers on the central axis. Category III are cliff tombs with three chambers on the central axis. Category IV are cliff tombs with more than three chambers on the central axis. Category V are cliff tombs with large extended side chambers. Category VI are cliff tombs with a transverse front chamber resembling a shrine. There have been attempts to trace the chronological development of the plan of the cliff tombs and to interpret the functions of the various burial chambers. It is generally believed that the early tombs, date between AD 6 and AD 39, are usually single chamber tombs. Larger and more complicated cliff tombs appeared in the 2nd century AD.[2] And as pointed out by Ma Xiaoliang, the early cliff tombs not only appeared exclusively in the western Sichuan Basin, including the Leshan and Pengshan areas, they have also been found throughout the Sichuan Basin, including the Fu 涪 River area, the Tuo 沱 River area, the Min 岷 River area and the Yangzi River area.[3]

It seems that the early adoption of the cliff tombs affected a wide range of areas, and the subsequent development of the cliff tomb with more complicated structures and forms varied from area to area. These local features were partly determined by geography, local tradition and local economy, as reflected by the features of the cliff tombs in four areas in Sichuan, the Chengdu-Leshan area, the Fu River area, the southeastern Sichuan Basin and the Chongqing area.[4] The cliff tombs are primarily distributed along rivers, which constituted the major traffic routes, sources of irrigation and a large fishing industry. In other words, the cliff tombs are found mostly in the areas that had a certain scale of population and economy. The quality of the cliff tombs partly corresponds to the scale of the local economy as recorded in the textual sources. For example, in the Eastern Han, the Leshan area, where large scale cliff tombs are concentrated, 'had fertile farm land over 1000 *li* 里, …, also had the benefit of fishing, salt, copper and silver mining industries, and from the convenient water route transportation'.[5] The Wuyang 武陽 Prefecture of the Leshan area was well irrigated.[6] The Santai area, along the Qi river, where many elaborately decorated large cliff tombs have been found, was also a wealthy region in the Eastern Han, as recorded in the *Huangyang guozhi*: 'It had prosperous salt well production. … The powerful families of Gao 高 and Ma 馬 had owned private armies for generations'.[7] For regions distant from Chengdu, the political and economic centre of the Eastern Han Sichuan area, such as the Chongqing area, and the Yibin 宜賓 area in the southern Sichuan Basin, the cliff tombs are often smaller, and of lesser quality.

The local features of the cliff tombs were also affected by the types of the mountain rock in the area. As Peter Rockwell points out, the characteristics of the stone have great influence on its workability, which can be classified as the 'present condition of the stone, hardness, characteristics caused by the stone's geological formation, reaction to tools and colour'.[8] The cliff tombs in Sichuan are cut into sandstone cliffs, which are relatively soft and easy to carve. The hardness and the colour of the sandstone vary to some extent, contributing to the diverse appearances of the cliff tombs in different areas. Most of the sandstone within the four major distributions of the cliff tombs in Sichuan is red. Some of the sandstone in the Fu River area is gray or somewhat between gray and red. This kind of sandstone is more resistant to weathering and the texture allows more delicate carving by comparison with the red sandstone. As a result, more elaborate cliff tombs are found in the Fu River area, especially in Santai. In the Chongqing area, the cliff usually contains both sandstone and conglomerate, which increases the hardness of the cliff and the difficulty for carvers.[9] By comparison with other areas, the tombs in Chongqing are usually smaller and have fewer pictorial carvings.

---
[1] Luo Erhu 1988: 137-141.
[2] Ma Xiaoliang 2012: 84-85.
[3] Ma Xiaoliang 2012: 84.
[4] When discussing the local features of the cliff tombs in Sichuan, Fan Xiaoping considers the cliff tombs in these four areas. See Fan Xiaoping 2006: 39-68.
[5] '沃野千里, … 又有魚鹽銅銀之利,浮水轉漕之便'. *Hou Han shu*: 535.
[6] '借江為大埝,灌郡下'. *Huayang*: 279.
[7] '富國井鹽. … 又有高,馬家,世掌部曲'. *Huayang*: 263.
[8] Rockwell 1993: 17.
[9] Many of the cliff tombs in the Chongqing area are located in the Danxia 丹霞 landform area, which is characterized by 'spectacular red cliffs'. See http://whc.unesco.org/en/list/1335. Accessed on 8 Feb 2013.

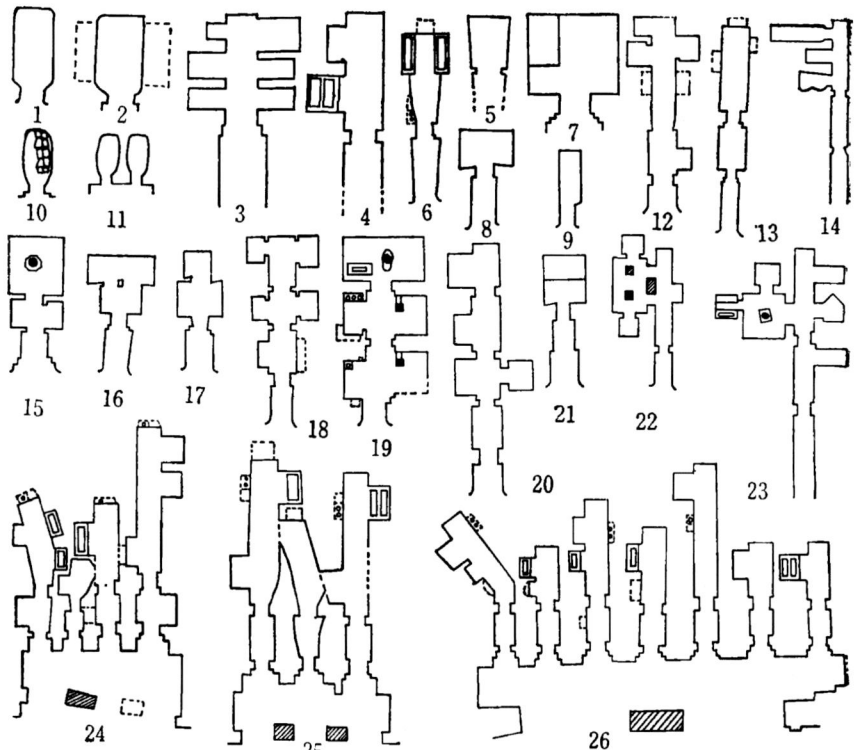

FIGURE 24. CATEGORIES OF CLIFF TOMB STRUCTURES. AFTER LUO ERHU 1988: FIG. 5.

Fan Xiaoping has made a comprehensive summary of the major features of the cliff tombs in different areas of Sichuan as follows (figure 25).[10]

2. Stone as Building Material

Interest in the Use of Stone

The exploitation of mountain rock for tomb construction was not invented in Sichuan. Early in the 2nd century BC, in the Western Han (206 BC-AD 8), large scale rock-cut tombs were used by the kings of the Western Han kingdoms in eastern China, mainly in present northern Jiangsu, eastern Henan, southern Shandong and Hebei.[11]

Such royal rock-cut tombs were usually cut horizontally into the mountain to create a series of burial chambers with different functions, similar to the dwelling for the living. For example, the Beidongshan 北洞山 tomb belonging to a king of the Chu kingdom in Xuzhou is cut horizontally into the mountain rock, with a 56 metres long central path on its axis and numerous side chambers, a rear chamber and an auxiliary hall connected to the central corridor.[12] It is notable that the auxiliary hall is made of stone slabs. It is actually a stone building attached to the rock-cut tomb modelled on the dwelling for the living. The use of slabs was probably a result of the workmen discovering they had dug into an area with insufficient rock to cut out for the large side chamber.[13]

Jessica Rawson suggests that the royal rock-cut tombs in the Western Han were an important stage in the development of Han tombs with a horizontal plan in place of the earlier vertical pit tombs. Moreover they are one of several manifestations of the Han interest in the use of stone.[14] Ann Paludan and Wu Hung also point out that it

---
[10] Based on the table by Fan Xiaoping 2006: 67.
[11] The Western Han kingdoms were assigned by the emperor of the Western Han to certain members of the royal family. The administrative duty of the king was equal to that of a prefect. For the sources of the rock-cut tombs of the Western Han kings discovered so far, see Appendix 1 in Miller 2011. According to Miller's survey, so far 43 rock-cut tombs of the Western Han kings have been discovered. 14 belonged to the kings of the Chu kingdom in Jiangsu. 11 belonged to the kings of the Liang 梁 kingdom in east Henan. 1 belonged to the king of the Jibei 濟北 kingdom in Shandong. 13 belonged to the kings of the Lu 魯 kingdom in Shandong. 2 belonged to the kings of the Zhongshan 中山 kingdom in Hebei. 1 belonged to the king of the Nanyue kingdom in Guangdong. 1 belonged to the king of the Ji'nan kingdom in Shandong. Important discoveries include the Mancheng 滿城 tomb in Hebei (Zhongguo shehui kexue yuan kaogu yanjiu suo 1980), the Beidongshan tomb (Xuzhou bowuguan and Nanjing daxue lishi xue xi kaogu zhuanye 2003) and the Shizishan 獅子山 tomb in Xuzhou (Shizishan Chuwangling kaogu dui 1998), and the Bao'anshan 保安山 tomb M2 in Henan (Henan sheng Shangqiu shi wenwu guanli weiyuanhui 2001: 40-71). Miller suggests that the emergence of the princely rock-cut tombs in the Western Han was influenced by Emperor Wen's (202-157 BC) tomb type, who intended to use the burial type of the rock-cut tomb as one of the strategies to reorganize the imperial ruling.

[12] For the archaeological report see Xuzhou bowuguan and Nanjing daxue lishi xue xi kaogu zhuanye 2003: 6-28.
[13] In the case of the Beidongshan tomb, the auxiliary hall made of stone slabs was also a step towards the use of stone masonry for lesser tombs. See Rawson 1999: 9-10. During the 1st and 2nd century AD, tombs with a horizontal plan constructed of stone or brick were built underground or half underground imitating dwellings for the living. They usually comprise several chambers and were covered under burial mounds. By and large, the introduction of the stone as the building material brought about the tombs of masonry structure, which gradually replaced the traditional wooden chamber (*muguo* 木槨) tombs. These tombs were especially prevalent in central and eastern China. They all resembled dwellings. Some indeed had doors and windows rendered in the interior.
[14] Rawson 1999: 9-10.

Area	Feature	Location and Geology	Tomb Structure	Important Feature
Chengdu-Leshan	Single chamber -multiple chambers; most consist of tunnel, door and burial chamber. In the plan of front and rear chamber or multiple chambers.	Secondary platform along the Min River and the Qingyi 青衣 River. Red sandstone. The tomb entrances are relatively low on the hills and high along the river.	6 types: 1. Rectangular single chamber tomb; 2. Single side chamber tomb; 3. Double-side chamber tomb; 4. Three-side chamber tomb; 5. Multiple-chamber tomb; 6. Irregular shaped tomb. The 'residential' function is salient. The sacrificial chamber is large, with multiple chambers in the rear.	Large scale family burial, with large amount of burial objects of various types. The chamber has drainage. The tunnel is long. The sacrificial chamber forms the front chamber of the family tomb.
Fu River area	Single chamber -multiple chambers. Most consist of tunnel, door and burial chamber.	Fu River area (central Sichuan Basin), along the Qi River. Red sandstone. Low tomb entrance.	6 types: 1. Rectangular single chamber tomb; 2. Single side chamber tomb; 3. Double-side chamber tomb; 4. Three-side chamber tomb; 5. Multiple-chamber tomb; 6. Irregular shaped tomb. Central pillars and coffin beds are often found in multiple-chamber tombs.	With pictorial carving and painting. The coloured paintings and carvings are usually in red and black. The carvings in the burial chambers have various content.
Southeastern Sichuan	Most are single chamber tombs. Multiple chamber tombs are very few.	Tuo River area (south Sichuan) and Yangtze River area (Jinsha 金沙 River and Min River). Red sandstone. Relatively high tomb entrance. Some are located on the wall of the cliff.	Appear in groups of single chamber tombs cut horizontally into the cliff; with short tomb tunnel, simple tomb structure. Multiple-chamber tombs are very few. Some reburials are found. Some Song and Mingy dynasty cliff tombs are found in the Nanguang River-Shicheng Mountain area.	Influenced largely by western Sichuan cliff tombs, and Sichuan-Yunnan and Sichuan-Guizhou cave burials. There is few interior decoration.
Chongqing area	Most are single chamber tombs.	Yangtze River and Jialing 嘉陵 River areas. Some are located in the Danxia 丹霞 landform area. Most are red and gray sandstone. Tomb entrances are relatively low on the hills and high along the rivers.	Most are grouped single chamber tombs; with short tunnel, simple structure. Double-chamber tombs are very few.	Influenced largely by western Sichuan and southern Sichuan cliff tomb structure. There are few relief carvings and decorations.

FIGURE 25. MAJOR FEATURES OF THE CLIFF TOMBS IN DIFFERENT AREAS OF SICHUAN.

was in the Han that people became interested in exploiting stone as a material for building and sculpture.[15] They both argue that the durable nature of stone was linked to some essential elements in Han belief: immortality and the West. The West is both a conceptual place where immortals dwell and a geographical area referring to the vast areas west of Han China, mainly Central and West Asia. Consequently, things borrowed from the West were related to immortals. The use of stone was almost certainly one of those borrowings, as well as some tomb reliefs and figurines with exotic features. Early in 1917, Victor Ségalen proposed that the cliff tombs in Sichuan may have originated in West Asia by giving the examples of the rock-cut tomb belonging to Darius I at Persepolis and some other West Asian tombs.[16] Later Chinese scholars including Gu Qiyi and Chen Mingda quoted the examples provided by Ségalen and re-examined the similarities and differences between the cliff tombs in Sichuan and the Western Asian rock-cut tombs.[17] Jessica Rawson further compares the facades of the tomb of Darius I and the cliff tomb Lijiagou M355 in Pengshan to show the potential West Asian influence on the cliff tombs in Sichuan (figure 26).[18] Both tombs feature a doorway framed by two columns and the decoration of the winged creatures above the door.[19]

---
[15] See Paludan 2006: 103-142; Wu 1995: 121-142. Robert Thorp and Wu Hung also point out that stone was an important material introduced from the West to the tomb constructions in China in the 2nd and 1st century BC. Before the Western Han (206 BC-AD 8), the major tomb building material in China was wood. See Thorp 1979: 128 and Wu 1995: 121-142.
[16] Ségalen 1917: 156.
[17] Gu Qiyi 1990: 186-188; Chen Mingda 2003b: 142-145.
[18] See Rawson 2012: 34. Her comparison also draws my attention to Schmidt's archaeological report on the rock-cut tomb at Naqsh-e Rustam.
[19] For the façade of the rock-cut tomb at Naqsh-e Rustam, see Schmidt 1970: 80-83. For the structure of the rock-cut tomb at Naqsh-e Rustam, see Schmidt 1970: 80-89. The tomb of Darius I at Naqsh-e Rustam 'consists of three basic units, namely vestibule, vault, and cist. The long axis of the vestibule is parallel, or was meant to be parallel, to the façade of the tomb. The vaults are alcoves of rectangular or approximately rectangular plan extending from the vestibule into the rock. The burial cists are rectangular cavities cut into the floors of the vaults' (Schmidt 1970: 87). The author of the archaeological report suggests that the tomb was 'prepared for a monarch and the closest members of his family group' and 'each cist was probably intended for one body' (Schmidt 1970: 88). In *A Global History of Architecture*, the authors suggest that the idea of building rock-cut tombs was an ancient one (Ching, Jarzombek and Prakash 2007: 164). So far rock-cut tombs have been found used in many ancient cultures in the world. The main areas include Thebes in Egypt (c. 1450 BC) (Strudwick and Taylor 2003 and Hawass and Vannini 2009),

Many western rock-cut tombs have extensively decorated façades imitating those of the classical palace architecture.

Lycia and Cyprus (c. 700 BC) (See Bean 1989: pls. 1-11 and pls. 29-30, Haspels 1971 and Roos 1972-1974), Etruria in Italy (c. 500 BC) (see Steingräber 2009), Persepolis in Iran (c. 480 BC) and Petra in Jordan (c. 100 AD) (McKenzie 2005 and Ossorio 2009). Though varying greatly in scale and belonging to tomb occupants of a variety of identities, these rock-cut tombs all feature plans and architectural details imitating those of the above ground palaces and dwellings. All these areas have appropriate geological formations for the construction of the rock-cut tombs. However, 'how the skills needed to create rock-cut architecture found such wide distribution is not known' (Ching, Jarzombek and Prakash 2007: 164).

In fact, not only researchers of the Han dynasty rock-cut tombs and cliff tombs have considered the origin of the rock-cut tomb in other regions, the researchers of the rock-cut tombs in other regions have also considered the possibility of the foreign influence on their rock-cut tombs. Stephan Steingräber examines the possible influence of the rock-cut tombs in Phrygia and Persepolis on the rock-cut tombs in Etruria. He then suggests that for typological reasons, the above mentioned rock-cut tombs cannot be regarded as prototypes of the Etruscan rock-cut tombs. In addition, the rock-cut tombs in Persepolis appeared later then the Etruscan tombs (Steingräber 2009: 67). He then comes to the conclusion that instead of being influenced by foreign models, the Etruscan rock-cut tombs were more likely mainly influenced by the local house and palace architecture (Steingräber 2009: 67-68). Furthermore, Steingräber proposes that the tradition of rock-cut tomb construction, 'which had been deeply rooted in some parts of Asia Minor since early times', 'may have given some impulse to the genesis of Etruscan rock tomb architecture, not so much in specific typology but in a more general conceptual way' (Steingräber 2009: 68). His main support for this hypothesis is that the oldest Etruscan rock-cut tombs were not the result of a long local development. They suddenly appeared in the well developed monumentalized form. The influence of rock-cut tomb tradition through the 'general conceptual way' can also be applied to the sudden popularity of the rock-cut tombs and cliff tombs in Han dynasty China.

On the rock-cut tombs in Petra in the 1st century AD, Judith McKenzie suggests that the development of these tombs could be influenced by foreign palace architecture, especially the façade of the classical palace architecture. Many rock-cut tombs in Petra feature extensively decorated facades. In some cases, 'the creation of facades which could not have been built free-standing was made possible by them being carved in the mountain side (from the top down)'. McKenzie suggests that this creativity could be resulted from 'the Nabataeans' lack of preconceptions about the conventions of classical architecture' (McKenzie 2005: 116-117).

When studying the rock-cut tombs at Etenna in southern Anatolia in comparison with the Lycian rock-cut tombs on the southern coast of Turkey dated to the 4th century BC, N. Cevik suggests that the basic similarity, 'such as the cutting of a tomb chamber in the rock, could occur without any influence from other cultural region'. The adoption of similar rock-cut tombs could be out of 'similar burial needs, similar natural materials or similar architectural knowledge'. 'The influences between the rock-cut tombs of different regions and periods must be seen in the particular details, and their relation to local burial customs.' See Cevik 2003: 114.

As seen from above, the rock-cut tombs and cliff tombs in Han dynasty China were probably also under the influence of foreign rock-cut tomb tradition through a conceptual way. Most of the architectural details of the Chinese local rock-cut tombs, however, were directly influenced by the local architecture. In the following brief discussion, I will touch upon two points on the potential foreign influence on the cliff tombs in Sichuan: one is about the influence through the conceptual way; one is about the influence reflected through architectural details.

As already briefly mentioned in Chapter 1, the structure of the cliff tombs in Sichuan was probably adapted for the use of a large family over generations, which might be one of the reasons for their popularity among the locals. This nature of the rock-cut tomb for the use of a growing family had been exploited as early as the 13th century BC in Ancient Egypt. Peter Dorman notes that in the Theban Necropolis, the rock-cut tomb for family use usually shared a front chamber for memorial, which was the earliest part completed in the tomb. The burial chambers were then carved out behind the front memorial chamber, one after another, depending on the needs and the population of the later generations of the family (Dorman 2003). Though it is impossible to establish a link between the burial traditions in the Theban Necropolis and the cliff tombs in Sichuan, the exploitation of one of the significant natures of the rock-cut tombs indicates that the concept of building rock-cut tombs could have influence in the area with rocky mountain.

FIGURE 26. ILLUSTRATION OF THE FAÇADE OF THE CLIFF TOMB LIJIAGOU M355 IN PENGSHAN. AFTER CHEN MINGDA 2003A: FIG. 4.

For example, the rock-cut tombs in Lycia dated to the 8th century BC and the rock-cut tombs in Petra dated to the 1st century AD. Significant borrowing of the classical architectural elements includes the representation of the pediments and mouldings on the rock-cut tomb facades. Notably, some dubious representation of the pediments and mouldings are also found on the facades of the cliff tombs in Sichuan. On the façade of a cliff tomb in Leshan, a pediment-like image is carved above the two entrances to the tomb.[20] It seems that this façade is not imitating the traditional Chinese architecture, which does not have the pediment on the front. As for the representation of mouldings, some tomb doors with multiple layers of door frames are found in the cliff tombs in Changning (figure 27).[21] Jessica Rawson suggests that two completely different sets of ornamental system were used in China and the West.[22] 'In the West, structural principles derived from architecture determined the rules that governed the organization of the motifs'.[23] As suggested by J. Summerson, the classical architectural elements such as the capital styles, the pediments, the cornices and the mouldings had been integrated into the language of ornament as a result of long term development.[24] The reproduction of fragmentary classical architectural elements in the cliff tombs reveals that the western ornamental system was still foreign to the cliff tomb builders. Instead of systematically copying these classical architectural elements from the classical palace architecture, it is more likely that the cliff tomb builders transplanted these elements directly from the facades of the western rock-cut tombs.

Though it is difficult to reconstruct the exact route for the contacts between West Asia and Sichuan in the Han, as Jessica Rawson has suggested, one of the possible routes may have been through 'the great tributaries of the Yangzi River from Shaanxi through Sichuan to Hubei, and yet

---

[20] See Bishop 1916: fig. 146.
[21] Sichuan daxue lishi xi qiba ji kaogu shixi dui 1985.
[22] Rawson 2006.
[23] Rawson 2006: 380.
[24] Summerson 1980.

FIGURE 27. THE QIGEDONG CLIFF TOMBS IN CHANGNING IN SICHUAN. PHOTOGRAPH BY XUAN CHEN.

further south to the kingdom of Dian 滇 in Yunnan'.[25] It seems that due to the craving for the immortal West, images related to the West were continuously imported to Sichuan and central China after the borrowing of stone tomb construction, for example, the decorative elements with Buddhist influence in the beginning of the 1st century AD. It is very likely that some forms of Buddhist decoration were introduced into the Han tombs first, without the introduction of their religious meanings. The special location of Sichuan connecting eastern China and the trade route to the West made the penetration of the Western influence easier. The early Buddhist images found in Sichuan (mainly from burial goods and stone carvings in the cliff tombs) are closer to their sources of origin, compared to the early Buddhist images found in central and eastern China. Important images of Buddha include the seated figure on the pottery seat of the money tree found in the cliff tomb in Pengshan,[26] and the figure carved on the lintel at the entrance to a burial chamber in the cliff tomb Mahao I M1 in Leshan.[27]

Monumental Aspect

In addition to the borrowing of stone as a kind of tomb building material because of its representation of immortality, the monumental aspect of stone building was also explored in the Han. Wu Hung argues that in the Han, the graveyard became a centre of social activities. It consists of a series of monumental structures, including the tomb, shrine and the *que* pillar gates.[28] To some extent, the family graveyard was a 'monumental complex consisting of multiple commemorative structures'.[29] It is generally agreed by scholars that a monument 'serves to preserve memory, to structure history, to immortalize a figure, event, or institution, to consolidate a community or a public, to define a centre for political gatherings or ritual communication, to relate the living to the dead, and to connect the present with the future'.[30]

Similarly, Françoise Choay emphasizes the memory preserving function of a monument: 'the original meaning of the word is that of the latin [sic] *monumentum*, itself derived from *monere* (to warn, to recall), which calls upon the faculty of memory. The affective nature of its purpose is essential; it is not simply a question of informing, of calling to mind a neutral bit of information, but rather of stirring up, through the emotions, a living memory…. [O]ne would term a monument any artifact erected… to commemorate or to recall… individuals, events, sacrifices, practices or beliefs.'[31]

In this sense, a cemetery of cliff tombs can be regarded as a monumental complex and the individual cliff tombs serve the functions of a monument, as will be elaborated later in this chapter that they record the things that had happened in the family and established communications between different generations of the family. In addition, the cliff tomb was 'part of a dynamic web linking the past, the present, and the future, while also binding the world of the living and the world of the dead'.[32]

Colin Renfrew suggests that a monument was a result of the ongoing social activities. Through monument construction and a series of rituals and religious activities centring on a monument, the monument became the centre of a new community, which would not have come into being had it not endeavoured to make and use the monument. In addition, the monument has an 'affective power', which originated from the human endeavour devoted to the construction of the monument. The 'affective power' or the impressive 'material presence' of the monument often brings a sense of a place or becomes a 'territorial marker' of the community who constructed the monument.[33] The structure of the cliff tomb in Sichuan exhibits many characteristics of such a monument as will be discussed below.

It is common to find rows of planned cliff tombs located on the gentle sloping hillside facing a river, in large numbers, from several tens to several hundreds (figure 28). Adjacent tombs are seldom found intruding into each other's space, no matter how complicated are the structures of their internal spaces in the mountain rock (figure 29).[34] Such

---

[25] Rawson 1999: 22.
[26] Nanjing bowuyuan 1991: fig. 44.
[27] Tang Changshou 1990: 114-115. For the important book on the discussion of the southern 'silk road' linking Sichuan and areas west and south to China in the 1st and 2nd century AD see Sichuan daxue gudai nanfang sichou zhi lu zonghe kaocha ketizu 1990. For discussions in individual papers, see He Zhiguo 1991, Lei Yuhua 1998 and Wu Guibing 2002.
[28] Wu 1995: 120-122.
[29] Wu 1995: 190.

[30] Wu 1995: 4.
[31] Choay 2001: 6. I was directed to Choay's understanding of monument by a chapter in John Carlson's DPhil thesis at the University of Oxford.
[32] Dramer 2002: 19.
[33] Renfrew 2001: 108-109. He uses the large stone monuments like Stonehenge and Avebury as examples to explain how extraordinary that labour resources were concentrated for the construction of a large communal project and how a potential social unit could consequently emerge. In addition, there would be ongoing rituals and other social activities centring the monument to enhance the continuity of the social unit.
[34] For an example of an organized cliff tomb cemetery, see the Hutouwan 虎頭灣 cliff tombs at Mahao 麻浩 in Leshan in Sichuan (Luo Erhu

FIGURE 28. PLANNED CLIFF TOMBS AT QIJIANG IN SANTAI. PHOTOGRAPH BY XUAN CHEN.

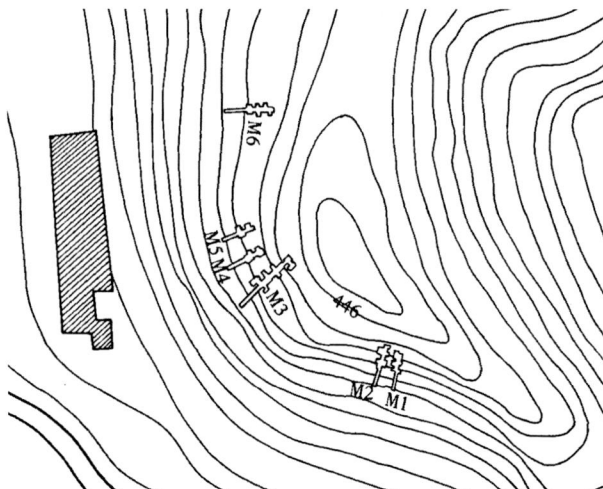

FIGURE 29. PLAN OF THE SITE CONTAINING THE TALIANGZI CLIFF TOMBS M1-M6 IN ZHONGJIANG. AFTER BEIJING SICHUAN SHENG WENWU KAOGU YANJIUYUAN, DEYANG SHI WENWU KAOGU YANJIUSUO AND ZHONGJIANG XIAN WENWU BAOHU GUANLI SUO 2008: FIG. 3.

a phenomenon indicates carful choosing and planning of the cemetery site for the cliff tombs. To some extent, the well-organized cliff tombs laid out in rows on a designated mountain slope can be regarded as a kind of 'ordered landscape', which symbolized the appropriation of the space while 'organizing and materializing social relationships and boundaries'.[35] A Han inscription found in Bazhou 巴州 in Sichuan reveals that a certain site on a hill or the whole hill could be purchased as a family cemetery for use for many generations.[36]

To form this 'ordered landscape', the site had to meet two standards: first, it had to have good *feng shui* 風水, that is, satisfying geomancy for the continuing benefit of the tomb occupants and their family members; second, the site had to have the proper sandstone for the excavation of the internal burial space.[37] These two standards further required people who had relevant professional knowledge to choose and plan the site for the cliff tombs.

It is generally believed that by the Han dynasty, certain standards of good *feng shui*, including the good *feng shui* for a cemetery, had been established.[38] For example, in the *Shi ji*, Sima Qian attributed the success of Han Xin 韓信 to the good *feng shui* of his mother's tomb. 'When I visited Huai-yin one of the men of the place told me that even when Han Hsin was still a commoner his ambitions were different from those of ordinary men. At the time of his mother's death he was so poor that he could not give her a proper burial, and yet he had her buried on a high, broad expanse of earth with room enough around to set up ten thousand households, this man said. I went to visit Han Hsin's mother's grave, and it was quite true.'[39] Seemingly, a high and broad open area was deemed as an ideal site for the tomb in the Han dynasty. In the *Hou Han shu*, Feng Yan 馮衍 also chose his tomb in an area which was 'high and broad' and 'overlooking a thousand *li*, watching over the old capital city'.[40] The sites of the cliff tombs are both high and broad, consistent with the basic standards of the site of good *feng shui*. We might suggest that the sites were selected by professionals according to *feng shui* principles with the cooperation of cliff workers, who knew the proper quality of the mountain rock for tomb construction.

It is important to note that when the whole cemetery can be considered as a monumental complex, it was the individual families who contributed their resources and efforts to their own family tombs at the cemetery. Though the income and the social status of these individual families might vary, their contribution within their means to the cemetery brought 'affective power' to the cemetery. Each tomb can be regarded as an independent monument, which commemorated the family history and located the family

---

1988: fig. 13) and the tombs at Liujiayan 劉家堰 at Qijiang 郪江 (Yang Cunguan 2000). On the hill slope of 100 by 30 metres, 66 cliff tombs are located neatly in three rows. The tombs M3, M4 and M5 at Taliangzi in Zhongjiang were well planned adjacent to each other, following a chronological order, starting from M5 as the earliest one, dated to the middle of Eastern Han, following by M4 and M3 dated to the late Eastern Han (Sichuan sheng wenwu kaogu yanjiuyuan, Deyang shi wenwu kaogu yanjiusuo and Zhongjiang xian wenwu baohu guanli suo 2008: 4, fig. 3, 19-40).

[35] See DeMarrais, Castillo and Earle 1996: 19. For the concept of 'ordered landscape', see Kus 1989.

[36] '地節二年□月,巴州民楊量買山,直錢千百作業冢.子孫永保. In the second year of Dijie (68 BC), Yang Liang, the resident of Bazhou, bought the hill at the cost of a 100,000 *qian* for a cemetery to be used by his offspring over generations.' Gao Wen and Gao Chenggang 1990: 3.

[37] Though some practices related to the concept of *feng shui* are recorded in Han texts, the term of *feng shui* was used much later. The early use of the term *feng shui* is found in the *Zang shu* 葬書, which was claimed to be the work of Guo Pu 郭璞 of the Western Jin period (AD 266-316), though was possibly written in the Tang (AD 618-907) or Nothern Song (AD 960-1127) period. For the study of the author and the time of the *Zang shu*, see Xu Wenfang and Wei Baowei 2005 and Yuan Fangming 2007.

[38] For the discussion on the development of the concept of *feng shui* in Han China based on textual records and archaeological evidence, see Zhang Qiming 2007.

[39] *Shi ji*: 2629-2630. '太史公曰:吾如淮陰,淮陰人為餘言,韓信雖為布衣時,其志與眾異.其母死,貧無以葬,然乃行營高敞地,令其旁可置萬家.餘視其母塚,良然.' The translation is after Watson 1971: 232.

[40] *Hou Han shu*: 986. '地勢高廠,...通視千里,覽見舊都.'

in a wider social context as embodied by the cemetery. To exhibit the impressive material presence that is essential to a monument, a high stone cutting technique for making good cliff tombs was very much appreciated during this time.

The accumulation of the relevant knowledge of sandstone cutting was very mature in Eastern Han Sichuan. Such knowledge may have first developed in other fields and then been manipulated by a group of professional cliff tomb builders in Sichuan. According to the *Houhan shu*, in Eastern Han, the people of the Yi 益 Region in Sichuan had already been able to tunnel 20 *li* into the mountain rock to channel water from the Pi River to irrigate the field in Guangdu 廣都.[41] At the end of the 4th century BC, before the army of the Qin State intruded into the Shu State in Sichuan, the local people were coaxed into building roads for the Qin army by cutting through the rocky mountain.[42] In the 3d century BC, the irrigation project at Dujiangyan 都江堰 led by Li Bing 李冰, the grand administrator of the Shu Commandery, also involved cutting away the mountain rock along the river.[43] In the Western Han, officials and workers in Sichuan were already regarded as very experienced in stone work, and they were ordered by Emperor Wu to cut out a stone path of over 2000 *li*, connecting Nanzhong 南中 with the Sichuan area.[44]

Not only from the long tradition of stone tunneling and working, a geological knowledge of stone may also have come from salt mining, a major means of gaining salt in the area. In Sichuan, the depth of the underground brine vaired, from several tens of metres to over a thousand metres.[45] To locate salt and to drill salt-brine wells required an understanding of the local geology and the development of relevant tools. Salt production was a main source of wealth for the local powerful families in Eastern Han, which was also well illustrated on many stone carvings or bricks in a burial context.[46]

Based on the scarce sources on the possible background of the cliff tomb excavation technique, we can see that the cliff tomb appeared with the development of other local industries, which encouraged the growth of the local powerful families and also the prosperity of the tomb construction business.

As in Eastern Han southern Shandong and northern Jiangsu areas, where master artisans' work of stone burial monuments were much valued,[47] cliff tombs built by well-known master artisans at a large cost were highly appreciated in Sichuan. The master artisan's name was usually carved at the entrance to the cliff tomb together with the cost and the date of construction, for example, the inscription at the entrance of the cliff tomb at Nanchuan 南川 in Chongqing: '陽嘉二年王師作值十萬 (Made by master artisan Wang in the second year of Yangjia (AD 133), worth 100,000 *qian*)',[48] the format of which is comparable to the inscriptions found on the stone burial monument in Eastern Han Shandong, such as the inscription on the stone pillar of the Wu family shrine at Jiaxiangin Shandong: '使石工孟李,李弟卯此闕,直錢十五萬 (Masons Meng Li and Li Dimao were ordered to make this stone pillar, worth 150,000 *qian*)'.[49] Sometimes, the inscription on the cliff tomb only included the name of the artisan, without mentioning the title *shi* 師 (master), for example, the inscription on the Qigongzui 七拱咀 cliff tomb in Qijiang 綦江 reads: '光和四年三月二日平路元立作冢萬五千 (The tomb was built by Ping Luyuan on the second day of the third month in the fourth year of Guanghe (AD 181), worth 15,000 *qian*)'.[50] It seems that the cost of hiring a master artisan was much higher than that for an ordinary one, as we can see here, a difference between 100,000 and 15,000 *qian*. In some cases, only the date of construction or the name and the title of the tomb occupant are mentioned in the inscription, for example, the inscription on the cliff tomb at Hutouwan 虎頭灣 in Leshan: '陽嘉三年 (the third year of Yangjia (AD 134))',[51] and the one at Shuangliu in Chengdu: '藍田令楊子輿所處穴 (the tomb for the governor of Lantian, Yang Ziyu)'.[52] These tombs were very likely done by mundane hands, whose names were not worthy to mention.

It is noteworthy that some large scale cliff tombs with pictorial carvings do not include inscriptions showing the master artisan's name, such as the well-known Mahao I M1 in Leshan. In contrast, the previously mentioned 100,000 *qian* worth cliff tomb built by the master artisan at Nanchuan is only a small single chamber tomb. One reason for this could be that the construction of a cliff tomb was done by a group of workers under the supervision of

---

[41] '鑿石二十裡,取郫江水灌廣都田. Stone was excavated over a distance of 20 *li*, the Pi River was channeled to irrigate the field of Guangdu.' *Houhan shu*: 3509.
[42] '秦惠王欲伐蜀,乃刻五石牛.置金其後,蜀人見之,以為牛便金牛下.有養卒以此天牛也,能便金.蜀王以為然,即發卒千人,使丁力士拖牛成道. The king Hui of the Qin state wanted to invade into the Shu state. So he had five stone oxen carved and put gold behind them. The Shu people saw this and thought that the gold were excreted from the oxen Some people thought that the oxen were from heaven, so they could excrete gold. The king of the Shu state was convinced and ordered a thousand people and Wu Ding to drag the oxen. Consequently, a road was built.' *Quan Han wen*: 540-541.
[43] *Huayang*: 202.
[44] '乃鑿石開閣,以通南中,迄于建寧,二千餘里,山道廣丈餘,深三四尺,其塹鑿之跡猶存'. Consequently, a stone path was cut to connect Nanzhong. The path started from Jianning, in a length of over 2000 *li*. The mountain path was over one *zhang* in width and three to four *chi* in depth. Traces of stone cutting still remained.' *Shuijing zhu*: 770.
[45] Luo Erhu 1987: 36.
[46] For example of the pictorial brick on salt mining, see Lim 1987: 99, pl. 14.

[47] For important studies on the stone burial monument workers in Eastern Han Shandong and Jiangsu, see Powers 1991: 104-128, Barbieri-Low 2007: 67-115 and Xing Yitian 1996.
[48] For the archaeological report see Miao Yongshu 1989.
[49] Miao Yongshu 1989: 26.
[50] Gao Wen and Gao Chenggang 1990: 33. According to the collections of the Han inscriptions found in Sichuan in Gao Wen and Gao Chenggang 1990, the artisan's name is usually followed by the cost, while the name of the tomb occupant is usually followed by other information without mentioning the cost. For example, the tomb occupant's name is recorded in the inscription on the cliff tomb at Xiaoba in Leshan: '延熹二年三月十日,佐孟机为子男造此家,端行九章左右,有四穴□入八尺当□由世中出. On the tenth day of the third month in the second year of Yanxi (AD 159), Zuo Mengji made this tomb for his son Zuo Nan. The *duan hang* on left and right measures nine *zhang*. There are four caves (*xue*) at the length of eight *chi*, tunnelled into the middle of the *shi*.' See Gao Wen and Gao Chenggang 1990: 25.
[51] Gao Wen and Gao Chenggang 1990:18.
[52] Gao Wen and Gao Chenggang 1990: 38.

a senior worker, who could either be a master artisan or an ordinary one. The overall scale and quality of the cliff tomb was more dependent on the number and competence of the workers in the group. To the wealthy families, who could afford to hire a large number of competent workers, there was no need to boast their endeavours in tomb construction, because the impressive material presence of the grand cliff tombs spoke for themselves. For the families who had fewer resources, the master artisan they hired became the most important evidence of their efforts in tomb construction. In this sense, the cemetery as a monumental complex was the achievement of communal endeavours of families from a variety of social classes or economic levels. On the other hand, they accepted the same material form as their burial monument, which was crucial for the formation of a community based on a communal monumental complex. In Colin Renfrew's example, the resources of a group of people contributed communally into a monumental project and consequently a community emerged.[53] Here, though the resources were not assigned by a central governing body, the resources of individual families were voluntarily devoted to their individual monuments which culminated in a communal monumental complex symbolizing the 'territorial marker' of the community. A common value on the family tomb and cemetery was shared by a community, as well as the procedures involved in cliff tomb construction.

A key group of people participating in the cliff tomb construction were the sculptors. These workers were a part of the larger group of people involved in the business of death in Eastern Han Sichuan. The major burial types of Eastern Han Sichuan – the cliff tomb and the brick tomb, and their burial goods show traces of commercialization and mass production.[54] Compared with brick tomb construction, cliff tomb construction involved a completely different set of techniques and procedures. Though no textual record is available, the remaining structure of the cliff tomb, the traces of tool marks and a few tomb inscriptions provide us with some general information on the tomb construction process.

First, a suitable area for a particular cliff tomb on the site was located. Next, a plan of the proposed tomb would have had to be drawn up. To some extent, though many cliff tombs were built to the same general plan, slight variations gave each some degree of individuality, which is very likely the result of the communication between the builders and the patrons. For example, the Taliangzi M4 and M5 with the same basic plan are next to each other, with M5 built around half a century earlier. Both tombs have two main chambers on the central axis, two chambers for coffins attached to the right side of the main chambers respectively and a stove built on the left side of the front chamber.[55] The major difference between the two tombs is that M4 has one additional left chamber for a coffin. Such a difference reflects the difference in the number of family members in individual families. The third step was to cut the tomb out of the solid rock, which required sharp iron tools. By comparison with the process of tomb construction in New Kingdom (1550-1077 BC) Egypt, the reconstruction of the process of cliff tomb construction here is very sketchy. However, the Egyptian rock-cut tomb, which involved similar stone cutting procedures, provides us with ideas on the possible tools and methods used in breaking and cutting away stone. For the Egyptian worker, breaking up the stone required the set of a spike and a mallet. The solid rock would be split by pounding a mallet on a spike.[56] For the cliff tomb, similar methods may have been adopted. According to the pictorial stones found in the Eastern Han stone tombs in eastern China, when quarrying stone for stone tomb construction, the artisans used similar set of tools as the mallet and spike. Pictorial stones found in the offering halls at Wuzhaishan 五寨山 in Jiaxiang in Shandong depicted artisans wielding sledgehammers, directing them at pointed chisels. 'Once a slot was opened up in the rock, he forced one or more iron wedges into the crevice and pounded them forcefully to cleave off a huge chunk of limestone.'[57] There are some examples of the tools, including the chisels and hammerheads, from such quarrying or stone-dressing sites.[58] Ancient Egyptian tomb builders may also have used a bronze hoe, 'which would have been wielded like a modern pick-axe'.[59] The builders of the cliff tombs in Sichuan could use a hammer in a similar way to break the stone. The hammer could be held in both hands overhead or in a single hand at a lower position.[60]

The following step was to evacuate the stone blocks from the tomb at the same time.[61] The larger the spaces in the cliff tomb the greater the work, since each burial chamber is made by carving out the interior. For large cliff tombs with a length over 20 metres, such as the Tianhuishan M3 in Chengdu and the Mahao I M1 in Leshan (figure 30), removing stone blocks require much labour. The workmen could also be the sculptors of the cliff tombs, or they might only be in charge of removing stone, which did not require much skill.

Peter Rockwell points out that the cliff tomb is a kind of carving without quarrying, the technical problems of which are mainly sculptural rather than architectural.[62]

---

[53] Renfrew 2001: 108-110.
[54] For the discussion of the funeral related market in Eastern Han, see Barberi-Low 2005 and Tang Guangxiao 2002. Tang Guangxiao's work focuses on the funeral related market in Eastern Sichuan in particular.
[55] For the archaeological reports, see Sichuan sheng wenwu kaogu yanjiuyuan, Deyang shi wenwu kaogu yanjiusuo and Zhongjiang xian wenwu baohu guanli suo 2008: 34-41.
[56] Biebrier 1982: 46-47, 47, fig. 28 shows the workman using the spike and mallet breaking up the stone.
[57] Barbieri-Low 2007: 84-85, 85, fig. 3.9.
[58] Examples are provided in Barbieri-Low 2007: 85, fig. 3.8.
[59] Biebrier 1982: 46.
[60] Luo Erhu suggests that there could be an alternative method to excavate the cliff tomb based on the paired holes with the diameters of around 10 centimetres found on the opposite walls in the tomb in some cases. According to his suggestion, a cross bar was fixed to the cliff through the paired holes and a wooden log equipped with an iron chisel was hung on the cross bar. The workers could swing the wooden log to hit the rock with the chisel repeatedly and consequently a cave was excavated (Luo Erhu 1987).
[61] Černý's (1973: 19) has pointed out the similar situation in the process of rock-cut tomb construction in Ancient Egypt.
[62] Rockwell 1993: 188.

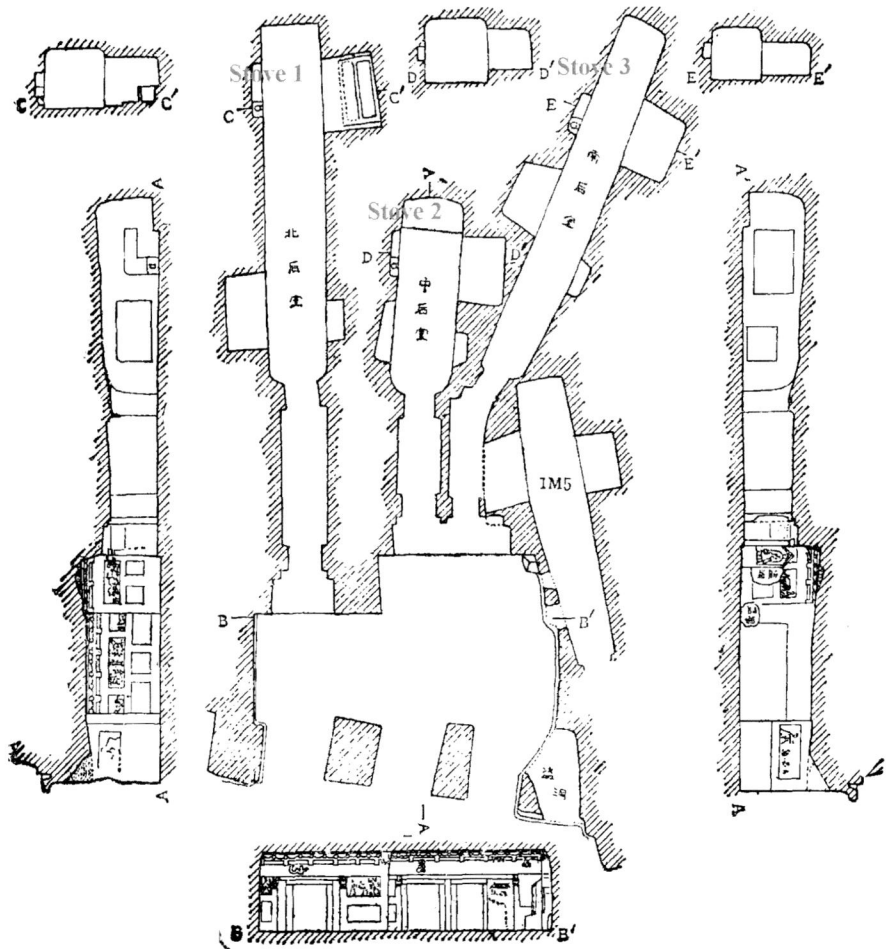

Figure 30. Plan of the Mahao I M1 in Leshan. After Tang Changshou 1990: fig. 1.

Unlike the contemporary brick and stone chamber stones, the problem is about carving something out of a mass of stone rather than putting things together into something. Consequently, the planning of tomb construction is simplified: 'no quarrying, transport, lifting into place, or putting together, no need for the structural planning other than that which is normal for ensuring that the stone will not be carved too thin to hold together'.[63] The consequent technical advantage of this is that, both the organizational work and technical work are simplified. Only one class of workers, the sculptors, is needed. 'All the rest have been made redundant by the choice of carving into the living rock',[64] for example, transporting and placing together the stone blocks. A further advantage is that this type of work allows the carving of large size monuments without a major structural problem, as long as the quality of the stone and the shape of the cliff meet the necessary standards of stability. And it is cheaper and easier to make large monuments by 'carving direct into the rock'.[65] In this sense, the prevalence of the cliff tombs among commoners and the relatively wealthy people, who were no richer than some owners of the more elaborately decorated brick or stone tombs, has an explanation from an economic aspect.

When considering the cliff tombs among the various tomb types prevalent in Eastern Han China, it is notable that even the largest and most elaborately decorated cliff tombs are less good in quality compared to some high quality brick and stone tombs. For example, the stone gate pillars of Gao Yi 高頤 at Ya'an 雅安 in Sichuan represent a much higher standard of stone burial sculpture than the stone carvings found in the elaborately decorated cliff tombs (figure 31).[66] According to the inscription on the pillars, they belong to a contemporary grand administrator of Yi 益, which was much higher in rank than the prefect of Lantian 藍田, the only official position recorded in the cliff tomb inscription found so far.[67] Though the official position of the tomb occupant cannot be entirely connected to his wealth, we can see the gap between both the official positions and the levels of wealth of tomb occupants of the high quality cliff tomb and the high quality brick or stone chamber tomb. It is a pity that the structure of the cliff tomb with the inscription 'Prefect of Lantian' is unknown. However, we have found the inscription recording the name of a commoner in an elaborately decorated large cliff tomb Bailinpo M1 in Santai in Sichuan (figure 32),

---

[63] Rockwell 1993: 188.
[64] Rockwell 1993: 188.
[65] Rockwell 1993: 188.

[66] Chongqing shi wenhua ju and Chongqing shi bowuguan 1992: 32 and 106, fig. 89. The stone *que* pillars are usually built above ground, in front of the burial mounds of the brick or stone chamber tomb.
[67] Gao Wen and Gao Chenggang 1990: 38.

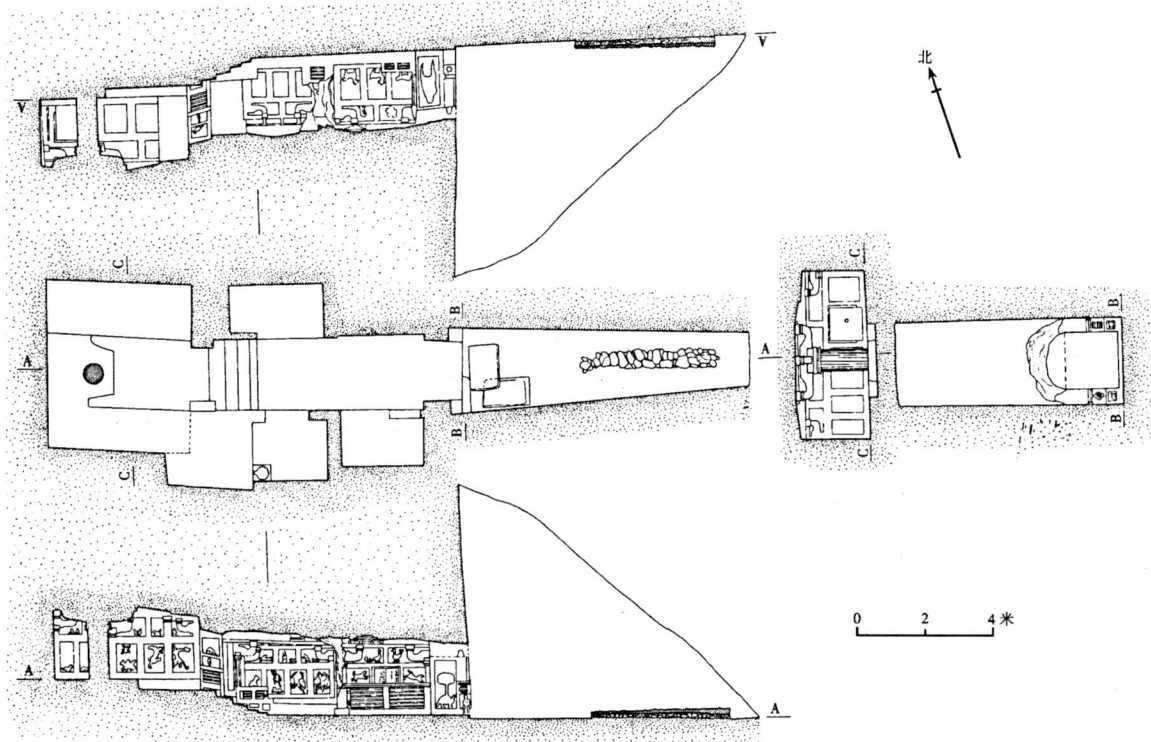

FIGURE 32. PLAN OF THE BAILINPO M1 IN SANTAI. AFTER SICHUAN SHENG WENWU KAOGU YANJIUYUAN, MIANYANG SHI BOWUGUAN AND SANTAI XIAN WENWU GUANLI SUO 2007: FIG. 179.

FIGURE 31. THE *QUE* PILLARS OF GAO YI IN YA'AN IN SICHUAN. AFTER CHONGQING SHI WENHUA JU AND CHONGQING SHI BOWUGUAN 1992: FIG. 89.

which may be regarded as one of the grandest cliff tombs in Sichuan. The inscription records '元初四年九月□日齊公冢 (The ninth month of the fourth year of Yuanchu (AD 117), Tomb of Mr Qi)'.[68] However, the quality of sculpture in this tomb is still not comparable to that of the stone gate pillars of Gao Yi, if we observe the sculptural details. It is important to note that though both the cliff tombs and the stone or brick chamber tombs vary in scale and quality due to the different social status and incomes of the tomb occupants, the tomb occupants of the cliff tombs seemed to have had a lower social status and income compared with those occupants of the stone or brick chamber tombs.

There is also a major disadvantage of this type of carving without quarrying as pointed out by Rockwell that 'a structure that is made entirely by carving from a mountainside cannot be organized so that the work is carried out by teams working at the same time in the way that a constructed building can' and therefore the work process is 'constrained by a combination of the chronology of actual carving of each section with the sequence of the exterior and interior spaces'.[69]

The cliff tombs in Sichuan avoided this disadvantage through developing a working schedule for more than one generation, as can be observed in some large scale cliff tombs. More importantly, the time consuming tomb construction project carried on for generations was essential to exhibit the longevity and prosperity of a family or a clan. Many large scale cliff tombs in Leshan, such as the Shiziwan M1 and the Mahao I M1, have the

---

[68] Sichuan sheng wenwu kaogu yanjiuyuan, Mianyang shi bowuguan, and Santai xian wenwu guanli suo 2007: 158. In Eastern Han, if the tomb occupant had an official title, it was usually recorded in the inscription. Therefore, we can be sure that the tomb occupant of Bailinpo M3 was a commoner, since the only respectful title for him was *gong* 公, no other official title was mentioned.

[69] Rockwell 1993: 189. He provides the example of a two-chambered cliff tomb at Cervetern to show that the second room could only be carved after the first had been excavated. The case of the cliff tomb in Sichuan is very similar.

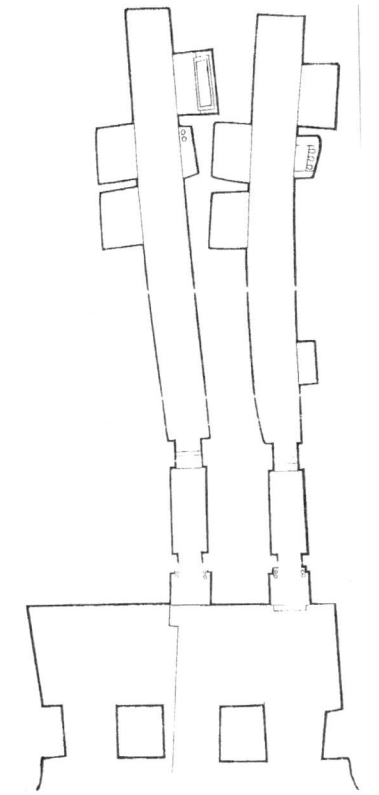

Figure 33. Plan of the Shiziwan no. 1 in Leshan. Redrawn after Tang 1997: fig. 2, by Xuan Chen.

structure of a rectangular front hall shared with three side by side burial chambers tunnelled into the rear wall of the hall (figure 33).[70] It is generally thought that the front hall was a communal shrine shared by three families buried respectively in the rear chambers.[71] According to the traces of construction and the decorative style in the cliff tombs, the burial chambers attached to the front hall were built consecutively. Tang Changshou, the author of the archaeological report on the Mahao I M1, suggests that the southern burial chamber of Mahao M1 was built first, followed by the middle chamber and then the northern chamber. There was a gap of around a few decades between the construction of each individual burial chamber.[72] The structure of the Shiziwan 柿子灣 M1 confirms this type of construction sequence. Though only two adjacent burial chambers were built into the rear wall of the front hall, a third burial chamber was intended to be tunnelled, as the incised outline of its intended entranceway is still discernable.[73] In addition, the front hall has three entrances to suggest the three burial chambers tunnelled into its back wall. In this sense, it is very likely that a shrine and a burial chamber were first built by the family of the first generation, then the other burial chambers were constructed by the later generations based on the original plan.

---
[70] Tang 1997: 73, fig. 2 and Tang Changshou 1990: fig. 1.
[71] See the argument in Chen Mingda 2003a: 72, Tang Changshou 1990: 115 and Huang Xiaofen 2003: 149. This point will be further elaborated later in this chapter.
[72] Tang Changshou 1990: 115.
[73] Tang 1997: 72.

In fact, it is very common for a large cliff tomb to contain several tomb occupants, who were probably from different generations of a large and prosperous family. The most notable example is Tianhuishan M3 in Chengdu, which contains a total number of 14 coffins, which were distributed in different burial chambers.[74] A cliff tomb inscription recorded how a cliff tomb was built and expanded in different periods for several generations of a family: '維兮本造此穿者張賓公妻,子偉伯,伯妻孫陵在此右方曲內中.維兮張偉伯子長仲以建初二年六月十二日與少子叔元俱下世,長子元益,為之祖父穿中造內,棲柱作崖棺,葬父及弟叔元'. The burial chamber (*chuan*) was first established by Zhang Bingong. His wife, his son Zhang Weibo and the wife of his son Sun Ling are interred in the L-shaped chamber (*nei*) on the right. The son of Zhang Weibo, Zhang Changzhong, and the youngest son Shuyuan were both interred on the twelfth day of the sixth month in the second year of Jianchu (AD 77). The eldest son Yuanyi built the *nei* chamber in the *chuan* chamber for his grandfather and built the stone coffin next to the column to inter his father and his younger brother Shuyuan.'[75] Actual traces of tomb expansion for the new generation in the tomb have been found in some cliff tombs containing multiple burial chambers. For example, the ceiling decoration of the front chamber of Dongzipai 洞子排 M1 is similar to that of Bailinpo M1 (figure 34 and 35), which is dated to AD 117 according to its inscription '元初四年 (the fourth year of Yuanchu)',[76] however, the excavation of the left side chamber of the front chamber of Dongzipai M1 broke into the original pseudo timber architectural stone carvings on the left wall of the front chamber. In addition, the style of the bracket set decoration inside this side chamber is usually observed on stone pillars dated to the end of the 2nd century and beginning of the 3rd century AD. Therefore, this side chamber may have been added several decades after the completion of the tomb. As in the richly decorated main chambers, this additional side chamber is also thoroughly decorated with stone carvings imitating timber architecture and is equipped with a built-in pictorial stone coffin and a built-in stove. The decorative style of the whole tomb continued in this additional chamber, though with some new contemporary decorative elements of the time. As will be explained later in the chapter, the built-in stove in the cliff tomb had an association with the unit of a family. Thus this additional side chamber may have symbolized the continuity of the large clan in the form of more and more sub-families for generations, with the tradition of the large clan being maintained.

Some inscriptions found in the cliff tombs imply that the cliff tomb construction was a family project continuing

---
[74] Liu Zhiyuan 1958: 90-93, 91, fig. 3. The tomb contains a front chamber and rear chamber laid out on an east-west axis. The front chamber has a side chamber on the south. The rear chamber has two small side chambers on the south and one large side chamber on the north. The large side chamber also has side chambers. One is on the north, the other one is on the east. A central pillar is located in the large side chamber.
[75] *Li shi*: 148-149. See Li Rusen 1996: 20 for the interpretation of the tomb inscription recorded in the *Li shi*.
[76] Sichuan sheng wenwu kaogu yanjiuyuan, Mianyang shi bowuguan and Santai xian wenwu guanli suo 2007: 154-179; 279-285.

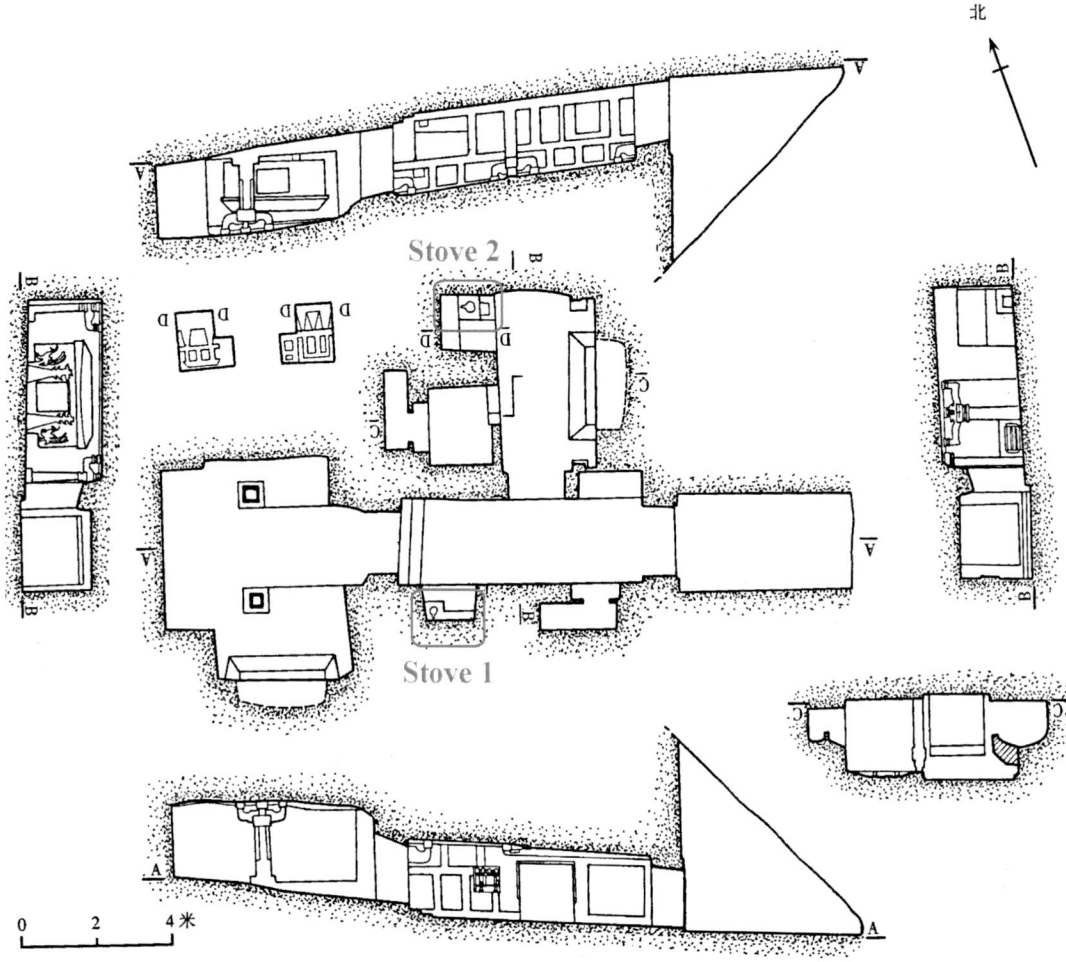

Figure 34. Plan of the tomb Dongzipai M1 in Santai. After Sichuan sheng wenwu kaogu yanjiuyuan, Mianyang shi bowuguan and Santai xian wenwu guanli suo 2007: fig. 281.

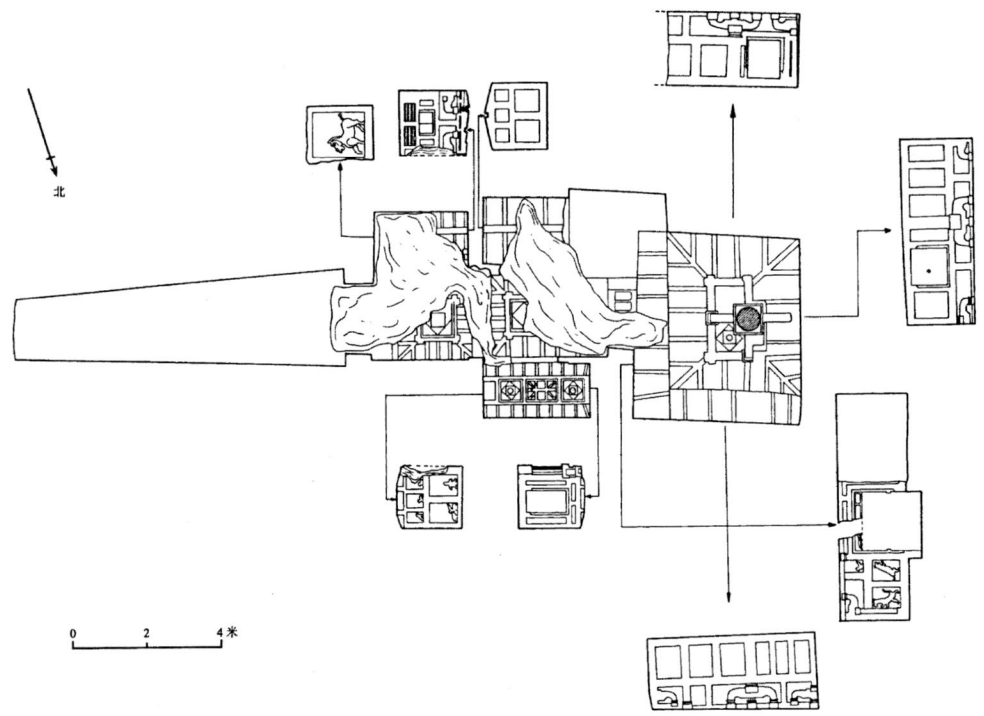

Figure 35. Bottom view of the Bailinpo M1 in Santai. After Sichuan sheng wenwu kaogu yanjiuyuan, Mianyang shi bowuguan and Santai xian wenwu guanli suo 2007: fig. 180.

for generations. The inscription found in the cliff tomb at Xinfusi 新服寺 in Leshan revealed the way in which the tomb was intended for many generations and for potential extension: '建和三年正月廿日造此冢,□行十丈□門三丈,川戶一丈,人川戶右方,穴八丈,有枚枚.周代造此冢,后子孫率來 (The tomb was made on the twentieth day of the first month in the third year of Jianhe (AD 149). The *hang* 行 measures ten *zhang* 丈. The door measures three *zhang* 丈. The entrance to the side burial chamber (*chuan* 穿) measures one *zhang* 丈. The chamber (*chuan* 穿) for coffin is located on the right. The cave (*xue* 穴) measures eight *zhang* 丈. There are several *mei* 枚. The tomb was made for Zhou Dai and for his offspring to use for generations.)'.[77] The two inscriptions in the Dayunao 大雲坳 cliff tomb M76 in Qingshen 青神 further confirm that the tomb was to be continuously in use for several generations. The first inscription reads: '建初元年十月造. Built in the tenth month in the first year of Jianchu (AD 76).' The second one reads: '元初五年十一月廿七日楊得采藏. Yang Decai was interred on the twenty seventh day of the eleventh month in the fifth year of Yuanchu (AD 118).' The tomb has two burial chambers. The front one contains a built-in coffin. According to the plan of the burial chamber and burial facilities, the tomb contained at least three tomb occupants (figure 36). Referring to the tomb inscriptions, we can see that after the tomb was built and was initially filled with tomb occupants, another tomb occupant Yang Decai was interred 42 years later.[78]

The measurements and the functions of the main architectural sections are sometimes indicated clearly in the inscription, which seemed to serve as a reference for later workers in the tomb extension project, since the original idea of tomb planning might have been lost over decades. A similar inscription containing measurement information for later planners and workers was also found in the cliff tomb at Xiaoba in Leshan: '延熹二年三月十日,佐孟机为子男造此冢,端行九章左右,有四穴□入八尺当□由世中出. On the tenth day of the third month in the second year of Yanxi (AD 159), Zuo Mengji made this tomb for his son Zuo Nan. The *duan* 端 *hang* 行 on left and right measures nine *zhang* 丈.' There are four caves (*xue* 穴) at the length of eight *chi* 尺, tunnelled into the middle of the *shi* 世.'[79] In this inscription, the main plan and the measurement of the main architectural sections of the *duan hang* and the *xue* are also indicated clearly. The previously mentioned 'Zhang Bingong 張賓公' inscription quoted from the *Li shi* indicates the occupants of the individual chambers or coffins, which further indicates the relationship between different architectural structures for the later workers as references for an extension. In addition, the inscription informs us that there were specific terms to describe burial chambers of different forms and functions, such as *chuan* 穿 and *nei* 內. Together with the characters used in the previous two cliff tomb inscriptions (which also use *chuan* and *nei*), *duan hang*, *xue*, *mei* and *shi*, it seems that there was a set of terms used by the cliff tomb

FIGURE 36. PLAN OF THE DAYUNAO TOMB NO. 76 IN QINGSHEN IN SICHUAN. AFTER TANG CHANGSHOU 1993: FIG. 5.

builders in their work.[80] The terms carved inside the cliff tomb not only exhibited the professionalization of the cliff tomb construction industry in Eastern Han Sichuan, but also established the continuous communication between the cliff tomb builders in different decades and between the different generations of the tomb occupants' family.[81]

In this sense, the large cliff tomb can be regarded as a monument that involved the participation and contribution of a large number of family members from a long established clan as well as the tomb builders. The large multi-chamber cliff tomb itself commemorated and celebrated the longevity and prosperity of a large clan. In contrast, the small single-chamber tombs exhibited the small and medium families whose clan did not last for a long time. However, these small cliff tombs were also the result of the participation and devotion of the lesser families. Consequently, the cemetery containing cliff tombs of various scales can be seen as a monumental complex formed through the endeavour of a whole community containing families of different social status. In other words, we can see an emerging community which adopted the same burial form through looking at the monumental complex of the community, the cliff tomb cemetery. It is also notable that the grandest cliff tombs were usually a

---

[77] Gao Wen and Gao Chenggang 1990: 23.
[78] Tang Changshou 1993: 80.
[79] Gao Wen and Gao Chenggang 1990: 25.
[80] Most of the meanings of these terms have been lost today. However, according to the meaning of the whole text, *chuan* and *nei* clearly indicate the burial chamber in the cliff tomb and there were further differences between the *chuan* chamber and the *nei* chamber, in probably their functions and scales. Chen Mingda (2003a: 69-70) pointed out that *nei* was usually used to describe the room of wealthy people's dwelling in Han textual sources. The use of the term *nei* in the description of the cliff tomb chamber suggests the intention of the cliff tomb builders to imitate an ample dwelling.
[81] Similar inscription of memo for tomb builders is also found carved in the pillars in the front chamber of the stone tomb at Cangshan 蒼山 in Shandong, dated to AD 151. See Shandong sheng bowuguan and Cangshan xian wenhuaguan 1975 for the archaeological report. The long inscription containing 324 characters describes the content and the pictorial scheme of the tomb carvings in the tomb chambers section by section. There appeared many terms used by professional stone carvers. It is regarded by scholars as the guide manual for the stone carvers (Li Falin 1985; Wang Entian 1989).

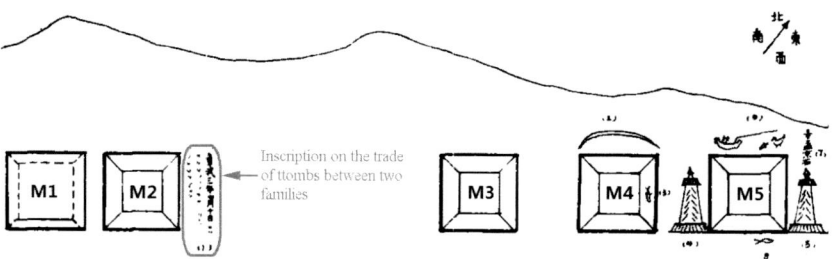

FIGURE 37. PLAN OF THE SITE OF THE CLIFF TOMBS M1, M2, M4 AND M5 (FROM LEFT TO RIGHT) AT TONGBANKOU IN XISHUI IN GUIZHOU. AFTER HUANG SITING 1986: FIG. 1.

project carried out by and for several families or several generations, which forms a great contrast to some of the most elaborate stone or brick chamber tombs of the same date, which were mainly dedicated to one tomb occupant or to a couple.[82] On one hand, this reflects the lesser social status and economic condition of the high-end cliff tomb occupant compared to those of the stone or brick chamber tombs; on the other hand, this shows the importance of the cliff tomb in reinforcing the ties between generations and families through incorporating them into a communal project.

It is also notable that sometimes the fall of a large family or a large clan is also revealed by their tombs. For example, an inscription found in the Tongbankou 桐半口 cliff tomb in Xishui 習水 in Guizhou, which is adjacent to southern Sichuan, shows that a person sold one of his family burial chambers to another person to inter the parents of that person. The inscription reads: '章武三年七月十日,姚立從曾意買大父曾孝梁右一門,七十萬,畢.知者廖诚,杜六.葬姚胡(父)及母. On the tenth day of the seventh month in the third year of Zhangwu (AD 223), Yao Li bought a burial chamber from Zeng Yi. The burial chamber was located on the right of the burial chamber of Zeng Xiaoliang, the father of Zeng Yi. The price was 700,000 qian. [The transaction] was concluded. The witnesses were Liao Cheng and Du Liu. Yao's father and mother were interred.'[83] According to the archaeological report, the inscription is at the entrance of the tomb M2, which is located in the right hand part of a row of five neatly planned tombs (figure 37).[84] In this sense, these five tombs may have been at the Zeng's family cemetery, and the tomb of Zeng Yi's father was one of the three tombs located to the right of the tomb M2. The year AD 223 recorded in this deal was one of the years of chaos following closely the fall of the Eastern Han. It is very likely that under some economic pressure from a declining large family, Zeng Yi had to make the compromise to sell one of the tombs from his family cemetery. The witnesses recorded in the inscription imply the formality of this deal.

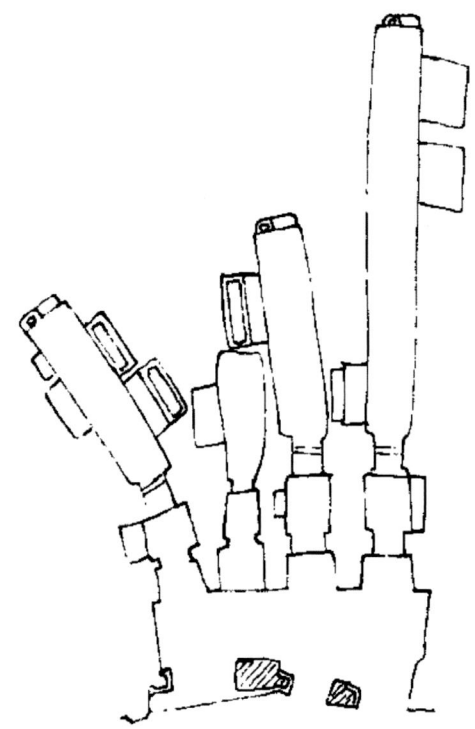

FIGURE 38. PLAN OF THE MAHAO II M99 IN LESHAN. AFTER TANG CHANGSHOU 1993: FIG. 6.

The above case could also to some extent explain why sometimes different surnames are found in a large cliff tomb or in adjacent cliff tombs. For example, in the Mahao III M99 in Leshan, seven pieces of inscriptions identifying the tomb occupants were carved in different burial chambers: '王鳳冢 (the tomb of Wang Feng)', '王景冢 (the tomb of Wang Jing)', '王□冢 (the tomb of Wang □)', '王景信父冢 (the tomb of Wang Jing and Wang Xin's father)', '王遂姒冢 (the tomb of Wang Sui's wife)', '鄧景達冢 (the tomb of Deng Jingda)' and '武陽趙國羊 (Zhao Guoyang from Wuyang)'.[85] The Mahao II M99 is a large scale tomb constituted by a rectangular front hall shared by four individual burial chambers tunnelled into the rear wall of the front hall, similar to the previously mentioned Mahao I M1 (figure 38). Each individual burial chamber is further divided into several small chambers containing built-in stoves and coffins.[86] Though the locations of these inscriptions recording the tomb occupants in Mahao II M99

---

[82] For examples of the most elaborate stone chamber tombs or the stone chamber tombs combined with some brick structures, see the Dahuting M1 in Mixian in Henan (Henan sheng wenwu yanjiusuo 1993) and the Yi'nan M1 in Shandong (Zeng Zhaoyu, Jiang Baogeng and Li Zhongyi 1956), which are all very likely belong to a high ranking official or a high ranking official together with his wife.
[83] Huang Siting 1986: 68.
[84] Huang Siting 1986: 68.

[85] Tang Changshou 1993: 81.
[86] Tang Changshou 1993: 34, fig. 6.

is not provided by Tang Changshou when he describes this tomb and there is no archaeological report on this tomb,[87] it is very likely that the whole tomb was originally built for the prosperous Wang family with a shared ancestral shrine and that some of the burial chambers were later sold to some members from the Deng and Zhao families, like the deal between the Yao and Zeng families at the Tongbankou cliff tomb in Guizhou.[88]

3. Wooden Architecture as Framework of Representation

Zhong Changtong's 仲長統 description offers us a glimpse of the ideal life of a wealthy landowner:

> May I live in a place with good fields and an ample house, with hills to the back and facing a stream, surrounded by waterways, encircled by bamboo and trees.

使居有良田廣宅,背山臨流,溝池環匝,竹木周布.[89]

The records in the *Hou Han shu* on how the powerful official 梁冀 and his wife Sun Shou 孫壽 spent lavishly on house construction show us what a spacious house looked like. The couple spent large amounts of money to build houses including multiple connected buildings with decorated walls and pillars. Both the reception section and the bedroom section in their houses have multiple chambers.[90]

Architectural elements of such spacious houses, including columns and coffers, were widely represented in cliff tombs. The use of these architectural features as visual clues may have led the viewers to project a house onto the tomb and evoked the illusion of the tomb as a luxurious dwelling.[91] The illusion was created by people's expectations of the dwelling of the wealthy people.[92] In addition, the funerary context of the representation of these architectural features created conditions of illusion, as tombs were often thought to be the dwellings for the deceased in the Eastern Han as mentioned in Chapter 1.[93] As will be discussed in the following sections, the representation of the dwelling for the living in the cliff tomb relied on 'the mutual reinforcement of illusion and expectation'.[94] To indicate the dwelling, tomb workers only carved a few architectural elements and furnishings, but there were three things they clearly emphasized—the column with brackets, the coffer and the stove. It is through these indications that the viewers of the tomb were led to interpret the representation. At the same time, the viewers were led to detach their projection of a house from the tomb and to recapture the burial context. As will be shown in the following sections, auspicious images associated with the heavenly world and images of exorcism in the funeral were often illustrated on columns and coffers in the tomb. It was through this act of 'switching' between a house and a burial context that the embodiment of a house in the tomb was reinforced.

Column with Bracket Set

Bracket sets originated in the construction of large wooden buildings. However, we have no evidence of any major examples surviving from before the Tang (AD 618-907). Yang Hongxun points out that the high ranking buildings were usually large in scale and were built on high platform made of rammed earth. To shelter the earthen platform from rain, large projecting eaves are required. Consequently, a new architectural solution to supporting the projecting eaves was needed.[95] The bracket sets work as cantilevers to assist the columns with supporting the roof. A bracket set usually consists of a block as the base and a pair of brackets or several brackets. The traditional wooden architecture functions mainly through three component parts, the column, the bracket set and the roof, among which the bracket set plays a crucial part in realizing the mechanical function of the wooden architecture.[96] Bracket sets and columns are represented in many places of the cliff tombs. They appear in the rear and middle of the burial chamber (figure 39); they are connected to the low walls to divide the burial space; they frame the entrances to cliff tombs; they are enshrined in the niches of the tomb and they appear in the places where auspicious icons are usually located (figure 40). Some locations and decorations of the bracket set draw our attention to the possible auspicious meanings embedded in the construction of the bracket set. For example, as a combination, the column and the bracket set are found enshrined in the niche carved in the Jinzhongshan 金鐘山 II M4 in Santai.[97] In the Zhaizishan 寨子山 M530 in Pengshan

---

[87] Tang Changshou 1993: 81.
[88] Wang Jiayou (1985) suggests that the reason for the appearing of different surnames in a cliff tomb is that the tomb occupants were non-Han people. When they started to be assimilated into the Han culture, they began to use Han surnames and changed their surnames from time to time. However, Tang Changshou (1993: 81-82) suggests that the Han people also changed their surnames sometimes for particular reasons. Therefore, the different surnames do not necessarily reflect the non-Han origin of the tomb occupants.
[89] *Hou Han shu*: 1644. The translation is after Ebrey 1987: 624.
[90] '冀乃大起第舍,而壽亦對街為宅,殫極土木,互相誇競.堂寢皆有陰陽奧室,連房洞戶,柱壁雕鏤,加以銅漆,窗牖皆有綺疏青瑣,圖以雲氣仙靈. Ji then started to build extravagant houses. Shou also built houses across the street. They used the best timber and competed for the lavish expenditure. The living rooms and the bed chambers of their houses all contained multiple small rooms. Multiple buildings were connected. The pillars and walls were decorated with pictorial carvings with bronze gilt. Both the windows and doors were hollowed out with patterns illustrating cloud scrolls and immortals.' *Hou Han shu*: 1181-1182.
[91] E. H. Gombrich suggested that representation to some extent relies on 'guided projection'. For example, 'when we say that the blots and brushstrokes of the impressionist landscapes "suddenly come to life", we mean we have been led to project a landscape into these dabs of pigment'. Gombrich 2009: 170.
[92] Gombrich argued that 'expectation created illusion'. Gombrich 2009: 171.
[93] Gombrich provided an example of cult images in such context, in which the faithful bathed and clothed them, and carried them in procession. There was an illusion that these images were smiling, frowning or nodding. Gombrich 2009: 172.
[94] Gombrich 2009: 173.
[95] Yang Hongxun 1987: 254-257.
[96] The English translations of the terms in traditional Chinese wooden architecture follow the translations in Guo Qinghua's PhD thesis (1999), *The Structure of Chinese Timber Architecture*, Chalmers University of Technology.
[97] Sichuan sheng wenwu kaogu yanjiuyuan, Mianyang shi bowuguan and Santai xian wenwu guanli suo 2007: 24-30.

FIGURE 39. THE REAR PILLAR IN THE HUJIAWAN M1 IN SANTAI. PHOTOGRAPH BY XUAN CHEN.

in Sichuan, auspicious icons are found on the *dougong* structure on top of the octagonal column (figure 41).[98] On the block, is carved a bow-shaped icon, which is usually thought to be a symbol of the presence of the Queen Mother of the West and therefore regarded as auspicious.[99] On the body of the bracket, a fish is carved with an unidentified creature on its back. As well as the bow-shaped icon, the fish is believed to be an auspicious symbol in the Han pictorial schema. In the tomb Bailinpo M5 in Santai, a squatting bear is carved in the middle of a bracket set.[100] A similar squatting bear in the tomb Yuanbaoshan 元寶山 M1 in Santai is identified by Susan Erickson as a *fangshi* 方士 or *fangxiangshi* 方相士, demon expellers who led exorcisms and rites that were associated with protecting the tomb from unfavorable influences.[101] She suggests that 'in general, the squatting bear with a frontal view of its face can be seen as a powerful apotropaic image, meant to protect the tomb and ward off anything harmful'.[102] The bracket set also appears independently on the lintel above the entrance to the cliff tomb, where usually auspicious icons are carved, such as the ram, the dragon and the *bi* disc, which suggests that the bracket set could also have been an auspicious icon.[103]

As in the cliff tombs in Sichuan, the columns with the bracket sets are also elaborately represented in stone carving and sculpture in some stone tombs in central and eastern China, which have led scholars to make assumptions on the auspicious meanings of the bracket sets. In the example of the Yi'nan tomb in Shandong, Lydia Thompson argues that the central columns in the front and middle chambers serve as the axis mundi, which connected the tomb with the heavenly sphere for the tomb occupant. The central columns are sometimes interpreted as Mount Kunlun (*Kunlun shan* 昆侖山) which leads the way to the immortal world where the Queen Mother of the West (*Xiwangmu* 西王母) resides.[104] She further suggests that the central column in a tomb chamber provides the tomb with the central point for locating the tomb in the cosmos oriented by the cardinal directions: the north, the south, the west and the east.[105] Part of her argument arises from the size, the quality and the elaborate sculpture of the column with bracket set in the Yi'nan tomb. The column together with the bracket set located in the centre of the middle chamber, reaches to a height of nearly two metres, with the bracket set flanked by a pair of elaborate dragon sculptures. People's attention would be naturally attracted to this affecting presence in the tomb. In addition, stone as the building material seems to have increased the attraction of the column with the bracket set. When discussing the stone sculpture in early China, Ann Paludan points out that 'even the most apparently secular figures were made for their intrinsic association with other-worldly powers'.[106] Moreover, as Wu Hung suggests, 'all the natural characteristics of stone-strength, plainness, and especially endurance-became analogous to eternity or immortality'.[107] In this sense, the stone column and bracket set modelled on the wooden structure are very likely to have been associated with the world of immortality.

Similar representation of the stone columns and the bracket sets can be found in the cliff tombs in Sichuan, where the central columns with the bracket sets constitute the main focus of some tombs. In the Bailipo M1 in Santai, a large central column in the rear chamber rises up from the floor to the ceiling, with a pair of wide brackets on top of its block on the capital (figure 42).[108] The rear chamber is square in

---

[98] Chen Mingda 2003a: 88.
[99] The bow-shaped icon is part of the headdress (*sheng* 勝) of the Queen Mother of the West. 'The *sheng* may be identified as a pair of discs that are linked by a straight rod (Loewe 1979: 105).' See also Knauer 2006: fig. 3.20. The *sheng* is 'a headdress or hair ornament which consists of two wheels with or without projections at either end of a thin stick which passes through the goddess's chignon. This headdress has symbolic significance, and has been variously interpreted as the ax of the magna mater cult, and the loom wheel of a spinning and silk cult (Cahill 1990: 99)'. See Knauer 2006: fig. 3.21 for the depictions of the looms. Frühauf further connects the *sheng* with the weaving of the universe (Frühauf 1999: 35).
[100] Sichuan sheng wenwu kaogu yanjiuyuan, Mianyang shi bowuguan and Santai xian wenwu guanli suo 2007: pls. 259 and 260.
[101] Erickson 2003: 440-441. Derk Bodde has made detailed discussion on the exorcisms and rites in the Han dynasty (Bodde 1975: 75-85). Bodde suggests that since the Zhou, the *fangxiangshi* performed as the demon expeller in important exorcisms, including exorcism during the funeral. According to the *Zhou li* 周禮, 'when there is a great funeral, the *fangxiangshi* goes in advance of the coffin, and upon its arrival at the tomb, when it is being inserted into the burial chamber, he strikes the four corners of the chamber with his lance (Bodde 1975: 78-79)'.
[102] Erickson 2003: 443.
[103] For example, see the bracket set carved in the middle of the lintel above the entrance to the tomb Douyafanggou 豆芽房溝 M166 in Pengshan (Chen Mingda 2003a: 86).
[104] Thompson 1998: 155-162.
[105] Thompson 1998: 155-162.
[106] Paludan 2006: 16.
[107] Wu 1995: 122. He further points out that there is the dichotomy of the architecture of stone and the architecture of wood: 'those of wood used by the living, and those of stone dedicated to the dead'.
[108] Sichuan sheng wenwu kaogu yanjiuyuan, Mianyang shi bowuguan and Santai xian wenwu guanli suo 2007: 154-179.

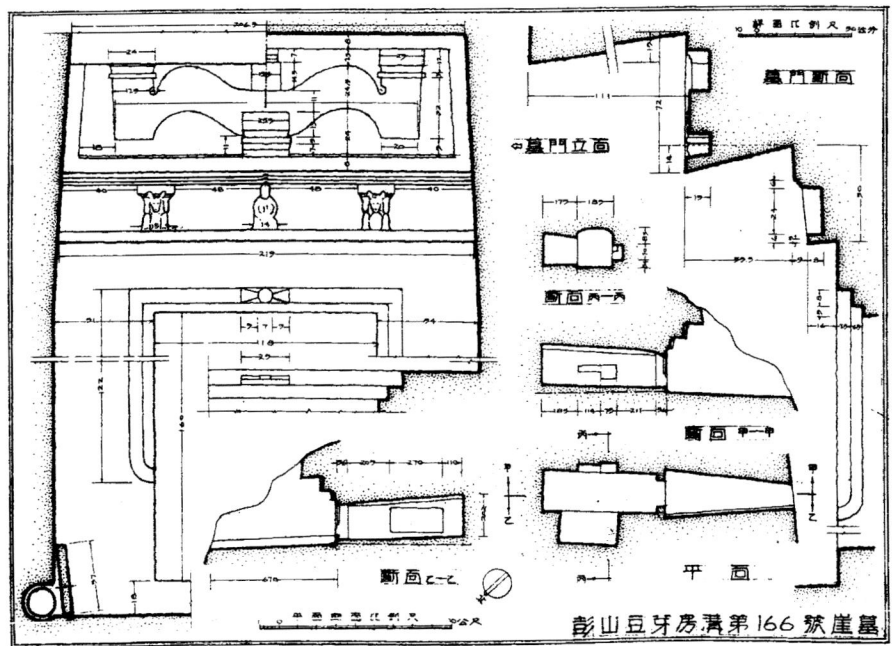

Figure 40. Illustration of the entrance of the Douyafanggou M166 in Pengshan. After Chen Mingda 2003a: fig. 16.

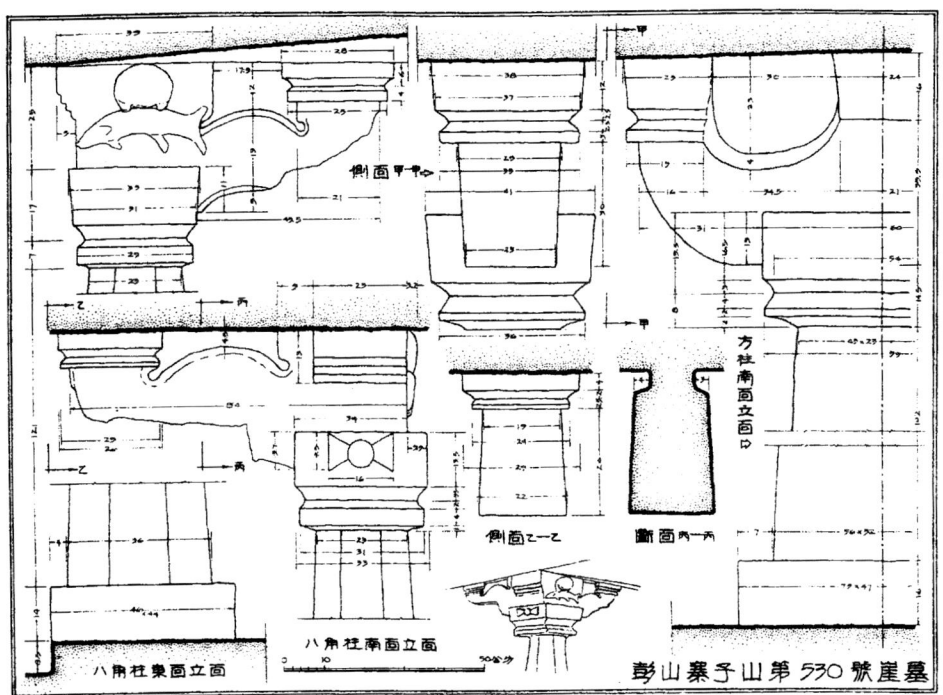

Figure 41. A pillar with the bow shaped icon and other auspicious images in the Zhaizishan M530 in Pengshan. After Chen Mingda 2003a: fig. 18.

shape, which further highlights the central position of the column. When one enters the rear chamber, one's attention would firstly be attracted to the large column and then to the wide brackets, which connect to the square coffer of the ceiling. In some cases, the structure of the column with the bracket set is further highlighted through the elaborate decoration of the animal-shaped column seat, which can be observed in the rear chamber of the Jinzhongshan I M4 and the façade of the cliff tomb Lijiagou 李家溝 M355 in Pengshan.[109] In addition, in some cliff tombs with simple

[109] Sichuan sheng wenwu kaogu yanjiuyuan, Mianyang shi bowuguan and Santai xian wenwu guanli suo 2007: 24-30; Chen Mingda 2003a: 68. Such animal-shaped column seat is also found in the brick tomb containing stone structures in the Xuzhen 許鎮 tomb in Deyang 德陽 in Sichuan (see Xinan bowuyuan choubeichu 1954: figs. 12 and 13) and in the stone tomb in Baiji 白集 in Xuzhou in Jiangsu (Nanjing bowuyuan 1981). Jessica Rawson uses the examples from the Baiji stone tomb in

FIGURE 42. A COLUMN IN A BURIAL CHAMBER OF THE BAILINPO M1 IN SANTAI. PHOTOGRAPH BY XUAN CHEN.

FIGURE 43. VIEW OF THE TOMB HUJIAWAN M1 IN SANTAI. AFTER SICHUAN SHENG WENWU KAOGU YANJIUYUAN, MIANYANG SHI BOWUGUAN AND SANTAI XIAN WENWU GUANLI SUO 2007: PL. 288.

structure and decoration, the elaborately sculpted columns and bracket sets naturally became the major attraction in the tomb. The importance of such structures may have been associated both with its importance in the grand dwelling for the living and its importance in the world of immortality. For example, the cliff tomb Hujiawan 胡家灣 M1 in Santai is a cliff tomb with very simple structure and decoration (figure 43). It comprises a passageway, a front chamber, a rear chamber, and two side chambers, in a total length of 16 metres.[110] Stone carvings only appear on the ceiling of the rear chamber and on the wall to resemble the wooden framed wall architecture. Consequently, the enormous column protruding from the rear wall with three-dimensional sculptures at the end of the long central axis of the tomb becomes the focus as the viewer enters the tomb. Seated on a stepped base, the octagonal column shaft is carved out of the rear wall of the tomb, with a capital composed by three pairs of brackets. Each pair of the brackets is set on a block. The whole column is carved from the living rock, connected to the rear wall, the ceiling and the floor of the tomb, forming an impressive visual effect. A similar representation of the rear column with the bracket set in a simple structured cliff tomb can be found in the cliff tomb Bailinpo M4 in Santai.[111]

Coffer

The *zaojing* or the coffer usually appears in the form of a well formed by corbelled layers on the ceiling of the cliff tomb. In wooden architecture, the *zaojing* is a part of a decorative ceiling. In traditional wooden architecture, the internal part under the roof is covered by a decorative ceiling which does not have any mechanical function. The bracket set structure is usually placed between the column and the roof. Part of the bracket set structure is deliberately exposed for aesthetic purposes. The major complicated part of the bracket sets structure is hidden from the viewers by the decorative ceiling under the roof. In a cliff tomb, the *zaojing* is represented in a similar way to how the bracket set is represented: both their association with a grand dwelling for the living and the other worldly power are emphasized.

The surface of the coffer (*zaojing*) in the cliff tomb is usually decorated with paintings or reliefs. Similar structures are mentioned in Eastern Han texts when describing palace architecture. The coffer (*zaojing*) is mentioned by Zhang Heng 張衡 (AD 78-139) in the *Xijing fu* 西京賦 (Western Metropolis Rhapsody) when describing the grand palace building of the *Weiyang gong* 未央宮 (Everlasting Hall) in Chang'an, the capital of the Western Han dynasty (206 BC-AD 8):

They ran crosswise long beams of the masculine arc,
Tied purlins and rafters to link them together,
Rooted inverted lotus stalks on the figured ceiling (*zaojing*),
Which bloomed with red flowers joined one to another.

亙雄虹之長梁，
結枆橑以相接，
蒂倒茄於藻井，
披紅葩之狎獵.[112]

The coffer is also evoked by Wang Yanshou 王延壽 (c. 124-148 AD) in the *Lu Lingguang dian fu* 魯靈光殿賦 (Rhapsody on the Hall of Luminous Brilliance in Lu) when describing the interior decoration of the grand palace building:

Xuzhou, the cliff tomb Jinzhongshan I M4 in Santai in Sichuan and the cliff tomb Lijiagou M355 in Pengshan in Sichuan to show the borrowing of animal-shaped column seat from the West (Rawson 2012: 34-35).
[110] For the archaeological report see Sichuan sheng wenwu kaogu yanjiuyuan, Mianyang shi bowuguan and Santai xian wenwu guanli suo 2007: 259-264.

[111] Sichuan sheng wenwu kaogu yanjiuyuan, Mianyang shi bowuguan and Santai xian wenwu guanli suo 2007: 154-179.
[112] *Wen xuan*: 38. The translation is after Knechtges 1982: 187-188. Quoted by Erickson (2003: 421), when she discusses the association of the coffer in the cliff tomb with that in the palace architecture.

In a round pool on the square well, invertly planted are lotus.

圓淵方井,反植荷葉.[113]

Indeed, as described in the above Eastern rhapsodies, some coffers (*zaojing*) in the cliff tombs are depicted with a relief of a lotus in stone.[114] Moreover, the lotus often appears together with the turtle in the corners of the coffer, which makes the coffer of the cliff tomb look exactly like an 'aquatic plant well'-the literal translation of *zaojing* in English (figure 44).[115] In addition to the lotus and the turtle, a melon is another decoration related to water that is often used on the coffer of the cliff tomb. For example, in the cliff tomb Baishabao M2 in Mianyang, the lotus and melon are carved respectively on two of the four corners of the coffer.[116] Sometimes, the melon appears independently in the centre of the coffer, for example, in the cliff tomb Hujiawan M1 in Santai.[117] According to Susan Erickson, the melon can be traced back to the image described in the *Shanhai jing* 山海經 (Classic of Mountains and Seas). 'According to the text, a cinnabar tree (*dan mu* 丹木) produces a fruit that is said to be like a melon. Its skin is red with black veins, and it was believed to provide protection against jaundice and to ward off fire.'[118] In the wooden buildings of the Eastern Han, fire could be of great concern. In this sense, the images related water decorated on the 'aquatic plant well' could have been desirable. Like the previously discussed column and bracket set, the coffer in the cliff is not only a pseudo architectural element, it is also embedded with auspicious meanings. In fact, in some cases, except for being an 'aquatic plant well', the coffer in the cliff tomb also has other meanings.

In the cliff tomb Bailinpo M1 in Santai, two coffers are carved side by side on the rectangular ceiling of a side chamber.[119] One coffer is carved with the relief decoration of a circle representing the sun, painted in red with some relics of black remaining in the middle.[120] The other coffer

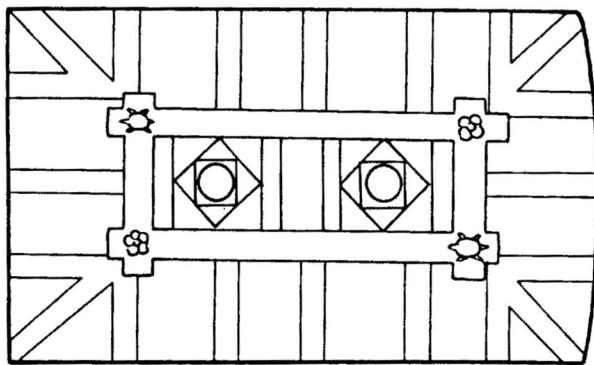

FIGURE 44. A CEILING IN THE TOMB ZIJINGWAN M3 IN SANTAI. AFTER SICHUAN SHENG WENWU KAOGU YANJIUYUAN, MIANYANG SHI BOWUGUAN AND SANTAI XIAN WENWU GUANLI SUO 2007: FIG. 107.

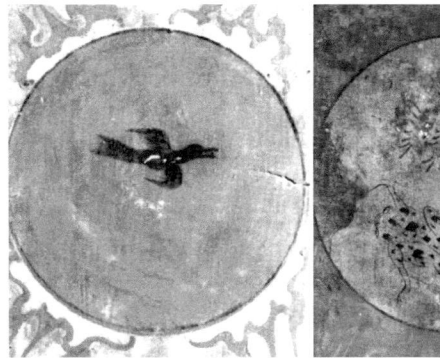

FIGURE 45. PAINTINGS OF THE SUN AND MOON ON THE CEILING OF THE BUQIANQIU TOMB IN LUOYANG IN HENAN (LATE WESTERN HAN). AFTER HUANG MINGLAN AND GUO YINQIANG 1996: PLS. 7 AND 18.

is carved with a circular relief representing the moon, which is painted in red with the rim painted in black. A black toad is depicted in the middle of the moon. Such arrangements of the sun and moon on coffers are common in cliff tombs in Sichuan.[121] Susan Erickson traces the depiction on the coffers as celestial bodies back to the brick tombs in central China dated to the middle of the 1st century BC.[122] She provides the example of the Buqianqiu 卜千秋 tomb in Luoyang in Henan, in which two ends of the apex of the ceiling are respectively painted with the circular sun and the moon (figure 45). Like the depiction of the sun and the moon in the cliff tomb, in the Buqianqiu tomb, a crow is painted in the red sun while a toad with a cinnamon tree is painted in the red moon. Between the sun and the moon are various creatures from the immortal

---

[113] *Wen xuan*: 170. The translation is after Knechtges 1987: 271-272. Quoted by Zeng Zhaoyu (Zeng Zhaoyu, Jiang Baogeng and Li Zhongyi 1956: 6), when she associated the coffer decoration of the lotus relief in the stone tomb the Yi'nan tomb in Shandong with that in the palace architecture.
[114] For example, see the cliff tombs Baishabao 白沙包 M2 in Mianyang (He Zhiguo 1988a), Zijingwan M1 in Santai (Sichuan sheng wenwu kaogu yanjiuyuan, Mianyang shi bowuguan and Santai xian wenwu guanli suo 2007: 70) and Zijingwan M3 in Santai (Sichuan sheng wenwu kaogu yanjiuyuan, Mianyang shi bowuguan and Santai xian wenwu guanli suo 2007: 82). In these tombs, the lotuses are carved in the corners of the coffers, instead of locating in the centre as described in the rhapsodies. In contrast, the lotus is usually carved in the centre of the coffer in the stone tombs in eastern China. For example, see the Yi'nan tomb (Zeng Zhaoyu, Jiang Baogeng and Li Zhongyi 1956: 6) in Shandong and the Lalishan 拉犁山 tomb in Xuzhou (Geng Jianjun 1990).
[115] The translation is after Erickson 2003: 421.
[116] He Zhiguo 1988a: fig. 4.
[117] Sichuan sheng wenwu kaogu yanjiuyuan, Mianyang shi bowuguan and Santai xian wenwu guanli suo 2007: pl. 290.
[118] Erickson 2003: 425. *Shanhai jing*: 38. '其上多丹木,...其實大如瓜, 赤符而黑理,食之已癉,可以禦火.'
[119] Sichuan sheng wenwu kaogu yanjiuyuan, Mianyang shi bowuguan and Santai xian wenwu guanli suo 2007: 159.
[120] According to the common pictorial scheme of the Han funerary mural paintings, the black part may have been a crow, which usually appears with the sun, called the *wu* 烏 (crow). For the association of the crow with the sun and the fire in the belief in early China, see Li Li 2004: 170-175.
[121] In some cases, only the sun appears in the centre of the coffer, which is located in the apex of the ceiling of the burial chamber. For example, see the cliff tomb Taliangzi M3 in Zhongjiang (Sichuan sheng wenwu kaogu yanjiuyuan, Deyang shi wenwu kaogu yanjiusuo and Zhongjiang xian wenwu baohu guanli suo 2008: pl. 17).
[122] Erickson 2003: 423-425. She further points out that the images of the sun and the moon are very usual in the Han tomb decoration by providing the example of the pictorial bricks from Peng Xian 彭縣 in Sichuan, on which the sun and the moon deities are represented (Erickson 2003: 423, 424, fig. 24).

world, in which the tomb occupant is identified to be the figure riding on the phoenix.[123]

In this sense, we can regard the coffers with the sun and the moon in the cliff tomb as the heavenly world prepared for the tomb occupant after his death. In this case, the coffer is no longer the 'aquatic plant well'. It turns out to be the depiction of heaven. The coffer decoration on the stone tomb the Yi'nan tomb further helps us to understand the coffer's association with heaven. A side chamber of the tomb has a coffer depicted with criss-cross pattern within a square frame.[124] Such a pattern is very common in the representation of a window in the tombs of the Han dynasty and the earlier times.[125] Wu Hung suggests that windows were created inside the tombs 'to facilitate the soul's movement'.[126] Similarly, we can see the windows represented on the coffer as the entrance to heaven or to the immortal world for the soul.

So far, we have seen several possible interpretations of the coffer in the cliff tomb. These interpretations are firstly established on the basis of the coffer as a decorative architectural element. In addition, we have discussed the roles of columns and bracket sets as both architectural features and as elements with other worldly associations. In fact, the link between an architectural feature and with the other worlds first appeared in dwellings for the living, where certain architectural elements of buildings were the subjects of sacrifices, the *wu si* 五祀 (Five Sacrifices).[127] The five subjects that received seasonal sacrifices from the residents were the *hu* 戶 (door), the *zao* 灶 (stove), the *zhongliu* 中霤 (Central Impluvium), the *men* 門 (gate) and the *jing* 井 (well), which were the deities of a dwelling who protected different aspects of the daily life of the resident families.[128] It is likely that the framework of the representation of the architectural elements in the cliff tomb was partly modelled on the sacrificial system embedded in the dwelling. In other words, the architecture of the cliff was designed to systematically resemble the dwelling, in which the sacrificial rites were made in an orderly sequence, among many other regulations that maintained the family organization. The following discussion on the stove in the cliff tomb, which was also one of the Five Sacrifices in Eastern Han, will further exhibit how the tomb furnishings were made to resemble the construction of the dwelling and to indicate the orderly rites that shaped and maintained the family organization.

The Stove and Family Organization

The cliff tombs are designed for many members of a family, sometimes, members of a small family which affiliated to a large family. Consequently, sometimes more than one stove or granary is found carved in the same cliff tomb, perhaps intended for the use of different small families within a larger clan that was embodied by the cliff tomb.[129] For example, in the Dongzipai M1 in Santai, two stoves are carved respectively in two chambers of the tomb.[130] Each area where the stove is located seems to suggest a kitchen for a specific family. The first stove is located on the right of the front chamber on the central axis of the tomb, seemingly built for the tomb occupant in the stone coffin located in the rear chamber on the central axis. The second stove is built in the side chamber on the right of the front chamber for the occupant in the stone coffin in the same chamber. Here the stoves were possibly built both for symbolizing a kitchen and for making seasonal sacrifices within a family as the basic unity for the activities.[131]

Similar arrangements of several stoves in the same cliff tomb can also be found in the Mahao M1 in Leshan. The cliff tomb is made by a rectangular front hall with three rear chambers tunnelled into its rear wall. Each rear chamber

---

[123] For the archaeological report, see Luoyang bowuguan 1977. The brick tomb the Luoyang 洛陽 M61 is another example that the sun and moon are painted together on the ceiling (Chaves 1968).
[124] Zeng Zhaoyu, Jiang Baogeng and Li Zhongyi 1956: 9, fig. 18.
[125] For example, see the drawing of the window in criss-cross pattern in the Eastern Han stone slab tomb the Houshiguo M1 in Mixian in Henan (Wu 2010: 229, fig. 223). See also Zhang Jianhua and Zhang Yuxia 2012: fig. 3.
[126] Wu 2010: 228-229. He also provides an earlier example of the windows represented on the wooden chamber of the Marquis Yi of Zeng dated to the 4th century BC (Wu 2010: 193, fig. 178).
[127] The records on the Five Sacrifices first appeared in the *Ji fa* 祭法 section in the *Li ji* 禮記, in which the Five Sacrifices were among the hierarchical sacrificial regulations made by the Lord. '諸侯為國立五祀 For the feudal lords he [the king] established the Five Sacrificial Cults for their states.' *Li ji*: 1305. The translation is after Chard 1990: 147. For the development and interpretation of the Five Sacrifices in the excavated and received texts, see the PhD thesis by Zou Junzhi (2008). The translation of the *zhongliu*, the *xing*, the *men* and the *hu* is after Chard 1990: 147.
[128] In some versions of the textual records, the *xing* (walkway) was one of the five sacrifices instead of the *jing* (well). Yang Hua (2004: 99) suggests that since in the *Baihu tong* 白虎通 edited by Ban Gu 班固 in Eastern Han placed the *jing* (well) instead of the *xing* 行 (walkway) among the Five Sacrifices, the *jing* (well) might start to replace the *xing* (walkway) in the Five Sacrifices in Eastern Han. '五祀者, 何謂也?謂門, 戶,井,竈,中霤也. What does "Five Sacrifical Cults" refer to? It refers to the gate, doorway, well, stove, and Central Impluvium.' *Baihu tong*: 77. The translation is after Chard 1990: 150.

[129] Larger families began to appear in Eastern Han. 'Some brothers lived together after they married and maintained an extended family, embracing such collateral relatives as uncles, nephews, and first cousins.' Ch'ü 1972: 9. For the structure of the family in Han, see Ch'ü 1972: 4-9.
[130] Sichuan sheng wenwu kaogu yanjiuyuan, Mianyang shi bowuguan and Santai xian wenwu guanli suo 2007: 279-284.
[131] Early regulations on the sacrifice to stove are found in the *Yi li* 儀禮, which dates from the time of Zhou Gong 周公 (c. 1100 BC), the founder of the Zhou dynasty. The content consists of detailed descriptions of the rituals of a *shi* 士, 'the low level member of the aristocracy' (Boltz 1993: 234). '尸卒食,而祭饎爨,雍爨 When the personator has finished eating, the female assistant makes an offering to the stove in which the millet was cooked, and the cook offers to the stove in which the meat was cooked.' *Yi li*: 891. The translation is after Steele 1917: 158. In Han, sacrifice to stove was among the Five Sacrifices and the Seven Sacrifices (*qi si* 七祀), as one of the standard seasonal domestic rituals, which were partly related to the ancestral ritual. Sacrifice to stove among the Five Sacrifices can be found in the *Monthly Instructions for the Four People* (*Si min yue ling* 四民月令), which was written in Eastern Han, thought to be a manual of family management for landowners (for detailed discussion of this text, see Ebrey 1974). '十二月…,遂臘先祖五祀. In the twelfth month…, the *la* sacrifice is offered to ancestors and to the five deities.' *Si min yueling*: 74. The translation is after Hsu 1980: 227. Though the Five Sacrifices are not specified in the text, they are identified in the 'ritual prescriptions for each month' in the *Li ji* (Chard 1990: 149). '仲夏之月,…其祀灶,祭先肺. In summer (the fourth and fifth months) it is the stove, and the lung is put first.' *Li ji*: 498. The translation is after Chard 1990: 149.
For the role of stove in food preparing for rituals in Han and pre-Han period, see Sterckx 2006. For the development of the cult of stove, see Yang Kun 1944 and Chard 1990. For the practice of the cult of stove in the imperial period, which is established on the basis of early period, see Chard 1995.

Chapter 2 Tomb Structure

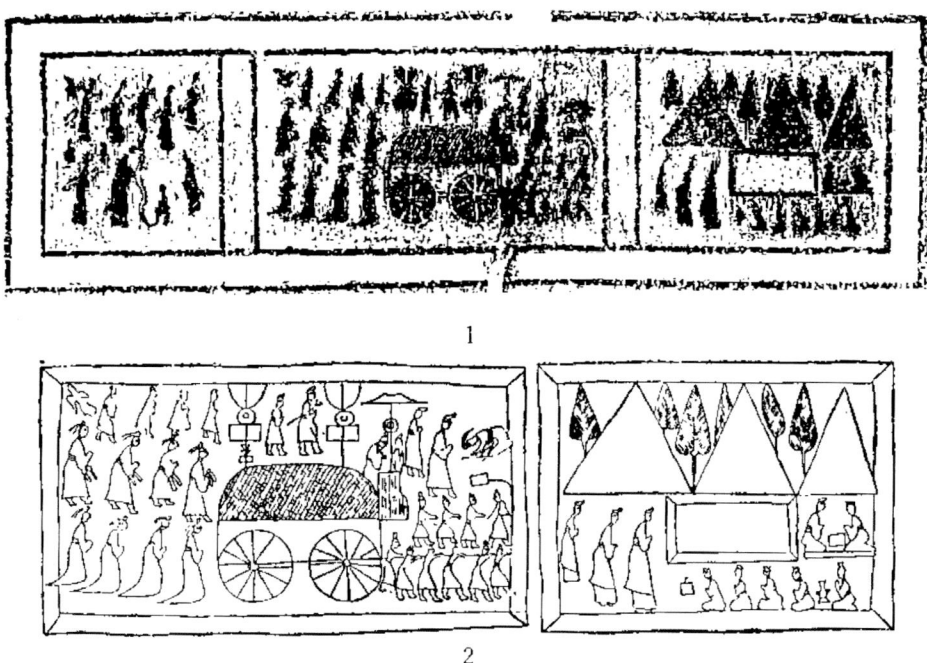

Figure 46. Rubbing and illustration of an Eastern Han pictorial stone illustrating funerary scene from Weishan in Shandong. After Xin Lixiang 2000: fig. 115.

is equipped with a stove together with relevant kitchen furnishings. The individual kitchen settings coincide with the plan of the tomb, suggesting three related families who shared the same sacrificial hall that might be dedicated to their communal ancestors.[132]

As Robert Chard suggests that 'the stove itself is the symbol of a single family unit'. 'The expression "divide stoves (fen zao 分灶)", which entails the ritual division of the ashes, denotes the breaking up of a household into smaller units'.[133] Though the expression 'divide stoves' came much later than the Han in imperial China, Chard suggests that the canonical prescriptions on stove sacrifice in Han provided the basis for the later beliefs in stove in imperial China down to the Qing period (AD 1644-1912). In this sense, in the Eastern Han, the stove may well have become one of the symbols of the family as a unit, which is extensively depicted and emphasized in the cliff tombs in Sichuan.

When studying the miniature buildings in Northern Song and Liao China, Chen Xin noted the 'ambiguity nature of the model'. Firstly, it is recognizable. But 'it functions outside the standard functions of a full sized object'. Yet 'a strong degree of resemblance – recalling the full sized object is essential'.[134] The cliff tomb here has a similar effect in modeling the wooden dwelling. In the cliff tomb, the architectural features continued to contribute to the ways in which 'viewers assessed the relative importance of various structures and their intended purposes and meanings'.[135]

Though the cliff tomb is not the actual wooden dwelling for the living, it has functions that require references to architectural uses. The nature of the wooden architecture carved in stone guides the movement and imagination of the viewers of the tomb.[136] Wooden architecture carved in stone provides the viewers with a special environment to understand the family organization and hierarchical orders of a large family in the framework of columns, ceilings and bracket sets and through furnishings like the stove.[137] Important architectural elements and furnishings are emphasized through stone sculptures to guide the viewers in realizing the important conmponents of the family organization.

4. Important Structure for Ritual and Sacrifice

An early Eastern Han pictorial stone from a tomb in Weishan 微山, Shandong illustrates a funeral scene, in which a carriage carrying a coffin is shown driving to the tomb, accompanied by a mourning procession. Some family members of the deceased are already at the burial site receiving the mourners. Some tomb builders seem still to be sitting at the side of the newly dug burial pit (figure 46).[138] This picture provides us with a direct knowledge of the role of the tomb in a funeral, which involved the

---

[132] Tang Changshou 1990: 112, fig. 1.
[133] Chard 1990: 10.
[134] Chen 2011: 147.
[135] Chen 2011: 151.
[136] Chen Xin suggests that two aspects of the viewers' engagement are closely related to the complete function of a model: movement and imagination. See Chen 2011: 170.
[137] Similar frameworks of the wooden architecture are also found in a 4th century earthen tomb in Gaotai 高臺 in Gansu. The wooden architectural details are carved elaborately into the earthen cave in a very similar way as the 1st and 2nd century cliff tombs in Sichuan. See Gansu sheng wenwu kaogu yanjiusuo and Gaotai xian bowuguan 2008.
[138] For the pictorial stone and the interpretation of the picture see Xin Lixiang 2000: 218-219.

deceased, the family members of the deceased, the funerary procession, the mourners and the tomb builders. Though the tomb depicted in this pictorial stone is not similar to the cliff tomb in Sichuan, we can imagine a similar role for the cliff tomb in funeral and other sacrifices around the same period in Eastern Han.

The argument of this section gathers much support from Wu Hung's contention that 'the tomb – as opposed to the family shrine – became the focus of ceremonial activity during the Han'. 'This custom developed, he maintains, because activities at the tomb emphasized devotion to the deceased, while activities at the family temple emphasized a person's ultimate lineage. Since the Han emperors were not of royal ancestry, they gained little from emphasizing their ancestry and instead focused on their filial devotion to immediate ancestors.'[139] Clearly, the local residents of the large agricultural estate would benefit from the same advantage of displaying their filial piety to their close ancestors. Consequently, the tomb became an important venue for the public display of the virtue of filial piety, which further facilitated the establishment of a beneficial relationship between members of the large clan, the wealthy landowners and the local officials.[140] Important activities including funerals and sacrifices centred on the tomb.

Compared with funerals at the tomb, as shown in the scene depicted in the pictorial stone from Shandong, sacrifices at the tomb were confined to a more exclusive social group. When the tomb was re-opened for sacrificial ritual, usually only the tomb occupants' family members could enter into the tomb for ritual, as revealed by the inscription carved by the entrance of the cliff tomb at Banbianjie 半邊街 in Pengshan: '永元十四年三月廿六日王叔蹈造, 子孫當開,他人不得 (Wang Shudao built this tomb on the twenty sixth day of the third month in the fourteenth year of Yongyuan. It should be opened by the offspring, not others.)'.[141] The inscription seems to imply that the tomb could be opened after the funeral and the offspring had an obligation to re-open the tomb to make sacrifices.[142]

Though the access to the tomb was confined to family members, a sacrifice still functioned as a public activity which corresponded to the close tie between family members and the responsibility of family members to maintain the tradition and fame of the already well-established family. The inscription in the cliff tomb HM3 at Xindu in Chengdu exhibited the importance of the cliff tomb as a venue for sacrifice: '惟自舊□,段本東州.祖考徠西,乃遷于慈.因處廣漢,造墓定基.魂靈不寧,於斯革之.永建三年八月,段仲孟造此萬歲之宅,刻勒石門,以示

---
[139] Powers 1991: 108-109.
[140] For the role of the public practice of mourning in forging beneficial relationships in a person's social network, see Brown 2007: 85-104.
[141] Gao Wen and Gao Chenggang 1990: 12.
[142] Inscription suggesting that the tomb could be accessed and viewed is also found elsewhere in the Eastern Han. See example from the inscription found in the Eastern Han tomb at the Baizi village 百子村, Xunyi 旬邑 in Shaanxi (Shaaxi sheng wenwuju and Shanghai bowuguan 2004: 99). The inscriptions advise the visitors to take off their shoes before entering into the tomb.

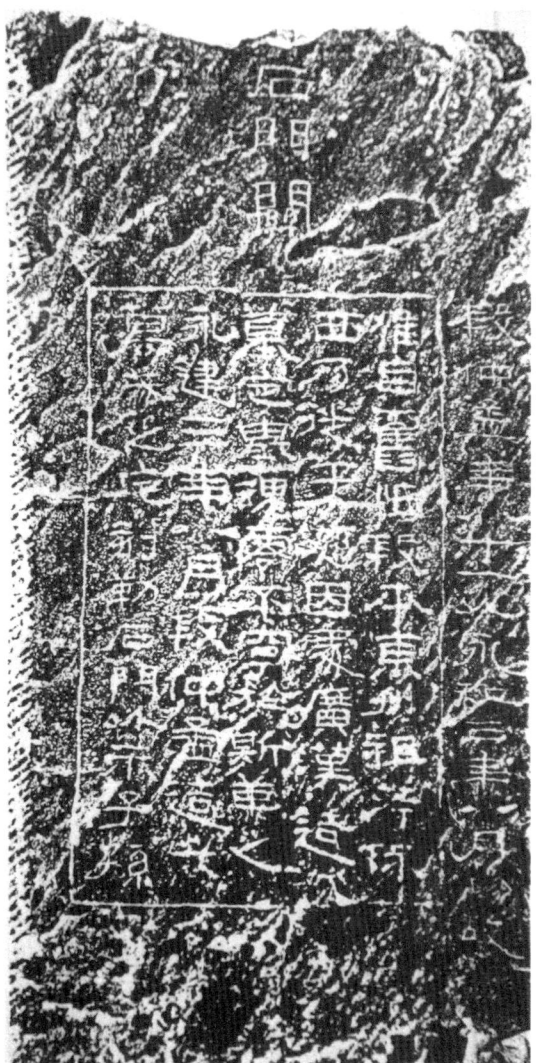

FIGURE 47. THE TOMB DOOR WITH INSCRIPTION FROM THE CLIFF TOMB HM3 IN XINDU IN SICHUAN. AFTER GAO WEN 2011: 184.

子孫. The ancestor of the Duan family was from the eastern province. After the ancestors came to the west, they moved the household to this place. Since we resided in Guanghan, we built tombs here to establish our roots. The situation that the souls were unrest had been changed since then. In the eighth month of the third year of Yongjian (AD 129), Duan Mengzhong built this dwelling for afterlife. The inscription was carved on the stone door to be shown to the offspring (figure 47).'[143] Above this passage, the characters '石門關 (stone barrier)' are carved. It is notable that these three inscriptions are carved on the stone door panel of the tomb entrance, facing the burial chamber. When the door was closed after sacrifice, the teaching for the offspring on the back of the door was religiously conserved together with the tomb occupants inside, who had already become ancestors of the family. And when the family members entered into the tomb, as a part of the sacrificial ritual, they could show their respect to the inscriptions recording the growth and establishment of their family due to the effort of their ancestors.

---
[143] Chen Yunhong, Zhang Yuxin and Wang Bo 2007: 41.

Some structures outside the cliff tomb further shows other possible sacrifices were carried out in the cemetery. Chen Mingda suggested that the square and flat ground outside the cliff tomb entrance was particularly excavated for use as a venue for sacrifice. It functioned similarly to the above ground stone shrine in front of the stone chamber tomb in Shandong and northern Jiangsu in Eastern Han. Such a venue is still discernable at many cliff tombs in Pengshan, such as tomb M505, M515 and M600.[144] Small caves were tunnelled into the cliff at the side of the venue for sacrifices, adjacent to the cliff tomb, and for placing ceremonial objects during the sacrifice. Two bowls containing several Han coins were found in one such small cave at tomb M600 in Pengshan.[145]

5. Conclusion

The depiction of monumentality and immortality in the cliff tomb has been thoroughly exploited by its users. In some cases, especially when the timber structure is sculpted in stone with spiritual images, the depiction of immortality in the cliff tomb structure also served to enhance its role as a monument. Through the representation of the timber architecture in stone, institutions in the community of the cliff tomb users were systematically illustrated and monumentalized. Furthermore, the characteristics of cliff tomb structures ensured that tombs could be constructed at a relatively low cost, which very likely culminated in the popularity of cliff tombs among a wide range of people. Though this chapter mainly focuses on discussing the grand cliff tombs, the lesser cliff tombs reflect a similar principle of tomb planning. As a result, a cemetery of cliff tombs of different scales exhibits the monumentalization of both the relationship within individual families and the relationship between the various families in a community. Through the continuous tomb construction, ritual and sacrifice taken place in the cemetery, the continuous communication between the past and future in a community was also carried on and on.

---

[144] Chen Mingda 2003a: 71-72.
[145] Chen Mingda 2003a: 72-73.

Chapter 3
Pictorial Carvings

This chapter is concerned with the pictorial carvings in the cliff tombs. The pictorial carvings usually appear in the form of various figures and images in low relief on the wall and at the entrance of the tomb. Occasionally, the decoration in the cliff tomb also appears in the form of coloured brush painting on the wall. Through analyzing the meaning of these pictorial carvings, the function of the whole cliff tomb and its individual component parts will be further revealed. Consequently, we can obtain a deeper insight into the factors underlying the popularity of the cliff tomb. As will be discussed in this chapter, many elements and schemes of the pictorial carvings in the cliff tombs are directly borrowed from those in contemporary brick or stone chamber tombs. Moreover, in the cliff tombs, some of these borrowed elements and schemes are particularly popular. The reasons for the prevalence of certain elements and schemes will be discussed. Subsequently, we can further understand how the cliff tombs came into being and became popular based on various already existing burial forms.

According to the 289 reported cliff tombs so far listed in Appendix 3, 52 cliff tombs were found decorated with pictorial carvings. The discussion in this chapter is primarily based on these cliff tombs and some other cliff tombs with pictorial carvings mentioned in two important regional surveys of the cliff tombs in Pengshan and Leshan.[1] None of these cliff tombs is entirely decorated with pictorial carvings on the main walls like some extensively decorated stone chamber tombs, such as the Yi'nan tomb and the Anqiu 安丘 tomb in Shandong.[2] Instead, most of these cliff tombs are only carved or painted with a few figures or images on the walls of one or two burial chambers, or on the walls near the entrance, especially the lintel above the entrance. Among all the 52 cliff tombs with pictorial carvings listed in Appendix 3, 17 are found with carvings on the lintels. This phenomenon will be discussed later and will be considered together with the frequently found pictorial carvings near the entrance of the cliff tomb. Before discussing the meaning of the pictorial carvings and their locations in the cliff tombs, it is important to consider the schema of the pictorial carvings in the contemporary brick or stone chamber tombs first. These are the major sources of the pictorial carvings in the cliff tombs.[3]

1. Pictorial Carvings in Stone and Brick Chamber Tombs: Communication between Sichuan and East China

As will be discussed in this section, the content and scheme of the pictorial carvings in the stone and brick chamber tombs in Sichuan are similar to those in east China in Shandong and Henan. The similarities are rooted in the similar plans of the burial chambers and the cemetery. It is very likely that communication about the pictorial carvings in the tomb and the plans of the cemeteries between these two distant areas was made through the people who took official positions in east China and were then buried in their adopted hometown in Sichuan as will be explained later in this section. Much content and arrangement of the pictorial carvings in the cliff tombs can be traced to those in the stone and brick chamber tombs, though with many variants adapted to the specific needs of the cliff tomb occupants. It is more likely that the pictorial carvings in the stone and brick chamber tombs in Sichuan instead of east China were the direct sources of the pictorial carvings in the cliff tombs.

Comparisons will be made between the stone chamber tombs in Sichuan and those in eastern China. The major tombs involved in the comparison are the Yangzishan tomb in Chengdu in Sichuan, the Zengjiabao tomb M1 and M2 in Chengdu in Sichuan, a stone chamber tomb in Hechuan in Sichuan, the Dahuiting tomb M1 in Mixian in Henan, a stone tomb in Cangshan in Shandong and the Yi'nan tomb M1 in Shandong.

At a first glance, there are many pictorial carvings with the same content in Sichuan and in eastern China. However the style of carving and the plan of a narrative scene are usually very different. For example, the pictorial carvings

---

[1] For the two regional surveys, see Tang Changshou 1993 and Chen Mingda 2003a and b. Tang Changshou made thorough survey of the cliff tombs in Pengshan and Leshan and compared the different features of the cliff tombs in these two areas (Tang Changshou 1993). Chen Mingda introduced the major features of the cliff tombs in Pemgshan in detail based on the archaeological excavation of the tombs in the area in the 1940s (Chen Mingda 2003a and b). Chen Mingda's work was not published until 2003 when Yin Lixin edited Chen Mingda's draft in the archive of the Chongqing China Three Gorges Museum. Many pictorial carvings in the cliff tombs can also be found in *Zhongguo Huaxiangshi quanji vol. 2* 中國畫像石全集第二卷 (Zhongguo huaxiangshi quanji bianji weiyuanhui 2000a).

[2] For the archaeological reports, see Zeng Zhaoyu, Jiang Baogeng and Li Zhongyi 1956 and Anqiu xian wenhuaju 1992. Details on the Yi'an tomb will be discussed later in the chapter. The Dongjiazhuang tomb in Anqiu is a multi-chambered tomb, built on a level plane, constructed of stone posts and lintels together with trapezoidal and rectangular stone slabs. The tomb has a cantilevered roof, which is supported by pillars. There are three main chambers, which are laid out on a north-south axis in a length of 8.7 metres. The widest main chamber is 7.55 metres in width. Carriage processions are illustrated in the front chamber. Scenes of entertainment and homage are depicted in the middle chamber. There is a landscape with immortals and deer in the rear chamber. The pillars in the tomb are also extensively decorated with immortal creatures and figures.

[3] Xin Lixiang also points out that the funerary pictorial carvings in Sichuan, which appeared later in the beginning of the 1st century AD were strongly influenced by those in Shandong and Henan. Xin Lixiang 2000: 230.

of the sages Fu Xi 伏羲 and Nü Wa 女媧 have been found frequently in the stone and brick chamber tombs in both Sichuan and east China, though the styles of carving in the two areas form a stark contrast.[4] Martin Powers has drawn our attention to the comparison of a pictorial brick excavated from Sichuan and a piece of pictorial stone from Suining 遂寧, near Xuzhou in Jiangsu.[5] The Sichuan brick illustrates Fu Xi who is holding the sun corresponding to his cosmic force of *yang* and Nü Wa who is holding the moon corresponding to her cosmic force of *yin*. The Xuzhou stone depicts Fu Xi and Nü Wa with their tails intertwining, accompanied by their children, who are the products of their union. A sense of liveliness and volume is depicted in the Sichuan brick while a rigid character can be discerned in the Xuzhou stone. Martin Powers traces this contrast to the different carving traditions in Sichuan and in the Northern Plain in east China. In Sichuan, the impression of movement and the sense of volume are the result of the perfect integration of the lines illustrating the contour and the lines depicting surface details. Take the sleeves of the Sichuan sages for example, the line of the contour of the cuff of the right sleeve of Nü Wa continues to define the contour of the scarf which is hanging down in front of her right cuff. The line delineating her left arm also continues to define the contour of her left cuff, which seems to be hanging down in front of her arm. To some extent, the contour line seems to be running around the figure, suggesting the free movement of the figure in and out in space. Rather than using light and shade, the contour line gives the sense of movement and volume. In addition, motion was depicted by the Sichuan artisan through capturing the marks of motion. For example, the knots of hair of Nü Wa fall backwards because she is moving forwards. In addition, the scarf on the left sleeve of Fu Xi is trailing forwards because he is lowering his arm. In contrast, the Xuzhou engravers seem to attempt to deliver an impression of flatness and rigidity. They executed the contour line and the incisions illustrating the surface details separately. As can been seen from the Xuzhou sages, a deep contour line was first cut to separate the figure from the ground. Then subdivisions were marked off within the contour through assigning them different surface patterns. For example, their lower sleeves are marked by wiggling lines while their shoulders are marked by a kind of striped pattern. In summary, the approach of the Sichuan artisan is profoundly synthetic while the approach taken by the Xuzhou artisan is essentially analytical.

In addition to the different styles of carving, the illustration of the same narrative scene can be different as well in between Sichuan and east China. The exhibition of Han relics from Sichuan held in San Francisco in 1987 has drawn our attention to the similar but different depictions of ascending to heaven with a deer on a pictorial brick from Pengxian 彭縣 in Sichuan and on a pictorial stone from Nanyang in Henan.[6] Both depictions can be traced to the tale described in a song by Cao Zhi 曹植 (AD 192-232):

> As I traveled over Qin Mountain one morning, clouds and mist were swirling. All of sudden I met two boys, both of brightness and beauty. Riding on a white deer, they were holding divine *lingzhi*. I realized they were immortals, and kneeled and begged for the Dao. 'Go west and climb the Jade Terrace. There are gold pavilions and corridors.' They gave me an immortal elixir, the Divine Sovereign had made it. They taught me how to take it, to replace my lost energy. 'Your longevity will match that of gold and jade, and you will never reach senility.'
>
> 晨游泰山.雲霧窈窕.忽逢二童.顏色鮮好.乘彼白鹿.手翳芝草.我知真人.長跪問道.西登玉台.金樓複道.授我仙藥.神皇所造.教我服食.還精補腦.壽同金石.永世難老.[7]

On the Sichuan brick, the deer suddenly stops when the man on its back sees a lady approaching him. Her clothes are elaborate, with her scarf flying in the breeze. She seems to be offering the *lingzhi* 靈芝 in her hands to suggest that the *lingzhi* will bring him longevity. On the Henan stone, all the elements in the tale, the deer, the rider, the immortals who hold the *lingzhi* are also illustrated. However, the way in which these elements are arranged is different. A chariot drawn by the deer is added. In addition, the number of the deer and the immortals are increased. Moreover, cloud scrolls are depicted around the deer chariot to emphasize the fact that the rider is ascending to heaven.

The above two case studies have explained how the pictorial carvings in Sichuan and eastern China are both similar and different. More common themes depicted on the pictorial carvings in these two areas can be analyzed in a similar way. Xin Lixiang has made a comprehensive summary of the common themes of the pictorial carvings in Eastern Han.[8] In fact, not only are the themes of the pictorial carvings in the stone and brick tombs in Sichuan and in east China similar, but so are the arrangement of these pictorial carvings in the tombs. The stone and brick

---
[4] Fu Xi was a sage king who invented many hallmarks of civilization. In Han pictorial art, he often appears as a male deity representing the cosmic force of the *yang*. Nü Wa saved mankind from extermination and was usually depicted as the female deity representing the cosmic force of the *yin*.
[5] Powers 1991: 112-117.
[6] Lim 1987: pl. 67, fig. 20.
[7] Zhao Youwen 1998: 397-398. The translation is based on Wu Hung's translation (Lim 1987: 173).
[8] Xin Lixiang 1986. The Han funerary pictorial pictorial carvings were categorized by him into 9 types with 55 sub-types. The main 9 types are 1) the major stages in the life of the tomb occupant, such as receiving the visits of officials, giving lessons and taking part in the war; 2) the entertainment scenes, such as feasting, watching performance and hunting; 3) the wealth of the tomb occupant, such as scenes of working on the farm or in the sideline industry; 4) religious images, such as the Queen Mother of the West, the thunder god and the four directional animals; 5) stories on the paragons of Confucius virtue; 6) images symbolizing auspicious omens; 7) architectural parts, such as the coffer, the bracket and the eave; 8) celestial bodies, such as the sun and the moon; and 9) decoration patterns. Though he admitted this categorization is problematic later in his research, his early research result to some extent reflects the large number of themes involved in the Han funerary pictorial carvings. He realizes that the above categorization cuts of the link between the mural painting and its location in the tomb. In addition, the relationship between different pictorial carvings in a tomb is omitted (Xin Lixiang 2000: 59-62).

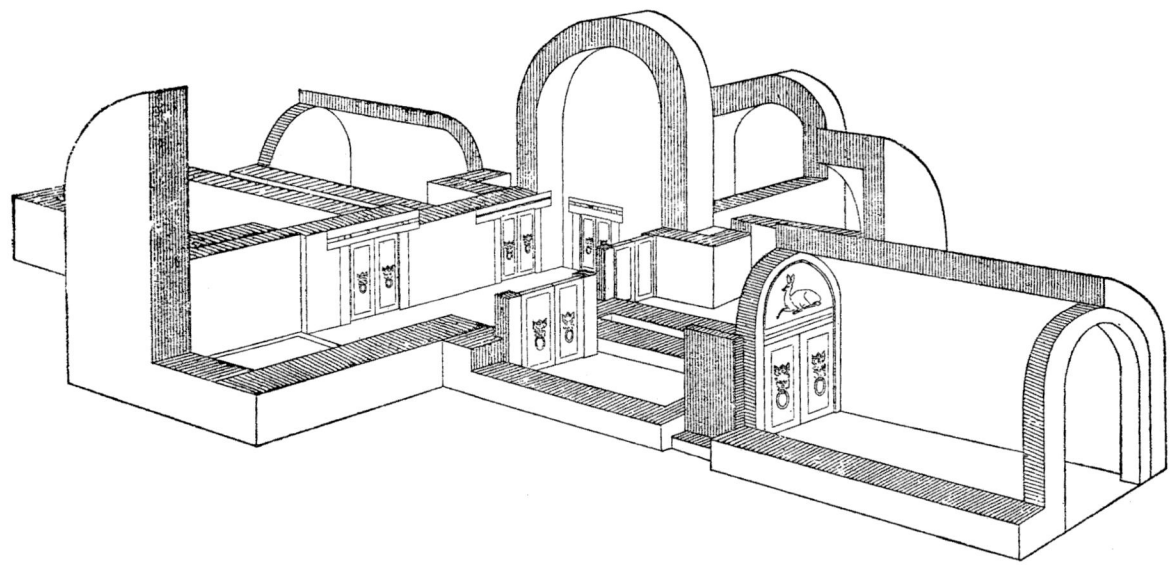

FIGURE 48. PANORAMIC VIEW OF THE DAHUTING TOMB NO. 1 IN MIXIAN IN HENAN.
AFTER HENAN SHENG WENWU YANJIUSUO 1993: FIG. 16.

tombs in both areas emphasizes the decoration of the tomb doors and illustrates the central burial chamber as the main space for ritual and transformation, which is to a large extent decided by their similar structure.

The Dahuting tomb M1 in Henan is a typical example of a large scale chamber tomb built built with both stone and brick with all its crucial structure constructed of stone and the rest constructed of brick (figure 48).[9] Six of the doors of its burial chambers are constructed of stone. Each door is consisted of two stone posts, a stone lintel and two door panels made of stone slabs. Each door slab has a door ring with an animal head appliqué carved on the surface to imitate the real door in the dwelling. The door lintels and posts are further carved with auspicious images. The main walls in the three main chambers and several side chambers are also made of massive stone slabs, carved with scenes exhibiting the daily life or the ideal afterlife of the tomb occupant. The rest of the structures are constructed by moulded bricks, including the upper part of the walls of the tomb chamber, the vaulted ceilings and the paved floors.

Compared with the large scale chamber tombs built with stone and brick in eastern China, large scale stone and brick tombs with elaborate decoration in Sichuan have much simpler plans, though the basic plan and the method of construction are the same. The Yangzishan tomb in Chengdu only has three burial chambers, the front chamber, the middle and the rear chamber, which are laid out on a north-south axis.[10] The tomb door is made of stone, consisting of a lintel, two door posts and two door panels. The two main walls in the middle chamber are constructed of two large stone slabs, which are elaborately carved with a long procession of riders and carriages, forming the main decoration of the tomb. The other parts of the tomb,

including the three vaulted ceilings of the three burial chambers, are constructed with bricks. The Zengjiabao tomb M1 and M2 in Chengdu feature a plan similar to the Yangzishan tomb (figure 49).[11] The only difference is that the rear chamber of the Zengjiabao tombs is further partitioned by a wall into two adjacent burial chambers for the placing of the coffins. The doors of both the tombs at Zengjiabao are constructed of stone, consisting of two door posts, a door lintel and two door panels. The rear walls of the two rear chambers of the tomb M1 are constructed by two whole pieces of stone slabs respectively, carved with vivid scenes of working on the farm and life in an ample dwelling with a courtyard, which form the largest part with pictorial carvings in the tomb (figure 50). The doors of both the tombs are extensively decorated. The back of the door panels of the tomb M1 are carved with a pair of Red Birds on the upper part, two figures holding weapons and one figure holding a fan on the lower part.[12] Both the front and back sides of the door panels of the tomb M2 are decorated.[13] On the front side, a pair of deer is carved on the upper part (figure 51). Two figures, seemingly the tomb occupants, are receiving greetings from two relatively small figures. On the back side, a weapon shelf is carved together with a dog, three figures holding weapons and a Red Bird. In addition, the front side of the lintel of the door of the tomb M2 is carved with a Red Bird.[14]

As for the chamber tomb constructed entirely of stone in Sichuan, the decoration also focuses on the doors and several main walls of the burial chamber. For example, the door of the central burial chamber of the Hechuan 合川 tomb in Sichuan is constructed by three pieces of decorated stone slabs, consisting of a door lintel and two

---

[9] Henan sheng wenwu yanjiusuo 1993: 6-26, figs. 4-16.
[10] Lim 1987: 191.
[11] Chengdu shi wenwu guanlichu 1981: 26-27.
[12] Chengdu shi wenwu guanlichu 1981: pls. 4.2 and 4.5.
[13] Chengdu shi wenwu guanlichu 1981: pls. 4.1, 4.3 and 4.4.
[14] Chengdu shi wenwu guanlichu 1981: 29, fig. 11.

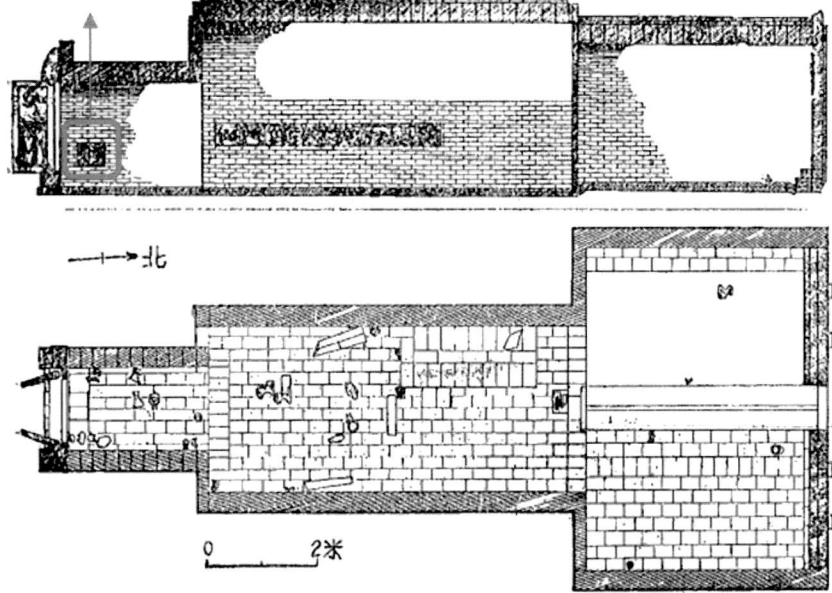

FIGURE 49. ELEVATION AND PLAN OF ZENGJIABAO NO. 2 IN CHENGDU IN SICHUAN.
AFTER CHENGDU SHI WENWU GUANLICHU 1981: FIG. 3.

FIGURE 50. RUBBINGS OF THE RELIEFS ON THE REAR WALLS OF THE TWO REAR CHAMBERS OF ZENGJIABAO NO. 1
IN CHENGDU. AFTER CHENGDU SHI WENWU GUANLICHU 1981: FIGS. 4 AND 5.

door posts (figure 52 and 53).[15] On the lintel, a dragon and a tiger are striving for a *bi* disc.[16] On the door posts, the door rings with the animal head appliqués are carved together with the Red Birds, seemingly to imitate the door panels in a dwelling for the living. On the sides of the two door posts, which face each other, the Green Dragon and the White Tiger are carved in low relief respectively.[17] The door of the rear chamber is also constructed with decorated stone pieces. On the lintel, there is carved the scene of Jing Ke, who is trying to assassinate the king of the Qin state and a figure who is shooting a tiger (figure 54).[18] One of the door posts is carved with Fu Xi holding the sun (figure 55).[19] Images with auspicious meanings are carved on several main walls in the tomb. A squatting sheep is carved in the niche on the east wall of the front chamber (figure 56).[20] The pronunciation of sheep (*yang* 羊) in Chinese is close to that of auspiciousness (*xiang* 祥). An immortal holding the *lingzhi* and a bottle of elixir

---

[15] Chongqing shi bowuguan tianye kaogu gongzuo xiaozu and Hechuan xian wenhuaguan tianye kaogu gongzuo xiaozu 1977: 66, fig. 11.
[16] Chongqing shi bowuguan tianye kaogu gongzuo xiaozu and Hechuan xian wenhuaguan tianye kaogu gongzuo xiaozu 1977: 66, fig. 9.
[17] Chongqing shi bowuguan tianye kaogu gongzuo xiaozu and Hechuan xian wenhuaguan tianye kaogu gongzuo xiaozu 1977: 66, figs. 13 and 14.

[18] Chongqing shi bowuguan tianye kaogu gongzuo xiaozu and Hechuan xian wenhuaguan tianye kaogu gongzuo xiaozu 1977: 67, fig. 18.
[19] Chongqing shi bowuguan tianye kaogu gongzuo xiaozu and Hechuan xian wenhuaguan tianye kaogu gongzuo xiaozu 1977: 67, fig. 20.
[20] Chongqing shi bowuguan tianye kaogu gongzuo xiaozu and Hechuan xian wenhuaguan tianye kaogu gongzuo xiaozu 1977: 66, fig. 6.

FIGURE 51. FRONT SIDE OF THE DOOR OF ZENGJIABAO NO. 2 IN CHENGDU. AFTER CHENGDU SHI WENWU GUANLICHU 1981: PL. 1.

FIGURE 52. ILLUSTRATION OF THE FRONT DOOR OF THE CENTRAL CHAMBER OF THE HECHUAN TOMB IN SICHUAN. AFTER CHONGQING SHI BOWUGUAN TIANYE KAOGU GONGZUO AND HECHUAN XIAN WENHUAGUAN TIANYE KAOGU GONGZUO XIAOZU 1977: FIG. 11.

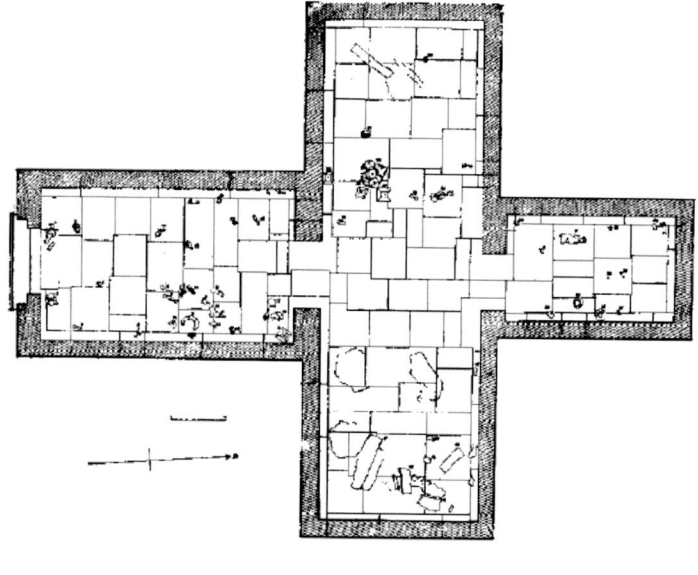

FIGURE 53. PLAN AND ELEVATION OF THE HECHUAN TOMB IN SICHUAN. AFTER CHONGQING SHI BOWUGUAN TIANYE KAOGU GONGZUO AND HECHUAN XIAN WENHUAGUAN TIANYE KAOGU GONGZUO XIAOZU 1977: FIGS. 1 AND 2.

is carved on the west wall of the front chamber (figure 57).[21] In the niche on the west wall of the central chamber, a figure playing a flute is carved (figure 58).[22] On the south wall of the west side chamber, is a carving of a bird holding a fish (figure 59).

It is notable that most of the pictures in the Hechuan tomb can find their counterparts in the cliff tombs in Sichuan.

---

[21] Chongqing shi bowuguan tianye kaogu gongzuo xiaozu and Hechuan xian wenhuaguan tianye kaogu gongzuo xiaozu 1977: 66, fig. 8.
[22] Chongqing shi bowuguan tianye kaogu gongzuo xiaozu and Hechuan xian wenhuaguan tianye kaogu gongzuo xiaozu 1977: 65, fig. 4.

Chapter 3 Pictorial Carvings

FIGURE 54. RUBBING OF THE LINTEL OF THE DOOR OF THE REAR CHAMBER OF THE HECHUAN TOMB IN SICHUAN. THE SCENE OF JING KE, WHO IS TRYING TO ASSASSINATE THE KING OF THE QIN IS IN THE MIDDLE. A FIGURE SHOOTING A TIGER IS ON THE RIGHT. AFTER CHONGQING SHI BOWUGUAN TIANYE KAOGU GONGZUO AND HECHUAN XIAN WENHUAGUAN TIANYE KAOGU GONGZUO XIAOZU 1977: FIG. 18.

FIGURE 55. ILLUSTRATION OF FU XI HOLDING THE SUN CARVED ON ONE OF THE DOOR POSTS OF THE DOOR TO THE REAR CHAMBER OF THE HECHUAN TOMB. AFTER CHONGQING SHI BOWUGUAN TIANYE KAOGU GONGZUO AND HECHUAN XIAN WENHUAGUAN TIANYE KAOGU GONGZUO XIAOZU 1977: FIG. 20.

FIGURE 57. RUBBING OF AN IMMORTAL HOLDING THE LINGZHI CARVED IN THE HECHUAN TOMB IN SICHUAN. AFTER CHONGQING SHI BOWUGUAN TIANYE KAOGU GONGZUO AND HECHUAN XIAN WENHUAGUAN TIANYE KAOGU GONGZUO XIAOZU 1977: FIG. 7.

FIGURE 56. ILLUSTRATION OF THE CARVING OF A SQUATTING SHEEP IN THE NICHE OF THE FRONT CHAMBER OF THE HECHUAN TOMB. AFTER CHONGQING SHI BOWUGUAN TIANYE KAOGU GONGZUO AND HECHUAN XIAN WENHUAGUAN TIANYE KAOGU GONGZUO XIAOZU 1977: FIG. 6.

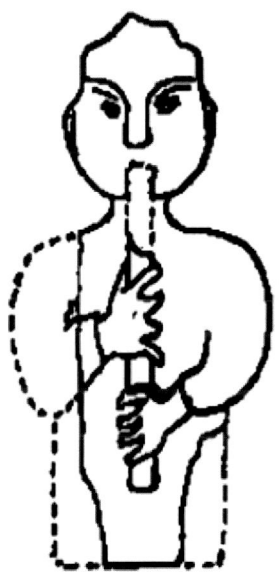

FIGURE 58. ILLUSTRATION OF A FLUTE PLAYING FIGURE CARVED IN THE HECHUAN TOMB IN SICHUAN. AFTER CHONGQING SHI BOWUGUAN TIANYE KAOGU GONGZUO AND HECHUAN XIAN WENHUAGUAN TIANYE KAOGU GONGZUO XIAOZU 1977: FIG. 4.

Figure 59. Rubbing of a bird holding a fish in the Hechuan tomb in Sichuan. After Chongqing shi bowuguan tianye kaogu gongzuo and Hechuan xian wenhuaguan tianye kaogu gongzuo xiaozu 1977: fig. 3.

Figure 61. A bird holding a fish carved in the cliff tomb Taliangzi M3 in Zhongjiang in Sichuan. After Beijing Sichuan sheng wenwu kaogu yanjiuyuan, Deyang shi wenwu kaogu yanjiusuo and Zhongjiang xian wenwu baohu guanli suo 2008: pl. 71.

Figure 60. Rubbing of a flute playing figure carved in a cliff tomb in Zhongjiang in Sichuan. After Zhongguo huaxiangshi quanji bianji weiyuanhui 2000b: pl. 9.

For example, a flute playing figure carved in almost the same style is found in a cliff tomb in Zhongjiang (figure 60).[23] The scene of a bird holding a fish is also frequently depicted in the cliff tombs (figure 61).[24] The squatting sheep have been found carved as a pair on the door lintel of the cliff tomb M535 in Pengshan (figure 62).[25] The image of Fu Xi holding the sun has been found carved on the door posts of the tomb doors of the Qigedong M1 and M7 in Changning (figure 63).[26] The door lintel carved with the dragon and the tiger striving for a *bi* disc in the Hechuan tomb can also find its counterpart in the cliff tomb, though with a subtle variation. For example, the door lintel of the cliff tomb M355 in Pengshan is carved with two winged dragons striving for a *bi* disc.[27] In addition, the scene illustrating the attempted assassination of the king of the Qin is the most frequently depicted story in the cliff tombs, especially in the Leshan area in Sichuan, in the front halls, which were used to commemorate the ancestors (figure 64).[28]

Next I will examine how and why these pictorial carvings were used in the Hechuan tomb in Sichuan and arranged in such way. Two stone chamber tombs in Shandong in east China with similar plans and richer information from their pictorial carvings and inscriptions are crucial to the discussion. The Cangshan 蒼山 tomb in Shandong consisted of a front chamber and two adjacent rear chambers, which are laid out on a north-south axis (figure 65).[29] The pictorial carvings of the tomb centre on the entrances to the front chamber and the two rear chambers, and the upper part of the surrounding walls of the front chamber. An inscription containing 324 words describing the content of the pictorial carvings in each section of the tomb carved on two of the stone posts in the front chamber is crucial to the reading of the pictorial programme of the

---

[23] Zhongguo huaxiangshi quanji bianji weiyuanhui 2000b: 12, fig. 39.
[24] For example, see Sichuan sheng wenwu kaogu yanjiuyuan, Deyang shi wenwu kaogu yanjiusuo and Zhongjiang xian wenwu baohu guanli suo 2008: pls. 70-75.
[25] Chen Mingda 2003a: 86, fig. 15.
[26] Luo Erhu 2005a: 281, fig. 3, 290, fig. 23.

[27] Chen Mingda 2003a: 68, fig. 4.
[28] For examples, see Tang 1997: fig. 5. The potential memorial function of the front halls in the cliff tombs in the Leshan area will be explained later in this chapter.
[29] Shandong sheng bowuguan and Cangshan xian wenhuaguan 1975: 124, fig. 1.

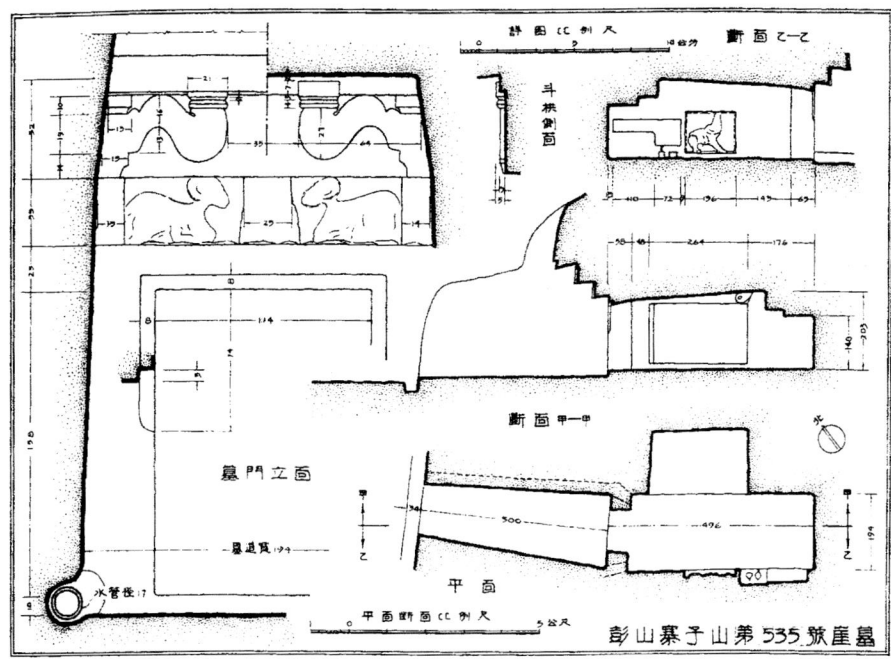

FIGURE 62. ILLUSTRATION OF THE ENTRANCE OF THE CLIFF TOMB ZHAIZISHAN NO. 535 IN PENGSHAN. TWO SHEEP AND TWO BRACKETS ARE CARVED ON THE LINTEL. AFTER CHEN MINGDA 2003A: FIG. 15.

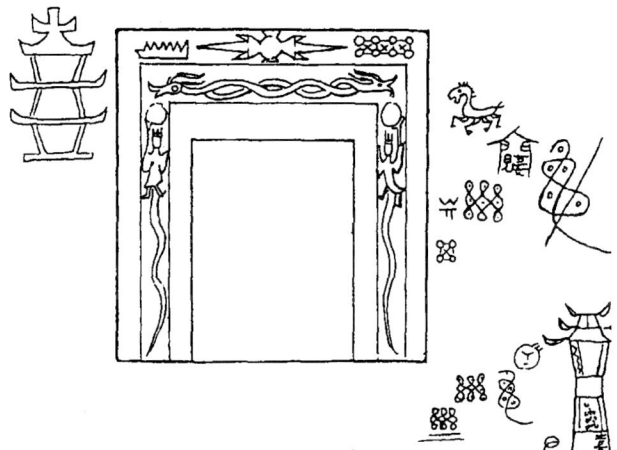

FIGURE 63. ILLUSTRATION OF THE DOOR OF THE CLIFF TOMB QIGEDONG M1 IN CHANGNING IN SICHUAN. AFTER LUO ERHU 2005: FIG. 3.

tomb.[30] The inscription was probably carved by the tomb builders to explain their design and indicates that the pictorial carvings in the tomb were planned in advance.[31]

Wu Hung has made a thorough discussion of how to read the pictorial programme of the Cangshan tomb according to the inscription.[32] He suggests that in the inscription, the description of the content of the pictures starts from the rear chamber and then gradually moves on to the front chamber and the tomb entrance. He argues that the whole pictorial programme was based on the perspective of the tomb occupants, since it began from the rear chamber, where the bodies of the deceased are located. As shown both by the sentence in the inscription and by the pictorial carving, the rear chamber is depicted as a microcosm for the deceased, constituted by the heavenly beasts and directional animals.[33]

The front chamber is an important place for the transformation of the soul of the deceased as shown by the depiction of the journeys in various forms on the surrounding walls.[34] According to the inscription, the journey experienced two stages, which were depicted on the upper parts of the western and the eastern walls of the front chamber respectively.[35] The first stage was in the

---

[30] Shandong sheng bowuguan and Cangshan xian wenhuaguan 1975: 126, figs. 4-5.
[31] Because the language used here is less literate than stele inscriptions which were usually composed by literati. In addition, there is no record on the life of the tomb occupant or any compliment in the inscription like those usually carved in the tomb chamber or on the stele. See Wu 1994: 92-93 and Li Falin 1985: 75.
[32] Wu 1994: 91-104.
[33] The inscription reads: '后當:朱爵(雀)對遊戲仙人,中行白虎後鳳凰.中直柱,雙結龍,主守中燎辟邪姎.室上姎:五子舉,僮女隨後駕鯉魚.前有青龍白虎車,後□被輪雷公君,從者推車,乎㮋(狐狸)宛廚(鴛鴦). The rear wall: The Red Bird encounters a roaming immortal Phoenixes trail after the White Tiger who is strolling in the middle. The central column [in front of the rear section]: Hee a pair of intertwining dragons, guard the tomb's heart and ward off evil. The ceiling of the [rear] chamber: A wuzi carriage is followed by servant girls who are driving carps; The chariot of the White Tiger and the Blue Dragon runs ahead; The Duke of Thunder on wheels brings up the rear; And those pushing the vehicle are assistants-foxes and mandarin ducks.' The translation is after Wu 1994: 93.
[34] Wu 1994: 100.
[35] The inscription reads: '上衛(渭)橋,尉車馬,前者功曹後主簿,亭長騎佐(左)胡使弩.下有深水多魚(漁)者;從兒刺舟渡諸母.使坐上,小車駢,驅馳相隨到都亭.游檄侯見謝自便.後有羊車橡(象)其㮋上即烏乘浮雲. [The lintel above the west chamber]: Ascending the bridge over the River Wei, here appear official chariots and horsemen. The Head Clerk is in front, and the Master of Records is behind. Together with them are the Chief of a Commune, the Assistant Commandant of Cavalry, and a

FIGURE 64. THE SCENE OF JING KE ASSASSINATING THE KING OF QIN CARVED ON THE WALL OF THE FRONT HALL OF THE MAHAO I M1 IN LESHAN. AFTER ZHONGGUO HUAXIANGSHI QUANJI BIANJI WEIYUANHUI 2000B: 1.

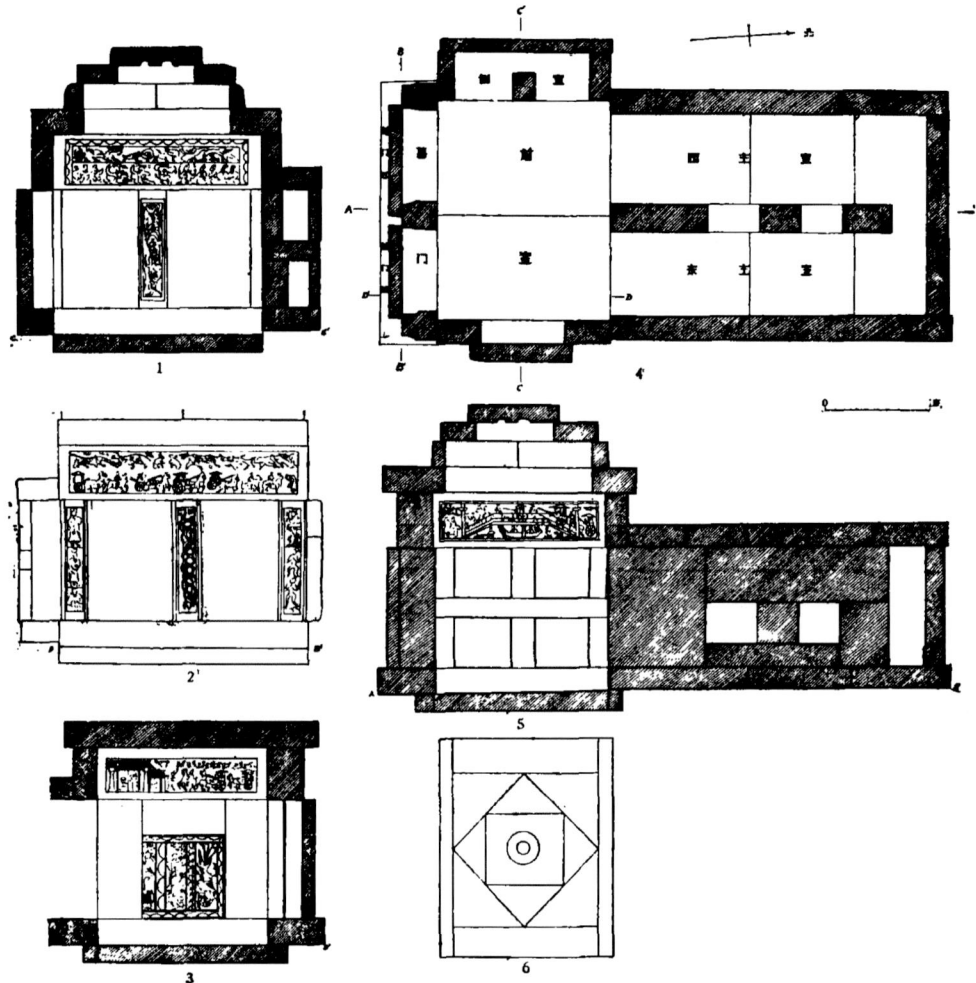

FIGURE 65. PLAN AND ELEVATION OF THE CANGSHAN TOMB IN SHANDONG. AFTER SHANDONG SHENG BOWUGUAN AND CANGSHAN XIAN WENHUAGUAN 1975: FIG. 1.

funerary procession on the bridge. The tomb occupant in the carriage was accompanied by numerous officials on horses across the Wei River (figure 66). The second stage was in the funerary procession on the land. The tomb occupant in the carriage was accompanied by his family members on his way to the other world to be received

barbarian drawing his cross-bow. Water flows under the bridge; a crowd of people are fishing. Servant boys are paddling a boat, ferrying [your] wives across the river. [The lintel above the east niche]: [The women] then sit in small ping-carriages; following one another, they gallop to a *ting* station. The awaiting officer *youxi* pays them an audience, and then apologizes for his departure. Behind [the procession], a ram-drawn carriage symbolizes a hearse; Above, divine birds are flying in drifting clouds.' The translation is after Wu 1994: 100.

by the figures in the half-open doors (figure 67). Wu Hung suggests that the carriages with the tomb occupant illustrated in the two stages are different. In the first stage, the carriage with the tomb occupant is a hearse, which carries the body of the tomb occupant.[36] After the body of the tomb occupant was transported to the funerary site, the second stage began. In the second stage, the carriage with the tomb occupant is a 'soul carriage', which carries the soul of the tomb occupant.[37] The second stage indicates

[36] Wu 1998: 22-23.

[37] Wu 1998: 23. Wu Hung suggests that the sheep carriage at the end of the procession depicted on the upper part of the east wall of the front chamber of the Cangshan tomb is the 'soul carriage'. The Chinese

FIGURE 66. CARVINGS ON THE WESTERN WALL OF THE MAIN CHAMBER OF THE CANGSHAN TOMB IN SHANDONG.
AFTER SHANDONG SHENG BOWUGUAN AND CANGSHAN XIAN WENHUAGUAN 1975: FIG. 7.1.

FIGURE 67. CARVINGS ON THE EASTERN WALL OF THE MAIN CHAMBER OF THE CANGSHAN TOMB IN SHANDONG.
AFTER SHANDONG SHENG BOWUGUAN AND CANGSHAN XIAN WENHUAGUAN 1975: FIG. 7.2.

that after the funeral, the soul of the tomb occupant needed to continue his journey to finally arrive in the heavenly world. It is notable that on the west and east walls in the same burial chamber, the carriages with the tomb occupant are travelling in opposite directions, which seems to emphasize the different destinations of the journeys at the two stages.

In the previously discussed Yangzishan tomb in Sichuan, two cases of travelling in opposite directions can also be observed. The long carriage processions carved on the two side walls of the middle chamber are travelling in opposite directions. Moreover, in the front chamber of the same tomb, there are two carriages travelling in opposite directions on the two pictorial bricks installed on the two side walls of the chamber respectively. Two *que* pillars are illustrated respectively on the two bricks which are installed at the entrance of the front chamber, seemingly to mark the start and the end of the two journeys in opposite directions.[38] In the Zengjiabao tomb M2 in Sichuan, a case of travelling in opposite directions can also be found in the middle chamber. The carriages travelling in opposite directions are depicted on two bricks respectively on the two side walls of the chamber.[39] The pictorial brick with the illustration of a *que* pillar near the entrance to the tomb in the front chamber seems to mark both the start and the end of the journey.

In the Cangshan tomb, after completing the two stages in the journey, the life in the other world continued in the way as depicted in the eastern niche.[40] In this pictorial carving, the tomb occupant was enjoying himself in a feast in the same way as in his lifetime (figure 68). At this point, from the rear chamber to the front chamber and then to the eastern niche, the tomb occupant completed his

---

pronunciation of sheep (羊) is similar to that of auspiciousness (祥), therefore, the sheep carriage is actually the 'auspicious carriage (*xiang che* 祥車)'. In the *Li ji*, the 'auspicious carriage' is recorded as the carriage whose seat should be left empty during a funeral, which means that the sheep carriage depicted in the procession is actually a 'soul carriage' for the invisible soul of the tomb occupant. See the annotation by Zheng Xuan in *Li ji*: 1253. '空神位也,祥車,葬之乘車. The carriage whose seat is left empty for spirit is an auspicious carriage, which is used for funeral.'

[38] Lim 1987: 192-193.
[39] The report of the Zengjiabao tomb M2 published in 1981 (Chengdu shi wenwu guanlichu 1981) does not provide the photos of the pictorial bricks in the tomb. However, the pictorial programme of the tomb can be reconstructed through the pictorial bricks from the tomb published in the catalogue, which is based on the exhibition on the Han relics in Sichuan held in San Franciso in 1987 (Lim 1987: pls. 9, 14, 15, 20, 21, 30, 31, 36, 47, and 48).
[40] The inscription reads: '其中畫,橡(像)家親,玉女執尊杯桉(案)柈(盤), 局尤穩好弱貌. The portrait inside [the east niche] represents you, the member of the family. The Jade Maidens are holding drinking vessels and serving boards-how fine, fragile and delicate they look!' The translation is after Wu 1994: 96.

FIGURE 68. RUBBING OF THE STONE ENGRAVINGS IN THE NICHE ON THE EASTERN WALL OF THE MAIN CHAMBER IN THE CANGSHAN TOMB IN SHANDONG. AFTER SHANDONG SHENG BOWUGUAN AND CANGSHAN XIAN WENHUAGUAN 1975: FIG. 8.2.

transformation from a newly deceased to a new member of the other world who continued to have the same enjoyment as in his lifetime.

Similarly, in the Yangzishan tomb in Sichuan, the life of the tomb occupant in the other world continued as depicted on the northern end of the east wall of the middle chamber, which is the destination of one of the long carriage processions, where the tomb occupant seems to be watching a performance of acrobats while eating and drinking with his guests.[41] In the Zengjiabao tomb M2 in Sichuan, the ideal afterlife is illustrated on the side walls of the middle chamber together with the carriages of the tomb occupant.[42] Various important aspects of an ideal afterlife are depicted respectively on individual pictorial bricks, including hunting and harvesting, salt mining, a city scene, playing the *liubo* 六博 game, feasting and entertaining, and the courtyard of an ample dwelling.[43]

The pictorial carvings at the entrances of the burial chambers in the Cangshan tomb are important in defining the front chamber and the rear chamber as functional spaces for rituals and for the transformation of the soul of the tomb occupant. On the front of the lintel of the tomb door, a grand procession of carriages and horses is carved (figure 69).[44] On the back side of the lintel, the tomb occupant was watching a dancing performance, in company with a Jade Maiden (figure 70).[45] Wu Hung suggests that these pictorial carvings on both sides of the lintel of the tomb door are the depictions of the joys of the tomb occupant in a grander scene, following the pictorial carvings in the eastern niche.[46] The pictorial carvings on the door posts were also regarded to be functional in the whole pictorial programme depicting the ritual for the transformation of the deceased. A pair of dragons are carved on the middle post at the entrance to the rear chamber to guard the body of the deceased.[47] Heavenly animals are carved on the middle door post at the entrance to the tomb to guard the front chamber.[48] Immortals and the offspring of the tomb occupant are carved respectively on the side door posts at the entrance to the tomb to mark the boundary between the world for the living and the world for the deceased.[49]

In the Hechuan tomb in Sichuan, we see a similar arrangement of meaningful pictorial carvings at the entrances to different burial chambers. The sage Fu Xi is carved on the side post of the door of the rear chamber to guard the body of the deceased.[50] Heavenly animals, the two dragons who are striving for a *bi* disc, are carved on the lintel of the door of the central chamber to guard the central chamber. Architectural elements used in the dwelling for the living and heavenly animals are carved respectively on the different sides of the door posts at the entrance to the central chamber to mark the boundary between the world for the living and the world for the deceased.[51]

---

[41] Lim 1987: 192-193. For the interpretation of the pictorial carvings, see Yu Haoliang 1955: 78.
[42] Chengdu shi wenwu guanlichu 1981: 26, fig. 3, 27-28.
[43] Lim 1987: pls. 9, 14, 15, 20, 36, 47 and 48.
[44] Shandong sheng bowuguan and Cangshan xian wenhuaguan 1975: 128, fig. 6.1.
[45] Shandong sheng bowuguan and Cangshan xian wenhuaguan 1975: 128, fig. 6.2. The inscription reads: '堂央外:君出遊,車馬導從騎吏留.都督在前后賊曹.上有龍虎銜利來,百鳥共持至錢財.其央外:有倡家,笙竽相和比吹蘆,龍雀除央鵒啄魚. The face of the door lintel: You are now taking a tour. Chariots are guiding the retinue out, while horsemen remain at the home. The *dudu* is in front, and the *zeicao* is at the rear. Above, tigers and dragons arrive with good fortune; a hundred birds fly over bringing abundant wealth. The back of the door lintel: Here are musicians and singing girls playing the wind-instruments *sheng* and *yu* in harmony, while the sound of a lu-pipe strikes up. Dragons and birds are driving evil away, and cranes are poking at fish.' The translation is after Wu 1994: 96.
[46] Shandong sheng bowuguan and Cangshan xian wenhuaguan 1975: 130, fig. 8.2. Wu 1994: 100.
[47] Shandong sheng bowuguan and Cangshan xian wenhuaguan 1975: 131, fig. 9.4. The inscription reads: '中直柱,雙結龍,主守中雷辟邪殃. The central column [in front of the rear section]: Here a pair of intertwining dragons, guard the tomb's heart and ward off evil.' The translation is after Wu 1994: 93.
[48] Shandong sheng bowuguan and Cangshan xian wenhuaguan 1975: 131, fig. 9.2.
[49] The inscription reads: '堂三柱:中直□龍飛翔,左有玉女與仙人,右柱□□請丞卿,新婦主侍給水漿. The three columns of the front hall: In the middle, dragons ward off evil; On the left, are the Jade Fairy and immortals; And on the right, the junior master is called upon, and drink is served by his newly wedded wife.' The translation is after Wu 1994: 96.
[50] In Sichuan, the rear chamber of the chamber tomb built by stone and brick was also used for placing the body of the deceased. For example, in the Yangzishan tomb, two skulls are found in the rear chamber. Yu Haoliang 1955: 77.
[51] Chongqing shi bowuguan tianye kaogu gongzuo xiaozu and Hechuan xian wenhuaguan tianye kaogu gongzuo xiaozu 1977: 66, figs. 11, 13, 14. The animal head appliqué holding rings carved on the front of the two door posts are the architectural elements used in the dwelling for the living. The heavenly animals, the White Tiger and the Green Dragon, are carved on the sides of the door posts.

Chapter 3 Pictorial Carvings

Figure 69. Rubbing of the front side of the lintel of the door of the Cangshan tomb in Shandong.
After Shandong sheng bowuguan and Cangshan xian wenhuaguan 1975: fig. 6.1.

Figure 70. Rubbing of the back side of the lintel of the door of the Cangshan tomb in Shandong.
After Shandong sheng bowuguan and Cangshan xian wenhuaguan 1975: fig. 6.2.

Though without any inscription evidence, the extensively decorated Yi'nan tomb in Shandong has rich pictorial information to testify that the doors of the burial chambers played an important role in defining the ritual space in the tomb. Lydia Thompson suggests that the central pillar in the middle chamber of the tomb is crucial to the understanding of the middle chamber as the major space for ritual and transformation.[52] Like the front chamber of the Cangshan tomb, there is also a scene on the journey, which starts from the northern wall of the middle chamber of the Yi'nan tomb (figure 71).[53] On the northern wall, a procession of carriages is travelling towards two *que* pillars, which are guarded by two officials (figure 72). Wu Hung agrees with Lydia Thompson's idea that the *que* pillars in the scene mark the entrance to the cemetery, thus the scene is centred on the funerary procession.[54] The journey continues on the upper part of the western wall and ends on the upper part of the southern wall of the middle chamber.[55] The journey on the western wall has become the journey of the soul of the tomb occupant, as suggested by a sacrificial table, the *ji* 幾 depicted at the end of the journey on the southern wall (figure 73). Some officials are bowing low before the *ji*. Lydia Thompson suggests that the *ji* table is a 'spirit rest'.[56] After being greeted by mourners at the *ji*, the soul of the tomb occupant continues his life as depicted on the eastern section of the southern wall and the eastern wall of the middle chamber.[57] Apparently, the overall plan of the middle chamber of the Yi'nan tomb as the major space for ritual is very similar to that of the front chamber of the Cangshan tomb.

Similarly, the entrance to the middle chamber of the Yi'nan tomb is framed by door posts and door lintels depicting heavenly animals guarding the main chamber for ritual.[58] The entrance to the two adjacent rear chambers is framed

---

[52] Zeng Zhaoyu, Jiang Baogeng and Li Zhongyi 1956: 4, fig. 3. Thompson 1998: 163. Lydia Thompson suggests that because of the iconic decoration of the Buddha-like figures, the Queen Mother of the West and the King Father of the East on the octagonal pillar and the focal position of the central pillar, the pillar can be viewed as the *axis mundi* connecting earth with heaven. When referring to Lydia Thompson's explanation of the central pillar in the Yi'nan tomb, Jessica Rawson suggests that when building tombs, the tomb builders also provided a cosmic setting (Rawson 1999: 13). Wu Hung suggests that a passage from the *Shenyi jing* 神異經 (Canon of Spirits and Oddities) could further support Lydia Thompson's interpretation of the central pillar in the Yi'nan tomb: 'On Kunlun there is a copper pillar which reaches heaven and so it is called the Pillar of Heaven. It is three thousand *li* wide and its winds around like crooked knife. Below there is the domain of the immortals. 昆侖山有銅柱,其高入天,所謂天柱也.圍三千里,圓回如削,下有仙人府 (cited from *Taiping yulan*: 187, translated by Wu Hung).' In this sense, the central pillar in the tomb could enable the soul of the tomb occupant to reach the immortal land (Wu 2010: 56-57).
[53] Zeng Zhaoyu, Jiang Baogeng and Li Zhongyi 1956: pl. 50.
[54] Wu 1998: 25. Because above each *que* pillar, there is 'a pole bearing a cross called a *biao* 表 – a funerary symbol'.
[55] Beijing 1956: pl. 49.
[56] Thompson 1998: 222. Thompson points out that in the *Tan Gong* 檀弓 section of the *Li ji*, the *ji* is identified as a 'spirit rest (幾依神也)' in the commentary (*Li ji*: 276). The commentary of this section further equates the *ji* with the soul of the deceased.
[57] Zeng Zhaoyu, Jiang Baogeng and Li Zhongyi 1956: pl. 48.
[58] Zeng Zhaoyu, Jiang Baogeng and Li Zhongyi 1956: pls. 32 and 33. The eastern and western door posts are respectively carved with a dragon.

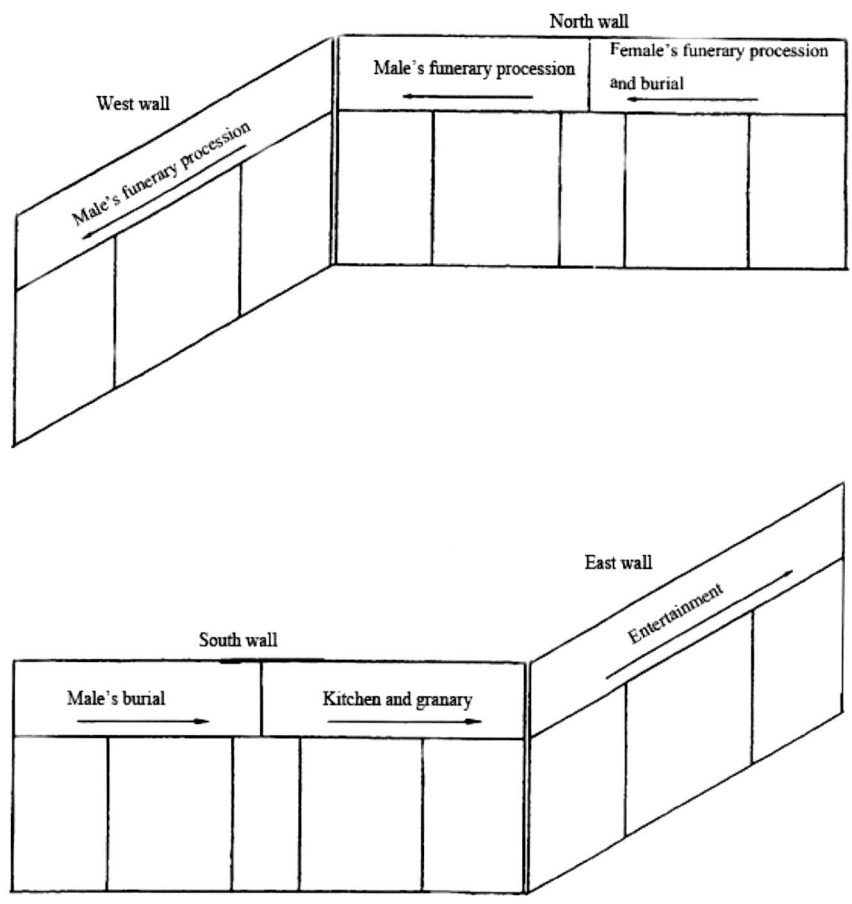

FIGURE 71. SCHEMATIC DRAWING OF THE MIDDLE CHAMBER OF THE YI'NAN TOMB. REDRAWN AFTER THOMPSON 1998: FIG. 5.24, BY XUAN CHEN.

FIGURE 72. CARRIAGE PROCESSION ON THE NORTHERN WALL OF THE MIDDLE CHAMBER OF THE YI'NAN TOMB. AFTER ZENG ZHAOYU, JIANG BAOGENG AND LI ZHONGYI 1956: PL. 49.

FIGURE 73. THE END OF THE PROCESSION AND THE *JI* TABLE ON THE SOUTHERN WALL OF THE MIDDLE CHAMBER OF THE YI'NAN TOMB. AFTER ZENG ZHAOYU, JIANG BAOGENG AND LI ZHONGYI 1956: PL. 49.

by door posts depicting guardian animals guarding the body of the deceased (figure 74).[59]

Let us return to the Hechuan tomb in Sichuan. It now seems clear that the stone and brick chamber tombs in Sichuan and eastern China indeed share many similarities on the content and plan of the pictorial programme. But how the information on the planning of the pictorial programme was communicated between these two distant areas comes into question. One hypothesis is that the information on the planning of tombs was brought back by the officials from east China to Sichuan. According to the *Huayang guozhi*, there were already many people of Sichuan origin taking high official positions in areas outside Sichuan.[60] Moreover, many of them took positions in Henan, Shandong and

---

[59] Zeng Zhaoyu, Jiang Baogeng and Li Zhongyi 1956: pl. 55. The bottom part of the eastern door post is illustrated with the White Tiger and the Green Dragon.

[60] See Appendix 2 on the Eastern Han high officials of Sichuan origin in the areas outside Sichuan.

Chapter 3 Pictorial Carvings

FIGURE 74. RUBBING OF THE RELIEF ON A DOOR POST OF THE ENTRANCE TO THE REAR CHAMBERS OF THE YI'NAN TOMB IN SHANDONG. AFTER AFTER ZENG ZHAOYU, JIANG BAOGENG AND LI ZHONGYI 1956: PL. 55.

Jiangsu in east China. There could be many opportunities for these officials of Sichuan origin to view how a tomb or a graveyard was planned when they attended a funeral in their local area. As mentioned in Chapter 1, a funeral at the graveyard was an important occasion for public display, and as suggested by Miranda Brown, the local political relationship was partly established on the various bonds of the obligations to attend a funeral.[61] When these officials retired and came back to their hometown, they might prefer to build their tombs after the one they used to view during an impressive funeral.

The que pillars are the major Eastern Han mortuary constructions with identifiable names of tomb occupants.[62]

And all the five pairs of que pillars with identifiable names belonged to high officials ranking 2000 shi 石.[63] As mentioned in Chapter 1, the que pillars usually mark the entrance to a graveyard which is constituted by a spiritual path flanked by stone guardian figures, a memorial shrine and chamber tombs covered under the burial mounds. Most of the Eastern Han graveyards that have been identified with such a plan are located in the areas in eastern China, in Hebei, Henan and Shandong.[64] It seems that the high officials of Sichuan origin had a preference for the graveyard plan that was popular in the east. In contrast, the cliff tombs in Sichuan were popular among the less wealthy groups. So far, the cliff tomb occupant identified with the highest official ranking is Yang Ziyu 楊子與, a prefect of the Lantian 藍田 Prefecture (in today's Shaanxi province).[65] In Eastern Han, a prefect usually ranked between 600 to 1000 shi, depending on the size of the population of the prefecture, much lower than the rank of 2000 shi.

Robert Thorp suggests that in the Han dynasty the development of the tomb types followed a scale-down

---

[61] Brown 2007: 85-104. Based mainly on the Eastern stele inscriptions, she suggests that many stelae reflect the various political relationships between the donors of the stele and the dedicatees, which can be regarded as the analogues of the relationship between father and son, friends, colleges, or teacher and pupil. The donors usually also attended the funeral. Patricia Ebrey also points out that the funeral might be one of the most important occasions in which local officials and elites could 'cement bonds of clientage': 'Wearing mourning for one's patron thus established the context in which patron-client ties can be interpreted: they were as strong, as natural, and as socially beneficial as the father-son or lord-minister tie.' Ebrey 1983: 539. See also her essay in Ebrey 1987: 626-648.

[62] So far, 20 pairs of que pillars have been found in the Sichuan area, in Mianyang, Deyang, Zitong 梓潼, Ya'an 雅安, Lushan 蘆山, Xichang 西昌, Jiajiang 夾江, Quxian 渠縣, Zhongxian 忠縣 and Chongiqng. Chongqing shi wenhua ju and Chongqing shi bowuguan 1992: 1.

[63] A pair of que pillars in Quxian 渠縣 is identified to belong to Feng Huan 馮煥, who was a Quxian local and used to be the Inspector of Youzhou 幽州 (in today's Hebei and Beijing). The son of Feng Huan, Feng Gun 馮緄 was also a high official. He used to be the Commandant of Justice (tingwei 廷尉), serving the central administration in Henan. Chongqing shi wenhua ju and Chongqing shi bowuguan 1992: 39. Inspector (cishi 刺史) in Eastern Han ranked 2000 shi, was the second highest official rank, only lower than the Three Exellencies (sangong 三公) that ranked 10,000 shi. Commandant of Justice also ranked 2000 shi. Shi was the unit to measure the official rank in the Han dynasty. It was originally a unit of the weight of grain. Shi could also be converted into cash in coins. According to the salary list of Eastern Han officials in Bielenstein 1980: 126, the highest rank is 10,000 shi and the lowest rank is 100 shi. Another three pairs of que pillars belonged to the Grand Administrators (taishou 太守, ranked 2000 shi) in the Sichuan area. The pair in Jiajiang belonged to Yang Zong 楊宗, a Grand Administrator of the Yi 益 Commandery (Chongqing shi wenhua ju and Chongqing shi bowuguan 1992: 36-38). The pair in Ya'an belonged to Gao Yi 高頤, a Grand Administrator of the Yi 益 Commandery as well (Chongqing shi wenhua ju and Chongqing shi bowuguan 1992: 31-34). The pair in Lushan belonged to Fan Min 樊敏, who used to be the Grand Administrator of the Ba 巴 Commandery (Chongqing shi wenhua ju and Chongqing shi bowuguan 1992: 34-35). The rest one is in Zhongxian, belonging to Ding Fang 丁房, who used to be the Chief Commandant (duwei 都尉, ranked 2000 shi), serving the central administration in Henan (Chongqing shi wenhua ju and Chongqing shi bowuguan 1992: 45-46).

[64] The important graveyards in the east include the Wu family graveyard in Jiaxiang in Shandong (Wu 1989b: 36-37), the Qin Fujun 秦府君 graveyard in Beijing (Beijing shi wenwu gongzuodui 1964) and the graveyard of the tomb of Yin Jian in Lushan in Henan (Wu 1989b: 30-31, also mentioned in the footnote in Chapter 1). Based on the records on the Yin Jian's graveyard in the Shuijing zhu, the plan of his graveyard is reconstructed by Wu Hung as shown in Diagram 2 in Wu 1989b: 31. According to the remaining stone pieces on the site of the Wu family graveyard in Jiaxiang and the transmitted rubbings and textual records on the pictorial stones from the site, Wu Hung has reconstructed the plan of the plan of the Wu family graveyard as shown in Diagram 4 in Wu 1989b: 36. Susan Erickson has further pointed out that the que pillars that mark the entrance to the Wu family graveyard had inherited a local tradition in the construction of the que pillars in the graveyard. Her suggestion is based on the comparison between the que pillars of the Wu family and the que pillar dated to AD 84 from Pingyi 平邑, a county located 50 kilometres east to Jixiang (Erickson 2008: 110-128).

[65] The name and official title of Yang Ziyu was carved in the Banbianjie 半邊街 cliff tomb in Shuangliu 雙流, near Chengdu, in Sichuan. The inscription was already destroyed. For the rubbing, see Gao Wen and Gao Chenggang 1990: 38.

model, in which new tomb types were first applied among the imperial members and social elites and then filtered down to lower classes.[66] Though the cliff tombs in Sichuan did not seem to appear first among the social elites, some features of the local chamber tombs of the social elites indeed had filtered down to the cliff tombs. For example, there are many large scale cliff tombs in Leshan, featuring a spacious front hall with a façade carved with the *que* pillars in low relief.[67] These 'pseudo' *que* pillars might be a low cost reproduction of those *que* pillars found at the graveyards of the local high officials. The front hall behind the pseudo *que* pillars was probably intended to imitate the memorial shrine in the graveyard marked by the *que* pillars. As will be elaborated in the case studies of two such front halls in Leshan later in this chapter, the pictorial scheme in the front hall, focusing on the exhibition of the stories of the filial sons is very similar to that in the shrines in the graveyard in eastern China. The Wu Liang shrine in the graveyard of the Wu family in Jiaxiang in Shandong will be cited as a major source for the content and arrangement of the stories of the filial sons in the front halls of the cliff tombs. Though no existing aboveground Eastern Han shrine has been found in Sichuan, the popularity of the graveyard marked by the *que* pillars among the high officials in Sichuan indicates that information on the mortuary constructions and their pictorial scheme could be communicated over long distances between Sichuan and eastern China.

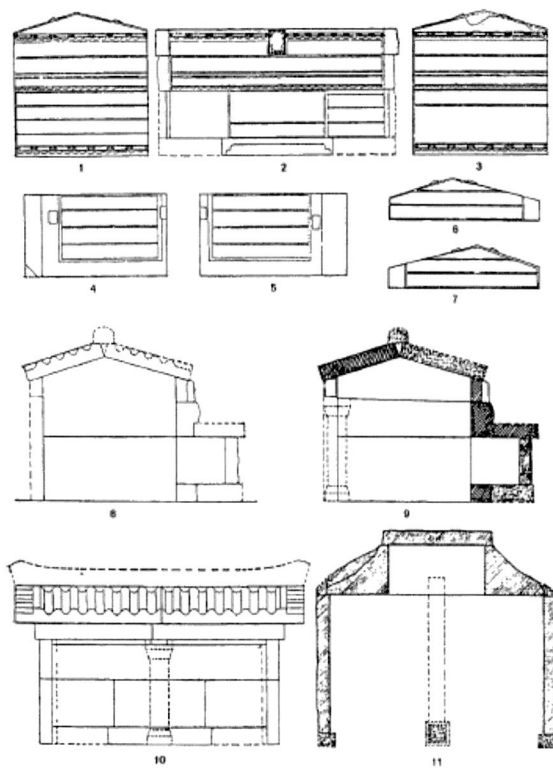

FIGURE 75. RECONSTRUCTION OF THE WU LIANG SHRINE BY JIANG YINGJU AND WU WENQI. AFTER JIANG YINGJU AND WU WENQI 1981: FIG. 5.

2. Pictorial Carvings in the Shrine

Pictorial carvings in the shrines are related to those in the tombs, while organized according to various different pictorial programmes. Xin Lixiang suggests that the pictorial carvings in the shrines originated from those in the ancestral temples, while the pictorial paintings in the tombs were based on the pictorial schemes of the earlier coffins.[68] The shrine as a constituent part of the mortuary structure on the cemetery was used for annual sacrificial rites after the funeral.[69] The different functions of the shrine and tomb further decide the different pictorial programmes in these two structures. Compared to the tomb sealed after the funeral, the shrine above ground was more of a public place, open to be visited and viewed by various people related the tomb occupant's family. Consequently, the pictorial carvings in the shrines played an important part in promoting the virtue and fame of the tomb occupant among the people in the social network of the family.[70]

[66] Thorp 1979: 187.
[67] For example, see the *que* pillars carved at the entrance to a cliff tomb in Leshan. Bishop 1916: fig. 150.
[68] Xin Lixiang 2000: 288, 190-197. Xin Lixiang points out that the plan of the pictorial carvings in the Han tombs were based on the pictorial scheme on the T-shaped tapestries covered on the wooden coffins dated to the Western Han. Important examples of such coffins include the coffins from the Mawangdui M1, M3 in Changsha in Hunan and the Jinqueshan 金雀山 M9 in Linyi 臨沂 in Shandong. The T-shaped tapestry illustrates the perspective on what would happen after death and the way to become immortal.
[69] Wu Hung has elaborated the transition of ancestral sacrificial rites from the ancestral temples to the shrines on the cemetery during the Han dynasty. See Wu 1989a.
[70] For how the funeral related activities maintained and reinforced the

To some extent, if we regard the pictorial carvings in the tomb as the narration of a ritual process, the pictorial carvings in the shrine could be seen as the exhibition of the perspectives of the tomb occupant on the world.

Stone shrines with pictorial carvings are mainly found in Shandong, northern Anhui and Jiangsu. So far, the most extensive study on the pictorial program of the carvings in a shrine has been carried out on the shrine of Wu Liang, located in Jiaxiang in Shandong. The Wu Liang shrine is a single-chambered building with a gabled roof (figure 75). Jiang Yingju and Wu Wenqi reconstructed the shrine from its scattered stone pieces in the 1980s. In his paper for the exhibition catalogue of the Wu family shrines published in 2008, Jiang Yingju re-examines the pictorial scheme of the Wu Liang shrine. He suggests that the pictorial scheme of the shrine can be divided into three sections (figure 76). 'Celestial beings and deities are shown on the ceilings, immortals on the triangular gables, and stories and events of human history on the three walls'.[71] The stories and events of human history on the three walls of the shrine are divided into four horizontal registers. The two upper registers are carved with the historical kings chronologically, and famous women and filial sons. The stories of the filial sons occupy the whole lower register of the upper part. The two lower registers are carved with the historical figures from the Eastern Zhou period. The

social network in the Han, see Brown 2007: 85-104.
[71] Jiang Yingju 2008: 171-173.

Chapter 3 Pictorial Carvings

Figure 76. Pictorial carvings in the Wu Liang shrine. After Xin Lixiang 2000: fig. 64.

figures include famous assassinators, loyal ministers and a wise woman. A pavilion is located in the centre of the lower part, breaking the continuity of the two lower registers. A figure is seated in the pavilion, receiving homage from the procession of carriages and figures around the pavilion.[72]

Such a scheme is 'in harmony with the Chinese cosmological perspective, images pertaining to a higher realm are placed higher (heaven/the ceilings), and those closer to the mundane world lower (historical figures/the walls); things of the past are placed higher, and present events are shown lower.'[73] Jiang Yinju further points out that the pictorial narrative of Wu Liang's life is also illustrated in the shrine, together with the sages and eminent figures in human history.[74] The chronological depiction of the sages and kings in history, and the stories symbolizing various virtues shows that Wu Liang accepted the traditional historical perspective of his time and valued all the virtues as depicted on the walls.

3. Pictorial Carvings and Memorial in the Cliff Tomb

A Case Study of the Shiziwan M1 in Leshan

As mentioned previously in the study, there are many cliff tombs in the Leshan area with the structure of a shared front hall and several individual burial chambers tunnelled into the rear wall of the front hall, for example, the tomb Shiziwan M1. Such a front hall is usually the only part of the tomb decorated with pictorial carvings. The most frequently carved scenes are stories of filial sons. So far, six stories have been identified. There are also two unidentified scenes, which are very likely also stories of filial sons, for they usually appear together with other carvings of such stories. These stories have been found carved in the front hall in the Mahao I M1, Mahao II M40, Shiziwan I M1 and Shiziwan II M22.[75] The stories of filial sons are usually carved in the middle section of the three walls enclosing the front hall, similar to the location of those carved in the Wu Liang shrine as mentioned previously.

The Shiziwan I M1 in Leshan is found to have most of the stories of filial sons in the front hall. A close examination of the pictorial programme in its front hall would be useful to understand the function of the front hall.[76] Seven scenes are carved on the middle of the surrounding walls of the front hall. Five of the scenes have been identified as the stories of filial sons.[77] Two framed images next to each other are carved on the left side wall. The left frame includes two stories carved in two scenes. Only the left scene containing three figures has been identified. It illustrates the story of the filial grandson, Yuan Gu 原穀 (figure 77). The figure on the left is Yuan Gu's father. The figure in the middle is Yuan Gu. He holds a carriage in his right hand and looks to his father on the left. The figure on the right is Yuan Gu's grandfather. He collapses on the ground, naked. The same story is also carved in the shrine of Wu Liang, where the three figures in the story are labeled with '孝孫 (the filial grandson)', '孝孫父 (the filial grandson's father)' and '孝孫祖父 (the filial grandson's grandfather)' respectively, which facilitates the identification of the same story carved in the Shiziwan M1. The story is recorded in the *Taiping*

---

[72] In *The Wu Liang Shrine: The Ideology of Early Chinese Pictorial Art*, Wu Hung has made thorough interpretation of the pictorial carvings on each part of the shrine. Wu 1989b: 142-217. Wu Hung suggests that the walls exhibit how Wu Liang read human history. The pictorial programme of the shrine of Wu Liang as a whole advertised Wu Liang's reading of the cosmos, which, according to him, was constituted by the cosmological orders, the world of the immortals and the history of human.
[73] Jiang Yingju 2008: 173.
[74] Jiang Yingju 2008: 172. Wu Liang is identified to be the figure kneeling before a carriage and facing an ox-drawn cart. The scene is carved on the east wall of the shrine. The inscription above the carriage reads 'District Official in the Bureau of Merit 縣功曹'. The inscription above the ox reads 'retired gentleman 處士'. These inscriptions coincide with Wu Liang's bibliography as recorded in his stele inscription: 'Having been called upon by commandery authorities to official posts, [Wu Liang] declined by reason of illness. Content with a simple life of humility, he took delight in learning as a free man.' See the stele inscription in *Li shi*: 168-169.

[75] See Tang Changshou 1993 and 2010.
[76] No report on this tomb has been published in Chinese academic journal. A detailed description of the tomb can be found in *Orientations*, September 1997. See Tang 1997.
[77] The following introduction of the stories of filial sons carved in the cliff tomb is based on the interpretation by Tang Changshou. See Tang Changshou 2010.

FIGURE 77. CARVING AND RUBBING OF THE STORY OF YUAN GU (LEFT) IN THE FRONT HALL OF THE CLIFF TOMB SHIZIWAN NO. 1 IN LESHAN. AFTER TANG CHANGSHOU 2010: FIG. 4.

FIGURE 78. RUBBING OF THE THREE STORIES ON FILIAL SONS CARVED IN THE FRONT HALL OF THE CLIFF TOMB SHIZIWAN NO. 1 IN LESHAN. AFTER TANG CHANGSHOU 2010: FIG. 2.

yulan 太平御覽, which quotes the anonymous *Xiaozi Zhuan* 孝子傳:

> 'The origin of Yuan Gu is unknown. When his grandfather was old, his parents detested the old man and wanted to abandon him. Gu, who was fifteen years old, entreated them piteously with tears, but his parents did not listen to him. They made a carriage and carried the grandfather away and abandoned him. Gu brought the carriage back. His father asked him, "What are you going to do with this inauspicious thing?" Gu replied: "I am afraid that when you get old, I will not be able to make a new carriage, and so I have brought it back." His father was moved and ashamed and carried the grandfather back and cared for him. He overcame his selfishness and criticized himself. He finally became a "purely [filial] son" and Gu became a "purely [filial] grandson".'[78]

The stories in the right frame cannot be identified. According to Tang Changshou, the carriage pulling scene in the left part of the frame is also very likely to be a story of the filial son, though it cannot be traced back to the series of filial son carvings in the shrine of Wu Liang. The similar pulling carriage scene also appears in the front hall of the Mahao I M1 together with other stories of filial sons.[79]

On the right side wall of the front hall, there are also two framed images carved next to each other. The left frame contains three stories, which are carved from right to left in the same scene (figure 78). On the right is an ox-drawn carriage, in which sits a crowned figure. The filial son, Min Ziqian 閔子騫 stands behind the carriage.[80] The scene can be found in the shrine of Wu Liang, which has inscriptions explaining the content of the carving: '閔子騫：與假母居,愛有偏移,子騫衣寒,御車失棰 (Min Ziqian: He lived together with his stepmother, Who favored [her own son]. Ziqian's clothes could not keep out the cold, And he dropped the horsewhip when he drove a chariot)'.

In addition, the main figures in the carving are labeled with '子騫後母弟 (the younger stepbrother of Ziqian)' and '子騫父 (the father of Ziqian)'.[81] The story is recorded in the *Yiwen leiju* 藝文類聚:

> 'Min Ziqian had a younger brother. After their mother died, their father remarried and had two other sons. Ziqian drove a chariot for his father and dropped the bridle. His father held his hands and [found] that he wore only thin clothing. The father then went home and called the sons of the stepmother. He held their hands and [found] that they were wearing thick, warm clothing. He blamed his wife, saying, "The reason that I married you was for my sons. Now you are cheating me and I cannot keep you here!" Ziqian went forth and said, "When mother is here, only one son is wearing thin clothing; if mother leaves, four sons will be in the cold." His father became silent. Therefore people say that Min Ziqian kept his mother at home by one word and made three sons warm by a second word.'[82]

Next to the story of Min Ziqian is the story of the filial son Laizi 萊子. In the middle of the scene, Laizi is face down on the ground. The parents of Laizi are sitting at the table, attended by Laizi's wife, watching Laizi. In the shrine of Wu Liang, a similar scene is carved with the inscription: '老萊子楚人也:侍親至孝,衣服斑連,嬰兒之態,另親有驩,君子嘉之,孝莫大焉. Elder Laizi was a native of Chu: He served his parents with the ultimate filial piety gesture. Wearing multicolored clothes and imitating an infant, he made his parents happy. Gentlemen praise him, because his filial piety is greatest of all.' The figures in the carving are also labeled with '萊子母 (the mother of Laizi)' and '萊子父 (the father of Laizi)'.[83] The story is recorded in the *Taiping yulan*, which quotes Shi Jueshou's 師覺授 *Xiaozi Zhuan*:

> 'Elder Laizi was a native of Chu. When he was seventy years old, his parents were both still alive. With the ultimate filial piety, he often wore multicolored clothes

---

[78] '原穀者,不知何許人.祖年老,父母厭患之,意欲棄之.穀年十五,涕泣苦諫.父母不從,乃作輿,异棄之.穀乃隨收輿归.父谓之曰："尔焉用此凶具？" 穀云："恐后父老,不能更作,是以取之尔."父感悟愧惧,乃載祖归侍养.克己自责,更成纯孝,穀为"纯孝孙".' *Taiping yulan*: 2360. The English translation is after Wu 1989b: 304-305.
[79] Tang 1997: 75.
[80] The standing figure is identified as Min Ziqian by Tang Changshou, as he thinks the illustration contains all the key elements of the story of Min Ziqian as carved in the shrine of Wu Liang. Tang Changshou 2010: 143.
[81] The translation of the inscriptions is after Wu 1989b: 278.
[82] '閔子騫,兄弟二人.母死,其父更娶,復有二子.子騫為其父御車,失轡,父持其手,衣甚單,父則歸,呼其後母兒,持其手,衣甚厚溫,即謂其婦曰："吾所以娶汝,乃為吾子.今汝欺我,去無留."子騫前曰："母在一子單,母去四子寒."其父默然.故曰:孝哉閔子騫,一言其母還,再言三子溫.' *Yiwen leiju*: 369. The translation is after Wu 1989b: 278.
[83] The translation of the inscriptions is after Wu 1989b: 280.

to serve his parents food in the main hall. Once he hurt his feet. Afraid to sadden his parents, he made himself tumble stiffly to the ground and bawled like an infant. Confucius remarked: "one does not use the word old when one's parents are getting old, because one fears this will make them grieve about their elderliness." A person like Elder Laizi can be called one who does not lose a child's heart.'[84]

On the left of the scene is depicted the story of Boyu 伯瑜. Boyu is kneeling on the ground, before his standing mother who is holding a stick. The similar scene is depicted in the shrine of Wu Liang, with the inscription: '伯瑜:傷親年老,氣力稍衰,笞之不慟,心懷楚悲. Boyu: He grieved for his mother's old age; Her strength had weakened. Being beaten he did not feel pain, He was sorrowful in his heart.' In addition, a figure is labeled with '瑜母 (the mother of Yu)'.[85] The story is recorded in the *Taiping yulan*:

> 'Boyu made a mistake and wept when his mother beat him with a stick. The mother asked him, saying, "I did not see you weep when I punished you before. Why do you cry today?" Boyu replied: "Before, when I offended you and you beat me with the stick, I often felt pain. But today your strength could not make me feel pain. That is why I am weeping."'[86]

In the right picture frame is carved the story of the filial son Dong Yong 董永 and a banquet scene. Dong Yong is working in the field, holding a hoe in the left hand and a fan (*bianmian* 便面) in the right hand. His father is resting in a cart parked in the shade of a tree. Dong Yong seems to be fanning his father with the fan. The similar scene in the shrine of Wu Liang is labeled with the inscriptions '永父 (the father of Yong)' and '董永千乘人也 (Dong Yong is a native of Qiancheng)'.[87] The story is also recorded in the *Taiping yulan* which quotes the *Xiaozi zhuan* by Liu Xiang:

> 'Dong Yong of the Former Han was a native of Qiancheng. Having lost his mother in childhood, he alone provided for his father. When his father died, he did not have money to arrange the funeral and so he took a loan of ten thousand cash from someone. Yong said to his creditor: "If I cannot repay the money later, I will give you my body and become your slave." The creditor was sympathetic. Yong got the money, buried his father, and then went to [the creditor's place to [become his slave. On his way he met a woman who asked him to take her as his wife. Yong said: "Now I am poor like this, and moreover I will become a slave. How can I humiliate you by taking you as my wife?" The woman replied: "It is my hope to become your wife; I will not regard being poor and lowly as a disgrace." Then Yong took the woman and went with her to [the creditor's place]. The creditor asked: "It was originally agreed that one person [would be my slave]. Why are there now two persons?" Yong replied: "According to our agreement you would have only one slave but now you have two-is there anything wrong with that?" The wife replied: "I can weave." The creditor said: "If you weave one thousand bolts of silk for me, then I will let you both go free." The wife then required natural silk [from the creditor]. Within ten days, one thousand bolts of silk were finished. The creditor was surprised and then released the couple. They went to the place where they had met. The wife told Yong: "I am the Weaving Maiden from heaven and was moved by your perfect filial piety. Heaven sent me to repay you. Now that your troubles have been settled, I cannot remain here long." After these words, clouds and fog descended, and she suddenly flew away.'[88]

There are more stories of filial sons found in other cliff tombs. In the front hall of the Mahao I M1, a seriously eroded scene is found carved with no fewer than five figures. They all kneel on the ground before an old lady who is standing with a stick. According to Tang Changshou, this may be the illustration of the seven filial sons from the poem *Kaifeng* 凱風 (Genial Wind) in the *Shi jing* 詩經, in which seven sons showed their gratitude to their mother who devoted herself to bringing them up.[89]

The above interpretation of the main pictorial carvings in the front chamber of the Shiziwan M1 is based on the pictorial carvings in the shrine of Wu Liang. However, the quality and quantity of the pictorial carvings in the Shizwan M1 are not comparable to those of the pictorial carvings in the Wu Liang shrine. In addition, there are 16 stories of filial sons carved in the Wu Liang shrine, while there are only six carved in the Shiziwan M1.[90] Moreover,

---

[84] '老萊子者,楚人也,行年七十,父母俱存.至孝蒸蒸,常著斑斕之衣,為親取飲,上堂腳跌,恐傷父母之心,因僵仆為嬰兒啼.孔子曰: "父母老,常言不稱老,為其傷老也."若老萊子可謂不失孺子之心矣.' *Taiping yulan*: 1907-1908. The translation is after Wu 1989b: 280.
[85] The translation is after Wu 1989b: 286.
[86] '伯瑜有過,其母笞之,泣,其母曰: "他日笞子未嘗見泣,今泣何也?" 對曰: "他日瑜得罪笞嘗痛,今母之力不能痛,是以泣."' *Taiping yulan*: 1907. The translation is after Wu 1989b: 287.
[87] The translation is after Wu 1989b: 289.

[88] '前漢董永,千乘人.小失母,獨養父.父亡無以葬,乃從人貸錢一萬.永謂錢主曰: "后若無錢還君,當以身作奴."主甚憐之.永得錢葬父畢,將往為奴,于路忽逢一婦人,求為永妻,永曰: "今貧若是,身復以為奴,何敢屈夫人之為妻."婦人曰: "原為君婦,不恥貧賤."永隨將婦人至.錢主曰: "本言一人,今何二?"永曰: "言一得二,于理乖乎!"主問永妻曰: "何能?" 妻曰: "能織耳."主曰: "為我織千匹絹,即放尔夫妻."於是索絲,十日之內,千匹絹足.主驚,遂放夫婦二人而去.行至本相逢處,乃謂永曰: "我是天之織女,感君之孝,天使我償之.今君事了,不能久停." 語訖,雲霧四垂,忽飛而去.' *Taiping yulan*: 1899. The translation is after Wu 1989b: 289-291.
[89] See Tang Changshou 2010: 144. '凱風自南,吹彼棘心.棘心夭夭,母氏劬勞. 凱風自南,吹彼棘薪.母氏圣善,我無令人.爰有寒泉.在浚之下.有子七人,母氏勞苦.睍睆黃鳥,載好其音.有了七人,莫慰母心. The genial wind from the south/ Blows on the heart of that jujube tree, / Till that heart looks tender and beautiful./ What toil and pain did our mother endure!/ The genial wind from the south/ Blows on the branches of that jujube tree, / Our mother is wise and good; But among us there is no good./ There is the cool spring/ Below [the city of] Tseun./ We are seven sons,/ And our mother is full of pain and suffering./ The beautiful yellow birds/ Give forth their pleasant notes,/ We are seven sons,/ And cannot compose our mother's heart.' *Shi jing*: 82. The English translation is after Legge 1960: 50-51.
[90] Wu Hung suggests that the 16 stories of filial sons in the Wu Liang shrine were illustrated based on the textual record in the *Xiaozi zhuan* (Biography of Filial Sons), edited by Liu Xiang 劉向 in the Western Han and probably revised in the Eastern Han. The *Xiaozi zhuan* was in continuous development and expansion over the period and finally became a series of 24 stories of filial sons representing the major aspects of filial piety in the Yuan dynasty. Wu 1989b: 273-275. It is probably out

the Wu Liang shrine also contains themes on the sages and kings, the righteous women, the loyal ministers and the assassinators, which are not touched upon by the pictorial carvings in the front hall of the Shiziwan M1. This observation required further examination.

Wu Hung suggests that the historical figures and stories carved chronologically in the Wu Liang shrine reflect the Han historical perspective. The walls of the shrine can be viewed as history encoded in important events, figures and virtues.[91] The large proportion of pavilion scenes located in the centre of the rear wall emphasizes the fact that crucial to this historical perspective is loyalty to the imperial ruler. The figure sitting in the pavilion receiving respect from the surrounding ministers symbolizes the proper relationship between the ruler and the ministers.[92]

Though certain content and arrangement of the pictorial carvings in the front hall of the Shiziwan M1 seem similar to the Wu Liang shrine, the designers of the Shiziwan M1 focused only on the theme of filial piety, instead of loyalty to the ruler and a series of virtues including filial piety that were regarded to be relevant to the most important virtue.[93] Moreover, some stories of the filial sons emphasize a well maintained relationship between family members in addition to filial piety. For example, in the story of Yuan Gu, Yuan Gu persuaded his father to be kind to his grandfather, and in the story of Jian Ziqian, Jian Ziqian persuaded his father to forgive his stepmother. In the story based on the poem *Kaifeng*, the virtue of filial piety was shown through the reciprocal affection between the mother and the sons.

It is noteworthy that the rear wall of the front hall of the Shiziwan M1 is connected to two individual burial chambers (a third one has yet to be excavated).[94] The two entrances and their two paired guards carved on the wall constitute the whole rear wall. Consequently, the tomb occupants in these burial chambers formed the sacrificial centre of the front hall. Compared to the stone shrines on the cemetery in eastern China, the cliff tomb with the front hall combined the sacrificial area, the sacrificial objects, and the tomb occupants more closely. The previous chapter on tomb structure has discussed the relationship between this kind of front hall and the multiple burial chambers. In this chapter, from the perspective of the pictorial programme, the front hall further shows how related households belonging to a large family were brought together through the design of the cliff tomb. In the shrine-like structure in the cliff tomb, the virtue of filial piety was much emphasized, for it was crucial to the cohesion of a family, which would subsequently contribute to the continuity and prosperity of a family.

A Case Study of the Taliangzi M3 in Zhongjiang

The cliff tomb with the front hall structure is popular mainly in the Leshan and the adjacent Qingshen area. In cliff tombs in other areas, the site for showing respect to the ancestors of the family was laid out in a side chamber. A side chamber in the Taliangzi M3 in Zhongjiang has two walls painted with the family history together with the relevant inscriptions (figure 79, 80 and 81).[95] The rear wall and the right side wall of the chamber are painted with two rows of eight framed images depicting a dining scene. The figures seated around the table with the dining set accompanied by attendants in each frame seem to be the members of the tomb occupants' family from different generations according to the 150 words inscriptions in three of the four frames in the upper row (figure 82). Though many characters are missing, due to erosion, some key facts can be deduced from the inscriptions. In addition, a chronological order of the frames from left to right, from the right side wall to the rear wall of the chamber can be told. The following interpretation is based on the transcription in the 2008 report and the interpretation by Wang Zijin and Gao Dalun.[96] The frames in the upper row are numbered 1, 3, 5, and 7 from left to right.

Frame 1:
According to the inscription in this frame, the early ancestor of the tomb occupant was the Commandant (*wei* 尉) of Nanyang. A later generation Jing Zibin 荊子賓, who was also called Jing Wenjun 荊文君, took the position of the Grand Herald (*da honglu* 大鴻臚). The son of Jing Zibin took the position of the Gentleman-in-Attendance of the Yellow Gates (*Huangmen shilang* 黃門侍郎). Jing Zibin stuck to his responsibilities in the post and thus offended some relatives of the empress and the emperor. He was exempted from being executed due to his success as the Grand Herald in suppressing the rebelling of the Qiang 羌 people. Instead, he was sent into exile in the west and died here in this district (*xiang* 鄉) of this prefecture (*xian* 縣) in the commandery (*jun* 郡) of this region (*zhou* 州).[97]

---

of economic consideration, several important stories of filial sons were selected from the contemporary collection to be carved in the front hall of the Shiziwan M1, since large areas of pictorial carvings were rare in the cliff tombs of the time.
[91] Wu 1989b: 142-217.
[92] Wu 1989b: 147-148.
[93] In some cases, the story of the assassinator Jing Ke 荊軻 is also carved in such front hall. For example, the Mahao I M1. However, in the Mahao I M1, this story is the only one on the assassinator and is carved together with other stories of filial sons, including the story of Dong Yong, the carriage pulling scene and the story illustrating the poem *Kaifeng*. For the report of the Mahao I M1, see Tang Changshou 1990. Jing Ke was sent by the prince of Yan 燕 to assassinate Ying Zheng 嬴政, the King of Qin 秦, for he threatened the living of other kingdoms including the Yan. Though Jing Ke finally failed to his mission and was executed by the King of Qin, he was remembered as a model of loyalty after the fall of the rule of Qin. For the record on Jing Ke, see *Shi ji*: 2534-2535. The scene carved in the Mahao I M1 illustrates the moment when Jing Ke threw the stab to the King of Qin, the stab unfortunately went into the pillar.
[94] See the previous chapter for detail.

[95] For the archaeological report see Sichuan sheng wenwu kaogu yanjiuyuan, Deyang shi wenwu kaogu yanjiusuo and Zhongjiang xian wenwu baohu guanli suo 2008: 19-34. The side chamber in Taliangzi M3 is so far the only case in the cliff tombs in Sichuan that is found with brush paintings on a layer of fine mud foundation on the wall together with inscriptions written in ink. Such method of tomb decoration is often used in the contemporary tombs in the Central Plain such as Henan and Shaanxi. The decoration in Taliangzi M3 may be related to the origin of the ancestor of the tomb occupant in Nanyang in Henan, as mentioned in the inscription. See Liu Zhangze and Li Zhaohe 2004.
[96] For the interpretation, see Wang Zijin and Gao Dalun 2004. The English translation of the official titles and the administrative divisions are after Bielenstein 1980.
[97] According to the transcription (Sichuan sheng wenwu kaogu yanjiuyuan, Deyang shi wenwu kaogu yanjiusuo and Zhongjiang xian

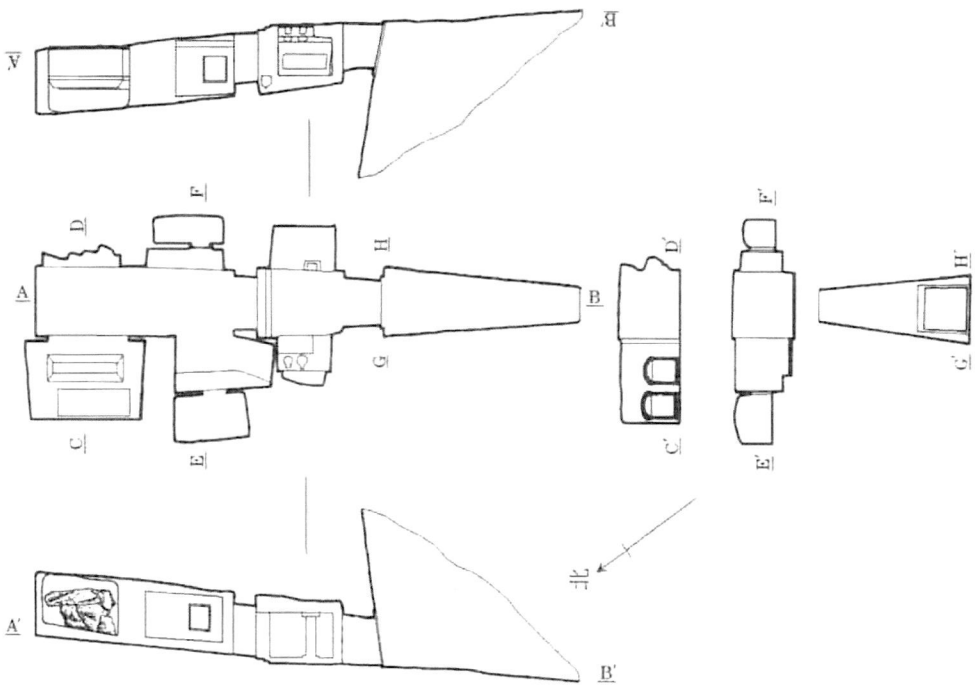

FIGURE 79. PLAN OF THE TALIANGZI M3 IN ZHONGJIANG. AFTER SICHUAN SHENG WENWU KAOGU YANJIUYUAN, DEYANG SHI WENWU KAOGU YANJIUSUO AND ZHONGJIANG XIAN WENWU BAOHU GUANLI SUO 2008: FIG. 15.

FIGURE 80. A SIDE CHAMBER WITH MURAL PAINTINGS ON THE TOMB OCCUPANT'S FAMILY HISTORY IN THE TALIANGZI M3 IN ZHONGJIANG. AFTER SICHUAN SHENG WENWU KAOGU YANJIUYUAN, DEYANG SHI WENWU KAOGU YANJIUSUO AND ZHONGJIANG XIAN WENWU BAOHU GUANLI SUO 2008: PL. 16.

Two figures are seated over the dining set in the scene, facing to the right. A small figure standing behind is holding a fan in one hand and a piece of cloth in the other hand. According to the location of the inscription describing the different identities of the main figures and the sitting order of the figures, the front figure is Jing Zibin, the figure in the middle is the son of Jing Zibin, and the smallest figure behind them is their servant. As the following framed images with inscriptions explain, the person who is elder wenwu baohu guanli suo 2008: 57), the inscription contains 13 lines: '先祖南陽尉□□/土鄉長□里漢太鴻/□文君子賓/子賓子中黃門侍郎/文君真坐與詔/外親內親相檢屬見/怨□□諸上頒頡諸/□□□□□絕肌則/骨當□□□父即/鴻蘆擁十萬眾/平羌有功赦死/西徙處/此州郡鄉卒'.

FIGURE 81. EXPANDED DIAGRAM OF THE SIDE CHAMBER IN THE TALIANGZI M3 IN ZHONGJIANG. AFTER SICHUAN SHENG WENWU KAOGU YANJIUYUAN, DEYANG SHI WENWU KAOGU YANJIUSUO AND ZHONGJIANG XIAN WENWU BAOHU GUANLI SUO 2008: FIG. 25.

Figure 82. Picture no.5 in the side chamber in the Taliangzi M3 in Zhongjiang. After Sichuan sheng wenwu kaogu yanjiuyuan, Deyang shi wenwu kaogu yanjiusuo and Zhongjiang xian wenwu baohu guanli suo 2008: pl. 52.

and of higher status is usually seated in the front and is illustrated larger in size.

Frame 5:
A similar dining scene is carved in this frame. Two large figures are seated facing each other across a dining table. Each of them has two attendants standing behind them. According to the inscription above, the large figure on the left, the figure is called Jing Zinü 荊子女, the father of the tomb occupant, Jing Zi'an. Jing Zinü used to work as an official in the office in charge of construction (*wa cao li* 瓦曹吏) in the Guanghan Commandery. Jing Zi'an built this tomb for his father.[98] The inscription above the figure on the right shows that the figure is called Jing Ziyuan 荊子元. He used to work as an assistant clerk for the grand administrator of the Shu Commandery.[99] Jing Ziyuan is probably the brother of Jing Zinü, since they are seated equally at the table.

Frame 7:
The tomb occupant couple are depicted in this frame, followed by three attendants. Each attendant is labeled with the title of their position.[100] According to the inscription above the front figure, who is facing to the left, the figure represents the tomb occupant Jing Zi'an, his other name is Jing Shengying 荊聖應.[101] The figure behind Jing Zi'an is his wife. Her name is not mentioned.[102]

Frame 3 and the frames in the lower row are all illustrated with similar dining scenes, though without inscriptions identifying the figures in the scene. It seems that there was a tradition that in the tombs or shrines of the Han period, the tomb occupant or the major figures who receive sacrifice are usually exhibited in the dining scene. For example, in the shrine of Zhu Wei 朱鮪 in Jinxiang 金鄉 in Shandong, the tomb occupant Zhu Wei is depicted in a grand dining scene occupying the whole rear wall of the shrine (figure 83). The scene includes people who are preparing food and several tables of guests sitting together.[103] In the Liangtai 涼臺 tomb in Zhucheng 諸城 in Shandong, the tomb occupant is illustrated in a grand dining scene as well. He is sitting at a table laden with various dishes in a pavilion, with servants around him, in front of many people showing respect to him (figure 84).[104] Such a pictorial scheme could be further traced to the tradition of arranging a dining set in front of the tomb occupant in the Han tomb. For example, in the cliff tomb Bailinpo M2 in Santai in Sichuan, a table with a set of cups is found placed in front of the body of the tomb occupant.[105] In the Western Han brick chamber tomb Wunüzhong 五女冢 M267 in Luoyang in Henan, a table set together with jars containing salt, rice, wheat and meat sauce are found placed in front of the wooden coffin in the tomb.[106]

A similar dining scene is also found illustrated on the wall of a side chamber in the cliff tomb Bailinpo M1 in Santai (figure 85).[107] In the dining scene, three figures are dining at a table. In addition, the side chamber contains the paintings of three individual figures labeled with their names on the surrounding walls.[108] It is very likely that this

---

[98] The inscription is: '廣□守丞瓦曹吏/創農諸□掾/□字子女長生荊/□□□ □□父造此墓'. Sichuan sheng wenwu kaogu yanjiuyuan, Deyang shi wenwu kaogu yanjiusuo and Zhongjiang xian wenwu baohu guanli suo 2008: 58-59.
[99] The inscription is: '蜀太守文魯掾縣/官嗇夫諸書掾/史堂子元/長生'. Sichuan sheng wenwu kaogu yanjiuyuan, Deyang shi wenwu kaogu yanjiusuo and Zhongjiang xian wenwu baohu guanli suo 2008: 59.
[100] '侍奴 (attending servant)', '從奴 (assistant servant)' and '從小 (minor assistant)' respectively.
[101] The inscription is: '荊子安字聖應主'. Sichuan sheng wenwu kaogu yanjiuyuan, Deyang shi wenwu kaogu yanjiusuo and Zhongjiang xian wenwu baohu guanli suo 2008: 60.
[102] The inscription is: '應婦'. Sichuan sheng wenwu kaogu yanjiuyuan, Deyang shi wenwu kaogu yanjiusuo and Zhongjiang xian wenwu baohu guanli suo 2008: 60.
[103] Zheng Yan 1998: 456, fig. 4.
[104] Ren Rixin 1981: 20, fig. 8.
[105] Sichuan sheng wenwu kaogu yanjiuyuan, Mianyang shi bowuguan, and Santai xian wenwu guanli suo 2007: 182.
[106] Luoyang shi wenwu gongzuodui 1996.
[107] Sichuan sheng wenwu kaogu yanjiuyuan, Mianyang shi bowuguan and Santai xian wenwu guanli suo 2007: 154-179.
[108] However, it is strange that the three figures have different surna-

Chapter 3 Pictorial Carvings

FIGURE 83. ILLUSTRATION OF THE CARVINGS ON THE REAR WALL OF THE SHRINE OF ZHU WEI IN JINXIANG IN SHANDONG. AFTER ZHENG YAN 1998: FIG. 4.

FIGURE 84. ILLUSTRATION OF THE CARVING OF THE TOMB OCCUPANT FROM THE QIANLIANGTAI TOMB IN ZHUCHENG IN SHANDONG. AFTER REN RIXIN 1981: FIG. 8.

FIGURE 85. MURAL PAINTING ON A DINING SCENE IN A SIDE CHAMBER OF THE BAILINPO M1 IN SANTAI. AFTER SICHUAN SHENG WENWU KAOGU YANJIUYUAN, MIANYANG SHI BOWUGUAN AND SANTAI XIAN WENWU GUANLI SUO 2007: PL. 172.

side chamber has the memorial function similar to the one in the Taliangzi M3.

Frame 7 in the side chamber of the Taliangzi M3 illustrating the tomb occupant, Jing Zi'an on the top right of the rear wall of the chamber, seems to be the focal point of the pictorial carvings in the chamber. It is also the starting point for reading the whole pictorial programme of the chamber. According to a reading from right to left, the viewer who enters the chamber would naturally start to look at the figure of the tomb occupant, and then trace back the family history to the tomb occupant's father on the left part of the rear wall and the earlier ancestors on the wall on the left side of the viewer. As suggested by Wu Hung, human history is illustrated on the walls in the Wu Liang shrine following the reading order from right to left.[109] The family history of Jing Zi'an is illustrated on the walls in a chamber in a similar way. Compared with a grand human

mes. According to the inscriptions, the names are '齊光 (Qi Guang)', '張庭平 (Zhang Tingping)' and '楊臣衡 (Yang Chenheng)' (Sichuan sheng wenwu kaogu yanjiuyuan, Mianyang shi bowuguan and Santai xian wenwu guanli suo 2007: 166). The inscription on the wall near the entrance of the tomb shows that the tomb belonged to Mr Qi (齊公) (Sichuan sheng wenwu kaogu yanjiuyuan, Mianyang shi bowuguan and Santai xian wenwu guanli suo 2007: 158).

[109] Wu 1989b: 142-143.

history full of sages, heroes and models of various virtues, the family history of Jing Zi'an is mundane. And through reading the inscriptions, we see the fall of a prosperous family. The official positions taken by the family members became lower over generations. In the generation of the tomb occupant, it seems that Jing Zi'an was only a commoner, since no official title was mentioned in the inscription on him, unlike other inscriptions describing the positions of the earlier family members. The turning point is the exile of an early high official in the family, Jing Wenjun to Sichuan, which reminds us of the role of Sichuan in the Han as a destination for exile and the previously mentioned inscription on the door of the cliff tomb HM3 in Xindu, which also records the migration to Sichuan in the family history. In this sense, the pictorial carvings in this side chamber in the Taliangzi M3 has a two-fold meaning: to make the offspring of the family proud of the family's glorious past; and to remind the offspring of the difficulties experienced by the family, thus reminding them of their responsibilities to revive the family.

Compared with the previously mentioned stories of filial sons carved in the front hall of the tomb, the side chamber illustrated with the family history emphasized the responsibilities of family members and reinforced the bond between family members over generations through a different approach. Both the above constructions with pictorial carvings contributed to the continuity and prosperity of the family.

4. Pictorial carvings and the Representation of Ritual in the Cliff Tomb

Pictorial carvings are very often found near the entrance to the cliff tomb. In the cliff tombs with several chambers, the entrance to each chamber is often the focus of the decoration. In many cases, the only decorated area in the cliff tomb is the entrance to the tomb and to the burial chambers inside the tomb. The entrance decoration can be divided into four categories according to their location at the entrance: 1) decoration on the door lintel; 2) decoration on the door post; 3) decoration on the walls next to the tomb door; and 4) decoration on the side walls of the doorway. The decoration involves various icons, images and figures. Many of them are often used in the pictorial carvings in the contemporary stone or brick chamber tombs and the cliff tombs.

For example, in the cliff tomb M460 in Pengshan, the only pictorial carvings of the tomb are found on the lintel of the tomb door, which is carved into three elaborately decorated steps toward the doorway.[110] On the top and exterior step, a *dougong* bracket set is carved in low relief, occupying the whole area of the step. On the middle step, there are two sheep facing each other, with a squatting bear in between. On the bottom and interior step, a bow-like icon is carved in the centre. The lintel seems to be an area for the assembly of various auspicious icons. As mentioned in the previous chapter, the *dougong* bracket set has special auspicious meanings in the cliff tomb; the bear is often interpreted as the incarnation of the *fangxiangshi*, the exorcist; and the bow-like icon symbolizes the presence of the Queen Mother of the West, who is an immortal in charge of the heavenly world. The pair of sheep also symbolizes auspiciousness as mentioned earlier. Such cliff tombs with the focus of pictorial carvings on the tomb door lintel are very often found in the Pengshan area.

The prevalence of pictorial carvings at tomb entrances in the cliff tombs in Sichuan has its counterpart in the contemporary stone or brick chamber tombs in central and eastern China as mentioned earlier in the chapter. Focusing on several case studies of the stone and brick chamber tombs in central and eastern China, Kim Dramer suggests the tomb door played an important role in the ritual performed in the tomb. As will be discussed in the following section of the chapter, the doors of the cliff tombs in Sichuan played a similar important role, though with many local features. And my discussion is mainly based on the pictorial carvings on the door.

The tomb door is an important venue for ritual. Kim Dramer suggests that a pictorial carving in the Yi'nan tomb depicts the mortuary ritual, the grain sacrifice at the tomb door (figure 86).[111] In the picture, the chief mourner is kneeling on the ground, followed by five rows of participants. Another kneeling figure, the liturgist is holding a mat with three rows of grain on it, facing the chief mourner. In front of the liturgist is a low offering table with additional grain on it, exposed to two open doors decorated with door rings. Dramer pinpoints the location of this scene at the entrance to the tomb through quoting Jonathan Chaves: '[the doors are] quite obviously meant to represent the entrance to the tomb itself before which sacrificial rites are being conducted…Actual tomb doors of a Han date with ring-heads are quite frequently encountered.'[112]

FIGURE 86. RUBBING OF THE SCENE ON SACRIFICE AT TOMB DOOR CARVED IN THE YI'NAN TOMB IN SHANDONG. AFTER ZHONGGUO HUAXIANGSHI QUANJI BIANJI WEIYUANHUI 2000C: PL. 186.

Some scholars have suggested that some pictorial carvings in the Han tombs exhibited attempts to visualize the ritual

---

[110] Nanjing bowuyuan 1991: 7.
[111] Dramer 2002: 1.
[112] Dramer 2002: 1. Chaves 1968: 20. Chaves makes this suggestion based on his observation of the tomb decoration in a Han brick chamber tomb in Luoyang in Henan.

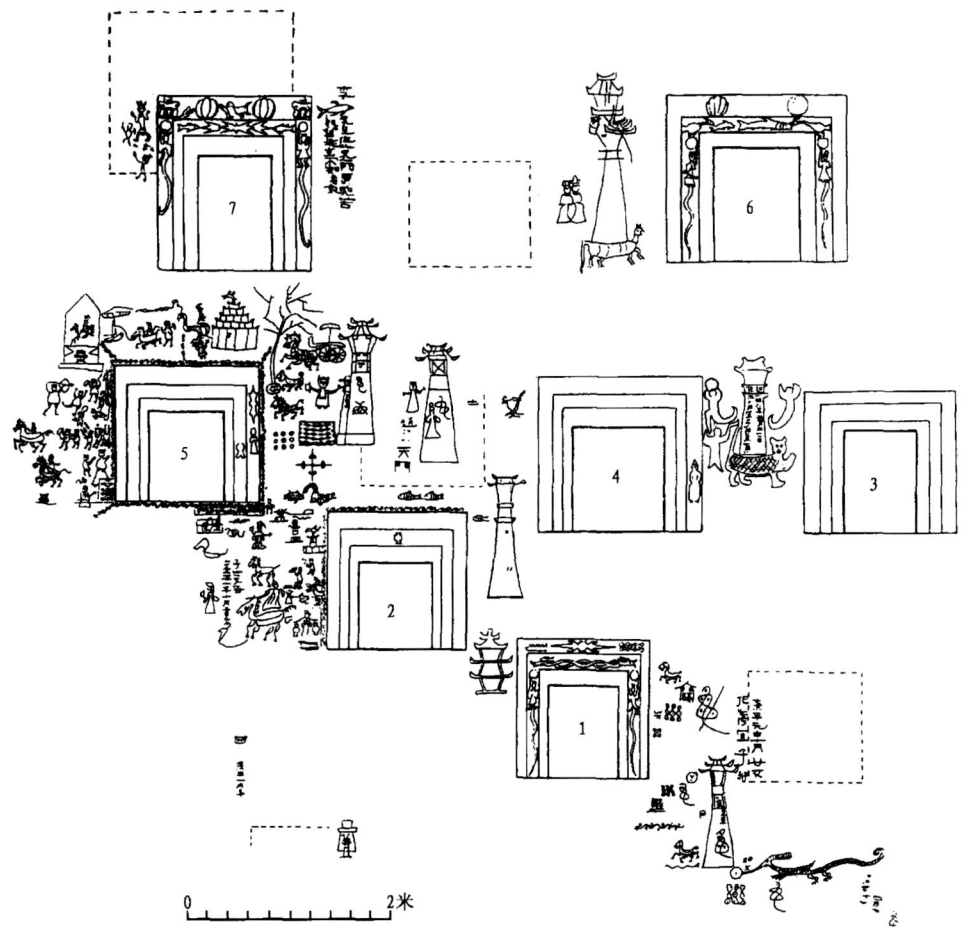

FIGURE 87. PLAN OF THE FAÇADE OF THE SEVEN CAVES (THE QIGEDONG CLIFF TOMBS) IN CHANGNING IN SICHUAN. AFTER LUO ERHU 2005: FIG. 1.

performed in the tomb and to show the completion of the ritual to the tomb occupants.[113] The first section of this chapter has provided two examples on how the ritual is depicted in the stone chamber tombs, the Cangshan tomb and the Yi'nan tomb.

In the cliff tombs in Sichuan, some pictorial carvings near the tomb entrance also seem to show the ritual performed at the tomb door. There are a group of seven cliff tombs excavated close to each other on the almost vertical cliff side in Changning in Sichuan, known as the 'seven caves (*qigedong* 七個洞)' by the local people (figure 87).[114] Four of the seven tombs have extensive decorations on the doors and on the surface of the cliff near the doors, though few pictorial carvings are found inside the tombs. The door posts are depicted as the *que* pillars and the lintels and the surrounding areas are carved with various auspicious animals and images. Two icons like a knot of twisted rope are carved on the cliff left of the entrance to the tomb M1. Luo Weixian identifies these icons as the representation of the sacrifice to the god of the earth and grain (*she ji* 社稷) and the spirit of *xuanwu* 玄武 (the turtle-shaped god

of the north),[115] which further shows the possibility that some rituals, including the grain sacrifice, were performed at the tomb door and the relevant icons were carved at the door as evidence of the completion of these rituals. The knot-like icon identified by Luo Weixian as the sacrifice to

[113] See Berger 1980: 207-215; Wu 1994: 91-100; Thompson 1998: 211-241; Dramer 2002: 18-39.
[114] For the archaeological report, see Sichuan daxue lishi xi qiba ji kaogu shixi dui 1985.
[115] Luo Weixian 1986. Luo Weixian suggests that the icon on the left includes nine sections divided by the twisted lines, which coincide the nine regions (*jiu zhou* 九州) of the territory of the ruling power. And the lines represent the rivers surrounding these regions. Traditionally, nine is regarded to be the number of regions in the control of the ruling power. The nine dots spread respectively in the centres of the nine sections represent the grain growing in the area. In this sense, the sections formed by the lines represent *she* 社, the earth, and the dots within the sections represent *ji* 稷, the grain.
There are several textual records on the *she ji* and the *jiu zhou* can be related to this icon as suggested by Luo Weixian (1986). The *Zhou li* 周禮 records that '以血祭祭社稷 (blood should be used for the sacrifice to the *she* and *ji*)', which is annotated by Zheng Xuan 鄭玄 that: '社稷, 土穀之神, 有德者配食焉. The *she* and *ji* are the gods of the earth and grain, only the virtuous ones can be guarded.' *Zhou li*: 456. The *Shi ji* describes the *jiu zhou* as: '中國外如赤縣神州者九, 乃所謂九州也, 於是有裨海環之…如一區中者乃為一州, 如此者九, 乃有大瀛海環其外, 天地之際焉. There are nine holy regions outside the central area, known as the *jiu zhou*, which are surrounded by water… each region is located in the centre of a water, there are nine such regions, and all are surrounded by the sea, at the border between the sky and land.' *Shi ji*: 2344. The relationship between the nine regions and the nine grains is recorded in the *Zhou li* as: '掌天下之圖, 以掌天下之地……與其財用九穀, 六畜之數要. To control the territory needs to master the map of the territory…to acquire wealth needs to know the method to manage the nine grains and the six farm animals.' *Zhou li*: 869.

the god of the earth and grain is also found on a pictorial brick illustrating the *que* pillar gates in the Yangzishan in Chengdu,[116] Since the *que* pillar gates usually indicate the entrance to a tomb or a cemetery in mortuary art, the illustration of the icon symbolizing the sacrifice to the god of the earth and grain in the same scene may imply the performance of the relevant ritual at the tomb door. Moreover, this brick is located in the doorway just next to the tomb door.

One reason for the importance of the tomb door as the venue for ritual can be explained by the role of doors in the Han society. The doors 'were closely related to the social-political structure as well as the rituals and customs of everyday life'.[117] Liu Tseng-kuei points out that, as early as the Spring and Autumn period, the *men* 門 and the *hu* 戶 were used to together as *menhu* 門戶 to denote a clan, *jiazu* 家族.[118] There were sumptuary laws regulating the use of different doors in the families of different social status, which consequently led to the expressions of *gao men da hu* 高門大戶 (high lintel and big door leaves) and *zhu hu* 朱戶 (vermilion door) 'as metaphors for families of high social status'.[119] Since the appearance of the door could exhibit the status of a family to a large extent, it is natural that the door of the cliff tomb that was built based on the dwelling for the living became the focus of mural decoration. The tomb door of the cliff tomb M355 in Pengshan is framed by a pair of pillars with the *dougong* bracket sets on top.[120] As mentioned in the previous chapter, the *dougong* structure was usually used in the grand buildings for the living. Hence the carving of the *dougong* at the tomb door was a public display of the status of the tomb occupant's family. In the Xiaoba II M80 in Leshan, the tomb door is framed by a pair of *que* pillar gates (figure 88).[121] In addition to the association with the entrance to the heavenly world, the *que* pillar gates in the Han society are a symbol of high social status. As recorded in the *Baihu tong* 白虎通: '門必有闕者何?闕者,所以飾門,別尊卑也. There are "towers" *ch'üeh* on the gates, as an adornment and to distinguish between the high and the lowly.'[122]

Due to the social-political meanings of the doors in both the tomb and the dwelling for the living, there were a series of regulations regarding the use of the door. Liu Tseng-kuei notes that the door in the dwelling for a family was one of the symbols of the patriarch. The main door in the centre symbolizes the honoured positions in the household and thus was reserved for the patriarch.[123] Dramer further points out that in the Han, the doors had 'the ability to change the social status and identity of those who passed

FIGURE 88. ENTRANCE TO THE XIAOBA II M80 IN LESHAN. AFTER TANG CHANGSHOU 1993: FIG. 12.

though them'.[124] At the doors of the tombs, there were also changes of the identities of the people who passed through them, namely, 'the paired rebirths of the chief mourner and his father'. Passing through the tomb door, the son as the chief mourner became the new patriarch of the family and the father as the deceased became a new member of the ancestors of the family.[125] Thus, the act of crossing the tomb door changed the social status of the living and the dead and became a 'social regeneration of the living and the dead'.[126] Consequently, the tomb door contains symbols of fecundity in its pictorial programme. For example, a kissing couple was found occupying the centre of the tomb door lintel of the cliff tomb M550 in Pengshan (figure 89).[127] The couple are naked, sitting on the ground and embracing each other. The man's hand is fondling the woman's breast while the woman's hand is resting on the man's shoulder. Chen Minda and Tang Changshou relate this image to some other sexual scenes depicted in the Han tombs in Sichuan and suggest that the kissing couple might symbolize reproduction and regeneration.[128] In the cliff tomb M6 and M7 from the group of seven tombs in Changning, the door lintels are carved with paired melons or pumpkins in high relief. Such melons or pumpkins have also been found carved on the ceiling of the burial chamber in the Hujiawan tomb M1 in Santai as mentioned in the previous chapter. One interpretation

---

[116] Yu Haoliang 1955: 71, fig. 1,2.
[117] Dramer 2002: 55.
[118] Liu Tseng-kuei 1997: 817. Both the *men* and the *hu* have the meaning of door. The early Chinese usually used *hu* to refer to the doors with one leaf, and used *men* to refer to the doors with double leaves.
[119] See Dramer 2001: 56 and Liu Tseng-kuei 1997: 856-858.
[120] Chen Mingda 2003a: 68, fig. 4.
[121] Tang Changshou 1993: 46, fig. 12.
[122] *Baihu tong*: 596. The translation is after Tjan 1952: 656.
[123] Liu Tseng-kuei 1997: 864.

[124] Dramer 2002: 56. She quotes textual record from the *Shi ji* on King Wu, who marked his victory in the Muye 牧野 battle on the gate of the village of Shang Rong, to show that as early as the Zhou, doors were used as signboards to exhibit the change of one's status.
[125] Dramer 2002: 40-41. She notes that in the *Tan Gong* 檀弓 section of the *Li ji*, the chief mourner was to present the burial gifts to the deceased after whose interment. '既封,主人贈,而祝宿虞尸. When the coffin has been let down into the grave, the chief mourner presents the (ruler's) gifts (to the dead in the grave).' *Li ji*: 272. The translation is after Legge 1967: 170. Zheng Xuan's 鄭玄 annotation of this section says that the gifts were offered by the chief mourner in the tomb. '送死者於壙也. Gifts were presented to the deceased in the tomb.' *Li ji*: 272.
[126] Dramer 2002: 73.
[127] Tang Changshou 1993: pl. 5. A similar image is found on the back of a sheep carved on the tomb door lintel of the Mahao I M1 in Leshan.
[128] Chen Mingda 2003b: 131 and Tang Changshou 1993: 61-62.

FIGURE 89. A KISSING COUPLE CARVED ON THE TOMB DOOR LINTEL OF THE CLIFF TOMB M550 IN PENGSHAN. AFTER NANJING BOWUYUAN 1991: PL. 12.

FIGURE 90. A BUDDHA IMAGE ON THE DOOR LINTEL OF THE MAHAO I M1 IN LESHAN. PHOTOGRAPH BY XUAN CHEN.

of this image is that melons or pumpkins usually have numerous seeds, which could have the implication for progeny.[129]

However, this 'social regeneration of the living and the dead' not only required proper rituals, but also could involve various dangers. In the Han period, ghosts of the deceased and various evil spirits were regarded as a main hazard to humans and the main impediment to the progress of the deceased to the heavenly world. To ensure the safety of the chief mourner and the completion of the mortuary ritual, exorcists were required to accompany the chief mourner to dispel the evil power at each door. Hence, the images of the *fangxiangshi* and various images with auspicious meanings are often found carved at the tomb door. On the cliff surrounding the group of seven cliff tombs in Changning, numerous auspicious images are carved together. It seems that there is no direct relationship between the individual images. However, the tomb occupant wanted to use as many as auspicious expressions to ensure the safety of his tomb and the mortuary ritual. The assembly of auspicious images includes the running tiger, the *que* pillar, the bird holding a fish in its beak, the icon of the persimmon leaves, the god and goddess, Fu Xi and Nü Wa, the dragon with the *bi* disk, and the exorcist.[130] They all appear to be coarsely carved by inexperienced hands, which suggests that their functions were much more valued than their quality.

It is notable that some images related to Buddhism also appear on the cliff tomb door lintels. For example, the Buddha-like images are found in the centre of the lintel of the entrance to the rear chamber in both the Mahao I M1 and the Shiziwan M1 in Leshan (figure 90).[131] The one in the Mahao I M1 is seated with his legs crossed and his right hand in the gesture of *abhaya mudra* (the gesture of fearlessness and reassurance). At the back of his head is a halo. Such a Buddha-like image could also be regarded as for the protection of the chief mourner and the tomb occupant from the harm of the evil spirit.[132] The Buddha-related images began to be imported into China in the 1st century AD. A south-western route from India to Sichuan and then to the Central Plain was one of the potential routes of dissemination. In this sense, the cliff tomb door lintel was up-to-date in incorporating new elements into its pictorial programme to assist with the mortuary ritual.

Inside the tombs, doors further 'marked the progress toward social transformation between the living and the dead' during the procession of the ritual.[133] In the previously discussed stone chamber tombs, the Yi'nan tomb and the Cangshan tomb, ritual was carried out along the central axis of the tomb, guided by the illustrations carved on the surrounding walls and lintels. The major recipients of this guidance were the chief mourner and the tomb occupant. Dramer points out that 'the visual cues incorporated in the tombs at the juncture of doorways also included aspects of the decorative programme such as changes in directionality or positionality or changes in motifs'.[134] As mentioned previously, the entrance to the rear chamber in the Cangshan tomb is framed by a pair of dragons, which

---

[129] Erickson 2003: 429.
[130] For the interpretation of these images, see Luo Erhu 2005a.
[131] Tang 1997: 77, figs. 15 and 16.
[132] Both Wu Hung and Tang Changshou suggest that the Buddha-like figures lost their original meanings in Buddhism in the pictorial programme of the cliff tomb. In the new context, they were treated like other immortals who were the protection of both the living and dead, such as the Queen Mother of the West. The main evidence is that the Buddha-like images are usually depicted with other auspicious images that were already common in the Han mortuary pictorial programme. See Wu 1986: 300-303 and Tang 1997: 77.
[133] Dramer 2002: 140.
[134] Dramer 2002: 140.

are the images related to the immortal world, instead of the guards from the world of the living like those carved near the front door, since, when the procession of the ritual in the tomb was getting closer to the rear chamber for the deceased after crossing one door after another, both the chief mourner and the deceased were closer to the immortal world. The rituals performed through crossing the doors and doorways in the tomb 'resulted in the activation of the decorative program and the mutual benefits achieved by the living and the dead'.[135] In addition, the act of ritual and the images carved on the doors 'reaffirmed and animated each other'.[136] The progression of ritual can be observed in the cliff tombs containing multiple burial chambers with decorated doors and doorways. These decorated doors and doorways regulated the progression of the ritual and were activated by the ritual at the same time.

The cliff tomb Taliangzi M3 in Zhongjiang (a decorated side chamber of which has been discussed previously), has three decorated doors and three decorated doorways playing important roles in regulating the progress of the ritual in the tomb.[137] The whole tomb has five main burial chambers on the east-west central axis and six side chambers, in a total length of 33 metres. The entrance to the second main chamber on the central axis is carved with a standing figure wearing a long robe and a hat, with a sword at his waist. The figure is slightly bending his body forward and his hands are held together in front, seemingly bowing to the visitors. The archaeological report identifies the figure as a door guardian.[138]

The entrance to the next main chamber has two standing figures carved on the two sides respectively. One is holding a long scepter in one hand while playing the flute.[139] The archaeological report notices that this figure might be foreign, since he is wearing a pointed hat, has a thick beard and is playing a *hu jia* 胡笳 (foreign flute), a musical instrument. The other figure is carved with a lying dog in the front and a flying bird above.[140] In the doorway, a group of dancing figures are carved in low relief with coloured paint on one side (figure 91).[141] The archaeological report regards these figures as foreign people due to the inscription of '裏人 *xiang ren* (the Xiang people)' written above.[142] Xie Chong'an further traces the origin of these people to the Qiang 羌 people in Huangzhong 湟中 in the

FIGURE 91. DANCING FOREIGNERS CARVED IN THE TALIANGZI M3 IN ZHONGJIANG. AFTER SICHUAN SHENG WENWU KAOGU YANJIUYUAN, DEYANG SHI WENWU KAOGU YANJIUSUO AND ZHONGJIANG XIAN WENWU BAOHU GUANLI SUO 2008: PL. 61.

Hexi 河西 corridor. The main evidence is that they wear short clothes and pointed hats, which were often worn by the foreign people of Indo-European origin.[143] In addition, the illustration of these people is right in front of the previously mentioned side chamber for the memorial, in which was placed a family ancestor well-known for his victory in the battle against the Qiang people. It seems that the illustration of the foreign figures in the doorway and at the entrance was intended to be the prelude to the upcoming memorial in the adjacent side chamber.

The entrance to the fourth main chamber has a large dragon carved on one side, seemingly to indicate the final resting place for the deceased, since this entrance is much closer to the large house-shaped coffin, which is cut into the end of the tomb on one side.[144] In the doorway, two birds holding a fish in their beaks are carved on the two side walls, offering meanings of regeneration and good fortune.[145] The entrance to the last main chamber is carved with some architectural details, mainly the eaves, without any figures. In the doorway to the last chamber, a mother goose with a baby goose is carved on one side, which might also have the meaning of regeneration and fecundity.[146]

As described above, the pictorial programme of the doors and doorways in the Taliangzi M3 begins with illustrating the images existing in the world for the living. As the ritual procession progressed from the outer doors to the inner doors in the tomb, the images on the doors become those relevant to the world of immortality. At the same time, the

---

[135] Dramer 2002: 140-141.
[136] Dramer 2002: 141.
[137] Sichuan sheng wenwu kaogu yanjiuyuan, Deyang shi wenwu kaogu yanjiusuo and Zhongjiang xian wenwu baohu guanli suo 2008: 19-34.
[138] Sichuan sheng wenwu kaogu yanjiuyuan, Deyang shi wenwu kaogu yanjiusuo and Zhongjiang xian wenwu baohu guanli suo 2008: 65, fig. 72, pl. 62.
[139] Sichuan sheng wenwu kaogu yanjiuyuan, Deyang shi wenwu kaogu yanjiusuo and Zhongjiang xian wenwu baohu guanli suo 2008: 26, fig. 22.
[140] Sichuan sheng wenwu kaogu yanjiuyuan, Deyang shi wenwu kaogu yanjiusuo and Zhongjiang xian wenwu baohu guanli suo 2008: 64-65. The pointed hat of this figure forms a stark contrast to the flat hat of the previous door guard. In this sense, the carvers seemed to emphasize the foreign features through certain details.
[141] Sichuan sheng wenwu kaogu yanjiuyuan, Deyang shi wenwu kaogu yanjiusuo and Zhongjiang xian wenwu baohu guanli suo 2008: pl. 61.
[142] Sichuan sheng wenwu kaogu yanjiuyuan, Deyang shi wenwu kaogu yanjiusuo and Zhongjiang xian wenwu baohu guanli suo 2008: 20.

[143] Xie Chong'an 2005. He also notes that their big eyes and thick beards are highlighted by paint, which might be intended to emphasize their foreign origin. In addition, their dance might be the 踏歌 *ta ge* (stepping with song) dance, which were popular among the minority groups in midwest China.
[144] Sichuan sheng wenwu kaogu yanjiuyuan, Deyang shi wenwu kaogu yanjiusuo and Zhongjiang xian wenwu baohu guanli suo 2008: 30, fig. 28, 33, fig. 31.
[145] Sichuan sheng wenwu kaogu yanjiuyuan, Deyang shi wenwu kaogu yanjiusuo and Zhongjiang xian wenwu baohu guanli suo 2008: pls. 70 and 71.
[146] Sichuan sheng wenwu kaogu yanjiuyuan, Deyang shi wenwu kaogu yanjiusuo and Zhongjiang xian wenwu baohu guanli suo 2008: pl. 78.

images on the doors guided the progress of the ritual, for example, the door and the doorway to the burial chamber for the memorial of the family ancestors drew the attention of the chief mourner and the participants in the ritual to the background of the experience of an outstanding ancestor of the family. Furthermore, there are thresholds built at all the entrances to the main burial chambers on the central axis of the tomb, which may have been intended to emphasize the progress of the ritual from the tomb door to the innermost burial chamber. Every time, another door was crossed in the ritual procession, the 'social transformation between the living and the dead' was one step closer to completion.[147]

A similar arrangement of the pictorial programmes at different doors in the cliff tomb can be observed in the previously mentioned Shiziwan M1. On the lintel over the entrance to the tomb, secular life scenes of dancing and entertainments are carved.[148] In the southern entranceway, each side wall is carved with an equestrian figure, who faces the outside of the tomb, seemingly welcoming the arrival of the chief mourner, the tomb occupant and the other participants of the ritual.[149] These equestrian figures may play a role similar to the bowing guard carved at the outer door of the tomb Taliangzi M3. After this entranceway is the front hall, which functioned as a shrine, as discussed previously. On the rear wall of the front hall, where the rear burial chambers are located, guards with features from the world of immortality are carved. Each burial chamber has two immortal guards carved on the two sides of its entrance.[150] One is identified as the tomb-pacifying god, who has the body of a man and the head of a beast.[151] He has two horns and ears of a pig. His eyes are large and bulging. He also has fangs and a long hanging tongue reaching to his belly. He holds an axe in one hand and a snake in the other hand.[152] People in the Sichuan area believed that snakes were demons from the underworld and could be beaten by pigs. Therefore, this figure is regarded as the pig-headed god, who could protect the tomb occupants from the harm of demons.[153] The other figure is regarded as the tomb-pacifying god's assistant. He holds a broom in one hand and a dust basket in the other hand, representing the 'sweeping away of evil influences'.[154] To some extent, the paired tomb-pacifying

FIGURE 92. ENTRANCE TO THE COFFIN CHAMBER OF THE TALIANGZI M3 IN ZHONGJIANG. AFTER SICHUAN SHENG WENWU KAOGU YANJIUYUAN, DEYANG SHI WENWU KAOGU YANJIUSUO AND ZHONGJIANG XIAN WENWU BAOHU GUANLI SUO 2008: FIG. 28.

god here played a role similar to the large dragon carved at the entrance to the burial chamber with the house-shaped coffin in the Taliangzi M3 (figure 92).[155] Through the use of such conventionalized displays, information was unambiguously communicated in the pictorial programme at the doors and during the mortuary ritual in the tomb.

5. Conclusion

Though at the first glance, the pictorial carvings inside the cliff tombs are scarce and scattered randomly, there is an underlying logic in the design and arrangement of these paintings. The pictorial carvings in the cliff tombs were concentrated in two main areas, the chamber for memorial of the family ancestors, and the doors and doorways. Because these two areas played important roles in the rituals performed at the tomb, they reinforced the cohesion of the tomb occupant's family and contributed to the continuity and prosperity of the family.

Through pictorial carvings, the burial chamber for the memorial of the family ancestors emphasized the important virtues for the cohesion and continuity of the family, and showed a sense of pride in the family's past. The pictorial carvings on the doors and in the doorways guided the progress of the ritual at the tomb and clarified the main relationships involved in the ritual, which was about the transitions to the roles of the family's patriarch

---

[147] Dramer 2002: 140.
[148] Tang 1997: 73. However, according to the author, due to the severe erosion of the lintel carvings, no picture is provided.
[149] Tang 1997: 73, fig. 4.
[150] Tang 1997: 74, fig. 6, 76, figs. 13 and 14.
[151] Tang 1997: 76-77.
[152] This tomb-pacifying god with long tongue also appears in the form of pottery figurine among the burial objects in the Eastern Han tombs in the Sichuan area. For a general study of this long tongue god in the Sichuan area, see Fu 2006. Fu Juan's research shows that there are mainly two kinds of pottery figurines featuring long tongue in the Sichuan area, the standing figure with a beast head and the squatting dog. These figurines have been found mainly in the Chengdu plain and the Chongqing area. More long tongue dogs and less long tongue figures have found in Chongqing. She suggests that such long tongue figurines might be influenced by the earlier Chu culture, in which some wooden figures with long tongues have been found.
[153] Tang 1997: 76-77.
[154] Tang 1997: 77. Tang Changshou notes that in 'his annotation to the *Rong you* 戎右 section in the *Xia guan* 夏官 division in the *Zhou li*, which deals with the proper rituals and procedures for military officials, the Han dynasty scholar Zheng Xuan 鄭玄 also mentions the use of the peach-wood broom to ward off evil influences'.
[155] According to Tang Changshou, the paired tomb-pacifying god is standard tomb door carving in the cliff tombs in Sichuan. Examples of these images have been found in the Shiziwan tombs no.22, 27 and 28 in Leshan, and the tomb no.46 at Jiangkou in Pengshan (Tang 1997: 77). However, no report on these cliff tombs has been published.

and ancestor. The ultimate aim of the ritual performed through crossing the tomb doors was to promise the continuous growth of the family, to ensure that the eldest sons continued to become the patriarch, and the patriarchs continued to become members of the family ancestors. The decorated burial chamber for memorial was also involved in this ritual through being incorporated into the tomb architecture for ritual, which was regulated by doors and doorways, for example, the chamber for memorial in the Taliangzi M3 and the Shiziwan M1. 'In this way, the living and the dead were linked eternally by the mortuary rituals performed at doors and doorways within the tombs.'[156]

The previous chapter has discussed how the cliff tomb structure was intended for the continuous development of the family. This chapter shows that pictorial carvings of the cliff tombs were planned for the same purpose and were integrated into the tomb structure. The previous chapter analyzes how the construction of the cliff tomb and the cliff tomb structure affected the relationship and behaviour of people. This chapter further shows that ritual was an important medium, through which material presence exerted its influence on people. Pictorial carvings in the cliff tomb were important to the efficacy of the ritual performed. Consequently, the proper pictorial carvings in the chamber for memorial and at the doors made the rituals in the tomb a useful regulating mechanism, which ensured the smooth and efficient running of the families in the local society.[157]

Moreover, through the comparison between the contemporary mortuary pictorial carvings in east China and in the cliff tombs in Sichuan, we see that there were borrowings and development with local features,[158] which is useful for us to study how the cliff tomb as a burial form came into being and became popular with many localized conventional displays.[159]

---

[156] Dramer 2002: 106.

[157] Dramer 2002: 107. She also points out that mortuary ritual was a tool of good government (Dramer 2002: 123).

[158] Many local features in the pictorial carvings in the cliff tombs were exhibited through some localized figures and images, such as the previously mentioned kissing couple, Buddha-like figure, and pig-head tomb-pacifying god, the origin of which rooted in the geography, tradition and history of the area.

[159] It seems that the concentration of pictorial carvings on the doors in the cliff tombs had its origin in the stone or brick chamber tombs in the Central Plain and east China. A group of chamber tombs constructed by the combination of stone and brick at Dabaodang 大保當 in Shenmu 神木 in Shaanxi more directly reflect the borrowing and the development with local feature. There is an Eastern Han city site together with an adjacent cemetery found in Dabaodang. On the cemetery, there are a group of 14 decorated chamber tombs, which were in use no earlier than AD 89 and no later than 140, a very short period when the area was not disturbed by the Xiongnu 匈奴 people from the north and the Qiang people. The 14 decorated tombs exhibit highly uniformed structures and pictorial programmes, with their door posts and lintels built by stone and the other parts by brick. All the pictorial carvings in the tombs are on the door posts and lintels, exactly like those late Western Han brick chamber tombs with decorated stone door posts and lintels in Nanyang in Henan. But the Dabaodang tombs had their own carving style and incorporated some elements with local features, for example, the illustration of the story on an early Western Han General Li Guang 李廣, who was well-known for his victory in the battle against the Xiongnu (Shaanxi sheng kaogu yanjiusuo and Yulin shi wenwu guanli weiyuanhui 2001: 36-37, figs. 37 and 38). During the short peaceful period, a group of people migrated to Dabaodang and brought the standard traditional burial form, while even in the very short period, the standard burial form became to have some local elements. For the archaeological report see Shaanxi sheng kaogu yanjiusuo and Yulin shi wenwu guanli weiyuanhui 2001: 35-110.

Chapter 4
Burial Objects

This chapter is concerned with how the burial objects were planned and arranged in a cliff tomb, interred with multiple occupants from different generations and related in various ways. The hypothesis is that there are certain principles to follow to establish an institutional relationship within the cliff tomb through the material presence of the burial objects. In addition, the burial objects were arranged in relation to the tomb structure and pictorial carvings to make the cliff tomb function as an integrated entity.

The general underlying logic of burial objects preparation for the tombs in the Han dynasty was to provide the deceased with what he would need in the afterlife which is largely modelled on this life. In this sense, burial objects in the Han tomb mainly fall into 4 categories. 1) pottery models of the things used in daily life, including vessels, buildings, figurines of servants and performers, models of horses and farm animals, sets of wells, stoves, toilets and warehouses. 2) Things treasured by the tomb occupants when they were alive, such as stationery and accessories. 3) Things used in ceremonies, such as chariot parts, weapons and scepters. 4) Tomb appeasing pieces, such as figurines, models of beasts, funerary land contracts.[1]

However, burial objects not only reflect the needs modelled on the life of the living, but in some cases, also the hope of the tomb occupants to enter the heavenly world, which is inhabited by the immortals, who do not need those things of the ordinary mortals. The heavenly world is widely depicted on some burial objects such as the money trees and the stone coffins that have been found in many Eastern Han tombs in Sichuan, especially in cliff tombs.

1. Plan of Burial Objects

An example of the types of burial objects and their spatiality in the tomb is provided by an unplundered cliff tomb in Zhongxian 忠縣 in Chongqing. The cliff tomb Tujing 涂井 M5 is a medium scale two-chamber tomb with a total length of 7.2 metres (figure 93).[2] A niche is carved at the right side of the front chamber and a stove is carved at the right side of the rear chamber, close to the front chamber. Two tomb occupants are located in the centre of the front chamber and one is located in the centre of the rear chamber. Though no remains of skeletons are left, three iron swords mark the locations of the three tomb occupants respectively. The sword in the rear chamber is found adjacent to some red lacquer paints and ashes of a black board, which may be the remains of the lacquered wooden coffin, as suggested by the author of the archaeological report.[3] Personal belongings, including two silver hair pins, a silver bracelet, a silver ring and the previously mentioned three iron swords, were found at the locations of the tomb occupants, as well as piles of coins. Most of the remaining 130 burial objects were pottery models representing the prosperous life on the farm, distributed in various locations in the tomb. Among them, 64 are pottery figurines illustrating attendants, chefs, a story teller, a dancer, a groom and soldiers. They are placed in mainly five groups in the two burial chambers. The single group in the rear chamber seems to serve the only occupant in the chamber. Among the remaining groups, two are located on the opposite sides of the front chamber respectively, one is near the entrance to the front chamber, and one is near the rear corner of the front chamber, at the entrance to the rear chamber. The only pottery figure of a groom is placed in the passageway to the tomb, together with a pottery horse. Most of the remaining pottery models are models of farm houses, wells, ponds and farm animals, distributed among the pottery figurines. In addition, some pottery vessels are found occupying the area against the rear wall of the tomb.

What is especially noteworthy is that, the only money tree in the tomb is placed near the rear corner of the front chamber and near the entrance to the rear chamber, a focal point for all the three tomb occupants. Jiang Yuxiang suggests that this arrangement symbolized that the head of the family led his family members making sacrifices to the money tree.[4] What the significance of the money tree was and what it was used for will be discussed in detail later.

This tomb provides us with the general idea that burial objects, mainly pottery models for the satisfaction of the *po* for the afterlife of the deceased, were individually gathered around a specific member in the tomb. Other burial objects, such as money trees, were shared by all members in the tomb. The individual identities of the individual members and the collective identity of all the members in the tomb were established through the symbolism of different objects.[5] The money tree and the stone coffin will be discussed as the major clues to understanding how this dialectical relationship was established in the tomb.

2. The Money Tree

The money tree is one of the most characteristic burial objects in the tombs in Eastern Han Sichuan (figure 94). They were distributed mainly in the Sichuan Basin; some are also found in the adjacent areas in northern Yunnan

---
[1] This categorization is based on Huang Xiaofen 2003:203-204.
[2] Zhang Caijun 1985: fig. 17.
[3] Zhang Caijun 1985: 54.
[4] Jiang Yuxiang 2000: 13.
[5] For the dialectical relationship between individual and collective identity, see Jenkins 2008: 46-47.

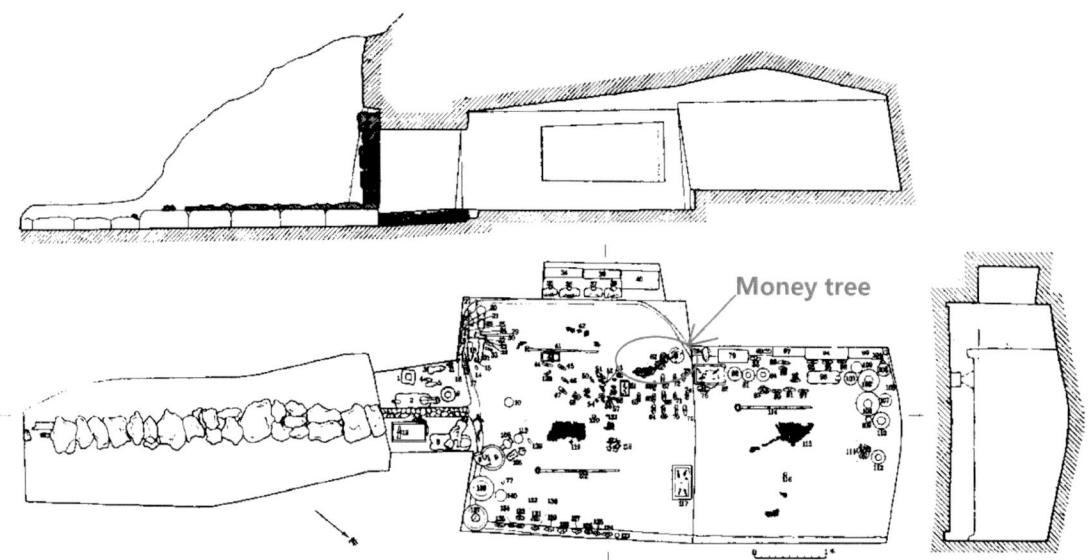

FIGURE 93. PLAN OF THE CLIFF TOMB TUJING NO. 5 IN ZHONGXIAN IN SICHUAN. AFTER ZHANG CAIJUN 1985: FIG. 17.

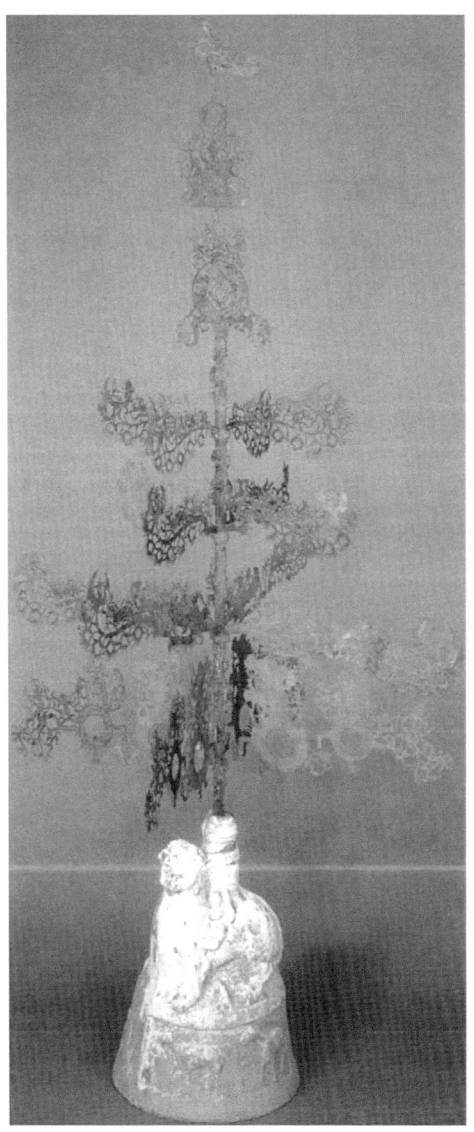

FIGURE 94. MONEY TREE FROM THE HEJIASHAN M2 IN MIANYANG IN SICHUAN. AFTER HE ZHIGUO 2006A: FIG. 5.51.

and Guizhou, western Hubei, and southern Shaanxi, Qinghai and Gansu. By 2006, information on 189 money trees had become available.[6] Many of them were found in cliff tombs. Some of them were from brick tombs. The money tree is made up of two parts, a pottery base in the shape of a mountain or an animal, and a bronze tree trunk with branches decorated with coins and auspicious images.[7] The name 'money tree' is derived from the coins, which look as though they grow out of the bronze tree. The term was first used by archaeologist to describe such an object during the 1940s, in the excavation of the cliff tombs in Pengshan in Sichuan.[8] So far, there have been many studies on the meaning and function of this artifact. The discussion is mainly focused on the meaning of the tree and coins, and the seemingly religious images carved all over the tree branches, trunk and base.[9] This chapter, however, will mainly look at the sense of volume and the visual complexity of the money tree and argue that the local people attempted to create a distinctive ritual object of their own. Consequently, the money tree functioned as a crucial part in symbolizing the collective identity of the occupants in a tomb.

[6] See He Zhiguo 2006a: 5 and a list of all the money trees with their locations, features and references in He Zhiguo 2006a: 271-296.
[7] In a few cases, the base is made of stone or bronze. For example, money tree no. 2 in He Zhiguo 2006a: 271, no. 31 in He 2006a: 274, no. 44 in He Zhiguo 2006a: 276 and no. 53 in He Zhiguo 2006a: 277.
[8] He Zhiguo 2006a: 7. The term 'money tree (qianshu 錢樹)' was first proposed by Feng Hanji to describe such frequently found burial object in the cliff tombs during excavation. See also the archaeological report on the 1940s excavation published in the 1990s based on the remaining drafts (Nanjing bowuyuan 1991: 35-37).
[9] For important studies on money tree, see Erickson 1994, He Zhiguo 2006a and Yu Haoliang 1961. Yu Haoliang was the first archeologist making thorough discussion on the potential function of the money tree as a burial object. Susan Erickson was the first western scholar who carries out comprehensive studies on the money tree from the aspects of its origin, manufacture, pictorial scheme, meaning and function. He Zhiguo has collected the most detailed information on the remaining money trees so far and focuses his discussion on the potential religious meaning of the money tree (He Zhiguo 2006a: 173-254).

Major Interpretations of the Money Tree

Based on previous research on the money tree, the meaning and function of it can be mainly summarized as follows: 1) The money tree was a source of money for the tomb occupants in their afterlife;[10] 2) The money tree was an axis mundi, through which the soul of the occupant was guided to heaven.[11]

These two functions represented the collective needs of the tomb occupants to satisfy both their *hun* and *po*. And as will be discussed below, a symbol of these collective needs was invented to materialize the collective identity of the occupants in a tomb.

An invented Symbol

The height of the money tree, including both its base and trunk, ranges from 1.2 to 2 metres. The tallest one found so far is the one from the collection of the National Museum China, reaching to a height of 2.01 metres.[12] Compared with the other burial objects in the tomb, the size of the money tree is extraordinary. Moreover, the height of medium to large scale cliff tombs is usually no more than 2 metres. Consequently, the money tree must have been a major focus in the tomb. Like the previously mentioned cliff tomb Tujing M5, in most cases, only one money tree is found in a tomb, and it is usually in the centre, surrounded by the tomb occupants.[13] For example, in the cliff tomb at Baozishan in Xinjin, a money tree was found in the centre of the area between the two rows of stone coffins. Each row has two stone coffins.[14]

In addition, the visual complexity of the money tree made it an impressive presence in the tomb. The branches sprout from the trunk in various directions. Each branch is decorated with elaborately carved coins, auspicious birds, people involved in various activities and sometimes, the Queen Mother of the West. Layer after layer of branches reach to the apex of the tree, where perches a large auspicious bird or sits the Queen Mother of the West with the auspicious bird. Not only the height, but also a sense of volume and the aesthetic illustration attract people's attention to the money tree in the tomb. Unlike pottery figures found in the cliff tombs, the standard of money trees is stable. In tombs where coarse pottery figurines were found, if sections of a money tree have survived, they appeared to be elaborate. To some extent, money trees appear more important as a burial object than the pottery models. This may be partly due to its dedication to the whole tomb occupants' family instead of the individuals. It is a pity that for most of the money trees only sections of the bronze trunk or branches, or the pottery base have remained in tombs. In some disturbed tombs, only one or two bronze pieces or the pottery base remained. Most of the intact money trees in the collection were reconstructed by archaeologists piece by piece. In this sense, it is easy to overlook the original sense of volume that a money tree delivered in the tomb, which was possibly what the patrons of the tomb wanted to achieve.

On the other hand, the fragility of the money tree reflects its special construction, made of numerous individual parts. These parts could be easily put together to form a tree, but easily fell apart as well. To install or to reconstruct a money tree, we first need to insert the tree trunk into the pottery base. The tubular tree trunk was usually made of four to six long tubes, which were hollow inside and had a slightly narrow end. Therefore, the tubes can be inserted into each other to form a whole trunk. Each branch is then individually hooked to the sockets cast on the trunk. Take the money tree found in the cliff tomb Hejiashan 何家山 M2 in Mianyang for example,[15] there are four layers of tree branches installed on the trunk. Each layer contains four sections of branches sprouting in four different directions. Finally, on top of the tree, a piece of bronze cast with seated Queen Mother of the West with a bird and a *bi* disc is inserted into the top tube of the trunk.

Though all the branches and the top decoration are two dimensional pieces, they form a three dimensional visual effect, after they are together. In the case of the money tree at Wanfu 萬福 in Guanghan, smaller independent pieces of branches are further erected on the four sprouting branches on the same layer to reinforce the sense of volume and complexity.[16] In addition, the four branches on each layer are cast from the same mould, with the same decoration. As a result, though the combination of the tree branches makes the money tree look complicated, the tree contains only five different patterns. Moreover, the top three layers of the tree branches follow a similar scheme, with a row of coins hanging below, a row of figures in motion above, and an auspicious bird perching on the end.

Lothar Ledderose points out that there was a module system in China to 'assemble objects from standardized parts', which were 'prefabricated in great quantity and could be put together quickly in different combinations, creating an extensive variety of units from a limited repertoire of components'.[17] The tree trunk and branches of the money tree can be regarded as modules, prefabricated to make

---
[10] Nylan 2003: 377. Nylan suggests that the money tree is literally composed of coins, which was a 'money-making venture' in the tomb.
[11] Erickson 1994: 27-29 and He Zhiguo 2006a: 157-162. He Zhiguo agrees with Erickson's interpretation of the money tree as the axis mundi and further develops her idea through incorporating the images on the money tree base, trunk, branches and leaves into a cosmological system, through which, as he suggests, the tomb occupant could ascend to heaven.
[12] He Zhiguo 2006a: 21. The tree was collected by the museum from personal collectors. For more information, see Xi Yuying 2006. Xi Yuying has made comparisons between this money tree and the ones from the cliff tomb Hejiashan 何家山 M1 and M2 in Mianyang in Sichuan and the cliff tombs in Hanzhong in southern Shaanxi, adjacent to the northern Sichuan Basin. He suggests that the bronze tree branches and leaves are close to those of the Hejiashan money trees and the pottery base is similar to those of the Hanzhong money trees.
[13] In the cliff tomb Hejiashan M2 in Mianyang (He Zhiguo 1991b), pieces from two money trees were found. So far, no more than two money trees have been found in a tomb.
[14] Li Xingyu 1993: 28.

[15] Bagley 2001: pl. 97.
[16] Bagley 2001: pl. 98.
[17] Ledderose 2000: 1.

an object of impressive material presence. Ledderose also suggests that the module system could meet the demands of the customers who 'expected high quality for a low price'.[18] In addition, the accessibility of the high quality product to a wider range of people contributed to the 'fostering of social homogeneity and cultural and political coherence'.[19] The popularity of the money tree among a wide range of tombs shows that the manufacturing cost of a money tree was affordable to tomb occupants of various economic means, including those with the tombs containing less good pottery burial objects. In fact, the modular manufacture system seen in the money tree not only made it economically affordable, but also made it easier to be transported to the tomb, given its height, shape and fragility. It is even possible that assembling the money tree piece by piece in the tomb became a part of the ritual in the tomb. Or we can think it the other way round, the money tree was originally designed in this height and shape together with its modular manufacture system at the same time. There could be several expectations for a new local ritual object in the tomb: first, it should be large and elaborate to become the focus of the burial space; second, it should be economically affordable to a community of families with various economic means; third, it should be possible to transport it to the tomb at a reasonable cost. Based on these expectations, a modular manufacture system was developed for the money tree, which culminated in the material form of the money tree as we found today. It is also important to note that the popularity of the money tree was in a wide context in which burial objects became commodities and were accessible to a wide range of people, which brought about a wide social influence from the material goods.[20]

A close examination of the way in which the tree branches and top decorations were cast further reveals the motivation for the creation of this novel burial object. The casting of money trees is usually linked to the casting of the *wuzhu* 五銖 coin in the Han (figure 95). One reason is that coins have been found in large quantities on all money trees, and many of them are cast with the *wuzhu* characters, just as they are cast on the real coins, but smaller and thinner.[21] Moreover, the archaeological discovery of the Han *wuzhu* coin mould suggests that the shape of the money tree may

FIGURE 95. BRONZE MOLD FOR THE CASTING OF THE HAN *WUZHU* COIN. AFTER HE ZHIGUO 2006A: FIG. 3.3.

have been inspired by the method used in coinage. Susan Erickson suggests that the notion of 'money growing on trees' may had its basis from the stack casting process, in which 'coins were cast in moulds which could be arranged in layers enabling the caster to produce many coins in one pour' (Figure 96).[22] 'A central channel branched out to smaller, individual channels which led to the coins. After the coins were cast, they were still linked to the channels and had the appearance of a branch with coins attached. Considering the size of the coin in relation to the branch and the placement of the coins to the side of the main channel, the mould and also the cast form before the coins were broken away from the centre channel, may have inspired the idea of the coins growing from branches.'[23]

However, there is still a big discrepancy between the shape of the money tree and the way that several layers of coins are attached to the channels of the mould. In fact, the most direct borrowing of the creation of the money tree seems to be from the coinage using stacked moulds, which greatly increased the work efficiency. In a similar way, the identical branches attached to the money tree trunk could be produced through one pour into some stacked moulds.[24] The inscription of '*zhu zhu* 鑄株 (money tree)'

---

[18] Ledderose 2000: 1.
[19] Ledderose 2000: 5. To explain on this point, Ledderose provides two examples: 'a petty Shang aristocrat owning a few small bronzes could take pride in the fact that his vessels displayed the same kind of décor and were cast in the same technique as the gorgeous bronze sets of the mightiest ruler'; 'a minor Qing-dynasty official serving food to his guests on porcelain plates made in Jingdezhen could relish the thought that the emperor in his palace also used dinner sets from Jingdezhen, even if those differed in decoration and quality'.
[20] For the study of the market of burial objects and the tombs and burial objects as commodities, see Tang Guangxiao 2002. Tang Guangxiao suggests that there was a highly developed funerary market in Eastern Han Sichuan. Many pottery burial objects produced from the same moulds have been found in tombs in different areas in Sichuan, indicating that the scale of the production of burial objects was relatively large and a local funerary market had formed.
[21] For the comparison of the *wuzhu* characters on the coins of the money trees and the real coins, see He Zhiguo 2006a: 73-75. For the process of coin manufacture in early China see the illustrations from the studies on the *Tiangong kaiwu* 天工開物 (Pan Jixing 1989: figs. 3.5 and 3.6).

[22] Erickson 1994: 14.
[23] Erickson 1994: 14.
[24] For more information on moulds and stacked moulds for metallurgical works in the Eastern Han, see Joseph Needham's *Science and Civilization in China*, volume 5, part II on early metallurgy (Wagner 2008: 150-158). Moulds and stacked moulds for metallurgical works had been highly developed in Eastern Han. Individual moulds were fabricated in the same way as pictorial bricks, by pressing wet clay into 'pattern boxes (模盒)', then removing, drying and baking. (This has well explained the similar pictorial styles on the money trees and the local pictorial bricks.) See also Li Jinghua 1985: 51. Then identical moulds are stacked, 'with a common casting gate, so that a very large number of castings can be made in a single pour, saving time, labour, metal, fuel, and refractory material' (Wagner 2008: 154). 500 mould-stacks were found on the site of a Han

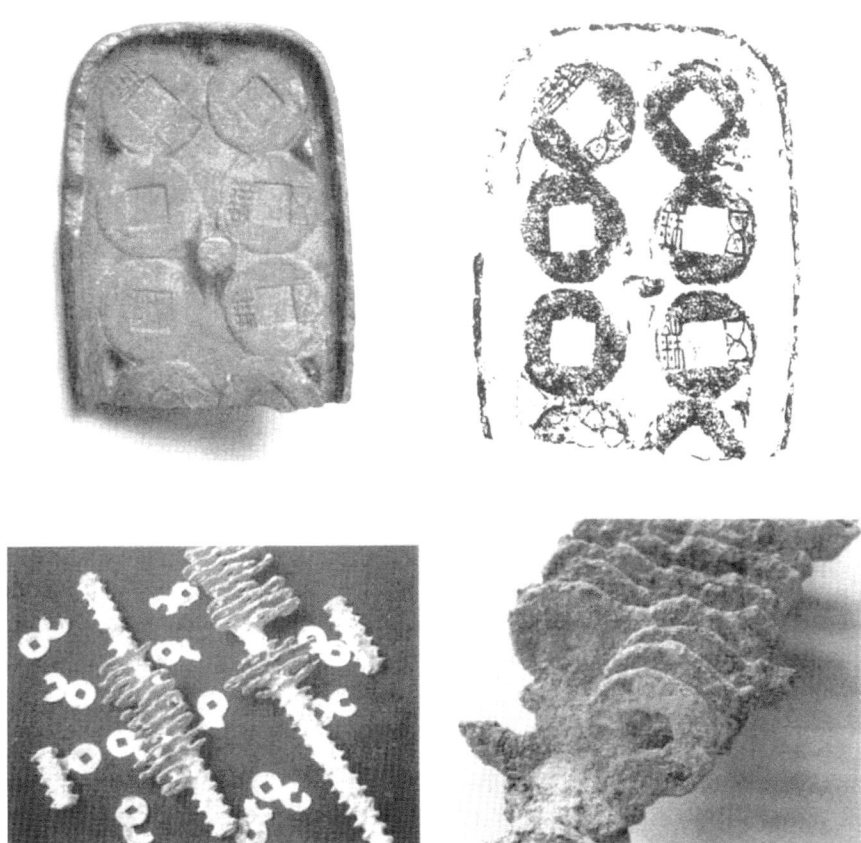

FIGURE 96. BRONZE MOULD FOR THE CASTING OF THE *WUZHU* COIN FROM XICHANG IN SICHUAN AND PRODUCTS OF THE *WUZHU* COINS FROM XICHANG. AFTER HE ZHIGUO 2006A: FIGS. 3.10, 3.11, 3.12 AND 3.13.

FIGURE 97. RUBBING OF THE RELIEF ON ONE SIDE OF THE STONE COFFIN NO. 3 FROM JIANYANG IN SICHUAN, WITH THE INSCRIPTION OF "*ZHUZHU* 鑄株". AFTER NEIJIANG SHI WENGUANSUO AND JIANYANG XIAN WENHUAGUAN 1991: FIG. 11.

beside a money tree-like image on the stone coffin in an Eastern Han tomb in Jianyang 簡陽 in Sichuan is often quoted by researchers as the evidence of the symbolic meaning of the three-dimensional bronze money (figure 97).[25] It seems that the inscription also suggests that the two-dimensional bronze pieces of the money tree were inspired by the appearance of the contemporary coin with two-dimensional inscriptions and square decoration.

foundry in Wenxian 溫縣 in Henan (Henan sheng bowuguan 1978). See Wagner 2008: 155, fig. 76 for an example of a stack-mould.

[25] Neijiang shi wenguansuo 內江市文管所 and Jianyang xian wenhuaguan 1991: 20-25, figs. 11 and 12.

Indeed, before the popularity of the money tree, individual illustrated two-dimensional bronze sections were rare. One example is a section of bronze tree branch with the illustrations of people and the *bi* discs, dated to the Western Han, found in a tomb in Yanyuan 鹽源 in Sichuan.[26] He Zhiguo suggests that this two-dimensional section might be the early stage in the development of the shape of the money tree, as both the Yanyuan section and the money tree feature two-dimensional representation of tree branches attached with figures and *bi* discs.[27] More importantly, this early section implies that there was a local tradition of making two-dimensional bronze sections for decoration, which was possibly developed later through the creation of the money tree as an assemblage of two-dimensional sections.

By and large, the money tree was designed to be economically produced in large numbers and at a reasonable quality. As long as there was an elaborately illustrated mould for the tree branches, equally good-looking money trees could be mass produced. In fact, some identical money tree branches have been found on different money trees located in separate areas.[28] Though the two-dimensional image might look less lively, it was technically easy to achieve and was relatively cheaper. And after artfully assembling the two-dimensional modules, a three-dimensional form delivered the viewers a complete sense of volume and visual complexity that is aesthetically pleasing.

Some researchers have noted that there are some similarities between the shapes of the money tree and the contemporary or earlier tree-shaped lamp found in a tomb.[29] A bronze tree-shaped lamp was found in the tomb of the king of the Zhongshan 中山 Kingdom in Pingshan 平山 in Hebei, dated to the late Warring States period.[30] Both the base and the upper part are made of bronze. Lamp cups are supported by 14 branches, on which three-dimensional figurines of birds and monkeys perch and play. The whole lamp was assembled from eight individual parts, which can be joined with their built-in tenon-and-mortise work. Susan Erickson further traces the tree-shaped object to the bronze tree found in Sanxingdui 三星堆 in Sichuan, dated to the Shang period.[31] The tree is nearly 4 metres high. It has nine branches, on which perch birds. A serpent-like creature is climbing the trunk. 'The base was cast in one piece, in a mould divided on the axes of the tripod legs. The trunk of the tree was made separately and joined to the base by running a separate pour of metal between them. The branches, assembled from about a hundred individually made components, were joined to the trunk in the same way.'[32]

Compared to the tree-shaped lamp and the Sanxingdui tree, the money tree is much simpler in production. In addition, its pottery base saved costs in casting or moulding a three-dimensional bronze base, similar to the bases of the tree-shaped lamp and the bronze tree. The use of two different materials - bronze and clay in one burial object is rarely seen in the Han or earlier. Again, this seems to be a local invention in an attempt to save manufacturing cost. Considering that the tombs containing the tree-shaped lamps usually belong to the royal family or high ranking official, it is more reasonable to regard the money tree as an economic invention dedicated to a wide range of people.[33] He Zhiguo suggests that the highest official positions of the tomb occupants of the tombs containing the money tree was the prefect. For the remaining ones, some were from powerful families, some were lesser commoners.[34]

Not only the novel way of production and assemblage reveals the tomb occupants' efforts to create a new ritual object of their own, but also the content of the illustration on the bronze tree and the pottery base. Growing money seems to be the most significant symbolic meaning of the money tree, as every money tree features large amount of coins on the branches, taking the place of the leaves. Many coins have inscriptions of the *wuzhu* characters, which make them closer to real money. Michael Nylan argues that the Eastern Han tombs in Sichuan were equipped to represent a well-protected home for the afterlife, based on real life. And the money tree was made to provide long-term financial support for the family after death.[35] An illustration of a money tree base from Yong'an 永安 in Santai can be regarded as self-explanatory regarding the meaning of money trees (figure 98).[36] On the main body of the pottery base, people are harvesting coins which are growing on the tree. In Eastern Han, this kind of blatant pursuit of money was only well depicted in the Sichuan area, which forms a stark contrast with the eastern part of the empire in southern Shandong and northern Jiangsu, where pictorial carvings in the stone tombs and shrines were important means to represent the tomb occupants as role models of Confucian scholars who despised money and fame.[37] The popularity of money trees among a wide range of people throughout the area can be seen as the legitimatization of this blatant pursuit.

---

[26] Liangshan zhou bowuguan 1999: 27, fig. 12. The Yanyuan bronze tree piece was found in a burial pit dated between the Warring States and Western Han. The height is between 0.16-0.20 metres. It illustrates two horses, three persons and four *bi* discs on the tree branches.
[27] He Zhiguo 2006a: 39.
[28] He Zhiguo 2006a: 123.
[29] Erickson 1994: 27-28 and He Zhiguo 2006a: 255-270.
[30] Li Xueqin 1986: 37 and pl. 104 .
[31] Erickson 1994: 28 and Bagley 2001: 116-118.
[32] Bagley 2001: 116.
[33] A bronze tree-shaped lamp with nine branches is found in tomb no. 1 in Guixian 桂縣 in Guangxi. The tomb occupant is identified to be a high ranking official in the Guilin 桂林 Commandery in the Nanyue 南越 Kingdom in early Western Han. See Guangxi zhuangzu zizhiqu bowuguan 1988: 91. Two bronze tree-shaped lamps with 12 branches and 13 branches respectively were found in an Eastern Han tomb at Leitai 雷臺 in Wuwei in Gansu. The tomb occupant is identified to be the governor of Zhangye 張掖. See Gansu sheng bowuguan 1974.
[34] He Zhiguo 2006a: 261. He Zhiguo's main evidence is from the tomb inscriptions recording the title and name of the tomb occupants. Most of the inscriptions on the tombs containing the money tree record the names of the tomb occupants without any official title. According to the Han tradition, if there was anyone with an official position, it would be mentioned in the tomb inscription.
[35] Nylan 2003: 377.
[36] He Zhiguo 2006a: 151, fig. 7.1.
[37] See Powers 1991: 41-50. Powers suggests that the pictorial carvings in the stone shrines and tombs in Eastern Han Shandong and Jiangsu do not 'merely mark rank or inspire awe but actually promotes certain points of view inherent in the classical texts' (Powers 1991: 41-42).

Figure 98. Rubbing of a pottery money tree base illustrating the scene of collecting coins from Yong'an in Santai. After He Zhiguo 2006a: fig. 3.2.

The other images on the base and on the tree surrounding the coins can be regarded as the further effort by the tomb occupants, who endeavoured to legitimatize their pursuit of money within an already well-established belief system. Many money trees follow a similar scheme of decoration, in which the Queen Mother of the West plays a major role. For example, the money tree found at Wanfu 萬福 in Guanghan in Sichuan contains six layers of branches.[38] The top layer has two main branches. Each of the five lower layers has four main branches. All the main branches have a Queen Mother of the West in the centre, sitting on her throne flanked by a tiger and a dragon. The money tree from the cliff tomb Hejiashan M2 in Mianyang in Sichuan has a Queen Mother of the West on the apex of the tree, sitting on a similar tiger and dragon throne.[39]

It is generally thought that by the end of the 1st century BC, the Queen Mother of the West had become the main almighty deity in the folk belief system. The following event in the spring of 3 BC recorded in the *Han shu* has been frequently quoted to prove this point: 'In the area east of the passes, the people were exchanging tokens in preparation for the advent of the Queen Mother of the West. They passed through the commanderies and kingdoms, moving west to within the passes and reaching the capital city. In addition, persons were assembling to worship the Queen Mother of the West, sometimes carrying fire to the rooftops by night, beating drums, shouting and frightening one another.'[40]

Based on studies over the last half century, Elfriede Knauer makes a brief summary of the records on the Queen Mother of the West in Chinese texts. 'The Queen Mother of the West can be traced through a period of more than two thousand years in Chinese texts and visual representations. She first appears as a directional deity on the oracle bones in the Shang period. After a long break, she becomes a powerful shaman and teacher of privileged human beings and a mediatrix between the earthly and heavenly realms during the Warring States. She is bestower of happiness, who imparts longevity and immortality to humankind, as well as an omnipotent cosmic deity during the Han and beyond.'[41]

The cult of the Queen Mother of the West developed with local variations, which can be discerned from her appearance on pictorial carvings on mortuary monuments and on burial objects. In southern Shandong and northern Jiangsu, the Queen Mother of the West is usually depicted as a lunar deity, paired with the King Father of the East, the solar deity. These two deities together were regarded as the 'talisman of cosmic bliss'.[42] In Sichuan, the Queen Mother of the West was the one and the only highest deity in control of the heavenly realm, as elaborately depicted on a tomb brick found at Xinfan 新繁 in Chengdu (figure 99).[43] In the centre of the picture is the Queen Mother of the West sitting on a throne flanked by a dragon and a tiger. On the left of the picture is a figure holding a *ge* 戈 scepter in his hands. This figure is usually believed to be the *Daxingbo* 大行伯, who is in charge of guiding the procession for the Queen Mother of the West and can protect the procession of the tomb occupant on his way to the heavenly realm. Next to the *Daxingbo* is the *Sanzuwu* 三足鳥, a bird with three legs, who is responsible for bringing food to the Queen Mother of the West. Below the bird is an ox-like beast, who stays on the mountain where the *Sanzuwu* lives. On the right of the picture is a fox with nine tails. It dwells on the mountain of the Queen Mother of the West and symbolizes prosperous offspring. Below the fox is a hare holding a *lingzhi* 靈芝, a kind of miraculas medicine, who is in charge of making herbal medicine for the Queen Mother of the West. Right below the Queen Mother of the West is a leaping toad, holding a bow in one hand, which corresponds to the Han and earlier folk tale that Chang E 嫦娥, the wife of archer Hou Yi 后羿, flied to the moon after stealing the panacea from the Queen Mother of the West and was transformed into a toad.[44]

---

[38] Bagley 2001: pl. 98.
[39] Bagley 2001: pl. 97.
[40] *Han shu*: 342. '關東民傳行西王母籌,經歷郡國,西入關至京師.民又會聚祠西王母.或夜持火上屋,擊鼓號呼相驚恐.' Another record says that 'the people were in a state of high excitement...running around hither and thither, exchanging tokens...and worshiping the Queen Mother of the West. 民相驚動,讙讙奔走,傳行詔籌祠西王母.' *Han shu*: 1312. There is a third record saying that: 'the population were running around in a state of alarm, each person carrying a manikin of straw or hemp. People exchange these emblems with one another, saying that they were carrying out the advent procession. Large numbers of persons, amounting to thousands, met in this way on the roadsides, some with disheveled hair or going barefoot... In the village settlements, the lanes, and paths across the fields they held services and set up gaming boards for a lucky throw, and they sang and danced in worship of the Queen Mother of the West. They also passed around a written message, saying, "the Mother tells the people that those who wear this talisman will not die."...By the autumn these practices had abated. 哀帝建平四年正月,民驚走,持或椒一枚,傳相付與,曰行詔籌.道中過逢多至千數,或被髮徒踐,或夜折關,或踰牆入,或乘車騎奔馳,以置驛傳行,經歷郡國二十六,至京師.其夏,京師郡國民聚會里巷仟佰,設張博具,歌舞祠西王母,又傳書曰:母告百姓,佩此書者不死.不信我言,視門樞下,當有白髮.至秋止.' *Han shu*: 1476. The translations are after Loewe 1979: 98-100.
[41] Knauer 2006: 62-63.
[42] Loewe 1979: 88.
[43] Liu Zhiyuan 1983: 132, fig. 103.
[44] Liu Zhiyuan 1983: 131-134.

Figure 99. Rubbing of a pictorial tomb brick illustrating the Queen Mother of the West and her attendants from Xinfan in Chengdu. After Chang Renxia, Jiang Yingju and Gao Wen 1988: pl. 248.

The figures on this pictorial brick cover the basic members in the local cult of the Queen Mother of the West, with minor changes from time to time. These figures are partly incorporated into the iconographic system centring on the Queen Mother of the West on the money tree. For example, a branch of the money tree from Gaocao 高草 in Xichang 西昌 in Sichuan shows a pair of attendants below the throne of the Queen Mother of the West (figure 100).[45] The attendant on the left is depicted as the hare making herbal medicine for the Queen Mother of the West. The attendant on the right is likely to be the toad, who is holding a square vessel in one hand to receive the elixir streaming out of the ganoderma-like plant. On the money tree branch from Maowen 茂汶 in Sichuan, we see a very similar arrangement of the hare and the toad as attendants of the Queen Mother of the West.[46]

The images that are prevalent in the tomb pictorial carvings, blessing the tomb occupants with a happy life in the heavenly realm, are also incorporated into the iconographic system of the money tree, under the control of the Queen Mother of the West. For example, on the money tree branch from Chengdu, acrobats and dancers are illustrated on the left of the Queen Mother of the West, providing entertainment in the heavenly realm as prevalently depicted on pictorial tomb stones and bricks.[47] The money tree branch from Mianxian 勉縣 in Shaanxi illustrates the procession of a carriage to the heavenly realm, another popular theme in Han tomb mural painting.[48] He Zhiguo further notes that the line drawing style on some thin bronze tree bronzes is very close to that on some pictorial tomb bricks in Eastern Han Sichuan.[49] It is very likely that the clay mould for

Figure 100. A money tree branch illustrating the Queen Mother of the West and her attendants from Gaocao in Xichang in Sichuan. After Liu Shixu 1987: fig. 1.

making money tree branch was borrowed directly from that for making tomb bricks. In this way, the pursuit of money was systematically incorporated into the already well-established belief system centring on the Queen Mother of the West. Consequently, a new distinguished local belief system obtained legitimacy.

It is notable that many Buddha-like figures have been found on the money trees. According to He Zhiguo, most of these Buddha-like figures are located on the tree trunk in a total number of 67 on 21 money trees (figure 101).[50] These figures feature a halo, knot on top of the head and symbolic postures of hands. They all wear a robe draping from their shoulders, with parallel lines depicting drapery. Wu Hung suggests that these representative Buddhist elements lost their original religious meaning. Instead, they were exploited to represent a local belief in immortality and the pursuit of a heavenly realm after death, as many Buddha-like figures are found in the context of a local depiction of the heavenly realm in the tomb.[51]

---

[45] He Zhiguo 2006a: 56-57, figs. 2.61 and 2.62.
[46] He Zhiguo 2006a: 228, fig. 10.8.
[47] He Zhiguo 2006a: 23, fig. 2.2.
[48] He Zhiguo 2006a: 63, fig. 2.69.
[49] He Zhiguo 2006a: 120-121. See also the techniques shared by making moulds for pictorial bricks and for metallurgical works in early China (Wagner 2008: 154), mentioned early in the footnote of this chapter.
[50] See He Zhiguo 2006a: 199-201 for more information on these tree trunks. Five are in private overseas collections. Three are from the cliff tomb no. 5 and no. 14 in Zhongxian in Chongqing (Zhang Caijun 1985). Two are from the Baihuzui 白虎嘴 cliff tomb no. 19 and no. 49 in Mianyang (He Zhiguo 2004: 61-62). The rest are from Fengdu 豐都 (He Zhiguo 2002a), Kaixian 開縣 (Luo Erhu 2005b), Anxian 安縣 (He Zhiguo 2002b), Mianyang (He Zhiguo 1991b; He Zhiguo 2004: 66), Zitong (He Zhiguo 2006b), Qingzhen 清鎮 (Luo Erhu 2001), Hanzhong (He Xincheng 1989), and the collection of the China National Museum.
[51] Wu 1986: 301-303.

FIGURE 101. A MONEY TREE TRUNK WITH THE IMAGE OF A BUDDHA FROM THE CLIFF TOMB HEJIASHAN M1 IN MIANYANG. AFTER HE ZHIGUO 1991C: FIG. 19.

FIGURE 102. A MONEY TREE BASE ILLUSTRATING A SEATED BUDDHA FROM PENGSHAN. AFTER NANJING BOWUYUAN 1991: FIG. 44.

And due to the unsystematic nature of the indigenous cults, 'the themes of Buddhist art were absorbed and used in a piecemeal manner, becoming isolated icons and symbols'.[52] For example, on a money tree base excavated from a cliff tomb in Pengshan sits a Buddha-like figure, whose location is usually occupied by the Queen Mother of the West on the money tree base (figure 102). It is very likely that to the local people the role of Buddha was equal to that of the Queen Mother of the West. On the lintel of the cliff tomb at Mahao in Leshan sits another Buddha-like figure, which is placed next to a dragon's head to suggest an entrance to an immortal world as elaborately illustrated in the front chamber.[53] In particular, on the trunks of some money trees, Buddha-like images are replaced by bear-like figures with a halo.[54] The bear-like figure is usually interpreted as the *fangxiangshi*, the exorcist, who often appears in the Han tomb art.[55] The interesting combination of the Buddhist element, the halo and the traditional figure may imply that the Buddha-like figure was understood as an exorcist in some cases. Compared to some occasional discoveries of Buddha-like figure on stone carvings in the tomb and on some pottery burial objects, Buddha-like figures are more frequently found on the money trees. If Buddha-like figures are perceived as borrowing the representational form from other religions, the money tree exhibits an effort to absorb various representational forms to enrich a newly created ritual object.

The most important representational feature of the money tree as a ritual object is the form of tree. In other words, the meaning of the money tree as a ritual object is embedded in the metaphor of tree, which according to Susan Erickson, symbolized the axis mundi.[56] She also notes that in the *Baihu tong* 白虎通, it mentioned that there should be a tree on the altar of the Gods of the Earth and of the Millet. Thus the people could see and worship it.[57] This is reminiscent of the possible ritual use of the money tree in the tomb, among the tomb occupants' family members. The scene is like a tree planted on an altar.

He Zhiguo further points out that the tree form of the money tree symbolizes fertility, the notion of which can be traced back to primitive time when people were still struggling to survive and were thus impressed by the vitality of the tree.[58] He provides two examples of the copulating scene on the branch and the base of the money tree to relate the money tree to the meaning of fertility. For example, the money tree branch from Hujiabian 胡家扁 in Santai in Sichuan shows two copulating horses, and the base of the money tree from Shitang 石塘 in Mianyang in Sichuan illustrates two copulating deer.[59] Moreover, he notes that on all Eastern Han pictorial tomb

---

[52] Wu 1986: 273.
[53] Wu 1986: 269-270.
[54] He Zhiguo 2006a: 111, fig. 5.9.
[55] Erickson 2003: 443.
[56] Erickson 1994: 27-33. Erickson mentions that in the *Huainan zi* 淮南子, the *jianmu* 建木 tree is mentioned as a cosmic tree. It grew on the peak of the Kunlun Mountain. The rising peak and the cosmic tree formed a vertical axis, via which one could ascend to the world of immortality. See *Huainan zi*: 432. '昆仑之丘,或上倍之,是谓凉风之山,登之而不死....建木在都广,...盖大地之中也. If one climbs to a height double that of the Kunlun Mountains, (that peak) is called Cool Wind Mountain. If one climbs it, one will not die. ...The Jian Tree on Mt. Duguang, ...It forms a canopy over the centre of the world.' The translation is after Major 1993: 158. Though the exact meaning of the money tree is yet to be explored, the illustrations on it confirm the notion of 'the tree as a pivot to connect the human and the spiritual worlds'. Erickson 1994: 30.
[57] Erickson 1994: 33. *Baihu tong*: 89. '社稷所以有樹何?尊而識之,使民望見即敬之. Why is there a tree on the altar of the Gods of the Earth and of the Millet? That it may [thereby] be honoured and recognized. [Thus] the people may see it from altar and worship it.' The translation is after Tjan 1952: 384.
[58] He Zhiguo 2006a: 164-166.
[59] He Zhiguo 2006a: 164, figs. 7.22 and 7.23.

bricks in Sichuan illustrating the copulating scene, a tree is present, implying the close link between the tree and fertility.[60] In this sense, the placement of the money tree in the centre of the tomb, surrounded by the tomb occupants' family, could convey the wishes for the continuity of the family through prosperous offspring, just as the cliff tomb structure, which was expected to be a continuous construction for a prosperous family. In addition, it could be imagined that when the cliff tomb was first built by the first generation of the family, placing the one and the only money tree for the family into the tomb would be a meaningful act, as it symbolized the initial establishment of the family and heralded the family's prosperous future. The meaning of that act could be just like the sense delivered by the inscription in the cliff tomb HM3 at Xindu in Chengdu mentioned in the previous chapter: 'The ancestor of the Duan family was from the eastern province. After the ancestors came to the west, they moved the household to this place. Since we resided in Guanghan, we built tombs here to establish our roots. The situation that the souls were homeless has been changed since then. In the eighth month of the third year of Yongjian, Duan Mengzhong built this dwelling for the afterlife. The inscription was carved on the stone door to be shown to the offspring.'[61]

FIGURE 103. THE STONE COFFIN OF WANG HUI FROM LUSHAN IN SICHUAN. AFTER GAO WEN 2011: 211.

3. Stone Coffin

By contrast with the money tree, which symbolized the collective identity of the multiple tomb occupants in a tomb, the stone coffin was important to the exhibition of individual identity within the tomb (figure 103). Through examining the pictorial schemes on the stone coffins, we will see that though the pictorial carvings in the tomb and on important burial objects, such as the money tree, provided the tomb occupants with an overall environment to enter the heavenly world, individual tomb occupant still needed to take the journey to the heavenly world individually as depicted in the pictorial carvings on the stone coffin. In addition, the stone coffin displayed different statuses, preferences and the experiences of the individual tomb occupants. More importantly, the stone coffin is crucial to understanding the relationship between multiple tomb occupants in the tomb and the ways in which the cliff tomb functioned as an integrated entity through its structure, mural painting and burial objects.

Eastern Han stone coffins are mainly distributed in the Sichuan Basin. Many of them are in the cliff tombs. Some are also found in the brick tombs. A small portion of them have pictorial carvings on the surface. A total of 70 pictorial stone coffins have been published with their content in detail.[62] The rectangular body of the stone coffin is usually sculpted from a whole piece of sandstone, the same stone that the cliff tomb is tunnelled into. Some have carvings on the surface to resemble the timber framed walls of the dwelling. The thickness of the surrounding walls is around 10 centimeters. The bottom is thicker, between 15 and 20 centimetres. The lid is separately sculpted, with a thickness between 10 and 15 centimetres.[63] The shapes of the pictorial and non-pictorial stone coffins are basically the same. Pictorial carvings are usually on the outside of the surrounding walls, sometimes are also on the top and the two ends of the lid. Most of the carvings are in low relief with the details carved in intaglio lines. Sometimes, high reliefs are also used, especially when depicting the lid as the roof of a house.

Metaphor of Architecture

The themes of pictorial carvings on the stone coffins are mainly from those of the pictorial carvings in the stone or

---

[60] He Zhiguo 2006a: 165. See also Feng Xiuqi 1995 on the interpretation of such scenes illustrated on the Eastern Han pictorial bricks in Sichuan.
[61] Chen Yunhong, Zhang Yuxin and Wang Bo 2007: 41.
[62] The discovery and study of stone coffins in Sichuan are closely related to those of the cliff tombs. The earliest record on the stone coffin in Sichuan is in the *Li shi* 148-149: '棲柱作崖棺 (built stone coffin next to the pillar)', quoted previously on the cliff tomb in Pengshan containing the Zhang Bingong inscription. When the cliff tombs were re-discovered in the late 19th and early 20th century by the Western travelers and scholars, the stone coffins appear in their records on the cliff tombs. See Barber 1882; Bishop 1916; Segalen 1917; Bedford 1937. In the 1930s and 1940s, when more local surveys and excavations of the cliff tombs in Sichuan were made by trained local scholars and archaeologists, the function of the stone coffin was confirmed to be for burial purpose, and the pictorial carvings on the stone coffin became to be partially identified as various historical or mythological stories or figures. Many intact pictorial stone coffins with elaborate carvings were found during the period. For the most famous one, the coffin belonging to Wang Hui 王暉, found in Lushan 蘆山, see Gao Wen 2011: pl. 3. Since the 1950s, pictorial stone carvings have been published in the archaeological reports on the cliff tombs or brick tombs in Sichuan in archaeological journals. Some were also collected from the survey of the local relics organized by the local archaeological institutes. Most of the pictorial stone coffins have been collected in the following catalogues: Luo Erhu 2002, Gao Wen and Gao Chenggang 1996 and Gao Wen 2011. For a recent comprehensive study of the pictorial stone coffins in Sichuan see Luo Erhu 2000.
[63] Luo Erhu 2002: 222.

Figure 104. Rubbing of a coffin wall from Dayi in Sichuan. After Gao Wen 2011: 151.

brick chamber tombs and the cliff tombs as discussed in the previous chapter. Though carved only on a small area of the four surrounding walls of the coffin, sometimes also on the coffin lid, the themes involve various auspicious figures and images and many historical or mythological stories, which are organized to form a meaningful pictorial programme within the architectural framework of the stone coffin. Though sometimes the lid of the stone coffin is not carved to imitate a roof, there are many architectural parts or buildings carved on the surrounding walls of the coffin to establish the relationships between different figures and images through an architectural framework. For example, a pair of the *que* pillars are often carved on one end of the coffin,[64] and pavilions or dwellings for living with many architectural details, including the windows, pillars, eaves, doors and steps, are often illustrated on one of the long side walls of the coffin (figure 104).[65] A possible explanation of this phenomenon is that the pictorial stone coffin was influenced by the pictorial stone chamber tombs.[66] Consequently, the spatiality of the chamber tomb was transplanted to the stone coffin and the pictorial programme in the stone chamber tomb was condensed in the pictorial carvings on the stone coffin.[67]

As mentioned in the previous chapter, the pictorial scheme in the stone chamber tomb illustrates the journey of the tomb occupant to the heavenly world.[68] Similarly, the pictorial stone coffin can be viewed as a micro-stone chamber tomb, the pictorial carvings on which depicted the process for the individual occupant in the coffin to enter the heavenly world.[69] A stone coffin from a cliff tomb in Xinjin is a good example of this process.[70] On one of the long sides of the coffin, a carriage procession of the tomb occupants is proceeding to a *que* pillar gate on the left end of the picture, which may suggest the entrance to the heavenly world (figure 105).[71] There is a Red Bird (*zhuque* 朱雀) with an animal head appliqué holding a ring (*pushou* 鋪首) carved on one end, which may represent the beginning of the journey, since the *pushou* image often appears on the tomb door to represent the knocker. On the other end of the coffin, there are the god and goddess Fu Xi and Nü Wa, suggesting the successful arrival in the

---

[64] For examples, see Gao Wen 2011: 126, 147, 225, 227.
[65] For examples, see Gao Wen 2011: 123, 124, 137, 146, 149, 150, 151.
[66] Xin Lixiang suggests that the cardinal directions illustrated on the stone coffins are the same to those carved in the shrine and stone chamber tombs in east China. Xin Lixiang 2000: 280. The cardinal directions are usually exhibited through the carvings of four auspicious animals, the red bird, the white tiger, the turtle with snake, and the dragon. In addition, Wu Hung suggests that the 'positional significance' of the carvings in the Wu Liang shrine as suggested by W. Fairbank can also be found in the pictorial carvings on different sides of the stone coffin. Wu 1987: 14. Fairbank 1941: 35.
[67] A similar trend in imitating architecture can also be found on the Roman sarcophagi, which are described by Jas Elsner as 'body-sized micro-architecture'. The lid of the Roman sarcophagus is often carved to resemble a roof. Elsner 2010: 3. Sometimes figures or scenes are placed in columnar context 'to create a semblance of architecture in a physically restricted space'. The reference of these sarcophagi to actual buildings to some extent answered the 'emotional needs' of their occupants. It also entails debates on the identities of the patrons of these sarcophagi, who were 'seeking an appropriate form of burial' and had interests in 'architecture as a symbolic form'. What follows is the question of 'what kind of building is envisioned here': is it a temple, a house or a theatre? As 'architectural form helped with distinguishing' and was a form of self-representation. The use of the metaphor of architecture exhibits the deep understanding of the human body, life and death, as shown in an example of the carvings on the Velletri sarcophagus, on the lowest register of which is a 'metaphor of architectural support', illustrating a 'vivid image of the human burden in life and death' (Thomas 2010: 407).
[68] For examples, see the Yi'nan tomb and the Cangshan tomb in Shandong.
[69] Both Wu Hung and Xin Lixiang suggest that the pictorial stone coffin can be regarded as a micro-cosmos. See Wu 1987 and Xin Lixiang 2000: 280. Wu Hung uses the example of the stone coffin from a cliff tomb in Xinjin to show the relationship between the carvings on different sides of the coffin. The lid of the coffin is carved with the story of the cowherd (*niulang* 牛郎) and the weaving maiden (*zhinü* 織女), the celestial association of which determines its position on the coffin. The *que* pillar gates guarded by a rider carved on one end represents the entrance to the heavenly world, and the carriage procession of the tomb occupant carved on one of the long sides is proceeding to the entrance. The other end is carved Fu xi and Nü Wa, suggesting the arrival in the heavenly world. The other long side is illustrated with the scenes of the heavenly world, where the immortals are playing the *liubo* 六博 game.
[70] Gao Wen 2011: 197-200.
[71] Gao Wen 2011: 198. For the interpretation of the frequently found *que* image on the stone coffins in Sichuan, see Xin Lixiang 2000: 271-287.

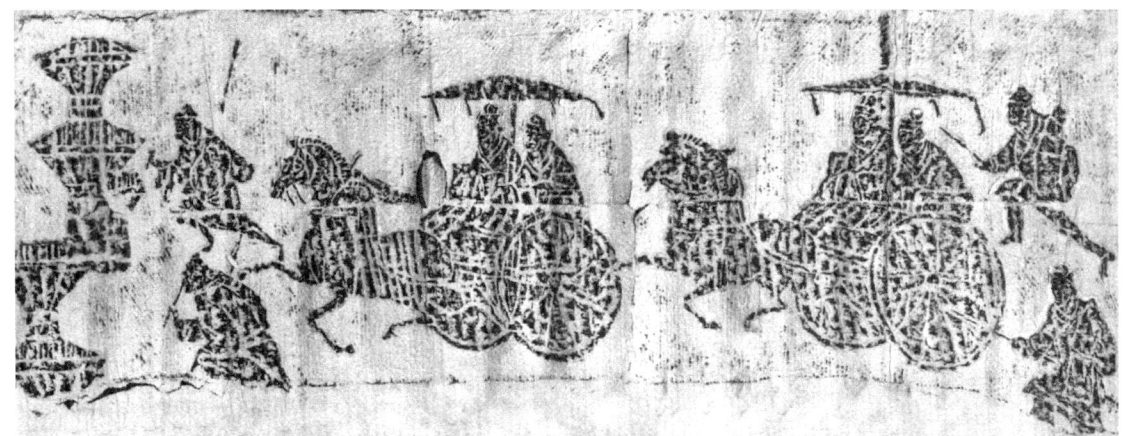

Figure 105. Rubbing of a coffin wall from Xinjin in Sichuan. After Gao Wen 2011: 198.

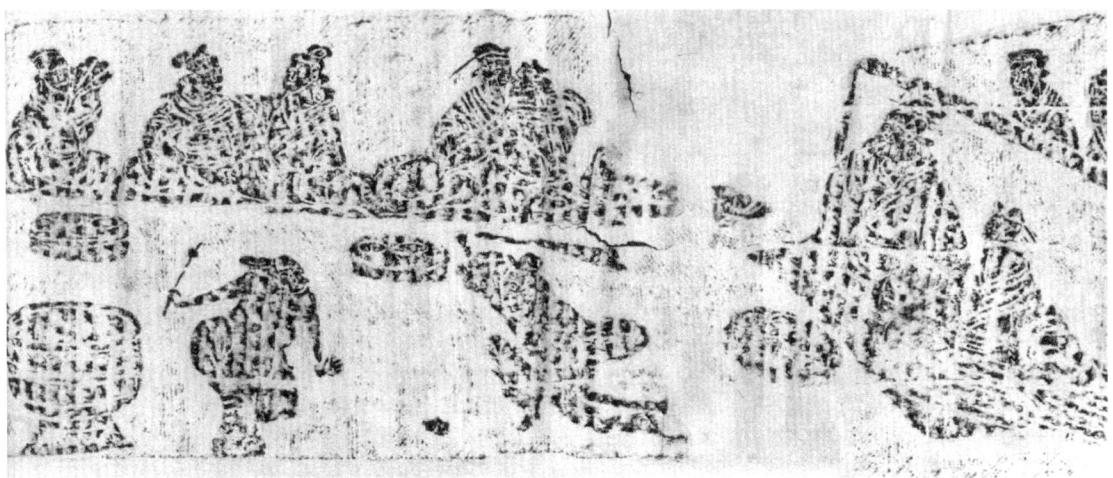

Figure 106. Rubbing of a coffin from Xinjin in Sichuan. After Gao Wen 2011: 197.

heavenly world. On the other long side of the coffin, the tomb occupant couple have completed their journey and have become members of the family ancestors, who are sitting over a low table with a drinking set, watching a performance, like those depicted in the burial chamber for memorial in the tomb (figure 106).

In some cases, the stone coffin is only carved to exhibit some architectural features without any narrative scenes showing details of the journey to the heavenly world. Instead, the transformation from a newly deceased to the member of the world of immortality is expressed through the metaphor of architecture. For example, a stone coffin found in Chengdu has a lid in the shape of a gabled roof. Only two of its surrounding walls carry carvings.[72] A *que* pillar is carved on one end. A façade of a dwelling is carved on one of the long sides (figure 107). A figure is standing in the half-open door in the centre of the façade. On top right is a window with railings carved in open-work. Two

birds are playing with an unidentified object. On the left are a weapon shelf and a lying dog.

The half-open door is crucial to the understanding of the structure of the stone coffin. It appears very often in Han mortuary art, especially on the pictorial stone coffins in Sichuan. On the stone coffin from Hejiang 合江, a half-open door with a figure inside is carved similarly in the middle of the long side of the coffin which illustrates the façade of a dwelling.[73] On the stone coffin of Wang Hui 王暉 in Lushan 蘆山, a winged immortal is looking outward from the half-open door carved on one end of the coffin (figure 108).[74] According to the location of the half-open door on the stone coffin, it possibly plays a role similar to that of the *que* pillar gate, which represents the entrance to the heavenly world.[75] The half-open state

---

[72] Chengdu wenwu kaogu yanjiusuo and Qingbaijiang qu wenwu baohu guanlisuo 2010: pls. 16 and 17.

[73] Gao Wen 2011: 345.
[74] Gao Wen 2011: pl. 3.
[75] For example, see the stone coffin found the cliff tomb no. 2 at Hongying 紅纓 in Neijiang 內江. The coffin lid is in the shaped of a gabled roof. The body of the coffin is consisted of 13 pieces of sandstone panels, with one end of the coffin in the shape of a pair of door panels which

Figure 107. Carvings and rubbing of one side of a stone coffin from Chengdu. After Chengdu wenwu kaogu yanjiusuo and Qingbaijiang qu wenwu baohu guanlisuo 2010: pl. 17.

Figure 108. Rubbing of the relief on one end of the stone coffin of Wang Hui from Lushan in Sichuan. After Zhongguo huaxiangshi quanji bianji weiyuanhui 2000b: pl. 91.

emphasizes the situation of a newly deceased who has not yet completed his journey to the heavenly world. In this sense, the half-open door is an architectural metaphor for a journey to the heavenly world, which is sometimes illustrated as the carriage procession on the stone coffin.[76]

Some coffins cut into the cliff in the cliff tomb also only exhibit architectural details in a similar way to the above mentioned stone coffin. They look like a small house-shaped tomb within a large tomb resembling a dwelling. For example, the built-in coffin in the tomb Tiantaishan 天臺山 M1 in Santai is tunnelled into the rear wall of the front side chamber of the tomb, right behind the chamber's entrance, which is framed by a pair of columns with bracket sets (figure 109).[77] The façade of the coffin is depicted as the front of a house, with a row of eaves on top and the window and door below. The window is carved with parallel horizontal railings, and a dog is lying by the side of the door. At the bottom of the façade are two toad-like creatures carrying the whole house-shaped coffin on their backs. If the whole cliff tomb is viewed as a courtyard dwelling for a large family, this stone coffin is the bedchamber for an individual household or a person in

---

can be opened or closed, which is reminiscent of the *que* pillar gates that usually appear at the same location suggesting the entrance to the heavenly world. Luo Erhu 2002: 227.

[76] The half-open door image in mortuary art of the Han and later periods has been extensively studied. It has been generally agreed that the meaning of this image varies, depending on its context. For the summary of the half-open door image in Han burials, see Goldin 2001. For a brief literature review of the studies on the half-open door image in mortuary art in China, see Deng 2011: 181. The half-open door image also appears in the previously mentioned stone chamber tomb in Cangshan in Shandong. On the east wall of the main burial chamber, a carriage is driving toward the half-open door. The figure standing inside the door seems to be prepared to receive the visitor. Wu Hung suggests that the half-open door here represents the great boundary between this life and the afterlife. Wu 1994: 100-103. This interpretation again relates the pictorial scheme of the stone chamber tomb to that of the stone coffin and the illustration of the architectural part is crucial to understand their relationship.

[77] Sichuan sheng wenwu kaogu yanjiuyuan, Mianyang shi bowuguan and Santai xian wenwu guanli suo 2007: pl. 83.

FIGURE 109. A BUILT-IN COFFIN IN THE TIANTAISHAN TOMB IN SANTAI. AFTER SICHUAN SHENG WENWU KAOGU YANJIUYUAN, MIANYANG SHI BOWUGUAN AND SANTAI XIAN WENWU GUANLI SUO 2007: PL. 83.

one of the courtyards. In fact, such built-in stone coffins in the cliff tombs have textual records like the 'cliff tomb inscription of Zhang Bingong' mentioned in the previous chapter. As recorded in the inscription, a built-in stone chamber next to the column in the tomb was specifically built for Zhang Yuanyi's father and younger brother.[78] The built-in stone coffin like the one in Tiantaishan M1 is very prevalent in Santai and Zhongjiang.[79]

By and large, the pictorial stone coffin represents a condensed understanding of the heavenly realm and ways to access it. First, it continued to adopt the notion that stone was related to immortality, which was also embedded in the cliff tomb architecture. Second, it presented the prosperous afterlife and the heavenly realm in the framework of architecture, as in the cliff tomb architecture, which emulated the dwelling for the living. Third, it used an architectural metaphor to pave the way for its occupant to achieve a place in the heavenly realm. Lillian Tseng suggests that 'to make the invisible visible, both artisans and viewers relied on tacit knowledge for coding and decoding'.[80] This process of coding and decoding and the common knowledge on the heavenly realm were well represented on the pictorial stone coffin.

Hierarchy and Distinction

The above observation entails the following questions. Why did the pictorial stone coffin imitate the tomb structure with architectural details? If the pictorial stone coffin was influenced by the pictorial stone chamber tomb, why did the pictorial stone coffin only become popular in Sichuan instead of in eastern China where the pictorial stone chamber tomb was prevalent?

A closer examination of the context where the stone coffin was found may provide some clues to this question. In the cliff tomb Tianhuishan M3 in Chengdu, 14 coffins made of different materials were found distributed in seven burial chambers. 11 are made of clay, two are made of stone and one is built of bricks.[81] One of the two stone coffins is built directly on the stone platform carved out of the wall of a northern side chamber in the cliff tomb, without any pictorial decoration on the surface. The other stone coffin is carved out of a whole piece of sandstone with a lid carved into the shape of gabled roof. The pictures on the surrounding walls of the coffin also partly depict the coffin as a house. On one side, an elevation of a house is depicted, with a scene of a kitchen and a scene of receiving guests in the living room. In the kitchen, a fish is hung from the rafter and a dog is tied up. The opposite side illustrates Fu Xi and Nü Wa holding the sun and the moon, accompanied by the *Zhuque* bird and a big fish. Two unidentified figures stand on the right hand part of the picture. One end of the body of the coffin depicts a pair of the *que* pillar gates, implying the entrance to the heavenly realm. The other end is an unfinished sketch of a house. Compared with the rest of the simple clay and brick coffins without any decoration, this house-shaped stone coffin is both labour and time consuming and aesthetically pleasing. The most extraordinary burial object in the tomb, a gilded iron book knife is found inside this coffin, which further

---

[78] *Li shi*: 148-149.
[79] For examples of the built-in coffins in Santai see Sichuan sheng wenwu kaogu yanjiuyuan, Mianyang shi bowuguan and Santai xian wenwu guanli suo 2007: pls. 83, 310 and 313. See Sichuan sheng wenwu kaogu yanjiuyuan, Deyang shi wenwu kaogu yanjiusuo and Zhongjiang xian wenwu baohu guanli suo 2008: pls. 5, 23 and 31 for examples in Zhongjiang.
[80] Tseng 2011: 9.

[81] Liu Zhiyuan 1958: 93-95. Only a pile of bricks were found on the location where the brick coffin was supposed to be.

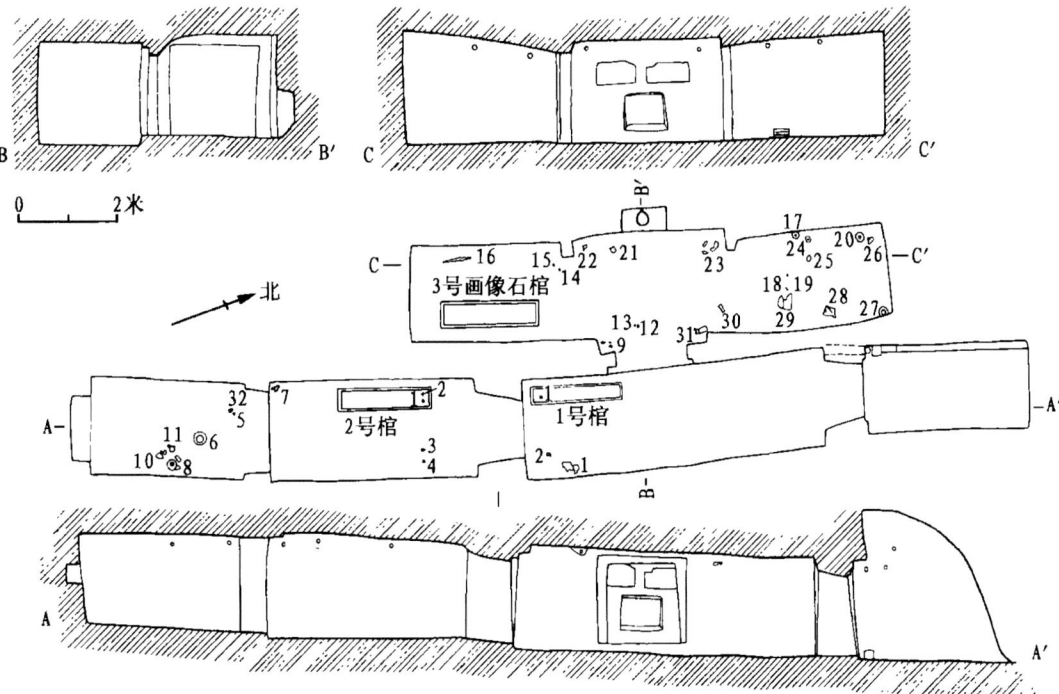

Figure 110. Plan of the cliff tomb HM3 in Xindu in Sichuan.
After Chen Yunhong, Zhang Yuxin and Wang Bo 2007: fig. 8.

distinguishes the occupant of this coffin from the rest of the occupants in lesser coffins.[82] Seemingly, the use of a stone coffin was crucial to establishing a hierarchy in the relationship between the large number of tomb occupants in one tomb. Even those tomb occupants who were from the same family or closely related in some way had their positions presented by their material representation.

Similar hierarchical order constructed by coffins of different materials and quality can be observed in many other cliff tombs containing several tomb occupants. In the cliff tomb HM3 in Chengdu, three coffins are found (figure 110).[83] The only pictorial stone coffin is located in one of the side chambers, next to a pottery coffin which was damaged (figure 111). The other two coffins are made of clay, located at the side of the main chamber. This tomb has been mentioned previously, as it is the one found with the 'inscription of Duan Mengzhong'. The author of the archaeological report attributes the pictorial stone coffin to Duan Mengzhong, since he had the highest status in the tomb.[84] The two clay coffins may have belonged to Duan Mengzhong's offspring, as this is what he wished in his inscription: '以示子孫 (to be shown to the offspring).' The styles of the pottery burial objects and the date in the inscription (AD 138) reveal that the tomb may have been in use from early to late Eastern Han, more than half a century,[85] which means that the founder Duan Mengzhong's wish for a prosperous family was to some extent realised. Duan Mengzhong's stone coffin also adopts the architectural metaphor, though the coffin lid was simplified as an arched roof instead of a more complicated gabled roof. One side of the body of the coffin is also illustrated with an elevation of a dwelling. From left to right, are a pavilion in which is tied a dog, an armory, a hall in which a *ding* vessel is flanked by two cranes, and a half-open door. The opposite side is carved with the Queen Mother of the West in the centre, sitting on her tiger and dragon throne, surrounded by her retinue. One end of the coffin is routinely carved with the *que* pillar gates. A plant, identified to be ganoderma, is carved on the other end.

The function of the stone coffin to distinguish its occupant is further enhanced by the inscription of '金棺 (gold coffin)' on the rim of the opening of a stone coffin in a brick tomb at Qingbai 青白 in Xindu 新都 in Sichuan.[86] The value of the material of the coffin, stone, was compared to that of gold. Consequently, the status of the occupant was exhibited through his 'gold coffin'. Sometimes, the pictorial stone coffins also distinguish themselves from the other non-pictorial stone coffins. For example, in a cliff tomb at Guitoushan 鬼頭山 in Jianyang, all the six coffins are found made of stone, four of which have pictorial carvings (figure 112).[87] According to the author of the

---

[82] Liu Zhiyuan 1958.1: 101. The inscription on the knife: '光和七年 (the seventh year of Guanghe) 廣漢工官□□□服者尊長保子孫宜侯王□宜□' dates the knife to AD 184 and confirms it as a product of the imperial workshop in Chengdu. In the Han, such gilded book knife was called the *jinma shudao* 金馬書刀 (gold horse book knife), was used to scrape off the incorrect characters on the bamboo slip. Usually, it was always brought along by the literati of the time. See Sun Ji 1991: 280.
[83] Chen Yunhong, Zhang Yuxin and Wang Bo 2007: 40-49.
[84] Chen Yunhong, Zhang Yuxin and Wang Bo 2007: 47.

[85] Chen Yunhong, Zhang Yuxin and Wang Bo 2007: 47.
[86] Luo Erhu 2002: 247. The complete inscription reads '永元八年四月廿日造此金棺. This gold coffin was made on the twentieth day of the fourth month in the eighth year of Yongyuan (AD 96)'.
[87] Neijiang shi wenguansuo and Jianyang xian wenhuaguan 1991: 21-25.

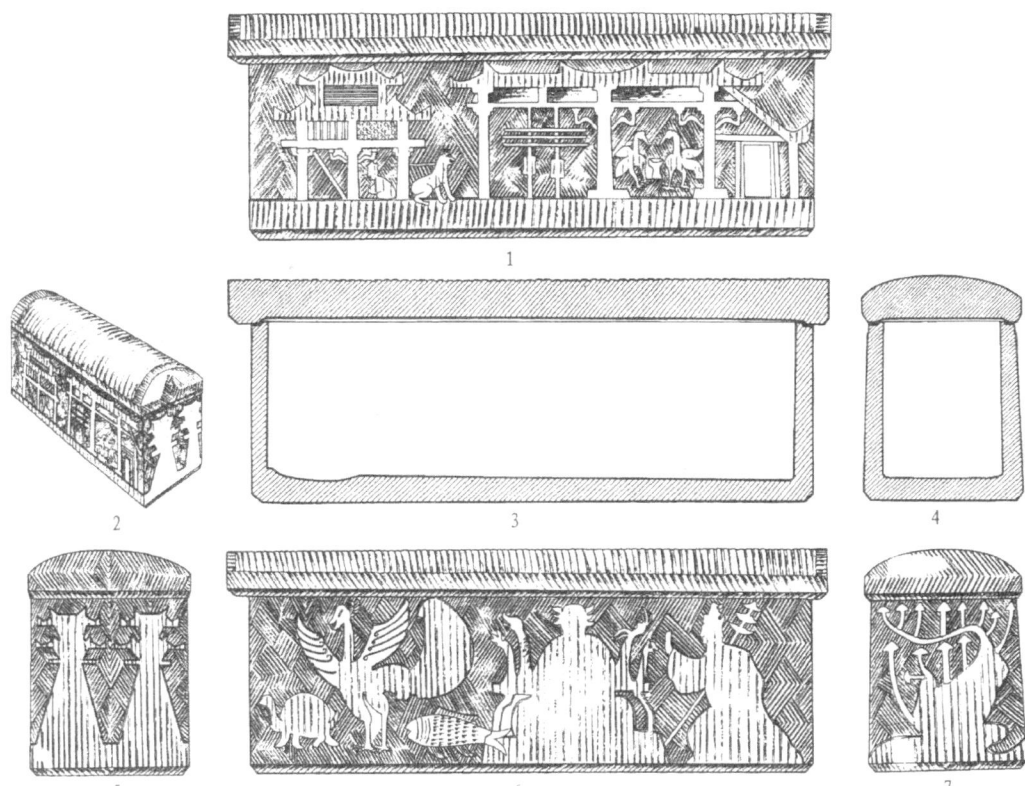

FIGURE 111. A PICTORIAL STONE COFFIN FROM THE CLIFF TOMB HM3 IN XINDU IN SICHUAN. AFTER CHEN YUNHONG, ZHANG YUXIN AND WANG BO 2007: FIG. 14.

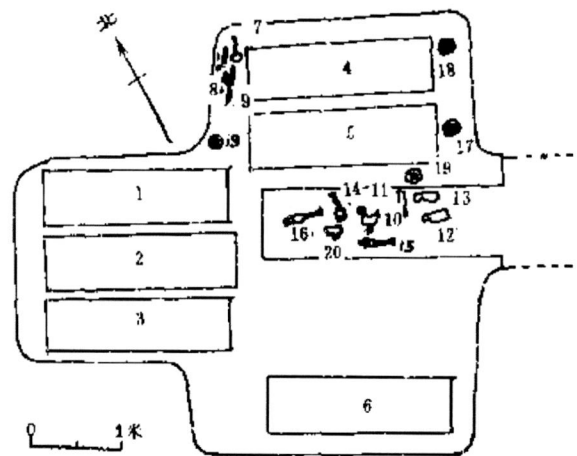

FIGURE 112. PLAN OF THE CLIFF TOMB AT GUITOUSHAN IN JIANYANG IN SICHUAN. AFTER NEIJIANG SHI WENGUANSUO AND JIANYANG XIAN WENHUAGUAN 1991: FIG. 2.

archaeological report, the tomb occupants were members of a large family who were interred at different times. Coffins 1 to 3, located side by side at the end of the tomb, were interred firstly, followed by coffins 4 to 6 located in the side niches of the tomb.[88] The earliest coffins 1 to 3, especially coffin 2 and coffin 3 may belong to the founders of the tomb, whose status may have been as high as the previously mentioned tomb founder Duan Mengzhong, who owned the most distinguished coffin, as coffin 2 and confin 3 exhibit the most elaborate and similar pictorial carvings. They both feature pictures accompanied by labels, which are extremely valuable for interpreting the various images appearing in the Han tomb art (figure 113).

Although pictorial stone coffin represented the special status of its occupant, the choice of making pictures on a single coffin instead of in the whole tomb reflected the relatively tight budget of the family.[89] As discussed in the previous chapter, few cliff tombs are extensively decorated and in the few cliff tombs with decoration, the pictorial carvings only appear in the most crucial part. Instead, the small area of decoration on individual stone coffins is more economical and feasible.

It was probably out of an economic consideration that the depiction of important images related to immortality and the heavenly realm were concentrated on the stone coffin of the most important member in the family. Later generations also had the chance to make their own pictorial coffins as long as they could afford it, just like the pictorial coffins 4 and 5 of the later generation in the previous mentioned cliff tomb at Guitoushan. To make a pictorial stone coffin or not was probably a personal choice. If one could not afford to make the whole tomb elaborately decorated, he could at least do something to his

---

[88] Neijiang shi wenguansuo and Jianyang xian wenhuaguan 1991: 25.

[89] Luo Erhu 2002: 246-247.

FIGURE 113. RUBBING OF THE RELIEF ON ONE SIDE OF THE STONE COFFIN NO. 2 FROM JIANYANG IN SICHUAN. AFTER NEIJIANG SHI WENGUANSUO AND JIANYANG XIAN WENHUAGUAN 1991: FIG. 9.

own coffin. In many cases, after the first generation built the tomb, what the later generation needed to do was only to build their own coffins. The picture on the stone coffin was thus both dedicated to the whole family and to the important individual.

Display of Individuality

Like the Han tomb pictorial carvings, the carvings on the pictorial stone coffins also have a set of existing motifs from which the artisans or the patrons could choose.[90] The previously mentioned architectural features are among these existing pictorial motifs. There were also historical and mythological stories from these existing pictorial motifs for the patrons to choose to display their individuality among the other family members interred in the cliff tomb. According to the biography of Zhao Qi 趙岐 in the *Hou Han shu*, he designed his own tomb when he was alive. Inside the tomb, he painted three wise ministers and a gentleman, Zi Chan 子產, Yan Ying 晏嬰, Shu Xiang 叔向 and Ji Zha 季札, 'as guests flanking his own portrait in the position of the host'.[91] All these figures are Confucian paragons from previous dynasties. Li Daoyuan (AD 472-527), who visited Zhao Qi's tomb in the 6th century, concluded that Zhao Qi 'expressed the values he had always admired' through designing the tomb mural.[92] Wu Hung suggests that the figures that Zhao Qi chose to use in his tomb were neither filial sons nor hermits, which 'constituted two lasting traditions' in the mortuary art. He suggests that the 'unconventional' figures chosen by Zhao Qi were the outcome of Zhao Qi's specific choice, related to his life experience. If we examine Zhao Qi's biography, we will see that he was forced to hide from political persecution in AD 158 and was later helped by a righteous man, Sun Song 孫嵩, who provided Zhao Qi with a place in which to hide until the end of the persecution. Zhao Qi finally regained his name as a respectable Confucius scholar. Wu Hung suggests that one of the figures painted in Zhao Qi's tomb is well-known

for his devotion toward a deceased friend and therefore could be dedicated to Sun Song by Zhao Qi to show his gratitude. The other three figures of the famous politicians from the past could allude to his political aspirations.[93]

Unfortunately, as Wu Hung points out that among the existing Han tombs, no pictorial carvings can be 'definitely identified as the outcome of the patron's specific intention', due to the lack of textual record of the tomb occupant's biography.[94] However, the potential personal preference can be identified through the choice of different historical stories on different pictorial stone coffins. And there is indeed a stark contrast between the pictorial carvings in the burial chambers of the cliff tombs, which are primarily the stories of the filial sons, and the stories carved on the stone coffins, which involve many other virtues, not only filial piety.

So far, ten stories with different themes have been identified on the Eastern Han pictorial stone coffins in Sichuan. The stone coffin no. 11 from Luzhou, the stone coffins no. 5, no. 7 and no. 11 from Changning are carved with the story on the First Emperor who obtained the *ding* 鼎 vessel from the Si 泗 River.[95] A built-in stone coffin from a cliff tomb in Xinjin contains the carvings of two stories (figure 114). One is on the meeting of Confucius with Laozi. The other one is about an eminent woman who righteously attended her widowed mother-in-law, but was wrongly put into prison.[96] The stone coffins no. 1 and no. 13 from a cliff tomb in Xinjin are both carved with the story of the eminent woman, Gaoxing 高行.[97] A stone coffin from Shehong 射洪 is carved with two stories: a story on Qiu Hu 秋胡 who did not recognize his wife and attempted to flirt with her; and a story on Ji Zha who kept his promise to his dead friend (figure 115).[98] The stone coffin no. 5 from a cliff tomb in Xinjin contains the carving of Emperor Wu of

---

[90] Xing Yitian uses the term '格套 *getao* (standard motif)' to describe the individual motifs from the assemblage of the frequently used motifs in Han mortuary art. Xing Yitian 2011. Wu Hung also notes the existence of the standard motifs on the pictorial stone coffins in Sichuan. Wu 1987: 79-80.
[91] *Hou Han shu*: 2124. '先自為壽藏,圖季札,子產,晏嬰,叔向四像居賓位,又自畫其像居主位,皆為讚頌.' The translation is after Wu 2010: 183.
[92] *Shuijing zhu*: 798. '敘其宿尚矣.' The translation is after Wu 2010: 183.

[93] Wu 2010: 183.
[94] Wu 2010: 183.
[95] Gao Wen 2011: 296-297, 307, 310-311.
[96] Gao Wen 2011: 412-413.
[97] Gao Wen 2011: 152, 187.
[98] Gao Wen 2011: 237-238. The story on Jizha also appears on the stone coffin no. 16 from a cliff tomb in Luzhou. Gao Wen 2011: 320-321. The story on Qiu Hu is also found on the stone coffin no. 4 from a cliff tomb in Xinjin and two built-in coffins in different cliff tombs in Xinjin. Gao Wen 2011: 160-161, 411, 415. The story of Shi Kuang is also carved on the stone coffin from Shehong and on a built-in coffin in a cliff tomb in Shehong. Gao Wen 2011: 238, 426-427.

FIGURE 114. ONE SIDE OF A BUILT-IN COFFIN IN A CLIFF TOMB IN XINJIN IN SICHUAN. AFTER WEN YOU 1955: FIG. 43.

FIGURE 115. RUBBING OF THE RELIEF ON ONE SIDE OF A STONE COFFIN FROM SHEHONG IN SICHUAN. THE STORY ON QIU HU'S WIFE IS ON THE LEFT. THE STORY ON JI ZHA IS ON THE RIGHT. AFTER GAO WEN 2011: 237.

the Western Han who sent an exorcist (*fangshi*) to visit and make sacrifice to a famous mountain (figure 116).[99] On the stone coffins no. 8 and no. 14 from a cliff tomb in Xinjin, there are scenes depicting Emperor Wu conferring a title on the alchemist Luan Da 欒大 (figure 117).[100] The story of the filial son Dong Yong 董永 is found carved on the stone coffin no. 22 from a tomb in Hejiang.[101] The popularity of the various stories on the pictorial stone coffins in Sichuan form a stark contrast to both the cliff tomb stone carvings of the filial sons and the popularity of the illustration of the stories of the 24 filial sons on stone coffins of the later periods in Luoyang in Henan.[102]

So far, there has been no discussion on this diverse choice of historical stories on the Eastern Han stone coffins in Sichuan. An examination of the content, the illustration and the location of these stories on the stone coffins may offer some insight. Among the ten stories, there are three stories on eminent women, on Gaoxing, the wife of Qiu Hu and the devoted daughter-in-law. These stories have not been found in the pictorial carvings in the burial chamber of the cliff tombs, but two of them appear among the eight stories on eminent women exhibiting standard Confucius virtues carved in the Wu Liang shrine. The stories on Gaoxing and the wife of Qiu Hu on the stone coffins in Sichuan are identified through the inscriptions in the Wu Liang shrine. According to the *Lienü zhuan* 列女傳 written by Liu Xiang 劉向 in the 1st century BC, Gaoxing was a widow in the Liang state. She was well-known for her beauty and was pursued by many noblemen even the king of Liang. However, she refused to remarry. She explained to the king of Liang that she had to take care of her children and be faithful to her dead husband. In order to show the determination, she cut off her nose with a knife.[103]

The story about the wife of Qiu Hu is also recorded in the *Lienü zhuan*.[104] Qiu Hu had left his wife to fill an office in another state. When he returned home after five years, he

---
[99] Gao Wen 2011: 166.
[100] Gao Wen 2011: 171, 188-189.
[101] Gao Wen 2011: 354-355.
[102] Some of the stories of the filial sons had already become standard motifs in the Eastern Han mortuary structures. 13 stories of the filial sons have been illustrated in the Wu Liang shrine. For detail, see Wu 1989b: 272-304. A standard version of the stories of the 24 filial sons formed both in textual record and in illustration since the Northern Wei (AD 386-557).

[103] *Lienü zhuan*: 58. For full text and translation see Appendix 1.
[104] *Lienü zhuan*: 68. For full text and translation see Appendix 1.

FIGURE 116. RUBBING OF THE RELIEF ON ONE SIDE OF THE STONE COFFIN NO. 5 FROM XINJIN IN SICHUAN.
AFTER GAO WEN 2011: 166.

FIGURE 117. RUBBING OF THE RELIEF ON ONE SIDE OF THE STONE COFFIN NO. 7 FROM XINJIN IN SICHUAN.
AFTER GAO WEN 2011: 171.

did not recognize his wife, who was picking mulberries by the roadside. He flirted with his wife and was rejected. His wife then scolded him because he did not fulfill his responsibility to his family, as a son and as a husband. Finally, his wife drowned herself in the river.

Compared to the other six stories about eminent women carved in the Wu Liang shrine,[105] the stories on Gaoxing and the wife of Qiu Hu not only praise the virtue of these two women, but also emphasize their roles as wives and mothers in the family. Gaoxing emphasized their responsibility to their children. The wife of Qiu Hu further pointed out the responsibility of a man as husband and father in the family. The illustration of these stories on the stone coffins may reflect the patron's admiration of the responsibilities to the family emphasized in the stories. In addition, the pictorial carvings on the coffin as a public display to the future mourners from the family into the tomb would remind the offspring to be dedicated to the continuous prosperity of the family. As mentioned previously in this chapter, the decorated stone coffin in a cliff tomb usually belonged to the most important member of the family, especially the founder of the tomb. Therefore, it is natural for the patron of the most elaborate coffin to emphasize the duties to the family through pictorial carvings on the coffin.

One example of the story on the wife of Qiu Hu is carved on the right of one of the long surrounding walls of the stone coffin in a cliff tomb in Xinjin.[106] In the picture, Qiu Hu's wife is picking mulberries from a tree. Her basket is on the ground. Qiu Hu is standing next to her, with a sword at his waist, seemingly to suggest his official position. The other four figures with sword at their waists on the same wall have not been identified. The whole pictorial scheme of the coffin provides the micro-cosmos and visual journey for the patron to get to the heavenly world, similar

---

[105] For detail of these stories, see Wu 1989b: 252-272.

[106] Gao Wen 2011: 160-161.

to the one also found in Xinjin described previously in this section. The two ends are carved with images of immortals. The paired deer and the auspicious beast, the *bixie* 辟邪, which are often illustrated together at the tomb entrance as tomb appeasing beasts, are carved on one side to suggest the beginning of the journey to the heavenly world. The winged spirits, *yumin* 羽民, are carved on the other side, to show the arrival at the heavenly world.[107] On the side opposite the story of the wife of Qiu Hu, the carriage of the tomb occupant is driving toward the heavenly world. Compared to the other coffin from Xinjin mentioned earlier, the only difference is that the scene of the heavenly world on the side opposite the carriage scene is replaced by this story. The patron might think that the heavenly world is already depicted on one end, showing the images of the winged immortals, and hence he could have more personal expressions illustrated on the coffin.

The story of Gaoxing on the coffin from a cliff tomb at Dengshuang 鄧雙 in Xinjin is depicted within the same pictorial scheme.[108] Unfortunately no information on the images on the two ends is available. It is possible those pictures have suffered severe erosion or do not exist. The story of Gaoxing is illustrated on the right side of a wall. There are two figures under a tree. The seated figure on the right is holding a mirror in one hand and a knife in the other hand, trying to cut off her nose. The standing figure on the left holding a scepter is the envoy sent by the king of Liang asking for marriage. There seems to be a story with three figures carved on the left side, which have not been identified. The story is carved opposite the side with the carriage scene, in which the tomb occupant is in the carriage driving to the entrance to the heavenly world carved on the right side.

It seems that several stories often appear together on the coffin, though only a few have been recognized. These stories very likely allude to the patron's virtues or the virtues he admired. On the coffin from Shehong, the story of the wife of Qiu Hu is illustrated together with the story of Ji Zha, which was also painted by Zhao Qi in his own tomb as a Confucian paragon, as mentioned earlier. The story of Qiu Hu with the horse and his wife picking mulberries is carved on the left side of the scene. Jizha is the figure on the right side, bowing to a tree with his sword hanging on the trunk. His story is recorded in the *Shi ji*: 'When Ji zha was on his way to the north as an envoy, he met the ruler of the Xu state, who admired Ji Zha's sword but did not dare to tell Ji Zha. Ji Zha knew this, however he did not give out his sword for he still had the mission. When he came back to the Xu state, the ruler of Xu was already dead. Ji Zha took off his sword and hung it on the tree at the tomb of the ruler of Xu. Ji Zha's attendant asked: "The ruler of Xu is already dead. Whom was this for?" Ji Zha said: "I decided to give this sword to him long time ago. The fact that he is already dead does not change my mind."'[109] Ji Zha had long been remembered for his commitment to his friend, which was probably admired by both Zhao Qi, who was helped by such a friend as mentioned earlier, and the patron of the coffin with the illustration of the story.

A built-in coffin in a cliff tomb in Xinjin exhibits the carvings on the coffin to some extent emulating those in the shrines, such as the Wu Liang shrine.[110] The pictorial coffin thus became a medium for the important family ancestor to present his historical perspective to the off-spring. On the front side of the coffin, the figures of Laozi, Confucius, Zengzi 曾子, Cangjie 倉頡, Shennong 神農, the young gentleman of Langmai 郎麥 and the governor of Donghai 東海 are carved sequentially from left to right. Each figure has an inscription above to be identified.[111] These figures constitute three main themes in human history as carved on the main wall of the Wu Liang shrine: the kings, the sages, and the paragons of Confucius virtue.[112]

In the middle of the scene on the coffin are Shennong and Cangjie, who were arranged among the ancient kings in the Wu Liang shrine to represent the most important figures in human history. Shennong was long regarded as the inventor of medicine and agricultural products. In the scene, he is trying a wild plant for the purpose of a medical test. Cangjie was believed to be the inventor of Chinese characters. In the scene, he is sitting on the ground, next to Shennong.

The three figures on the left illustrate the story between two sages, Laozi and Confucius. According to the *Shi ji*, Confucius used to go to the Zhou capital Luoyang with his students to visit Laozi. During the time, Laozi was a high ranking official. Confucius showed great respect to Laozi, which was vividly depicted on the coffin, where Confucius with his student Zengzi at the side is bowing to Laozi, who appeared as a more senior figure in the scene. In the end of the meeting, Laozi said that 'I have heard that the rich and great offer farewell gifts of money while the good offer advice. I am neither rich nor great but, unworthy as I am, have been called good; so let me offer you a few words of advice.' Then he said, 'a shrewd observer, prone to criticize others, riskes his own life. A learned man who exposes the faults of others endangers himself. A filial son must never thrust himself forward, and neither may a good subject.'[113]

---

[107] For the record on the *yumin*, see *Shanhai jing*: 183. '羽民國在其東南,其為人長頭,身生羽.一曰,在比翼鳥東南,其為人長頰. The kingdom of the *yumin* is in the southeast. They have head of human and feathers on the body. There is a saying that the paired birds are in the southeast, with faces of human.'
[108] Gao Wen 2011: 186-187.
[109] *Shi ji*: 1459. '季札之初使,北過徐君.徐君好季札劍,口弗敢言.季札心知之,為使上國,未獻.還至徐.徐君已死,於是乃解其寶劍.繫之徐君樹而去.從者曰: "徐君已死,尚誰予乎?"季子曰: "不然.始吾心已許之,豈以死倍吾心哉!"'
[110] Gao Wen 2011: 412-413.
[111] From left to right, the inscriptions are '老子 (Laozi)', '孔子 (Confucius)', '曾子 (Zengzi)', '倉頡 (Cangjie)', '神農 (Shennong)', '郎麥少君 (the young gentleman of Langmai)' '東海太守 (the grand administrator of Donghai)'. The inscription '郎麥少君' has been destroyed.
[112] For detail on how these themes are elaborated within a historical framework through carvings on the wall in the Wu Liang shrine, see the previous chapter and Wu 1989b: 142-217.
[113] *Shi ji*: 1909. '吾聞富貴者送人以財,仁者送人以言.吾不能富貴,竊仁人之號,送子以言,曰:聰明深察而近於死者,好議人者也.博辯廣大危其身者,發人之惡者也.為人子者毋以有己,為人臣者毋以有己.' The translation is after Yang and Yang 2008: 213.

Wu Hung suggests that the illustration of the story on Confucius and Laozi here emphasizes the higher status of Laozi as recorded in the *Shi ji*. However, in contemporary east China, where Confucianism was the dominant school of thinking, the depiction of the same story on the stone emphasizes the respect of Laozi for Confucius, in which Laozi walked outside to receive Confucius in person.[114] Wu Hung attributes this difference in illustrations to the prevalence of Daoism in Sichuan during the time, since Laozi was the sage of Daoism.[115] It is very likely that the patron of this coffin also believed in Daoism.

The two figures on the right side illustrate the story of an eminent woman in Donghai. Although this woman is not among the eight eminent women depicted in the Wu Liang shrine, she is described in the *Lienü zhuan*, which is a collection of the main stories of the eminent women of the time, and the *Han shu*.[116] The woman in Donghai became a widow at a young age and then lost her son. But she took care of her widowed mother-in-law devotedly. In order to reduce her burden, the mother-in-law committed suicide. The woman was accused to be the murderer and was executed. The governor of Donghai finally realized he made a serious mistake and made apology to this filial woman at her tomb.

To some extent, the pictures on this built-in coffin can be regarded as a condensed version of human history depicted in the Wu Liang shrine. The patron could select stories according to his personal life experience, belief and preference to fit into the three main themes to exhibit his own historical perspective to his offspring.

4. Conclusion

Huang Xiaofen suggests that the set of pottery models of the stove, the well, the granary and the toilet constituted the most important part of the Han burial objects, which continued to provide the tomb occupants with the necessities in their afterlife.[117] Many similar cases have been found in the cliff tombs in Sichuan. However, in the cliff tombs, many of these necessities, especially the stove and the granary were already carved into the cliff as parts of the tomb architecture. This brings up the question of whether the burial objects and the built-in facilities as parts of the tomb structure can substitute each other.

An examination of the burial objects of the stove and the stoves carved in the cliff tombs show that the burial objects and the tomb structure have separate functions. The stoves carved in the cliff tombs, as discussed in Chapter 2, establish an overall institutional relationship within the framework of the tomb structure. The burial objects of stoves represent individual needs embedded in this relationship. To some extent, the tomb structure exhibits the collective identity of the tomb occupants.

However, some burial objects, such as the money tree, which symbolizes the collective identity, function in a way similar to the tomb structure. The general relationship between the burial objects and the tomb structure is a dialogue between individual identity and collective identity, which together contribute to the representation and function of an organized community in the cliff tomb.

---

[114] For the scene, see the carving in the Wu Liang shrine. Wu 1989b: 43, fig. 25.
[115] Wu 1987: 79.
[116] *Han shu*: 3041-3042.

[117] Huang Xiaofen 2003: 217-227.

Chapter 5
Conclusion

In his book *Archaeology and Colonialism*, Chris Gosden mentions a small flask made in Corinth around 650 BC.[1] It was used for holding perfumed oil. It is decorated with curvilinear animal and human figures and motifs. The shape of the flask can be traced back to Cyprus in the 9th century BC. Its cable ornament and palmette decoration go back to Egyptian and Oriental stonework and metalwork, which makes the flask a part of the 'Orientalising' trend in Greek material culture. In addition, its decoration techniques also exhibit the 'Orientalising' trend. The black paint and the outline are acheived through incision. However, these techniques were originally used on metalwork. But now they are applied to pottery in a new manner. In this sense, he points out that 'a perfume flask does not exist on its own, but is held in a complex set of connections to earlier items, some of which were made in metal not pottery, and through links to many other contemporary items of metal, stone and pottery'.[2]

The studies on the characteristics of the cliff tomb also show that the cliff tomb was held in a complex set of connections to the development of the burial forms, and existed through links to many other contemporary burial forms, the brick chamber tomb, the stone chamber tomb, and the princely rock-cut tomb. These connections and links formed to a large extent through the incorporation of the Sichuan area into the empire which began in the 4th century BC. It was in this context, a series of factors contributed to the formation and popularity of the cliff tombs in Sichuan. The hilly topography and the soft sandstone, easy to cut, provided the natural condition for the development of the cliff tombs. The decision to make use of this natural condition was affected by many factors rooted in the social background, which are also the main focus of the analysis of the characteristics of the cliff tomb in this study.

An important characteristic of the cliff tomb is that it conformed to the imperial order of the empire that was reflected from the cultural aspect, namely the burial culture. It followed the contemporary trend in tomb construction to use stone as the building material. Though the form of the burial cave was not extensively used all over the empire, the use of the large scale rock-cut tomb by the imperial members in eastern China in an earlier period provided a model for the cliff tomb as a burial form. The cliff tomb was also used in the ways similar to that in the brick or stone chamber tombs in funeral and sacrifice, with similar perspectives on death and the afterlife, as can be viewed from similar themes in the pictorial carvings and the way that certain sets of burial objects were used. More importantly, the cliff tomb, like other contemporary burial forms, was exploited for public display, which might bring along positive contributions to the tomb occupant's family.

The major differences between the cliff tomb and other burial forms are rooted in their different tomb structures. The inherent nature of the cliff tomb structure was fully explored, which was then followed by a series of corresponding innovations on the pictorial carvings and the burial objects. In this sense, there is a consistent preference of the tomb occupants underlying the design of the cliff tomb structure, pictorial carvings and burial objects. The economical aspect of the cliff tomb structure was exploited by the local people. Since this structure required relatively low investment and could be used for many generations, this met the demands of a group of people, who were not very wealthy but wanted to reinforce the cohesion of their family through tomb construction. Some of the cliff tombs mentioned in the study may have been related to some local powerful families. But the quality of the tomb architecture, burial objects and pictorial carvings shows that the tomb occupants were more likely to be from some middle income families, who wanted their family to become powerful. Some of these tomb occupants had immigrant backgrounds, which was closely related to the role of Sichuan as a designated area for migration and exile during its incorporation into the empire. These tomb occupants usually had ancestors from really powerful families in the Central Plain, for example, the family of Jing Zi'an mentioned in Chapter 3.

In addition to the economic aspect, the meaning of a continuous family embedded in the cliff tomb structure was explored, as the construction of the tomb was the result of the continuous endeavours from many generations of the family, and the physical form of the cliff tomb was a metaphor for a prosperous family. Following this intention of the tomb occupants underlying the design of the cliff tomb structure, the pictorial carvings and the burial objects in the cliff tomb made adaptations to make the cliff tomb an embodiment of relations between different family members and different generations.

---

[1] Gosden 2004: 153-155.
[2] Gosden 2004: 154.

Bibliography

Anqiu xian wenhuaju 安丘縣文化局. 1992. *Anqiu Dongjiazhuang Han huaxiang shimu* 安丘董家莊漢畫像石墓. Ji'nan, Ji'nan chubanshe.

Baber, E. 1882. Travels and Researches in the Interior of China. In *Royal Geographical Society Supplementary Papers 1, part* 1: 129-139. London, John Murray.

Bagley, Robert. 2001. *Ancient Sichuan: Treasures from a Lost Civilization*. Seattle, Seattle Art Museum and Princeton University.

Baihu tong 白虎通, by Ban Gu 班固, c. early 2nd century AD. Annotated by Chen Li 陳立, early 19th century. Beijing, Zhonghua shuju, 1994.

Barbieri-Low, Anthony. 2005. Carving Out a Living: Stone-Monument Artisans during the Eastern Han Dynasty. In Cary Y. Liu, Michael Nylan and Anthony Barbieri-Low (eds.), *Recarving China's Past: Art, Archaeology, and Architecture of the 'Wu Family Shrines'*: 485-512. New Haven and London, Yale University Press.

Barbieri-Low, Anthony. 2007. *Artisans in Early Imperial China*. Washington, University of Washington Press.

Bean, George. 1989. *Lycian Turkey: An Archaeological Guide*. London, John Murray.

Bedford, O. H. 1937. Han Dynasty Cave Tombs in West China. *The China Journal* 26 (4): 175-176.

Beijing shi wenwu gongzuodui 北京市文物工作隊. 1964. Beijing xijiao faxian Han dai shique qingli jianbao 北京西郊發現漢代石闕清理簡報. *Wenwu* 文物 1964.11: 13-22.

Bielenstein, Hans. 1980. *The Bureaucracy of Han Times*. Cambridge, Cambridge University Press.

Bierbrier, Morris. 1982. *The Tomb-Builders of the Pharaohs*. London, British Museum Publications.

Bishop, Carl. 1916. The Expedition to the Far East. *The Museum Journal (University of Pennsylvania)* 7(2): 97-124.

Bodde, Derk. 1975. *Festivals in Classical China: New Year and Other Annual Observances during the Han Dynasty 206 BC-AD 220*. Princeton, Princeton University Press.

Boltz, William. 1993. I li 儀禮. In Michael Loewe (ed.), *Early Chinese Texts: A Bibliographic Guide*: 234-243. Berkley, Society for the study of early China and the Institute of East Asian Studies, University of California at Berkley.

Boyer, Pascal. 2001. *Religion Explained: the Human Instincts that Fashion Gods, Spirits and Ancestors*. London, Heinemann.

Brashier, K. E. 2001-2002. The Spirit Lord of Baishi Mountain: Feeding the Deities or Heeding the *Yinyang*. *Early China* 26-27: 159-231.

Brown, Miranda. 2007. *The Politics of Mourning in Early China*. Albany, N.Y., State University of New York Press.

Cahill, S. 1990. *The Image of the Goddess His Wang Mu in Medieval Chinese Literature*. Unpublished PhD thesis, University of California at Berkeley.

Černý, Jaroslav. 1973. *The Valley of the Kings: fragments d'un manuscrit inachevé*. Le Caire, Institut français d'archéologie orientale du Caire.

Cevik, N. 2003. New Rock-Cut Tombs at Etenna and the Rock-Cut Tomb Tradition in Southern Anatolia. *Anatolian Studies* 53: 97-116.

Chang Renxia 常任俠, Jiang Yingju 蔣英炬 and Gao Wen 高文. 1988. *Zhongguo meishu quanji: huaxiangshi huaxiangzhuan* 中國美術全集:畫像石畫像磚. Beijing, Wenwu chubanshe.

Chard, Robert. 1990. *Master of the Family: History and Development of the Chinese Cult of the Stove*. Unpublished PhD thesis, University of California at Berkeley.

Chard, Robert. 1995. Rituals and Scriptures of the Stove Cult. In David Johnson (ed.), *Ritual and Scripture in Chinese Popular Religion: Five Studies*: 3-54. Berkeley, Chinese Popular Culture Project.

Chaves, Jonathan. 1968. A Han Painted Tomb at Loyang. *Artibus Asiae* 30(1): 5-27.

Chen Mingda 陳明達. 2003a. Yamu jianzhu (shang) – Pengshan fajue baogao zhiyi 崖墓建築（上）——彭山發掘報告之一. *Jianzhu shi lunwen ji* 建築史論文集 17: 60-88.

Chen Mingda 陳明達. 2003b. Yamu jianzhu (xia) – Pengshan fajue baogao zhiyi 崖墓建築（下）——彭山發掘報告之一. *Jianzhu shi* 建築史 18: 125-150.

Chen Suzhen 陳蘇鎮. 2010. Donghan de haozu yu lizhi 東漢的豪族與吏治. *Wen shi zhe* 文史哲 2010.6: 41-58.

Chen, Xiandan. 1997. On the designation 'Money Tree'. *Orientations* 1997(9): 67-71.

Chen, Xin. 2011. *Minature Buildings in the Liao (907-1125) and the Northern Song (960-1127) Periods*. Unpublished DPhil. thesis, University of Oxford.

Chen Yunhong 陳雲洪, Zhang Yuxin 張俞新 and Wang Bo 王波. 2007. Chengdu shi Xindu qu Donghan yamu de fajue 成都市新都區東漢崖墓的發掘. *Kaogu* 考古 2007.9: 36-56.

Cheng Junying 程俊英 and Jiang Jianyuan 蔣見元. 1991. *Shi jing zhuxi* 詩經注析. Beijng, Zhonghua shuju.

Cheng, Te-Kun. 1957. *Archaeological Studies in Szechwan*. Cambridge, Cambridge University Press.

Chengdu shi wenwu guanlichu 成都市文物管理處. 1981. Sichuan Chengdu Zengjiabao Donghan huaxiang zhuanshi mu 四川成都曾家包東漢畫像磚石墓. *Wenwu* 文物 1981.10: 25-32.

Chengdu shi wenwu kaogu yanjiusuo 成都市文物考古研究所. 2004. Chengdu shi Xindu qu Huzhu cun Liangshui cun yamu fajue jianbao 成都市新都區互

助村、涼水村崖墓發掘簡報. In Chengdu shi wenwu kaogu yanjiusuo 成都市文物考古研究所 (ed.), *Chengdu kaogu faxian 2002* 成都考古發現 2002: 316-358. Beijing, Kexue chubanshe.

Chengdu shi wenwu kaogu yanjiusuo 成都市文物考古研究. 2010. Chengdu shi Shuangliu xian Miaoshan cun yamu fajue jianbao 成都市雙流縣廟山村崖墓發掘簡報. In Chengdu shi wenwu kaogu yanjiusuo 成都市文物考古研究所 (ed.), *Chengdu kaogu faxian* 2007 成都考古發現 2007: 271-281. Beijing, Kexue chubanshe.

Chengdu wenwu kaogu yanjiusuo 成都文物考古研究所 and Qingbaijiang qu wenwu baohu guanlisuo 青白江區文物保護管理所. 2010. Chengdu shi Qingbaijiang qu Datong linfeichang gongdi Hanmu fajue baogao 成都市青白江區大同磷肥廠工地漢墓發掘報告. In Chengdu shi wenwu kaogu yanjiusuo 成都市文物考古研究所 (ed.), *Chengdu kaogu faxian 2008* 成都考古發現 2008: 292-367. Beijing, Kexue chubanshe.

Ching, Francis, Jarzombek, Mark and Prakash, Vikramaditya (eds.) 2007. *A Global History of Architecture*. New Jersey, John Wiley & Sons, Inc.

Choay, Francoise. 2001. *The Invention of the Historic Monument*. Cambridge, Cambridge University Press.

Chongqing shi bowuguan tianye kaogu gongzuo xiaozu 重慶市博物館田野考古工作小組 and Hechuan xian wenhuaguan tianye kaogu gongzuo xiaozu 合川縣文化館田野考古工作小組. 1977. Hechuan Donghan huaxiangshi mu 合川東漢畫像石墓. *Wenwu* 文物 1977.2: 63-69.

Chongqing shi wenhua ju 重慶市文化局 and Chongqing shi bowuguan 重慶市博物館 (eds.) 1992. *Sichuan Han dai shique* 四川漢代石闕. Beijing, Wenwu chubanshe.

Ch'ü, T'ung-tsu. 1972. *Han Social Structure*. Seattle, University of Washington Press.

Dabaotai hanmu fajue zu 大葆臺漢墓發掘組 and Zhongguo shehui kexue yuan kaogu yanjiusuo 中國社會科學院考古發掘所. 1989. *Beijing Dabaotai hanmu* 北京大葆臺漢墓. Beijing, Wewu chubanshe.

DeMarrais, Elizabeth, Castillo, Luis and Earle, Timothy. 1996. Ideology, Materialization, and Power Strategies. *Current Anthropology* 37(1): 15-31.

Deng, Fei. 2011. *Understanding Efficacy: A Study of Decorated Tombs in Northern Song China (960-1127)*. Unpublishd DPhil thesis, University of Oxford.

Dorman, Peter. 2003. Family Burial and Commemoration in the Theban Necropolis. In Nigel Strudwick and John Taylor (eds.), *The Theban Necropolis: Past, Present and Future*: 30-41. London, The British Museum.

Dramer, Kim. 2002. *Between the Living and the Dead: Han Dynasty Stone Carved Tomb Doors*. Unpublished PhD thesis, Columbia University.

Ebrey, Patricia. 1974. Estate and Family Management in the Later Han as seen in the *Monthly Instructions for the Four Classes of People*. Journal of the Economics and Social History of the Orient 17: 173-205.

Ebrey, Patricia. 1983. Patron-Client Relations in the Late Han. *Journal of the American Oriental society* 103(3): 533-542.

Ebrey, Patricia. 1987. The Economic and Social History of Later Han. In Denis Twitchett and John K. Fairbank (eds.), *The Cambridge History of China vol.1: The Ch'in and Han Empires, 221 BC–AD 220*: 608-648. Cambridge, Cambridge University Press.

Edwards, Richard. 1954. The Cave Reliefs at Ma Hao. *Artibus Asiae* 17(1): 4-28.

Elsner, Jas (ed.) 2010. *Life, Death and Representation: Some New Work on Roman Sarcophagi*. Berlin and New York, De Gruyter.

Erickson, Susan. 1994. Money trees of the Eastern Han Dynasty. *The Museum of Far Eastern Antiquities Bulletin* 66: 5-115.

Erickson, Susan. 2003. Eastern Han Dynasty Cliff Tombs of Santai Xian, Sichuan Province. *Journal of East Asian Archaeology* 5(1-4): 401-469.

Erickson, Susan. 2008. *Que* Pillars at the Wu Family Cemetery and Related Structures in Shandong Province. In N. Richard (ed.), *Rethinking Recarving: Ideals, Practices and Problems of the 'Wu Family Shrines' and Han China*: 110-131. New Haven and London, Yale University Press.

Erickson, Susan. 2010. Han Dynasty Tomb Structures and Contents. In Michael Nylan and Michael Loewe (eds.), *China's Early Empires: a Re-appraisal*: 13-81. Cambridge, Cambridge University Press.

Fairbank, W. 1941. The Offering Shrine of Wu Liang Tzu. *Harvard Journal of Asiatic Studies* 6(1): 1-36.

Falkenhausen, Lothar von. 2006. *Chinese Society in the Age of Confucius (1000-250 BC): the archaeological evidence*. Los Angeles, Costsen Institute of Archaeology, University of California.

Fan Xiaoping 范小平. 2006. *Sichuan yamu yishu* 四川崖墓藝術. Chengdu, Sichuan chuban jituan.

Fang Jianguo 方建國 and Tang Zhaojun 唐朝君. 1992. Sichuan Jianyang xian Yeyuedong faxian Donghan yamu 四川簡陽縣夜月洞發現東漢崖墓. *Kaogu* 考古 1992.4: 383-384.

Feng Xiuqi 馮修齊. 1995. Sangjian yehe huaxiangzhuan kaoshi 桑間野合畫像磚考釋. *Sichuan wenwu* 四川文物 1995.3: 60-62.

Forke, Alfred. 1962. *Lun Heng*. New York, Paragon Book Gallery.

Frühauf, M. 1999. *Die koenigliche Mutter des Westens: Xiwangmu in alten Dokumenten Chinas*. Munich, Bochum Project.

Fu Juan 傅娟. 2006. Chuan Yu Donghan mu chutu tushe taosu zaoxiang chutan 川渝東漢墓出土吐舌陶塑造像初探. *Sichuan wenwu* 四川文物 2006.4: 75-80.

Gansu sheng bowuguan 甘肅省博物館. 1974. Wuwei Leitai Han mu 武威擂臺漢墓. *Kaogu xuebao* 考古學報 1974.2: 87-110

Gansu sheng wenwu kaogu yanjiusuo 甘肅省文物考古研究所 and Gaotai xian bowuguan 高臺縣博物館. 2008. Gansu Gaotai Digengpo Jin mu fajue jianbao 甘肅高臺地埂坡晉墓發掘簡報. *Wenwu* 文物 2008.9: 29-39.

Gao Wen 高文 and Gao Chenggang 高成剛. 1990. *Sichuan lidai beike* 四川歷代碑刻. Chengdu, Sichuan daxue chubanshe.

Gao Wen 高文 and Gao Chenggang 高成剛. 1996. *Zhongguo huaxiang shiguan yishu* 中國畫像石棺藝術. Taiyuan, Shanxi renmin chubanshe.

Gao Wen 高文. 2011. *Zhongguo huaxiang shiguan quanji* 中國畫像石棺全集. Taiyuan, Sanjin chubanshe.

Gariner, K. H. J. 1973. Standard Histories, Han to Sui. In Donald Leslie, Colin Mackerras, Gungwu Wang and C. P. Fitzgerald (eds.), *Essays on the Sources for Chinese History*: 42-52. Columbia: University of South Carolina Press.

Geng Jianjun 耿建軍. 1991. Xuzhou shi Lalishan erhao Donghan shishi mu 徐州市拉犁山二號東漢石室墓. In Zhongguo kaogu xuehui 中國考古學會 (ed.), *Zhongguo kaoguxue nianjian 1990* 中國考古學年鑒 1990: 208-209. Beijing, Wenwu chubanshe.

Goldin, Paul. 2001. The Motif of the Woman in the Doorway and Related Imagery in Traditional Chinese Funerary Art. *Journal of the American Oriental Society* 121(4): 539-548.

Gombrich, E. H. 2009. *Art and Illusion: A Study in the Psychology of Pictorial Representation* (Sixth edition). London and New York, Phaidon Press.

Gong Tingwan 龔廷萬, Gong Yu 龔玉 and Dai Jialing 戴嘉陵 (eds.) 1998. *Ba Shu Han dai huaxiang ji* 巴蜀漢代畫像集. Beijing, Wenwu chubanshe.

Gosden, Chris. 2004. *Archaeology and Colonialism: Cultural Contact from 5000 BC to the Present*. Cambridge, Cambridge University Press.

Gu Qiyi 辜其一. 1990. Leshan, Pengshan he Neijiang Donghan yamu jianzhu chutan 樂山、彭山和內江東漢崖墓建築初探. In Zhang Yuhuan 張宇寰 (ed.), *Zhonghua gu jianzhu* 中華古建築: 165-192. Beijing, Zhongguo kexue jishu chubanshe.

Guangxi zhuangzu zizhiqu bowuguan 廣西壯族自治區博物館. 1988. *Guangxi Guixian Luobowan Han mu* 廣西貴縣羅泊灣漢墓. Beijing, Wenwu chubanshe.

Guo Lizhong 郭立中. 1959. Sichuan Jiaoshan Weijiachong faxian Han dai yamu 四川焦山魏家沖發現漢代崖墓. *Kaogu* 考古 1959.8: 448.

Guo, Qinghua. 1999. *The Structure of Chinese Timber Architecture*. Unpublished PhD thesis, Chalmers University of Technology.

Guo Shude 郭蜀德 and Wang Xinnan 王新南. 1987. Chongqing shi shuini chang Donghan yanmu 重慶市水泥廠東漢巖墓. *Sichuan wenwu* 四川文物 1987.2: 58-61.

Han shu 漢書, by Ban Gu 班固, c. early 2nd century AD. Beijing, Zhonghua Shuju, 1970.

Haspels, C. 1971. *The Highlands of Phrygia: Sites and Monuments*. Princeton, Princeton University Press.

Hawass, Zahi and Vannini, Sandro. 2009. *The Lost Tombs of Thebes: Life in Paradise*. London, Thames & Hudson.

He Xincheng 何新成. 1989. Shaanxi Hanzhong shi Puzhen zhuanchang hanmu qingli jianbao 陝西漢中市鋪鎮磚廠漢墓清理簡報. *Kaogu xuebao* 考古學報 1989.6: 35-46.

He Zhiguo 何志國. 1988a. Sichuan Mianyang Hebian Donghan yamu 四川綿陽河邊東漢崖墓. *Kaogu* 考古 1988.3: 219-226.

He Zhiguo 何志國. 1988b. Mianyang Yangjiazhen Han dai yamu qingli jianbao 綿陽楊家鎮漢代崖墓清理簡報. *Sichuan wenwu* 四川文物 1988.5: 76-77.

He Zhiguo 何志國. 1991a. Shi tan Mianyang chutu Donghan foxiang ji qi xiangguan wenti 試談綿陽出土東漢佛像及其相關問題. *Sichuan wenwu* 四川文物 1991.5: 23-30.

He Zhiguo 何志國. 1991b. Sichuan Mianyang Hejiashan 2 hao Donghan yamu qingli jianbao 四川綿陽何家山2號東漢崖墓清理簡報. *Wenwu* 文物 1991.3: 9-19.

He Zhiguo 何志國. 1991c. Sichuan Mianyang Hejiashan 1 hao Donghan yamu qingli jianbao 四川綿陽何家山1號東漢崖墓清理簡報. *Wenwu* 文物 1991.3: 1-8.

He Zhiguo 何志國. 2002a. Fengdu Donghan jinian mu chutu foxiang de zhongyao yiyi 豐都東漢紀年墓出土佛像的重要意義. *Zhongguo wenwu bao* 中國文物報 2002.5.3.

He Zhiguo 何志國. 2002b. Sichuan Anxian wenguansuo shoucang de Donghan foxiang yaoqianshu 四川安縣文管所收藏的東漢佛像搖錢樹. *Wenwu* 文物 2002.6: 63-67.

He Zhiguo 何志國. 2004. Zhongguo nanfang zaoqi fojiao yishu chulun 中國南方早期佛教藝術初論. Beijing, Zhongguo wenlian chubanshe.

He Zhiguo 何志國. 2006a. *Han Wei yaoqianshu chubu yanjiu* 漢魏搖錢樹初步研究. Beijing, Kexue chubanshe.

He Zhiguo 何志國. 2006b. Sichuan Zitong Han mo yaoqianshu xiaoji 四川梓潼漢末搖錢樹小記. *Zhongyuan wenwu* 中原文物 2006.2: 75-79.

He Zhiguo 何志國. 2010. Lun yaoqianshu yu duozhideng de guanxi 論搖錢樹與多枝燈的關係. *Kaogu* 考古 2010.1: 81-89.

Henan sheng bowuguan 河南省博物館. 1978. *Handai diezhu: Wenxian hongfan yao de fajue he yanjiu* 漢代疊鑄:溫縣烘范窯的發掘和研究. Beijing, Wenwu chubanshe.

Henan sheng Shangqiu shi wenwu guanli weiyuanhui 河南省商丘市文物管理委員會. 2001. *Mangdangshan Xihan liangwang mudi* 芒碭山西漢梁王墓地. Beijing, Wenwu chubanshe.

Henan sheng wenhuaju wenwu gongzuodui 河南省文化局文物工作隊. 1960. Zhengzhou Nanguan 159 hao hanmu de fajue 鄭州南關159號漢墓的發掘. *Wenwu* 文物 1960.8-9: 19-24.

Henan sheng wenhuaju wenwu gongzuodui 河南省文化局文物工作隊. 1964. Henan Xiangcheng Cigou Han huaxiangshimu 河南襄城茨溝漢畫像石墓. *Kaogu xuebao* 考古學報 1964.1: 111-131.

Henan sheng wenwu yanjiusuo 河南省文物研究所. 1993. *Mixian Dahuting hanmu*. 密縣打虎亭漢墓. Beijing, Wenwu chubanshe.

Hou Han shu 後漢書, by Fan Ye 范曄, c. 225 AD. Beijing, Zhonghua Shuju, 1965.

Hsu, Cho-yun. 1980. *Han Agriculture: The Formation of Early Chinese Agrarian Economy (206 BC-AD 220)*. Seatle and London, University of Washinton Press.

Hu Changyu 胡長鈺 and Huang Jiaxiang 黃家祥. 1984. Sichuan Fuling Donghan yamu qingli jianbao 四川涪陵東漢崖墓清理簡報. *Kaogu* 考古 1984.12: 1085-1089.

Hu Renchao 胡人朝. 1958. Chongqing Hualong qiao Donghan zhuan mu de qingli 重慶化龍橋東漢磚墓的清理. *Kaogu* 考古 1958. 3: 42-43.

Hu Xueyuan 胡學元. 1988. Leshan Shizhongqu Gaosuntian yamu qingli jianbao 樂山市中區高筍田崖墓清理簡報. *Sichuan wenwu* 四川文物 1988.3: 76-77.

Hu Xueyuan 胡學元 and Yang Yi 楊翼. 1993. Sichuan Leshan shi Tuogouzui Donghan yamu qingli jianbao 四川樂山市沱溝嘴東漢崖墓清理簡報. *Wenwu* 文物 1993.1: 40-50.

Huanyang guozhi 華陽國志, by Chang Qu 常璩, c. 347 AD. Anotated by Liu Lin 劉琳. Chengdu, Bashu Shushe, 1984.

Huang Minglan 黃明蘭 and Guo Yinqiang 郭引強. 1996. *Luoyang Han mu bihua* 洛陽漢墓壁畫. Beijing, Wenwu chubanshe.

Huainan zi 淮南子. Anotated by Zhang Shuangli 張雙棣. Beijing, Beijing daxue chubanshe, 1997.

Huang Jiaxiang 黃家祥 and Wang Chaowei 王朝衛. 2003. Sichuan Yibin Hengjiang zhen Donghan yamu qingli jianbao 四川宜賓橫江鎮東漢崖墓清理簡報. *Huaxia kaogu* 華夏考古 2003.1: 3-17.

Huang Siting 黃泗亭. 1986. Guizhou Xishui xian faxian de Shu Han yamu he moya tiji ji yanhua 貴州習水縣發現的蜀漢崖墓和摩崖題記及岩畫. *Sichuan wenwu* 四川文物 1986.1: 67-69.

Huang Xiaofen 黃曉芬. 2003. *Han mu de kaoguxue yanjiu* 漢墓的考古學研究. Changsha, Yuelu chubanshe.

Huang Xueqian 黃學謙, Yang Yi 楊翼 and Hu Xueyuan 胡學元. 1991. Sichuan Leshan Shizhong qu Dawanzui yamu qingli jianbao 四川樂山市中區大灣嘴崖墓清理簡報. *Kaogu* 考古 1991.1: 23-32.

Huang Zhongyou 黃中幼 and Zhang Ronghua 張榮華. 1994. Jiangjin Shahe faxian Donghan jinian yamu 江津沙河發現東漢紀年崖墓. *Sichuan wenwu* 四川文物 1994.4: 65-66.

Hulsewé, A. F. P. 1993. *Han shu* 漢書. In Michael Loewe (ed.), *Early Chinese Texts: A Bibliographic Guide*: 129-136. Berkley, Society for the study of early China and the Institute of East Asian Studies, University of California.

Humphreys, S. C. 1993. *The Family, Women and Death*. Ann Arbor, The University of Michgan Press.

Hunan bowuguan 湖南博物館 and Zhongguo kexueyuan kaogu yanjiusuo 中國科學院考古研究所. 1973. *Changsha Mawangdui yihao Han mu* 長沙馬王堆一號漢墓. Beijing, Wenwu chubanshe.

Jenkins, Richard. 2008. *Social Identity*. London, Routledge.

Ji Bing 季兵. 1994. Mianyang shi Wujia Han dai yamu qingli jianbao 綿陽市吳家漢代崖墓清理簡報. *Sichuan wenwu* 四川文物 1994.5: 79-80.

Jiang Yingju. 2008. The Iconography of the 'Homage Scene' in Han Pictorial Carving. In N. Richard (ed.), *Rethinking Recarving: Ideals, Practices, and Problems of the 'Wu Family Shrines' and Han China*: 162-179. New Haven and London, Yale University Press.

Jiang Yingju 蔣英炬 and Wu Wenqi 吳文祺. 1981. Wu shi ci huaxiangshi jianzhu peizhi kao 武氏祠畫像石建築配置考. *Kaogu xuebao* 考古學報 1981.2: 165-184.

Jiang Yuxiang 江玉祥. 2000. Guanyu kaogu chutu yaoqianshu yanjiu zhong de jige wenti 關於考古出土搖錢樹研究中的幾個問題. *Sichuan wenwu* 四川文物 2000.4: 10-13.

Jing Zhuyou 景竹友. 1993. Santai Xinde xiang Donghan yamu qingli jianbao 三台縣新德鄉東漢崖墓清理簡報. *Sichuan wenwu* 四川文物 1993.5: 68-69.

Jing Zhuyou 景竹友. 1997. Santai Yongming xiang yamu diaocha jianbao 三台永明鄉崖墓調查簡報. *Sichuan wenwu* 四川文物 1997.1: 63-71.

Knauer, Elfriede. 2006. The Queen Mother of the West: A Study of the Influence of Western Prototypes on the Iconography of the Taoist Deity. In Victor Mair (ed.), *Contact and Exchange in the Ancient World*: 62-115. Honolulu, University of Hawaii Press.

Knechtges, David. 1982. *Wen xuan or Selections of Refined Literature, volume one: Rhapsodies on Metropolises and Capitals*. Princeton, Princeton University Press.

Knechtges, David. 1987. *Wen xuan or Selections of Refined Literature, volume two: Rhapsodies on Sacrifices, Hunting, Travel, Sightseeing, Palaces and Halls, Rivers and Seas*. Princeton, Princeton University Press.

Kus, Susan. 1982. Matters Material and Ideal. In Ian Hodder (ed.), *Symbolic and Structural Archaeology*: 47-62. Cambridge, Cambridge University Press.

Ledderose, Lothar. 2000. *Ten Thousand Things: Module and Mass Production in Chinese Art*. Princeton, N.J., Princeton University.

Legge, James. 1960. *The Chinese Classics*, vol. 4. Hong Kong, Hong Kong University Press.

Legge, James. 1967. *Li Chi Book of Rites: An Encyclopedia of Ancient Ceremonial Usages, Religious Creeds, and Social Institutions, Vol.1*. New York, University Books

Leslie, D. D. 1973. Local Gazetteers. In Donald Leslie, Colin Mackerras, Gungwu Wang and C.P. Fitzgerald (eds.), *Essays on the Sources for Chinese History*: 71-74. Columbia, University of South Carolina Press.

Lei Jianjin 雷建金. 1992. Neijiang shi Guanshengdian Donghan yamu huaxiang shiguan 內江市關升店東漢崖墓畫像石棺. *Sichuan wenwu* 四川文物 1992.3: 60-62.

Lei Jianjin 雷建金 and Zeng Jian 曾健. 1989. Neijiang Shizhong qu Hongying Dong Han yamu 內江市中區紅櫻東漢崖墓. *Sichuan wenwu* 四川文物 1989.1: 40-42.

Lei Yu 雷雨. 2006. Baoxing Qiaoqi Dandi Meidi Han dai zhuanshi mu ji Qiaofeng yamu fajue jianbao 寶興磽磧旦地美地漢代磚室墓及磽豐崖墓發掘簡報. *Sichuan wenwu* 四川文物 2006.4: 28-33.

Lei Yuhua 雷玉華. 1998. Sichuan zaoqi fojiao tanyuan 四川早期佛教探源. *Sichuan wenwu* 四川文物 1998. 5: 39-42.

Lewis, Mark. 2006. *The Construction of Space in Early China*. Albany, State University of New York Press.

Lewis, Mark. 2007. *The Early Chinese Empires: Qin and Han*. Cambridge, Mass. and London, Belknap Press of Harvard University.

Li Falin 李發林. 1982. *Shandong Han huaxiangshi yanjiu* 山東漢畫像石研究. Ji'nan, Qilu shushe.

Li Falin 李發林. 1985. Shandong Cangshan Yuanjia yuan nian huaxiangshimu tiji shishi 山東蒼山元嘉元年畫像石墓題記試釋. *Zhongyuan wenwu* 文物 1985.1: 72-75.

Li ji 禮記. Annotated by Zheng Xuan 鄭玄 (AD 127-200). Collected in *Shisan jing zhushu Li ji zhengyi* 十三經注疏禮記正義. Beijing, Beijing daxue chubanshe, 1999.

Li Jiafeng 李加鋒. 1991. Shuangliu Huayang Shahe cun yamu fajue jianbao 雙流華陽沙河村崖墓發掘簡報. *Sichuan wenwu* 四川文物 1991.6: 58-61.

Li Jinghua 李京華. 1985. Gudai hongfan gongyi 古代烘范工藝. In Zhongguo kexueyuan ziran kexueshi yanjiusuo 中國科學院自然科學史研究所 (ed.), *Kejishi wenji* 科技史文集: 47-53. Shanghai, Shanghai kexue jishu chubanshe.

Li li 李立. 2004. *Han mu shenhua yanjiu: shenhua yu shenhua yishu jingshen de kaocha yu fenxi* 漢墓神畫研究:神話與神話藝術精神的考察與分析. Shanghai, Shanghai guji chubanshe.

Li Rusen 李如森. 1996. Handai jiazu mudi yu yingyu shang sheshi de xingqi 漢代家族墓地與塋域上設施的興起. *Shixue jikan* 史學集刊 1996.1: 18-24.

Li shi 隸釋, by Hong Gua 洪适 (AD 1117-1184). Beijing, Zhonghua shuju, 1985.

Li Xingyu 李興玉. 1993. Xinjin xian chutu Dong Han yaoqianshu 新津縣出土東漢搖錢樹. *Chengdu wenwu* 成都文物 1993.2: 28.

Li Xueqin 李學勤 (ed.) 1986. *Zhongguo meishu quanji gongyi meishu bian 5 qingtongqi (xia)* 中國美術全集工藝美術編5青銅器(下). Beijing, wenwu chubanshe.

Liang, Sicheng. 1984. *A Pictorial History of Chinese Architecture: A Study of the Development of Its Structural System and the Evolution of Its Types*. Cambridge, Mass., MIT Press.

Liangshan zhou bowuguan 涼山州博物館. 1994. Yanyuan jinnian chutu de Zhanguo zhi Xi Han wenwu 鹽源近年出土的戰國至西漢文物. *Sichuan wenwu* 四川文物 1999.4: 23-32.

Lienü zhuan 列女傳, by Liu Xiang 劉向 (77-6 BC). Shanghai, Shangwu yinshuguan, 1937.

Lim, Lucy (ed.) 1987. *Stories from China's Past: Han Dynasty Pictorial Tomb Reliefs and Archaeological Objects from Sichuan Province, People's Republic of China*. San Francisco, Chinese Culture Foundation of San Francisco.

Liu Pansui 劉盼遂. 1957. *Lun heng jijie* 論衡集解. Beijing, Guji chubanshe.

Liu Shixu 劉世旭. 1987. Sichuan Xichang Gaocao chutu Han dai yaoqianshu canpian 四川西昌高草出土漢代搖錢樹殘片. *Kaogu* 考古 1987.3: 279-288.

Liu Tseng-kuei 劉增貴. 1997. Men hu yu zhong guo gudai shehui 門戶與中國古代社會. *Bulletin of the Institute of History and Philology* 68.4: 817-898.

Liu Zhangze 劉章澤 and Li Zhaohe 李昭和. 2004. Sichuan Zhongjiang Taliangzi yamu fajue jianbao 四川中江塔梁子崖墓發掘簡報. *Wenwu* 文物 2004.9: 4-33.

Liu Zhiyuan 劉志遠. 1958. Chengdu Tianhuishan yamu qingli ji 成都天回山崖墓清理記. *Kaogu xuebao* 考古學報 1958.1: 87-103.

Liu Zhiyuan 劉志遠. 1974. Sichuan Yanting Donghan yamu chutu wenwu jianji 四川鹽亭東漢崖墓出土文物簡記. *Wenwu* 文物 1974.5: 92-94.

Liu Zhiyuan 劉志遠 (ed.) 1983. *Sichuan Han dai huaxiangzhuan yu Han dai shehui* 四川漢代畫像磚與漢代社會. Beijing, Wenwu chubanshe.

Loewe, Michael. 1979. *Ways to Paradise: The Chinese Quest for Immortality*. London, Allen & Unwin.

Loewe, Michael. 1987. Introduction. In Denis Twitchett and John K. Fairbank (eds.), *The Cambridge History of China, Vol. 1: The Ch'in and Han Empires, 221 BC-AD 220*: 1-19. Cambridge, Cambridge University Press.

Los Angeles County Museum of Art and China Overseas Archaeological Exhibition Corporation. 1987. *The Quest for Eternity, Chinese Ceramic Sculptures from the People's Republic of China*. London, Thames & Hudson and Los Angeles County Museum of Art.

Lu Deliang 陸德良. 1958. Sichuan Xinjin xian Baozi shan yamu qingli jianbao 四川新津寶資山崖墓清理簡報. *Kaogu* 考古 1958. 8: 31-37.

Luo Weixian 羅偉先. 1986. Dui Changning Qigedong shike hua zhong liangzhong fuhao de shishi 對長寧七個洞石刻畫中兩種符號的試釋. *Kaogu yu wenwu* 考古與文物 1986.3: 82-85.

Luo Erhu 羅二虎. 1987. Sichuan yamu kaizao jishu tansuo 四川崖墓開鑿技術探索. *Sichuan wenwu* 四川文物 1987.2: 35-38.

Luo Erhu 羅二虎. 1988. Sichuan yamu de chubu yanjiu 四川崖墓的初步研究. *Kaogu xuebao* 考古學報 1988.2: 133-167.

Luo Erhu 羅二虎. 2000. Han dai huaxiang shiguan yanjiu 漢代畫像石棺研究. *Kaogu xuebao* 考古學報: 31-62.

Luo Erhu 羅二虎. 2001. Lue lun Guizhou Qingzhen Hanmu chutu de zaoqi foxiang 略論貴州清鎮漢墓出土的早期佛像. *Sichuan wenwu* 四川文物 2001.2: 49-52.

Luo Erhu 羅二虎. 2002. *Han dai huaxiang shiguan* 漢代畫像石棺. Chengdu, Bashu chubanshe.

Luo Erhu 羅二虎. 2005a. Changning qigedong yamu qun Han huaxiang yanjiu 長寧七個洞崖墓群漢畫像研究. *Kaogu xuebao* 考古學報 2005.3: 279-306.

Luo Erhu 羅二虎. 2005b. Lun Zhongguo xinan diqu de zaoqi foxiang 論中國西南地區的早期佛像. *Kaogu xuebao* 考古學報 2005.6: 66-73.

Luoyang bowuguan 洛陽博物館. 1977. Luoyang Xihan Buqianqiu mu bihua mu fajue jianbao 洛陽西漢卜千秋墓壁畫墓發掘簡報. *Wenwu* 文物 1977.6: 1-12.

Luoyang kaogu fajuedui 洛陽考古發掘隊. 1959. *Luoyang Shaogou hanmu* 洛陽燒溝漢墓. Beijing, Kexue chubanshe.

Luoyang shi wenwu gongzuodui 洛陽市文物工作隊. 1996 Luoyang Wunüzhong 267 hao Xin Mang mu fajue jianbao 洛陽五女冢267號新莽墓發掘簡報. *Wenwu* 文物 1996.7: 42-53.

Luo Renzhong 羅仁忠. 1996. Neijiang Qikongzi Han dai yamu qingli jianbao 內江七孔子漢代崖墓清理簡報. *Sichuan wenwu* 四川文物 1996.4: 64-66.

Ma Xiaoliang 馬曉亮. 2012. Sichuan zaoqi yamu ji xiangguan wenti tantao 四川早期崖墓及相關問題探討. *Kaogu* 考古 2012.1: 82-90.

Major, John. 1993. *Heaven and Earth in Early Han Thought: Chapters Three, Four, and Five of the Huainanzi*. Albany, State University of New York Press.

Miao Yongshu 繆永舒. 1989. Nanchuan xian Han yamu shike yanjiu 南川縣汉崖墓石刻研究. *Sichuan wenwu* 四川文物 1989.3: 25-28.

McKenzie, Judith. 2005. *The Architecture of Petra*. Oxford, Oxford University Press.

Miller, Allison. 2011. *Patronage, Politics, and the Emergence of Rock-Cut Tombs in Early Han China*. Unpublished PhD thesis, Harvard University.

Miller, Daniel. 2005. *Materiality*. Durham and London, Duke University Press.

Mo Honggui 莫洪貴. 2004. Jiange xian Yansheng zhen Jieshan cun yamu fajue jianbao 劍閣縣演聖鎮截山村發掘簡報. *Sichuan wenwu* 四川文物 2004.3: 3-5.

Morris, Ian. 1992. *Death-Ritual and Social Structure in Classical Antiquity*. Cambridge, Cambridge University Press.

Nanjing bowuyuan 南京博物院. 1981. Xuzhou Qingshanquan Baiji Donghan huaxiangshi mu 徐州青山泉白集東漢畫像石墓. *Kaogu* 考古 1981.2: 137-150.

Nanjing bowuyuan 南京博物院. 1991. *Sichuan Pengshan Han dai yamu* 四川彭山漢代崖墓. Beijing, Wenwu chubanshe.

Nanyang diqu wenwu dui 南陽地區文物隊 and Nanyang bowuguan 南陽博物館. 1980. Tanghe Han Yuping dayin Fengjun Ruren huaxiang shi mu 唐河漢郁平大尹馮君孺人畫像石墓. *Kaogu xuebao* 考古學報 1980.2: 239-262.

Nanyang Han huaxiangshi bianweihui 南陽漢畫像石編委會. 1982. Tanghe xian Dianchang Han huaxiangshimu 唐河縣電廠漢畫像石墓. *Zhongyuan wenwu* 中原文物 1982.1: 5-11.

Neijiang shi wenguansuo 內江市文管所 and Jianyang xian wenhuaguan 簡陽縣文化館. 1991. Sichuan Jianyang xian Guitoushan Dong Han yamu 四川簡陽縣鬼頭山東漢崖墓. *Wenwu* 文物 1991.3: 20-25.

Nylan, Michael. 2001. The Legacies of the Chengdu Plain. In Robert Bagley (ed.), *Ancient Sichuan: Treasures from a Lost Civilization*: 309-325. Seattle, Seattle Art Museum and Princeton University.

Nylan, Michael. 2003. The Archaeological Record of Han Sichuan. *Journal of East Asian Archaeology* 5(1-4): 375-400.

Ossorio, Francesca. 2009. *Petra: Splendor of the Nabataean Civilization*. Vercelli, Italy, White Star Publishers.

Paludan, Ann. 1994. *Chinese Tomb Figurines*. Hong Kong and Oxford, Oxford University Press.

Paludan, Ann. 2006. *Chinese Sculpture: A Great Tradition*. Chicago, Serindia Publications.

Pan Jixing 潘吉星. 1989. *Tiangong kaiwu jiaozhu ji yanjiu* 天工開物校注及研究. Chengdu, Bashu shushe.

Pirazzoli-t'Serstevens, Michèle. 2001. Sichuan in the Warring States and Han Periods. In Robert Bagley (ed.), *Ancient Sichuan: Treasures from a Lost Civilization*: 39-57. Seattle, Seattle Art Museum and Princeton University.

Poo, Mu-chou. 1998. *In Search of Personal Welfare: A View of Ancient Chinese Religion*. Albany, N.Y., State University of New York.

Powers, Martin. 1984. Pictorial Art and Its Public Issues in Early Imperial China. *Art History* 7.2: 135-163.

Powers, Martin. 1991. *Art and Political Expression in Early China*. New Haven and London, Yale University Press.

Quan Han wen 全漢文. Edited by Yan Kejun 嚴可均 (AD 1762-1843). Beijing, Shangwu yinshuguan, 1999.

Rawson, Jessica. 1998. Chinese Burial Patterns: Sources of Information on Thought and Belief. In Chris Scarre and Colin Renfrew (eds.), *Cognition and Culture: the Archaeology of Symbolic Storage*: 107-133. Cambridge, McDonald Institute for Archaeological Research.

Rawson, Jessica. 1999. The Eternal Palaces of the Western Han: A New View of the Universe. *Artibus Asiae* 59(1/2): 5-58.

Rawson, Jessica. 2006. Ornament as System: Chinese Bird-and-Flower Design. *The Burlington Magazine* 2006(6): 380-389.

Rawson, Jessica. 2012. The Han Empire and its Northern Neighbours: The Fascination of the Exotic. In James Lin (ed.), *The Search for Immortality: Tomb Treasures of Han China*: 23-36. New Haven and London, Yale University Press.

Ren Rixin 任日新. 1981. Shandong Zhucheng Han mu huaxiangshi 山東諸城漢墓畫像石. *Wenwu* 文物 1981.10: 14-21.

Renfrew, Colin. 2011. Commodification and Institution in Group-Oriented and Individualising Societies. In W. G. Runciman (ed.), *The Origin of Human Social Institution*: 93-117. London, British Academy.

Renfrew, Colin. 2005. Towards a Theory of Material Engagement. In E. Demarrais, Chris Gosden and Colin Renfrew (eds.), *Rethinking Materiality: The Engagement of Mind with the Material World*: 23-31. Cambridge, McDonald Institute for Archaeological Research.

Rockwell, Peter. 1993. *The Art of Stone Carving: A Reference Guide*. Cambridge, Cambridge University Press.

Roos, Paavo. 1972-1974. *The Rock Tombs of Caunus*. Göteborg, P. Åströms.

Rudolph, Richard and Wen, Yu. 1951. *Han Tomb Art of West China: a Collection of First- and Second-century Reliefs*. Berkeley, University of California Press.

Santai xian wenhuaguan 三臺縣文化館. 1976. Sichuan Santai xian faxian Donghan mu 四川三台縣發現東漢墓. *Kaogu* 考古 1976.6: 395.

Schmidt, Erich. 1970. *Persepolis* Volume III. Chicago, University of Chicago Press.

Ségalen, Victor. 1917. Recent discoveries in Ancient Chinese Sculpture. *Journal of the North China Branch of the Royal Asiatic Society* 48: 145-162.

Ségalen, Victor. 1923. *Mission archéologique en Chine, atlas, vol. 1: La sculpture et les monuments funéraires*. Paris, Paul Geuthner.

Seidel, Anna. 1987. Traces of Han Religion in Funeral Texts Found in Tombs. In Akizuki Kanei 秋月觀英 (ed.), *Dokyo to shukyo bunka* 道教と宗教文化: 21-57. Tokyo, Hirakawa.

Shaanxi sheng kaogu yanjiusuo 陝西省考古研究所 and Yulin shi wenwu guanli weiyuanhui 榆林市文物管理委員會 (eds.) 2001. *Shenmu Dabaodang Han dai chengzhi yu muzang kaogu baogao* 神木大保當漢代城址與墓葬考古報告. Beijing, Kexue chubanshe.

Shandong sheng bowuguan 山東省博物館 and Cangshan xian wenhuaguan 蒼山縣文化館. 1975. Shandong Cangshan Yuanjia yuan nian huaxiangshimu 山東蒼山元嘉元年畫像石墓. *Kaogu* 考古 1975.2: 124-134.

Shanhai jing 山海經. Annotated by Yuan Ke 袁珂. Shanghai, Shanghai guji chubanshe, 1985.

Shaanxi sheng wenwuju 陝西省文物局 and Shanghai bowuguan 上海博物館. 2004. *Zhou Qin Han Tang wenming* 周秦漢唐文明. Shanghai, Shanghai shuhua chubanshe.

Shi ji 史記, by Sima Qian 司馬遷, c. 91 BC. Beijing, Zhonghua shuju, 1959.

Shizishan Chuwangling kaogu dui 獅子山楚王陵考古隊. 1998. Xuzhou Shizishan Xihan Chuwang ling fajue jianbao 徐州獅子山西漢楚王陵發掘簡報. *Wenwu* 文物 1998.8: 4-33.

Shuijing zhu 水經注, by Li Daoyuan 酈道元, c. early 6th century. Annotated by Chen Qiaoyi 陳橋驛. Beijing, Zhonghua shuju, 2007.

Sichuan daxue gudai nanfang sichou zhi lu zonghe kaocha ketizu 四川大學古代南方絲綢之路綜合考察課題組. 1990. *Gudai xinan sichou zhi lu yanjiu* 古代西南絲綢之路研究. Chengdu, Sichuan daxue chubanshe.

Sichuan daxue lishi xi qiba ji kaogu shixi dui deng 四川大學歷史系七八級考古實習隊等. 1984. Sichuan Yibin Huangsan yamu diaocha ji qingli jianbao 四川宜賓黃傘崖墓調查及清理簡報. *Kaogu yu wenwu* 考古與文物 1984.6: 12-21.

Sichuan daxue lishi xi qiba ji kaogu shixi dui 四川大學歷史系七八級考古實習隊. 1985. Sichuan Changning Qigedong Donghan jinian huaxiang yamu 四川長寧七個洞東漢紀年畫像崖墓. *Kaogu yu wenwu* 考古與文物 1985.5: 43-55.

Sichuan Pixian wenhuaguan 四川郫縣文化館. 1979. Sichuan Pixian Donghan zhuanmu de shiguan huaxiang 四川郫縣東漢磚墓的石棺畫像. *Kaogu* 考古 1979.6: 495-505.

Sichuan sheng bowuguan 四川省博物館. 1985a. Xindu Majiashan yamu fajue jianbao 新都馬家山崖墓發掘簡報. In Wenwu bianji weiyuanhui 文物編輯委員會 (ed.), *Wenwu ziliao congkan di jiu ji* 文物資料叢刊第九集: 93-121. Beijing, Wenwu chubanshe.

Sichuan sheng bowuguan 四川省博物館. 1985b. Yibin Shanguci Han dai yamu qingli jianbao 宜賓山谷祠漢代崖墓清理簡報. In Wenwu bianji weiyuanhui 文物編輯委員會 (ed.), *Wenwu ziliao congkan di jiu ji* 文物資料叢刊第九集: 133-137. Beijing, Wenwu chubanshe.

Sichuan sheng bowuguan 四川省博物館. 1985c. Suining Bijiashan yamu qingli jianbao 遂寧筆架山崖墓清理簡報. In Wenwu bianji weiyuanhui 文物編輯委員會 (ed.), *Wenwu ziliao congkan di jiu ji* 文物資料叢刊第九集: 122-132. Beijing, Wenwu chubanshe.

Sichuan sheng bowuguan 四川省博物館 (ed.) 1992. *Sichuan sheng bowuguan* 四川省博物館. Beijing, Wenwu chubanshe.

Sichuan sheng weguanhui 四川省文管會. 1985. Sichuan Yingjing shuikangou yamu 四川滎經水坎溝崖墓. *Wenwu* 文物 1985.5: 23-28.

Sichuan sheng wenwu kaogu yanjiu suo 四川省文物考古研究所 and Luzhou shi bowuguan 瀘州市博物館. 2006. Sichuan Luzhou Hekoutou Han dai yamu qingli jianbao 四川瀘州河口頭漢代崖墓清理簡報. *Sichuan wenwu* 四川文物 2006.5: 25-30.

Sichuan sheng wenwu kaogu yanjiusuo 四川省文物考古研究所 and Mianyang bowuguan 綿陽博物館. 2006. *Mianyang Shuangbaoshan Han mu* 綿陽雙包山漢墓. Beijing, Wenwu chubanshe.

Sichuan sheng wenwu kaogu yanjiuyuan 四川省文物考古研究院, Deyang shi wenwu kaogu yanjiusuo 德陽市文物考古研究所 and Zhongjiang xian wenwu baohu guanli suo 中江縣文物保護管理所 (eds.) 2008. *Zhongjiang Taliangzi yamu* 中江塔梁子崖墓. Beijing, Wenwu chubanshe.

Sichuan sheng wenwu kaogu yanjiuyuan 四川省文物考古研究院, Guang'an shi wenwu guanlisuo 廣安市文物管理所, Wusheng xian wenhua tiyuju 武勝縣文化體育局 and Wusheng xian wenwu guanlisuo 武勝縣文物管理所. 2010. Sichuan Wusheng Shanshui yan yamu qun fajue baogao 四川武勝山水巖崖墓群發掘報告. *Sichuan wenwu* 四川文物 2010.1: 3-26.

Sichuan sheng wenwu kaogu yanjiuyuan 四川省文物考古研究院, Mianyang shi bowuguan 綿陽市博物館 and Santai xian wenwu guanli suo 三台縣文物管理所 (eds.) 2007. *Santai Qijiang yamu* 三台郪江崖墓. Beijing, Wenwu chubanshe.

Si min yueling 四民月令, by Cui Shi 崔寔 (c. 103-170 AD). Anotated by Shi Hansheng 石漢聲. Beijing, Zhonghua shuju, 1965.

Steele, John. 1917. *The I-Li or Book of Etiquette and Ceremonial, Vol. II*. London, Probsthain & CO.

Steingräber, Stephan. 2009. Etruscan Rock-cut Tombs: Origins, Characteristics, Local and Foreign Elements. In J. Swaddling and P. Perkins (eds.), *Etruscan by Definition: The Cultural, Regional and Personal Identity of the Etruscans: Papers in Hounour of Sybille Haynes, MBE*: 64-68. London, British Museum Research Publication.

Stercks, Roel. 2006. Sages, Cooks, and Flavors in Warring States and Han China. *Monumenta Serica* 54: 1-46.

Strudwick, Nigel and Taylor, John (eds.) 2003. *The Theban Necropolis: Past, Present and Future*. London, The British Museum.

Summerson, J. 1980. *The Classical Language of Architecture*. London, Thames and Hudson.

Sun Hua 孫華. 1987. Ba Shu fuhao chu lun 巴蜀符號初論. In Xu Zhongshu 徐仲殊 (ed.), *Ba Shu kaogu lunwen ji* 巴蜀考古論文集: 89-100. Beijing, Wenwu chubanshe.

Sun Ji 孫機. 1991. *Han dai wuzhi wenhua ziliao tushuo* 漢代物質文化資料圖說. Beijing, Wenwu chubanshe.

Taiping yulan 太平御覽, by Li Fang 李昉, c. 10th century. Beijing, Zhonghua shuju, 1960.

Tang Changshou 唐長壽. 1990. Sichuan Leshan Mahao yihao yamu 四川樂山麻浩一號崖墓. *Kaogu* 考古 1990.2: 111-122.

Tang Changshou 唐長壽. 1993. *Leshan yamu he Pengshan yamu* 樂山崖墓和彭山崖墓. Chengdu, Dianzi keji daxue chubanshe.

Tang, Changshou. 1997. Shiziwan Cliff Tomb No. 1. *Orientations* 1997(9): 72-77.

Tang Changshou 唐長壽. 2010. Leshan yanmu zhong de xiaozitu shidu 樂山崖墓中的孝子圖釋讀. In Zhongguo Han hua xuehui 中國漢畫學會 and Sichuan bowuyuan 四川博物院 (eds.), *Zhongguo Han hua xuehui dishier jie nianhui lunwenji* 中國漢畫學會第十二屆年會論文集: 143-145. Hong Kong, Zhongguo guoji wenhua chubanshe.

Tang Guangxiao 唐光孝. 2002. Shi xi Sichuan Han dai zangsu zhong de shangpin hua wenti 試析四川漢代葬俗中的商品化問題. *Sichuan wenwu* 四川文物 2002.5: 53-60.

Tang Guangxiao 唐光孝. 2003. Sichuan Mianyang shi Zhujialiangzi Donghan yamu 四川綿陽市朱家梁子東漢崖墓. *Kaogu* 考古 2003.1: 39-49.

Thomas, Edmund. 2010. 'Houses of the dead'? Columnar Sarcophagi as 'micro-architecture'. In Jas Elsner (ed.), *Life, Death and Representation: Some New Work on Roman Sarcophagi*: 387-436. Berlin and New York, De Gruyter.

Thompson, Lydia. 1998. *The Yi'nan Tomb: Narrative and Ritual in Pictorial Art of the Eastern Han (25-220 C. E.)*. Unpublished PhD thesis, New York University.

Thorp, Robert. 1979. *Mortuary Art and Architecture of Early Imperial China*. Unpublished PhD thesis, University of Kansas.

Thote, Alan. 2001. The Archaeology of Eastern Sichuan at the Bronze Age (5th to 3rd Century BC). In Robert Bagley (ed.), *Ancient Sichuan: Treasures from a Lost Civilization*: 203-252. Seattle, Seattle Art Museum and Princeton University.

Tjan, Tjoe Som. 1952. *Po Hu T'ung: The Comprehensive Discussions in the White Tiger Hall*. Leiden, E. J. Brill.

Torrance, T. 1910. Burial Customs in Sz-chuan. *Journal of the North China Branch of the Royal Asiatic Society* 41: 57-75.

Torrance, T. 1930-1931. Notes on the Cave Tombs and Ancient Burial Mounds of Western Szechuan. *Journal of the West China Border Research Society* 4: 88-96.

Trigger, Bruce. 2006. *A History of Archaeological Thought*. Cambridge, Cambridge University Press.

Tseng Lan-ying 曾藍瑩. 2000. Zuofang getao yu diyu zi chuantong: cong Shandong Anqiu Dongjiazhuang Han mu de zhizuo henji tanqi 作坊、格套與地域子傳統：從山東安丘董家莊漢墓的製作痕跡談起. *Guoli Taiwan daxue meishushi yanjiu jikan* 國立臺灣大學美術史研究集刊 8: 33-86.

Tseng, Lillian. 2011. *Picturing Heaven in Early China*. Cambridge and London, Harvard University Press.

Wagner, Donald. 2008. *Joseph Needham Science and Civilization in China, volume 5, part II Ferrous Metallurgy*. Cambridge, Cambridge University Press.

Wang Entian 王恩田. 1989. Cangshan Yuanjia yuan nian huaxiangshimu kao 蒼山元嘉元年畫像石墓考. *Sichuan wenwu* 四川文物 1989.4: 3-10.

Wang Chaowei 王朝衛. 2003. Sichuan Yibin Zhenwushan faxian yizuo Donghan yamu 四川宜賓真武山發現一座東漢崖墓. *Huaxia kaogu* 華夏考古 2003.1: 18-20.

Wang Qipeng 王啟鵬 and Wang Kongzhi 王孔智. 1989. Zhongjiang xian Yugui xiang Dong han yamu diaocha jianbao 中江縣玉桂鄉東漢崖墓調查簡報. *Sichuan wenwu* 四川文物 1989.5: 64-65.

Wang Tingfu 王庭福 and Li Yihong 李一洪. 1995. Hejiang Zhangjiagou erhao yamu huaxiang shiguan fajue jianbao 合江張家溝二號崖墓畫像石棺發掘簡報. *Sichuan wenwu* 四川文物 1995.5: 65-66.

Wang Zijin 王子今 and Gao Dalun 高大倫. 2004. *Zhongjiang Taliangzi yamu bihua bangti kaolun* 中江塔梁子崖墓壁畫榜題考論. *Wenwu* 文物 2004.9: 64-73.

Watson, Burton. 1971. *Records of the Grand Historian of China*. New York, Columbia University Press.

Wen xuan 文選, reprint of 1810 ed., with index. Beijing, Zhonghua Shuju, 1977.

Wen You 聞宥. 1955. *Sichuan Han dai huaxiang xuanji* 四川漢代畫像選集. Shanghai, Qunlian chubanshe.

Wu Guibing 吳桂兵. 2002. Zhongxian Tujing M5 yu Shu di zaoqi fojiao chuanbo 忠縣涂井M5与蜀地早期佛教传播. *Sichuan wenwu* 四川文物 2002.5: 65-71.

Wu, Hung. 1986. Buddhist Elements in Early Chinese Art (2nd and 3rd Century AD). *Artibus Asiae* 47(3/4): 263-352.

Wu, Hung. 1987. Myths and Legends in Han Funerary Art: Their Pictorial Structure and Symbolic Meanings as Reflected in Carvings on Sichuan Sarcophagi. In Lucy Lim (ed.), *Stories from China's Past*: 72-82. San Francisco, The Chinese Culture Foundation of San Francisco.

Wu, Hung. 1989a. From Temple to Tomb: Ancient Chinese Art and Religion in Transition. *Early China* 14: 78-114.

Wu, Hung. 1989b. *The Wu Liang Shrine: The Ideology of Early Chinese Pictorial Art*. Standford, Stanford University Press.

Wu, Hung. 1994. Beyond the 'Great Boundary': Funerary Narraive in the Cangshan Tomb. In John Hay (ed.), *Boundaries in China*: 81-104. London, Reaktion.

Wu, Hung. 1995. *Moumentality in Early Chinese Art and Architecture*. Stanford, California, Stanford University Press.

Wu, Hung. 1998. Where Are They Going? Where Did They Come from? – Hearse and 'Soul-Carriage' in Han Dynasty Tomb Art. *Orientations* 1998(6): 22-31.

Wu, Hung 巫鴻. 2000. Diyu kaogu yu dui 'wudoumijiao' meishu chuantong de chonggou' 地域考古與對五門米美術傳統的重構. In Wu Hung 巫鴻 (ed.), *Han Tang zhijian de zongjiao yishu yu kaogu* 漢唐之間的宗教藝術與考古: 431-455. Beijing, Wenwu chubanshe.

Wu, Hung. 2010. *The Art of the Yellow Spring: Understanding Chinese Tombs*. London, Reaktion Books Ltd.

Xi Yuying 習育英. 2006. Guojia bowuguan cang tongqianshu 國家博物館藏銅錢樹. *Zhongguo lishi wenwu* 中國歷史文物 2006.4: 51-67.

Xie Chong'an 謝崇安. 2005. Zhongjiang Taliangzi Donghan yamu huren bihua diaoxiang kaoshi 中江塔梁子東漢崖墓胡人壁畫雕像考釋. *Sichuan wenwu* 四川文物 2005.5: 34-39.

Xie Yanxiang 謝雁翔. 1974. Sichuan Pixian Xipu chutu de Donghan can bei 四川郫縣犀浦出土的東漢殘碑. *Wenwu* 文物 1974. 4: 67-71.

Xin Lixiang 信立祥. 1986. Han huaxiangshi de fenqu yu fenqi yanjiu 漢畫像石的分區與分期研究. In Yu Weichao 俞偉超 (ed.), *Kaogu leixingxue de lilun yu shijian* 考古類型學的理論與實踐: 234-306. Beijing, Wenwu chubanshe.

Xin Lixiang 信立祥. 2000. *Handai huaxiangshi zonghe yanji* 漢代畫像石綜合研究. Beijing, Wenwu chubanshe.

Xinan bowuyuan choubeichu 西南博物院籌備處. 1954. Baocheng tielu xiuzhu gongcheng zhong faxian de wenwu jianjie 寶成鐵路修築工程中發現的文物簡介. *Wenwu* 文物 1954.3: 10-34.

Xindu xian wenwu guanlisuo 新都縣文物管理所. 1984. Xindu Majiashan 22 hao mu qingli jianbao 新都馬家山22號墓清理簡報. *Sichuan wenwu* 四川文物 1984.4: 63-64.

Xing Yitian 邢義田. 1996. Han bei, Han hua he shigong de guanxi 漢碑漢畫和石工的關係. *Gugong wenwu yuekan* 故宮文物月刊14.4: 44-59.

Xing Yitian 邢義田. 2011. Getao bangti wenxian yu huaxiang jieshi 格套榜題文獻與畫像解釋. In Xing Yitian 邢義田 (ed.), *Hua wei xinsheng* 畫為心聲: 92-137. Beijing, Zhonghua shuju.

Xu Zhongshu 徐仲殊. 1982. *Lun Ba Shu wenhua* 論巴蜀文化. Chengdu, Sichuan renmin chubanshe.

Xu Wenfang 許文芳 and Wei Baowei 韋寶畏. 2005. Zang shu zuozhe ji chengshu shidai kaobian 葬書作者及成書時代考辯. *Yili jiaoyu xueyuan xuebao* 伊犁教育學院學報 18.4: 8-10.

Xuzhou bowuguan 徐州博物館 and Nanjing daxue lishi xue xi kaogu zhuanye 南京大學歷史學系考古專業. 2003. *Xuzhou Beidongshan Xihan chuwang mu* 徐州北洞山西漢楚王墓. Beiing, Wenwu chubanshe.

Yantie lun 鹽鐵論, by Huan Kuan 桓寬, c. 1st century BC. Annotated by Wang Liqi 王利器. Beijing, Zhonghua shuju, 1992.

Yang Chonghua 楊重華. 1992. Sichuan Santai faxian yizuo Donghan mu 四川三台發現一座東漢墓. *Kaogu* 考古 1992.9: 860-862.

Yang Cunguan 楊存貫. 2000. Santai diaocha Qijiang Han Jin yamu qun wenwu yicun 三台調查郪江漢晉崖墓群文化遺存. *Zhongguo wenwu bao* 中國文物報 2000.8.23.

Yang Hongxun 楊鴻勳. 1987. Dougou qiyuan kaocha 斗拱起源考察. In Yang Hongxun 楊鴻勳 (ed.), *Jianzhu kaoguxue lunwen ji* 建築考古學論文集: 253-267. Beijing, Wenwu chubanshe.

Yang Hua 楊華. 2004.Wu si jidao yu Chu Han wenhua de chuancheng 五祀祭禱與楚漢文化的傳承. *Jiang Han luntan* 江漢論壇 2004.9: 95-101.

Yang, Hsien-i and Yang, Gladys. 2008. *Selections from Records of the Historian*. Beijing, Foreign Languages Press.

Yang Kun 楊堃. 1944. Zaoshen kao 灶神考. *Hanxue* 漢學 I: 108-168.

Yang Liansheng 楊聯陞. 1936. Donghan de haozu 東漢的豪族. *Qinghua xuebao* 清華學報 1936: 1007-1063.

Yi li 儀禮. Annotated by Zheng Xuan 鄭玄 (AD 127-200). Collected in *Shisan jing zhushu Yi li zhushu* 十三經注疏儀禮注疏. Beijing, Beijing daxue chubanshe, 1999.

Yiwen leiju 藝文類聚, by Ouyang Xun 歐陽詢 (AD 557-641). Shanghai: Zhonghua shuju, 1965.

Yu Haoliang 于豪亮. 1955. Ji Chengdu Yangzishan yihao mu 記成都揚子山一號墓. *Wenwu* 文物 1955.9: 70-84.

Yu Haoliang 于豪亮. 1961. Qianshu qianshu zuo he yu long manyan zhi xi 錢樹錢樹座和魚龍蔓延之戲. *Wenwu* 文物 1961.11: 43-45.

Yü, Ying-shih. 1987. 'O Soul, Come Back!' A Study in the Changing Conceptions of the Soul and Afterlife in Pre-Buddhist China. *Harvard Journal of Asiatic Studies* 47(2): 363-395.

Yuan Fangming 袁方明. 2007. Zang shu de zuozhe zhenwei kaozheng 葬書的作者真偽考證. *Kangding minzu shifan gaodeng zhuanke xuexiao xuebao* 康定民族師範高等專科學校學報 16.2: 47-49.

Zeng Zhaoyu 曾昭燏, Jiang Baogeng 蔣寶庚 and Li Zhongyi 黎忠義. 1956. *Yi'nan gu huaxiangshi mu fajue baogao* 沂南古畫像石墓發掘報告. Beijing, Wenhuabu wenwu guanliju.

Zhang Caijun 張才俊. 1983. Sichuan Suining Chuanshanpo yamu fajue jianbao 四川遂寧船山坡崖墓發掘簡報. *Kaogu yu wenwu* 考古與文物 1983.3: 31-33.

Zhang Caijun 張才俊. 1985. Sichuan Zhongxian Tujing Shuhan yamu 四川忠縣涂井蜀漢崖墓. *Wenwu* 文物 1985.7: 49-95.

Zhang Jianhua 張建華 and Zhang Yuxia 張玉霞. 2012. Henan Han dai fang mugou muzang de jianzhu xue yanjiu 河南漢代仿木構墓葬的建築學研究. *Zhongyuan wenwu* 中原文物 2012.5: 68-73.

Zhang Qiming 張齊明. 2007. Liang Han shiqi sangzang feng shui xinyang 兩漢時期喪葬風水信仰. *Nandu xuetan* 南都學壇 27.6: 10-15.

Zhang Xunliao 張勳燎 and Yuan Shuguang 袁曙光. 1994. Sichuan sheng bowuguan cang Han dai Lühou zuren muzang shike wenzi ji qi xiangguan wenti 四川省博物館藏漢代呂後族人墓葬石刻文字及其相關問題. In Sichuan daxue lishi xi 四川大學歷史系 (ed.), *Zhongguo xi'nan de gudai jiaotong yu wenhua* 中國西南的古代交通與文化: 106-109. Chengdu, Sichuan daxue chubanshe.

Zhao Youwen 趙幼文. 1998. *Cao Zhi ji jiaozhu* 曹植集校注. Beijing, Renmin wenxue chubanshe.

Zheng Yan 鄭岩. 1998. Muzhu huaxiang yanjiu 墓主畫像研究. In Shandong daxue kaoguxi 山東大學考古系 (ed.), *Liu Dunyuan xiansheng jinian wenji* 劉敦愿先生紀念文集: 450-468. Ji'nan, Shandong daxue chubanshe.

Zheng Yan 鄭岩. 2002. *Wei Jin Nan Bei chao bihuamu yanjiu* 魏晉南北朝壁畫墓研究. Beijing, Wenwu chubanshe.

Zhong Zhi 鍾治. 2008. Sichuan Santai Huangmingyue yihao huaxiang yamu 四川三台黃明月一號畫像崖墓. *Wenwu* 文物 2008.2: 69-71.

Zhongguo huaxiangshi quanji bianji weiyuanhui 中國畫像石全集編輯委員會. 2000a. *Zhongguo Huaxiangshi quanji vol. 2* 中國畫像石全集第二卷. Ji'nan, Shandong meishu chubanshe.

Zhongguo huaxiangshi quanji bianji weiyuanhui 中國畫像石全集編輯委員會. 2000b. *Zhongguo Huaxiangshi quanji vol. 7* 中國畫像石全集第七卷. Ji'nan, Shandong meishu chubanshe.

Zhongguo huaxiangshi quanji bianji weiyuanhui 中國畫像石全集編輯委員會. 2000c. *Zhongguo Huaxiangshi quanji vol. 1* 中國畫像石全集第一卷. Ji'nan, Shandong meishu chubanshe.

Zhongguo shehui kexue yuan kaogu yanjiu suo 中國社會科學院考古研究所. 1980. *Mancheng hanmu fajue baogao* 滿城漢墓發掘報告. Beijing, wenwu chubanshe.

Zhuang Wenbin 莊文彬. 1994. Sichuan Suining shi faxian liangzuo Donghan yamu 四川遂寧市發現兩座東漢崖墓". *Kaogu* 考古 1994.8: 760-761.

Zhou li 周禮. Annotated by Zheng Xuan 鄭玄 (AD 127-200). Collected in *Shisan jing zhushu Zhou li zhushu* 十三經注疏周禮注疏. Beijing, Beijing daxue chubanshe, 1999.

Zou Junzhi 鄒濬智. 2008. *Xihan yiqian jiazhai wu si jiqi xiangguan xinyang yanjiu: yi Chu di jianbo wenxian ziliao wei taolun jiaodian* 西漢以前家宅五祀及其相關信仰研究:以楚地簡帛文獻資料為討論焦點. Unpublished PhD thesis, National Taiwan Normal University.

Appendix 1
Stories of Filial Sons and Eminent Men and Women Carved in the Cliff tombs in Sichuan

Stories of Filial Sons

The stories of filial sons carved in the cliff tombs in Sichuan have been identified mainly based on the pictorial stone carvings with inscriptions in the Wu Liang shrine in Jiaxiang in Shandong. Wu Hung has introduced in detail on how the stories of the filial sons carved in the Wu Liang shrine can be traced to their various textural sources in The Wu Liang Shrine: The Ideology of Early Chinese Pictorial Art.[1] In the Western Han, Liu Xiang 劉向 compiled the *Xiaozi zhuan* 孝子傳 (Biographies of Filial Sons) with illustrations. The *Taiping yulan* 太平御覽, a Song encyclopedia cites biographies of two filial sons from the *Xiaozi zhuan* by Liu Xiang, which confirms the existence of the *Xiaozi zhuan* in Western Han.[2] Though the original version of the *Xiaozi zhuan* compiled by Liu Xiang was lost, various versions of the biographies of filial sons appeared during the period between the fall of the Eastern Han and the Sui (AD 220-588). As Wu Hung suggested, 'the development of the *Xiaozi zhuan*' is 'characterized by a continuous accumulation of stories and by the replacement of less famous earlier examples by popular or influential later ones'.[3] In this sense, there was no standard set of stories of filial sons in both textual records and pictorial carvings in funerary monuments.

1. Yuan Gu 元穀

The story of Yuan Gu is cited from the *Xiaozi zhuan* in the *Taiping yulan*.

> The origin of Yuan Gu is unknown. When his grandfather was old, his parents detested the old man and wanted to abandon him. Gu, who was fifteen years old, entreated them piteously with tears, but his parents did not listen to him. They made a carriage and carried the grandfather away and abandoned him. Gu brought the carriage back. His father asked him, 'What are you going to do with this inauspicious thing?' Gu replied: 'I am afraid that when you get old, I will not be able to make a new carriage, and so I have brought it back.' His father was moved and ashamed and carried the grandfather back and cared for him. He overcame his selfishness and criticized himself. He finally became a 'purely [filial] son' and Gu became a 'purely [filial] grandson'.

原穀者,不知何許人.祖年老,父母厭患之,意欲弃之.穀年十五,涕泣苦谏.父母不从,乃作舆,异弃之.穀乃随收舆归.父谓之曰:'尔焉用此凶具?'穀云:'恐后父老,不能更作,是以取之尔.'父感悟愧惧,乃载祖归侍养.克己自责,更成纯孝,穀为'纯孝孙'.[4]

2. Min Ziqian 閔子騫

The story of Min Ziqian is recorded in the *Yiwen leiju* 藝文類聚 by Ouyang Xun 歐陽詢.

> Min Ziqian had a younger brother. After their mother died, their father remarried and had two other sons. Ziqian drove a chariot for his father and dropped the bridle. His father held his hands and [found] that he wore only thin clothing. The father then went home and called the sons of the stepmother. He held their hands and [found] that they were wearing thick, warm clothing. He blamed his wife, saying, 'The reason that I married you was for my sons. Now you are cheating me and I cannot keep you here!' Ziqian went forth and said, 'When mother is here, only one son is wearing thin clothing; if mother leaves, four sons will be in the cold.' His father became silent. Therefore people say that Min Ziqian kept his mother home by one word and made three sons warm by a second word.

閔子騫,兄弟二人.母死,其父更娶,復有二子.子騫為其父御車,失轡,父持其手,衣甚單,父則歸,呼其後母兒,持其手,衣甚厚溫,即謂其婦曰:'吾所以娶汝,乃為吾子.今汝欺我,去無留.'子騫前曰:'母在一子單,母去四子寒.'其父默然.故曰:孝哉閔子騫,一言其母還,再言三子溫.[5]

3. Laizi 萊子

The story is recorded in the *Taiping yulan*, which quotes Shi Jueshou's 師覺授 *Xiaozi Zhuan*.

> Elder Laizi was a native of Chu. When he was seventy years old, his parents were both still alive. With the ultimate filial piety, he often wore multicolored clothes to serve his parents food in the main hall. Once he hurt his feet. Afraid to sadden his parents, he made himself tumble stiffly to the ground and bawled like an infant. Confucius remarked: 'one does not use the word "old" when one's parents are getting old, because one fears this will make them grieve about their elderliness.' A person like Elder Laizi can be called one who does not lose a child's heart.

---

[1] Wu 1989b: 272-276.
[2] Wu 1989b: 272.
[3] Wu 1989b: 73.
[4] *Taiping yulan*: 2360. The English translation is after Wu 1989b: 304-305.
[5] *Yiwen leiju*: 369. The translation is after Wu 1989b: 278.

老萊子者,楚人也,行年七十,父母俱存.至孝蒸蒸,常著斑斕之衣,為親取飲,上堂腳跌,恐傷父母之心,因僵仆為嬰兒啼.孔子曰: '父母老,常言不稱老,為其傷老也.' 若老萊子可謂不失孺子之心矣.[6]

4. Boyu 伯瑜

The story of Boyu is recorded in the *Taiping yulan*.

> Boyu made a mistake and wept when his mother beat him with a stick. The mother asked him, saying, 'I did not see you weep when I punished you before. Why do you cry today?' Boyu replied: 'Before, when I offended you and you beat me with the stick, I often felt pain. But today your strength could not make me feel pain. That is why I am weeping.'

伯瑜有過,其母笞之,泣,其母曰: '他日笞子未嘗見泣,今泣何也?' 對曰: '他日瑜得罪笞嘗痛,今母之力不能使痛,是以泣.'[7]

5. Dong Yong 董永

The story of Dong Yong is recorded in the *Taiping yulan* which quotes the *Xiaozi zhuan* by Liu Xiang.

> Dong Yong of the Former Han was a native of Qiancheng. Having lost his mother in childhood, he alone provided for his father. When his father died, he did not have money to arrange the funeral and so he took a loan of ten thousand cash from someone. Yong said to his creditor: 'If I cannot repay the money later, I will give you my body and become your slave.' The creditor was sympathetic. Yong got the money, buried his father, and then went to [the creditor's place to [become his slave. On his way he met a woman who asked him to take her as his wife. Yong said: 'Now I am poor like this, and moreover I will become a slave. How can I humiliate you by taking you as my wife?' The woman replied: 'It is my hope to become your wife; I will not regard being poor and lowly as a disgrace.' Then Yong took the woman and went with her to [the creditor's place]. The creditor asked: 'It was originally agreed that one person [would be my slave]. Why are there now two persons?' Yong replied: 'According to our agreement you would have only one slave but now you have two- is there anything wrong with that?' The wife replied: 'I can weave.' The creditor said: 'If you weave one thousand bolts of silk for me, then I will let you both go free.' The wife then required natural silk [from the creditor]. Within ten days, one thousand bolts of silk were finished. The creditor was surprised and then released the couple. They went to the place where they had met. The wife told Yong: 'I am the Weaving Maiden from heaven and was moved by your perfect filial piety. Heaven sent me to repay you. Now that your troubles have been settled, I cannot remain her long.' After these words, clouds and fog descended, and she suddenly flew away.

前漢董永,千乘人.小失母,獨養父.父亡無以葬,乃從人貸錢一萬.永謂錢主曰: '后若無錢還君,當以身作奴.' 主甚憐之.永得錢葬父畢,將往為奴,于路忽逢一婦人,求為永妻,永曰: '今貧若是,身復為奴,何敢屈夫人之為妻.' 婦人曰: '原為君婦,不恥貧賤.' 永隨將婦人至.錢主曰: '本言一人,今何二?' 永曰: '言一得二,于理乖乎!' 主問永妻曰: '何能?' 妻曰: '能織耳.' 主曰: '為我織千匹絹,即放尔夫妻.' 於是索絲,十日之內,千匹絹足.主驚,遂放夫婦二人而去.行至本相逢處,乃謂永曰: '我是天之織女,感君之孝,天使我償之.今君事了,不能久停.' 語訖,雲霧四垂,忽飛而去.[8]

6. *Kaifeng* 凱風 (Genial Wind)

The story of seven filial sons who showed their gratitude to their mother is recorded in the poem *Kaifeng* (Genial Wind) in the *Shi jing* 詩經.

> The genial wind from the south/ Blows on the heart of that jujube tree, / Till that heart looks tender and beautiful./ What toil and pain did our mother endure!/ The genial wind from the south/ Blows on the branches of that jujube tree, / Our mother is wise and good; But among us there is no good./ There is the cool spring/ Below [the city of] Tseun./ We are seven sons,/ And our mother is full of pain and suffering./ The beautiful yellow birds/ Give forth their pleasant notes,/ We are seven sons,/ And cannot compose our mother's heart.

凱風自南,吹彼棘心.棘心夭夭,母氏劬勞.凱風自南,吹彼棘薪.母氏聖善,我無令人.爰有寒泉,在浚之下.有子七人,母氏勞苦.睍睆黃鳥,載好其音.有子七人,莫慰母心.[9]

Eminent Men and Women

7. Liang Gaoxing 梁高行

The story of Liang Gaoxing is recorded in the *Lienü zhuan* 列女傳 written by Liu Xiang 劉向 in the 1st century BC.

> Gaoxing was a widow from the state of Liang. She was glorious in her beauty and praiseworthy in her conduct. Though her husband died, leaving her widowed early in life, she did not remarry. Many noblemen of Liang strove among themselves to marry her, but no one could win her. The king of Liang heard of this and sent his minister with betrothal gifts. Gaoxing said, 'My husband unfortunately died young; I live in widowhood to raise his orphans, and [I am afraid that] I have given them enough attention. Many honorable men have sought me, but I have fortunately succeeded in evading them. Today the king is seeking

---

[6] *Taiping yulan*: 1907-1908. The translation is after Wu 1989b: 280.
[7] *Taiping yulan*: 1907. The translation is after Wu 1989b: 287.
[8] *Taiping yulan*: 1899. The translation is after Wu 1989b: 289-291.
[9] *Shi jing*: 82. The English translation is after Legge 1960: 50-51.

my hand. I have learned that "the principle for a wife is that once having gone forth to marry, she will not change over, and that she may keep all the rules of chastity and faithfulness." To forget the dead and to run to the living is not faithfulness; to be honored and forget the lowly is not faithfulness; to be honored and forge the lowly is not chastity; and to abandon righteousness and follow gain is not worthy of a woman.' Then she took up a mirror and a knife, and cut off her nose, saying 'I have become a disfigured person. I did not commit suicide because I could not bear to see my children orphaned a second time. The king has sought me because of my beauty, but today, after having been disfigured, I may avoid the danger [of remarrying].' Thereupon, the minister made his report, and the king exalted her righteousness and praised her conduct.

高行者,梁之寡婦也.其為人榮與色而美與行.夫死早,寡不嫁.梁貴人多爭欲娶之者,不能得.梁王聞之,使相聘焉.高行曰:'妾夫不幸早死,死狗馬填溝壑,妾守養其孤幼,曾不得專意.貴人多求妾者,幸而得免,今王又重之.妾聞:"婦人之以,一往而不改,以全貞信之節."忘死而趨生,是不信也.貴而忘賤,是不貞也.棄義而從利,無以為人.'乃援鏡持刀以割其鼻曰:'妾已刑矣.所以不死者,不忍幼弱之重孤也.王之求妾者以其色也.今刑餘之人殆可釋矣.'於是相以報,王大其義,高其行,乃復其身,尊其號曰高行.[10]

8. Wife of Qiu Hu 秋胡

The story on the wife of Qiu Hu is also recorded in the *Lienü zhuan.*

> The Eminent Wife was the wife of Master Qiu Hu of Lu. When she had been married but five days, her husband went to fill an office in Chen and returned only after five year. When he had not yet reached his home, he saw a woman picking mulberries by the roadside. Qiu Hu was pleased with her, and he descended from his carriage and spoke to her: 'As it is very hot to pick mulberries and I have come a long journey, I hope you will allow me to spread out my cloak and rest in the shade of the mulberry tree.' The woman went on picking mulberries without stopping, and [again] Qiu Hu spoke to her: 'To labor in the field is not so good as to happen upon a good harvest; to pick mulberries is not so good as meeting the minister of the state. I have money that I desire to give you.' The woman said, 'Oh no! I use my strength to pick mulberries; I spin and weave in order to supply clothes and food; and I serve my parents-in-law and raise my husband's children. I do not want your money. I hope that you have no ulterior motive for I have no intention of giving in to lust. Take up your traveling cloak and your money!' After this, Qiu Hu departed.

> When he reached home, he presented the money to his mother and ordered someone to call his wife to him. Then the woman who was picking mulberries approached, and Qiu Hu was ashamed. The wife said, 'You bade farewell to your parents to fill an office when you bound up your hair, and only returned five years later. You ought to ride your horse to return happily, hurrying to arrive and raising a dust like wind. However, today you took a fancy to a woman by the roadside, threw down your cloak, and tried to give her your money. This is to forget your mother, and to forget your mother is unfilial. To admire the beauty of women and to give in to unrestrained lust is depraved conduct. Depraved conduct is not righteous. If you are unfilial in the service of your parents, you will be disloyal in the service of your sovereign; if your home life is not righteous, then the administration of your office will unprincipled. Filial piety and benignity have both gone to ruin, and this may not be allowed. I cannot bear to see these happen. You may take another wife, but I will not marry again.' Afterwards she departed and went eastward where she cast herself into a river and drowned.

潔婦者,魯秋胡子妻也.既納之五日,去而官於陳,五年乃歸.未至家,見路旁婦人採桑,秋胡子悅之,下車謂曰:'若曝採桑,吾行道遠,願托桑陰下□下賚休焉.'婦人採桑不輟,秋胡子謂曰:'力田不如逢豐年,力桑不如見國卿.吾有金,願以與夫人.'婦人曰:'嘻!夫採桑力作,紡績織紝,以供衣食,奉二親,養夫子.吾不願金,所願卿無有外意,妾亦無淫佚之志,收子之賚與笥金.'秋胡子遂去,至家,奉金遺母,使人喚婦至,乃向採桑者也,秋胡慚.婦曰:'子束髮辭親,往仕五年乃還,當所悅馳驟,揚塵疾至.今也乃悅路傍婦人,下子之裝,以金予之,是忘母也.忘母不孝,好色淫佚,是污行也,污行不義.夫事親不孝,則事君不忠.處家不義,則治官不理.孝義并亡,必不遂矣.妾不忍見,子改娶矣,妾亦不嫁.'遂去而東走,投河而死.[11]

9. The Filial Daughter-in-Law of Donghai 東海

The story of the filial daughter-in-law of Donghai is both recorded in the *Lienü zhuan* and the *Han shu.*

> In Donghai there was a filial daughter-in-law, who was widowed at a young age and lost her son. She attended her mother-in-law carefully. Her mother-in-law wanted her to get a new marriage. She refused. Her mother-in-law told the neighbors: 'My daughter-in-law devoted too much in attending me. I felt sorry for her loss of son and husband. Since I am already old there is no need to bother young person.' Then the mother-in-law committed suicide. Her daughter reported to the officer: 'My sister-in-law killed my mother.' The officer arrested the filial daughter-in-law, who refused to take the charge of murder. Yu Gong thought since this filial daughter-in-law attended her mother-in-law carefully for over ten

---

[10] *Lienü zhuan*: 58. The translation is after Wu 1989b: 253-254.

[11] *Lienü zhuan*: 68. The translation is after Wu 1989b: 255.

years, well-known for her filial piety, there was no reason to believe that she was the murderer. The grand administrator of the county did not accept Yu Gong's argument and finally sentenced the filial daughter-in-law to death. The county was affected by drought for three years after that. When the new grand administrator came, he consulted the exorcist for the reason of the drought. Yu Gong said: 'The filial daughter-in-law should not be executed. The previous grand administrator made the wrong decision.' Subsequently, the new grand administrator sacrificed cattle to the filial daughter-in-law at her tomb. It started to rain heavily right away. The people of the county thus showed their respect to Yu Gong.

東海有孝婦,少寡,亡子,養姑甚謹,姑欲嫁之,終不肯.姑謂鄰人曰:'孝婦事我勤苦,哀其亡子守寡,我老.久累丁壯,奈何?'其後姑自經死,姑女告吏:'婦殺我母.'吏捕孝婦,孝婦辭不殺姑.吏驗治,孝婦自誣服.具獄上府,于公以為此婦養姑十餘年,以孝聞,必不殺也.太守不聽,于公爭之,弗能得,乃抱其具獄,哭於府上,因辭疾去.太守竟論殺孝婦.郡中枯旱三年.後太守至,卜筮其故,于公曰:'孝婦不當死,前太守彊斷之.咎黨在是乎?'於是太守殺牛自祭孝婦,因表其墓,天立大雨,歲孰.郡中以此大敬重于公.¹²

10. Ji Zha 季札

The story of Ji Zha is recorded in the *Shi ji*.

When Ji zha was on his way to the north as an envoy, he met the ruler of the Xu state, who admired Ji Zha's sword but did not dare to tell Ji Zha. Ji Zha knew this, however he did not give out his sword for he still had the mission. When he came back to the Xu state, the ruler of Xu was already dead. Ji Zha took off his sword and hung it on the tree at the tomb of the ruler of Xu. Ji Zha's attendant asked: 'The ruler of Xu is already dead. Whom was this for?' Ji Zha said: 'I decided to give this sword to him long time ago. The fact that he is already dead would not change my mind.'

季札之初使,北過徐君.徐君好季札劍,口弗敢言.季札心知之,為使上國,未獻.還至徐.徐君已死,於是乃解其寶劍.繫之徐君樹而去.從者曰:'徐君已死,尚誰予乎?'季子曰:'不然.始吾心已許之,豈以死倍吾心哉!'¹³

---

¹² *Han shu*: 3041-3042.

¹³ *Shi ji*: 1459.

Appendix 2
Eastern Han High Officials of the Areas Outside Sichuan from the Sichuan Area[1]

Commandery of Origin	Name	Official Title (Area)	Reference
Shu 蜀	Ren Xun 任循	Grand Administrator 太守 of Changsha 長沙 (Hunan)	*Huayang*: 915
Shu 蜀	Ren Fang 任昉	Grand Minister of Agriculture 大司農 (Henan)	*Huayang*: 916
Shu 蜀	Ren Kai 任愷	Inspector 刺史 of Xuzhou 徐州 (Jiangsu)	*Huyang*: 916
Shu 蜀	Zhang Ba 張霸	Palace Attendant 侍中 (Henan)	*Huayang*: 916
Shu 蜀	Zhang Ling 張陵	Master of Writing 尚屬 (Henan)	*Huayang*: 916
Shu 蜀	Zhao Jie 趙戒	Grand Commandant 太尉 (Henan)	*Huayang*: 916
Shu 蜀	Zhao Dian 趙典	Grand Master of Ceremonies 太常 (Henan)	*Huayang*: 916
Shu 蜀	Zhao Qian 趙謙	Grand Commandant 太尉 (Henan)	*Huayang*: 916
Shu 蜀	Zhao Wen 趙溫	Minister over the Masses 司徒 (Henan)	*Huayang*: 916
Shu 蜀	Yang Ban 楊班	Erudit 博士 (Henan)	*Huayang*: 917
Shu 蜀	Liu Zong 柳宗	Prefect 令 of Meiyang 美陽 (Shaanxi)	*Huayang*: 917
Shu 蜀	He Ying 何英	Supervisor of the Internuncios 謁者僕射 (Henan)	*Huayang*: 917
Shu 蜀	Chang Qia 常洽	Palace Attendant 侍中 (Henan)	*Huayang*: 916
Shu 蜀	Chang Xu 常詡	Attending Secretary 侍禦史 (Henan)	*Huayang*: 916
Shu 蜀	Chang Zhu 常竺	Palace Attendant 侍中 (Henan)	*Huayang*: 919
Guanghan 廣漢	Zhai Pu 翟酺	將作大匠 Court Architect (Henan)	*Huayang*: 937
Guanghan 廣漢	Guo Jian 郭堅	Colonel 校尉 of Wuhuan 烏桓 (Inner-Mongolia)	*Huayang*: 936
Guanghan 廣漢	Guo He 郭賀	Colonel Director of the Retainers 司隸校尉 (Henan)	*Huayang*: 936
Guanghan 廣漢	Cai Gong 蔡弓	Grand Administrator 太守 of Lujiang 廬江 (Anhui)	*Huayang*: 936
Guanghan 廣漢	Li You 李尤	Chancellor 相 of Lejiang 樂江 (Jiangxi)	*Huayang*: 936
Guanghan 廣漢	Li Chong 李充	Gentleman of the Masters of Writing 尚書郎	*Huayang*: 936
Guanghan 廣漢	Zhang Jiang 張江	Grand Administrator 太守 of Wuwei 武威 (Gansu)	*Huayang*: 937
Guanghan 廣漢	Zhe Guo 折國	Grand Administrator 太守 of Yulin 郁林 (Guangxi)	*Huayang*: 937
Guanghan 廣漢	Yang Tong 楊統	Prefect 令 of Pengcheng 彭城 (Jiangsu)	*Huayang*: 936
Guanghan 廣漢	Yang Bo 楊博	Imperial Household Grandee 光祿大夫 (Henan)	*Huayang*: 936
Guanghan 廣漢	Yang Hou 楊厚	Palace Attendant 侍中 (Henan)	*Huayang*: 936
Guanghan 廣漢	Wang Huan 王渙	Prefect 令 of Luoyang 洛陽 (Henan)	*Huayang*: 937
Guanghan 廣漢	Tan Xian 鐔顯	Palace Attendant 侍中 (Henan)	*Huayang*: 936
Guanghan 廣漢	Yang Qi 羊期	Prefect 令 of Yewang 野王 (Henan)	*Huayang*: 937
Guanghan 廣漢	Wen Tun 文忳	Grand Administrator 太守 of Beihai 北海 (Shandong)	*Huayang*: 948
Guanghan 廣漢	Kou Qi 寇祺	Prefect 令 of Jiyin 濟陰 (Shandong)	*Huayang*: 948
Qianwei 犍為	Zhao Song 趙松	Grand Administrator 太守 of Shangdang 上黨 (Shanxi)	*Huayang*: 941
Qianwei 犍為	Yang Mang 楊莽	Inspector 刺史 of Yangzhou 揚州 (Jiangsu)	*Huayang*: 941
Qianwei 犍為	Yang Huan 楊渙	Colonel Director of the Retainers 司隸校尉 (Henan)	*Huayang*: 941
Qianwei 犍為	Yang Yingbo 楊穎伯	Inspector 刺史 of Jizhou 冀州 (Hebei)	*Huayang*: 941
Qianwei 犍為	Zhang Hao 張皓	Grand Minister of Works 大司空 (Henan)	*Huayang*: 941
Qianwei 犍為	Zhang Xu 張續	Master of Writing 尚書 (Henan)	*Huayang*: 942
Qianwei 犍為	Zhang Fang 張方	Inspector 刺史 of Yuzhou 豫州 (Henan)	*Huayang*: 942
Qianwei 犍為	Yang Huai 楊淮	Colonel Director of the Retainers 司隸校尉 (Henan)	*Huayang*: 941
Qianwei 犍為	Dong Jun 董均	Colonel of the City Gates 城門校尉 (Henan)	*Huayang*: 941
Qianwei 犍為	Zhao Qi 趙旂	Colonel Director of the Retainers 司隸校尉 (Henan)	*Huayang*: 942
Qianwei 犍為	Du Fu 杜撫	Prefect of the Majors in Charge of Official Carriages 公車令 (Henan)	*Huayang*: 942
Qianwei 犍為	FeikuYi 費貽	Grand Administrator 太守 of Hepu 合浦 (Guangxi)	*Huayang*: 941
Ba 巴	Ye Huan 謁煥	Grand Administrator 太守 of Runan 汝南 (Henan)	*Huayang*: 925
Ba 巴	Ran Wen 然溫	Governor 太守 of Guilin 桂林 (Guangxi)	*Huayang*: 925
Ba 巴	Ren Wengong 任文公	Assistant for the Minister of Works 司空掾 (Henan)	*Huayang*: 921
Ba 巴	Qiao Xuan 譙玄	Grand Palace Grandee 太中大夫 (Henan)	*Huayang*: 922
Ba 巴	Qiao Ying 譙瑛	Gentleman of the Grand Masters of Writing 尚書郎 (Henan)	*Huayang*: 922
Ba 巴	Zhao Hong 趙宏	Inspector 刺史 of Liangzhou 涼州 (Gansu)	*Huayang*: 922
Ba 巴	Yan Zun 嚴遵	Inspector 刺史 of Yangzhou 揚州 (Jiangsu)	*Huayang*: 924
Ba 巴	Yan Yu 嚴羽	Inspector 刺史 of Xuzhou 徐州 (Jiangsu)	*Huayang*: 924
Ba 巴	Wang Weiqing 王偉卿	Prefect 令 of Chang'an 長安 (Shaanxi)	*Huayang*: 924

[1] All the official titles here are translated after the Appendix on Han Dynasty Official Titles in Bielenstein 1980.

Commandery of Origin	Name	Official Title (Area)	Reference
Ba 巴	Zhao Shao 趙邵	Prefect 令 of Shangcai 上蔡 (Henan)	*Huayang*: 925
Ba 巴	Xuan He 玄賀	Grand Administrator 太守 of Pei 沛 (Jiangsu)	*Huayang*: 924
Ba 巴	Pang Xiong 龐雄	Grand Herald 大鴻臚 (Henan)	*Huayang*: 924
Ba 巴	Feng Huan 馮煥	Inspector 刺史 of Youzhou 幽州 (Hebei)	*Huayang*: 924
Ba 巴	Feng Gun 馮緄	General of Chariots and Calvary 車騎將軍 (Henan)	*Huayang*: 924
Ba 巴	Feng Yun 馮允	Colonel of Defeating Enemies 降虜校尉 (Henan)	*Huayang*: 924
Ba 巴	Feng Zun 馮遵	Gentleman of the Masters of Writing 尚書郎	*Huayang*: 924
Ba 巴	Li Wen 李溫	Grand Administrator 太守 of Guilin 桂林 (Guangxi)	Huayang: 925
Ba 巴	Shen □ 沈□	Prefect 令 of Xinfeng 新豐 (Shaanxi)	Chongqing shi wenhua ju and Chongqing shi bowuguan 1992: 40-41
Ba 巴	Gong Diao 龔調	Inspector 刺史 of Jingzhou 荊州 (Hubei)	*Huayang*: 925
Ba 巴	Chen Hong 陳宏	Grand Administrator 太守 of Shanggu 上穀 (Hebei)	*Huayang*: 925
Ba 巴	Zhao Yan 趙晏	Grand Administrator 太守 of Wei 魏 (Heinan)	*Huayang*: 925

Appendix 3
Eastern Han Cliff Tombs Excavated in the Sichuan Area

I: single chamber II: double-chamber III: more than two chambers

No.	Name	Place	Date	Type	Furnishings	Burial Instrument	Grave Goods — Pottery	Grave Goods — Bronzes	Grave Goods — Ceramics	Tomb Decoration	Source
1	Tianhuishan M1	Chengdu	late Eastern Han	III	drainage	pottery coffin	*guan, fu, bo,* lamp, well, figurines, animal	money tree		brick with stripe pattern	Liu Zhiyuan 1958
2	Tianhuishan M2	Chengdu	late Eastern Han	I	drainage	wooden coffin				brick with stripe pattern	Liu Zhiyuan 1958
3	Tianhuishan M3	Chengdu	late Eastern Han	III	drainage	pottery coffin, stone coffin, brick coffin	*guan, bo, pan,* lamp, well, paddy field, house, zither, figurines, animal	money tree		brick with stripe pattern, pictorial stone coffin	Liu Zhiyuan 1958
4	2002CHLM1	Chengdu	middle Eastern Han	I		pottery coffin	*pen, bo, wan, fu*				Chengdu shi wenwu kaogu yanjiusuo 2004
5	2002CHLM2	Chengdu	late Eastern Han	II	drainage, niche	pottery coffin	*fu,* figurine, dog				Chengdu shi wenwu kaogu yanjiusuo 2004
6	2002CHLM3	Chengdu	middle Eastern Han	II	drainage, niche, stove	pottery coffin, stone coffin	*guan, weng, bo,* granary, pond, house, figurine, wheel			carvings on coffin	Chengdu shi wenwu kaogu yanjiusuo 2004
7	2002CHLM4	Chengdu	middle Eastern Han	II	drainage	pottery coffin	*guan, fu, zeng,* house, figurine, paddy field				Chengdu shi wenwu kaogu yanjiusuo 2004
8	2002CXLM1	Chengdu	middle Eastern Han	II			*guan*				Chengdu shi wenwu kaogu yanjiusuo 2004
9	2002CXLM2	Chengdu	middle Eastern Han	II	niche		*guan, fu, weng, zhong,* figurine, animal, stove				Chengdu shi wenwu kaogu yanjiusuo 2004
10	2002CXLM3	Chengdu	middle Eastern Han	III	niche						Chengdu shi wenwu kaogu yanjiusuo 2004
11	2008CXMM1	Chengdu	early Eastern Han	II	niche		*bo, pen, gui, ganghu, fu, weng, guan,* cover				Chengdu shi wenwu kaogu yanjiusuo 2009
12	Shahecun M	Chengdu	middle Eastern Han	II		pottery coffin	*guan, bo, dou, fu,* well, *pen,* lamp, field, figurine, animal	crane			Li Jiafeng 1991
13	Xinshenggongshe M2	Pixan	Eastern Han	I		stone coffin	*guan, bo,* zither, aniaml, house	money tree		carvings on stone coffin	Sichuan Pixian wenhuaguan 1979
14	Yeyuedong M1	Jianyang	Eastern Han	I	niche		figurine, pond, *fu, dou, guan, pan,* animal	*xi*		carvings on lintel	Fang Jianguo and Tang Zhaojun 1992
15	Guitoushan M	Jianyang	late Eastern Han	I		stone coffin	figurine, chicken	support, applique, vessel, decoration		carvings on stone coffin	Neijiang shi wenguansuo and Jianyang xian wenhuaguan 1991
16	HM1	Xindu	early Eastern Han	I			*fu, pen, bo, wan*				Chen Yunhong, Zhang Yuxin and Wang Bo 2007
17	HM2	Xindu	late Eastern Han	II	niche	pottery coffin	*fu,* tomb appeasing figurine, chef figurine, dog				Chen Yunhong, Zhang Yuxin and Wang Bo 2007
18	HM3	Xindu	middle to late Eastern Han	II	drainage, niche, stove	pottery coffin	*guan, weng, bo,* figurine, pond, house, granary	money tree, ring		pictorial stone coffin	Chen Yunhong, Zhang Yuxin and Wang Bo 2007
19	HM4	Xindu	early to late Eastern Han	II			*guan, bo, fu, zeng,* paddy field, figurine, house, animal	money tree			Chen Yunhong, Zhang Yuxin and Wang Bo 2007
20	LM1	Xindu	middle or late Eastern Han	II		house-shaped stone coffin	*guan, fu, pen*			pictorial stone coffin	Chen Yunhong, Zhang Yuxin and Wang Bo 2007
21	LM2	Xindu	early Eastern Han	III	niche		*guan, fu, weng, zhong,* figurine, stove, animal				Chen Yunhong, Zhang Yuxin and Wang Bo 2007

Eastern Han (AD 25-220) Tombs in Sichuan

No.	Name	Place	Date	Type	Furnishings	Burial Instrument	Grave Goods Pottery	Grave Goods Bronzes	Grave Goods Ceramics	Tomb Decoration	Source
22	LM3	Xindu	early or Wang Mang Period to Late Eastern Han	III	niche		relics	arrowhead			Chen Yunhong, Zhang Yuxin and Wang Bo 2007
23	Majiashan M22	Xindu	early Eastern Han (AD 65)	II			figurine, table, *wan*				Xindu xian wenwu guanlisuo 1984
24	PM 127	Pengshan	early Eastern Han	I	drainage	wooden coffin	*guan, weng,*				Nanjing bowuyuan 1991
25	Jizhaodong A	Pengshan	early Eastern Han	I	niche	pottery coffin					Nanjing bowuyuan 1991
26	Fushoudong M	Pengshan	early Eastern Han	I		pottery coffin					Nanjing bowuyuan 1991
27	PM 131	Pengshan	early Eastern Han	I		pottery coffin	*wan*				Nanjing bowuyuan 1991
28	PM 164	Pengshan	early Eastern Han	I		pottery coffin				carvings on lintel	Nanjing bowuyuan 1991
29	PM 362	Pengshan	early Eastern Han	I		pottery coffin		spoon			Nanjing bowuyuan 1991
30	PM 705	Pengshan	early Eastern Han	I		pottery coffin					Nanjing bowuyuan 1991
31	PM 166	Pengshan	middle or late Eastern Han	II		pottery coffin	house, chicken, *fu*, figurine	money tree		carvings on lintel	Nanjing bowuyuan 1991
32	PM 369	Pengshan	middle or late Eastern Han	II		pottery coffin, wooden coffin	*wan*				Nanjing bowuyuan 1991
33	PM 460	Pengshan	middle or late Eastern Han	II	niche	stone coffin				carvings on lintel	Nanjing bowuyuan 1991
34	PM 556	Pengshan	middle or late Eastern Han	II	niche	pottery coffin, stone coffin	*fu, wan*, animal, figurine				Nanjing bowuyuan 1991
35	PM 561	Pengshan	middle or late Eastern Han	II			chicken, figurine				Nanjing bowuyuan 1991
36	PM 656	Pengshan	middle or late Eastern Han	II		stone coffin	*weng*, figurine				Nanjing bowuyuan 1991
37	PM 128	Pengshan	middle or late Eastern Han	II	niche, drainage	pottery coffin	*guan, fu,* well				Nanjing bowuyuan 1991
38	PM 153	Pengshan	middle or late Eastern Han	II	drainage	pottery coffin	*guan*, figurine				Nanjing bowuyuan 1991
39	PM 161	Pengshan	middle or late Eastern Han	II	drainage	pottery coffin	*guan, weng, fu, wan*, table, ear cup, *bo*, animal, figurine	needle			Nanjing bowuyuan 1991
40	PM 684	Pengshan	middle or late Eastern Han	II	niche, drainage	wooden coffin	*guan, zeng*, ear cup				Nanjing bowuyuan 1991
41	PM 666	Pengshan	middle or late Eastern Han	II	niche	stone coffin	*guan, weng, fu, zeng, wan*, table, *bo*, floodgate, animal, figurine	money tree			Nanjing bowuyuan 1991
42	PM 677	Pengshan	middle or late Eastern Han	II	niche		chicken, figurine				Nanjing bowuyuan 1991
43	PM 682	Pengshan	middle or late Eastern Han	II	niche		*guan, zeng*, table, pond, figurine				Nanjing bowuyuan 1991
44	PM 800	Pengshan	middle or late Eastern Han	II	niche		chicken, figurine				Nanjing bowuyuan 1991
45	PM 901	Pengshan	middle or late Eastern Han	II	niche	wooden coffin	house, animal, figurine				Nanjing bowuyuan 1991
46	PM 152	Pengshan	middle or late Eastern Han	II	niche		figurine	chariot fittings			Nanjing bowuyuan 1991
47	PM 167	Pengshan	middle or late Eastern Han	II	niche		animal, figurine			brick with stripe pattern	Nanjing bowuyuan 1991
48	PM 170	Pengshan	middle or late Eastern Han	II	niche						Nanjing bowuyuan 1991
49	PM 360	Pengshan	middle or late Eastern Han	II	niche		table				Nanjing bowuyuan 1991

APPENDIX 3

No.	Name	Place	Date	Type	Furnishings	Burial Instrument	Grave Goods Pottery	Grave Goods Bronzes	Grave Goods Ceramics	Tomb Decoration	Source
50	PM 364	Pengshan	middle or late Eastern Han	II	niche	stone coffin	*zeng*, table, ear cup, figurine	animal			Nanjing bowuyuan 1991
51	PM 601	Pengshan	middle or late Eastern Han	II	niche		*guan, fu, zeng, wan*, well, paddy field, pavilion, roof, animal, figurine	part of sword			Nanjing bowuyuan 1991
52	PM 661	Pengshan	middle or late Eastern Han	II	niche	stone coffin, wooden coffin	well, pavilion paddy field, animal, *guan, wan*, table, ear cup, *bo*, figurine				Nanjing bowuyuan 1991
53	PM 130	Pengshan	middle or late Eastern Han	II			*wan*, figurine				Nanjing bowuyuan 1991
54	PM 168	Pengshan	middle or late Eastern Han	II			*wan*, figurine			carvings on lintel	Nanjing bowuyuan 1991
55	PM 169	Pengshan	middle or late Eastern Han	II			*wan*, horse, figurine	hair pin		carvings on lintel	Nanjing bowuyuan 1991
56	PM 501	Pengshan	middle or late Eastern Han	II			*guan, zeng, wan*, well, chicken, figurine				Nanjing bowuyuan 1991
57	PM 530	Pengshan	middle or late Eastern Han	II							Nanjing bowuyuan 1991
58	PM 560	Pengshan	middle or late Eastern Han	II			figurine	money tree			Nanjing bowuyuan 1991
59	PM 176	Pengshan	middle or late Eastern Han	II	stove, niche, drainage	pottery coffin	table, *bo*, paddy field, chicken, figurine	money tree		carvings on lintel	Nanjing bowuyuan 1991
60	PM 365	Pengshan	middle or late Eastern Han	II			table, *bo*, pond, house, roof, chicken			brick with stripe pattern	Nanjing bowuyuan 1991
61	PM 900	Pengshan	middle or late Eastern Han	II		pottery coffin, wooden coffin	*fu*, table, ear cup, *bo*, figurine	bubble, peache-shaped piece, petal, chariot fittings			Nanjing bowuyuan 1991
62	PM 550	Pengshan	middle or late Eastern Han	II		wooden coffin	*guan, zeng, wan*, house, roof, animal, figurine	chariot fittings		carvings on lintel	Nanjing bowuyuan 1991
63	PM 669	Pengshan	middle or late Eastern Han	II		pottery coffin	figurine				Nanjing bowuyuan 1991
64	PM 45	Pengshan	Eastern Han		stove		*guan*, well, animal, figurine			carvings on lintel	Nanjing bowuyuan 1991
65	PM 171	Pengshan	Eastern Han								Nanjing bowuyuan 1991
66	PM 363	Pengshan	Eastern Han								Nanjing bowuyuan 1991
67	PM 370	Pengshan	Eastern Han				table, ear cup, figurine				Nanjing bowuyuan 1991
68	PM 480	Pengshan	Eastern Han				paddy field, figurine				Nanjing bowuyuan 1991
69	PM 505	Pengshan	Eastern Han				*bo*, figurine				Nanjing bowuyuan 1991
70	PM 515	Pengshan	Eastern Han							brick with stripe pattern	Nanjing bowuyuan 1991
71	PM 600	Pengshan	Eastern Han								Nanjing bowuyuan 1991
72	PM 668	Pengshan	Eastern Han								Nanjing bowuyuan 1991
73	PM 679	Pengshan	Eastern Han								Nanjing bowuyuan 1991
74	PM 680	Pengshan	Eastern Han								Nanjing bowuyuan 1991
75	PM 690	Pengshan	Eastern Han								Nanjing bowuyuan 1991
76	PM 700	Pengshan	Eastern Han				figurine				Nanjing bowuyuan 1991
77	PM 710	Pengshan	Eastern Han				*wan*				Nanjing bowuyuan 1991
78	PM 930	Pengshan	Eastern Han								Nanjing bowuyuan 1991
79	PM 150	Pengshan	Eastern Han								Nanjing bowuyuan 1991
80	PM 151	Pengshan	Eastern Han								Nanjing bowuyuan 1991
81	PM 162	Pengshan	Eastern Han								Nanjing bowuyuan 1991

No.	Name	Place	Date	Type	Furnishings	Burial Instrument	Grave Goods Pottery	Grave Goods Bronzes	Ceramics	Tomb Decoration	Source
82	PM 163	Pengshan	Eastern Han								Nanjing bowuyuan 1991
83	PM 165	Pengshan	Eastern Han								Nanjing bowuyuan 1991
84	PM 172	Pengshan	Eastern Han								Nanjing bowuyuan 1991
85	PM 173	Pengshan	Eastern Han								Nanjing bowuyuan 1991
86	PM 174	Pengshan	Eastern Han							carvings on lintel	Nanjing bowuyuan 1991
87	PM 175	Pengshan	Eastern Han							carvings on lintel	Nanjing bowuyuan 1991
88	PM 177	Pengshan	Eastern Han								Nanjing bowuyuan 1991
89	PM 366	Pengshan	Eastern Han							carvings on lintel	Nanjing bowuyuan 1991
90	PM 367	Pengshan	Eastern Han								Nanjing bowuyuan 1991
91	PM 368	Pengshan	Eastern Han								Nanjing bowuyuan 1991
92	PM 549	Pengshan	Eastern Han								Nanjing bowuyuan 1991
93	PM 654	Pengshan	Eastern Han								Nanjing bowuyuan 1991
94	PM 678	Pengshan	Eastern Han								Nanjing bowuyuan 1991
95	PM 662	Pengshan	Eastern Han								Nanjing bowuyuan 1991
96	PM 701	Pengshan	Eastern Han								Nanjing bowuyuan 1991
97	PM 951	Pengshan	Eastern Han								Nanjing bowuyuan 1991
98	PM 965	Pengshan	Eastern Han								Nanjing bowuyuan 1991
99	Jizhaodong B	Pengshan	Eastern Han								Nanjing bowuyuan 1991
100	Jizhaodong C	Pengshan	Eastern Han								Nanjing bowuyuan 1991
101	Dawanzui M1	Leshan	late Eastern Han	I	drainage						Huang Xueqian, Yang Yi and Hu Xueyuan 1991
102	Dawanzui M2	Leshan	late Eastern Han	I	stove						Huang Xueqian, Yang Yi and Hu Xueyuan 1991
103	Dawanzui M3	Leshan	late Eastern Han	I							Huang Xueqian, Yang Yi and Hu Xueyuan 1991
104	Dawanzui M4	Leshan	late Eastern Han	I	niche, stove	stone coffin, pottery coffin with tenon and mortise					Huang Xueqian, Yang Yi and Hu Xueyuan 1991
105	Dawanzui M5	Leshan	late Eastern Han	I	stove	pottery coffin with tenon and mortise					Huang Xueqian, Yang Yi and Hu Xueyuan 1991
106	Dawanzui M6	Leshan	late Eastern Han	I	stove						Huang Xueqian, Yang Yi and Hu Xueyuan 1991
107	Dawanzui M7	Leshan	late Eastern Han	I							Huang Xueqian, Yang Yi and Hu Xueyuan 1991
108	Dawanzui M8	Leshan	late Eastern Han	I			figurine, Queen Mother of the West (lamp), house, well, animal, mirror, dou, hu, zeng	mirror, bird			Huang Xueqian, Yang Yi and Hu Xueyuan 1991
109	Dawanzui M9	Leshan	late Eastern Han	I	stove						Huang Xueqian, Yang Yi and Hu Xueyuan 1991
110	Dawanzui M10	Leshan	late Eastern Han	I							Huang Xueqian, Yang Yi and Hu Xueyuan 1991
111	Dawanzui M11	Leshan	late Eastern Han	I	stove						Huang Xueqian, Yang Yi and Hu Xueyuan 1991
112	Dawanzui M12	Leshan	late Eastern Han	I							Huang Xueqian, Yang Yi and Hu Xueyuan 1991
113	Dawanzui M13	Leshan	late Eastern Han	I							Huang Xueqian, Yang Yi and Hu Xueyuan 1991
114	Dawanzui M14	Leshan	late Eastern Han	I							Huang Xueqian, Yang Yi and Hu Xueyuan 1991
115	Dawanzui M15	Leshan	late Eastern Han	I							Huang Xueqian, Yang Yi and Hu Xueyuan 1991
116	Dawanzui M16	Leshan	late Eastern Han	I							Huang Xueqian, Yang Yi and Hu Xueyuan 1991

APPENDIX 3

No.	Name	Place	Date	Type	Furnishings	Burial Instrument	Grave Goods			Tomb Decoration	Source
							Pottery	Bronzes	Ceramics		
117	Mahao M1	Leshan	late Eastern Han to Shuhan	IV	drainage, stove, niche	wall-attached stone coffin				carvings on wall and lintel	Huang Xueqian, Yang Yi and Hu Xueyuan 1991
118	Tuozuigou M	Leshan	Eastern Han	I	stove	house-shaped stone coffin	figurine	money tree		carvings on wall and stone coffin	Hu Xueyuan and Yang Yi 1993
119	Gaosuntian M1	Leshan	Eastern Han	II	niche	pottery coffin, wall-attached stone coffin	Queen Mother of the West, figurine, house, animal	money tree			Hu Xueyuan 1988
120	Gaosuntian M2	Leshan	Eastern Han	II	stove	pottery coffin					Hu Xueyuan 1988
121	96MBM1	Mianyang	early to middle Eastern Han	II	niche, stove	platform	ear cup, figurine, *guan*, *bo*	mirror			Tang Guangxiao 2003
122	96MBM2	Mianyang	early to middle Eastern Han	II	stove	platform	figurine, house, paddy field, *guan*, *fu*, *bo*				Tang Guangxiao 2003
123	96MBM3	Mianyang	early Eastern Han (AD 85)	I	stove	platform	figurine, house, paddy field, *guan*, *fu*, *bo*, chicken	mirror, ear cup			Tang Guangxiao 2003
124	96MBM4	Mianyang	early to middle Eastern Han	I			*fu*, *bo*				Tang Guangxiao 2003
125	96MBM5	Mianyang	early to middle Eastern Han	I			*guan*, *fu*, figurine, animal, house	pipe			Tang Guangxiao 2003
126	96MBM6	Mianyang	early to middle Eastern Han	I			*guan*, *pan*, *zeng*, *dou*, *fu*, animal, house, paddy field				Tang Guangxiao 2003
127	HM1	Mianyang	late Eastern Han	II		pottery coffin	*hu*, *fu*, *guan*, figurine, animal, paddy field, table	money tree, mirror, table, applique			He Zhiguo 1991c
128	HM2	Mianyang	late Eastern Han	I		platform	figurine, animal, house, stove, granary, lamp, *guan*, *fu*, pottery	horse, money tree		brick with stripe pattern	He Zhiguo 1991b
129	Wujia M1	Mianyang	Eastern Han	I			figurine				Ji Bing 1994
130	Wujia M2	Mianyang	Eastern Han	I			figurine, chicken, *guan*, *bo*, *hu*				Ji Bing 1994
131	Yangjiazhen M1	Mianyang	middle Eastern Han	I		brick coffin	figurine, *guan*, *fu*				He Zhiguo 1988b
132	Yangjiazhen M2	Mianyang	middle Eastern Han	I			figurine, animal				He Zhiguo 1988b
133	Jinzhongshan I M1	Santai	late Eastern Han	II	pillar					stone carvings on wall	Sichuan sheng wenwu kaogu yanjiuyuan, Mianyang shi bowuguan and Santai xian wenwu guanli suo 2007
134	Jinzhongshan I M2	Santai	late Eastern Han	II	pillar, stove					stone carvings on wall	Sichuan sheng wenwu kaogu yanjiuyuan, Mianyang shi bowuguan and Santai xian wenwu guanli suo 2007
135	Jinzhongshan I M3	Santai	late Eastern Han	III	pillar, stove		*guan*, figurine, animal, house			stone carvings on wall, brick with stripe pattern	Sichuan sheng wenwu kaogu yanjiuyuan, Mianyang shi bowuguan and Santai xian wenwu guanli suo 2007
136	Jin I M4	Santai	late Eastern Han	II	pillar, toilet, stove, stable, niche	stone coffin				stone carvings on wall	Sichuan sheng wenwu kaogu yanjiuyuan, Mianyang shi bowuguan and Santai xian wenwu guanli suo 2007
137	Jinzhongshan II M1	Santai	late Eastern Han	II	stove, pillar		figurine			carvings on wall	Sichuan sheng wenwu kaogu yanjiuyuan, Mianyang shi bowuguan and Santai xian wenwu guanli suo 2007

Eastern Han (AD 25-220) Tombs in Sichuan

No.	Name	Place	Date	Type	Furnishings	Burial Instrument	Grave Goods			Tomb Decoration	Source
							Pottery	Bronzes	Ceramics		
138	Jinzhongshan II M2	Santai	late Eastern Han	II	pillar, stove	stone coffin	bo, pan, figurine, dog	figurine		brick with stripe pattern, pictorial stone coffin, carvings on wall	Sichuan sheng wenwu kaogu yanjiuyuan, Mianyang shi bowuguan and Santai xian wenwu guanli suo 2007
139	Jinzhongshan II M3	Santai	late Eastern Han	II	stove		bo, pottery, figurine, chicken			brick with stripe pattern	Sichuan sheng wenwu kaogu yanjiuyuan, Mianyang shi bowuguan and Santai xian wenwu guanli suo 2007
140	Jinzhongshan II M4	Santai	late Eastern Han	II	niche		guan, weng, hu, plate, figurine	money tree, mirror, chariot fittings		brick with stripe pattern	Sichuan sheng wenwu kaogu yanjiuyuan, Mianyang shi bowuguan and Santai xian wenwu guanli suo 2007
141	Jinzhongshan II M5	Santai	late Eastern Han	II	pillar	house-shaped stone coffin	wan, figurine			carvings on wall	Sichuan sheng wenwu kaogu yanjiuyuan, Mianyang shi bowuguan and Santai xian wenwu guanli suo 2007
142	Tiantaishan M1	Santai	late Eastern Han	II	pillar, stove	niche-shaped coffin	wan, figurine, horse			carvings on wall and coffin, brick with stripe pattern	Sichuan sheng wenwu kaogu yanjiuyuan, Mianyang shi bowuguan and Santai xian wenwu guanli suo 2007
143	Zijingwan M1	Santai	late Eastern Han	II			bird			carvings on wall	Sichuan sheng wenwu kaogu yanjiuyuan, Mianyang shi bowuguan and Santai xian wenwu guanli suo 2007
144	Zijingwan M2	Santai	late Eastern Han	III	drainage, stove		guan, pen, table		cup	brick with stripe pattern	Sichuan sheng wenwu kaogu yanjiuyuan, Mianyang shi bowuguan and Santai xian wenwu guanli suo 2007
145	Zijingwan M3	Santai	late Eastern Han	III	pillar, stove		guan, pottery, figurine, animal		wan, lamp, cup	carvings on wall	Sichuan sheng wenwu kaogu yanjiuyuan, Mianyang shi bowuguan and Santai xian wenwu guanli suo 2007
146	Zijingwan M4	Santai	late Eastern Han	II	platform	stone coffin	dog	money tree		brick with stripe pattern	Sichuan sheng wenwu kaogu yanjiuyuan, Mianyang shi bowuguan and Santai xian wenwu guanli suo 2007
147	Zijingwan M5	Santai	middle Eastern Han	II	stove, pillar, niche	pottery coffin, brick coffin	guan, pen, bo, fu, cover, pottery, chariot fittings, cup, chariot fittings, figurine, animal	money tree, pipe		carvings on wall, brick with stripe pattern	Sichuan sheng wenwu kaogu yanjiuyuan, Mianyang shi bowuguan and Santai xian wenwu guanli suo 2007
148	Zijingwan M6	Santai	middle Eastern Han	II		stone coffin	weng, animal, figurine				Sichuan sheng wenwu kaogu yanjiuyuan, Mianyang shi bowuguan and Santai xian wenwu guanli suo 2007
149	Zijingwan M7	Santai	late Eastern Han	II	stove	pottery coffin	guan, pen, cup, lamp, table, chariot fittings, figurine, animal	money tree		carvings on wall, brick with stripe pattern	Sichuan sheng wenwu kaogu yanjiuyuan, Mianyang shi bowuguan and Santai xian wenwu guanli suo 2007
150	Zijingwan M8	Santai	late Eastern Han		stove	niche-shaped coffin, house-shaped coffin	cup, guan, dog			carvings on coffin	Sichuan sheng wenwu kaogu yanjiuyuan, Mianyang shi bowuguan and Santai xian wenwu guanli suo 2007

APPENDIX 3

No.	Name	Place	Date	Type	Furnishings	Burial Instrument	Grave Goods Pottery	Bronzes	Ceramics	Tomb Decoration	Source
151	Zijingwan M9	Santai									Sichuan sheng wenwu kaogu yanjiuyuan, Mianyang shi bowuguan and Santai xian wenwu guanli suo 2007
152	Zijingwan M10	Santai	late Eastern Han	III	stove, niche		figurine			brick with stripe pattern	Sichuan sheng wenwu kaogu yanjiuyuan, Mianyang shi bowuguan and Santai xian wenwu guanli suo 2007
153	Zijingwan M11	Santai	middle Eastern Han	III	niche, drainage		*guan*, figurine				Sichuan sheng wenwu kaogu yanjiuyuan, Mianyang shi bowuguan and Santai xian wenwu guanli suo 2007
154	Zijingwan M12	Santai	early Eastern Han	III		niche-shaped coffin	*guan, bo, weng, pen*, cover, box, *ding, hu*, well, pig			carvings on wall	Sichuan sheng wenwu kaogu yanjiuyuan, Mianyang shi bowuguan and Santai xian wenwu guanli suo 2007
155	Zijingwan M13	Santai	late Eastern Han	II	stove		*bo, guan, hu, pen*, lamp, cup, house, figurine, animal				Sichuan sheng wenwu kaogu yanjiuyuan, Mianyang shi bowuguan and Santai xian wenwu guanli suo 2007
156	Zijingwan M14	Santai	late Eastern Han	III	stove		*guan, bo*, cup			carvings on wall	Sichuan sheng wenwu kaogu yanjiuyuan, Mianyang shi bowuguan and Santai xian wenwu guanli suo 2007
157	Wujiawan M1	Santai	late Eastern Han	II			*guan, bo*			carvings on wall	Sichuan sheng wenwu kaogu yanjiuyuan, Mianyang shi bowuguan and Santai xian wenwu guanli suo 2007
158	Songlinzui M1	Santai	late Eastern Han	II	stove		*guan*, cover			carvings on wall	Sichuan sheng wenwu kaogu yanjiuyuan, Mianyang shi bowuguan and Santai xian wenwu guanli suo 2007
159	Bailinpo M1	Santai	middle Eastern Han (AD 117)	II	drainage, stove, pillar		*guan, weng, pen, zeng, bo*, lamp, table, handle, figurine, animal, house	chariot fittings		carvings on wall, brick with stripe pattern	Sichuan sheng wenwu kaogu yanjiuyuan, Mianyang shi bowuguan and Santai xian wenwu guanli suo 2007
160	Bailinpo M2	Santai	late Eastern Han	II	stable, stove	niche-shaped coffin	*guan, weng, zeng, bo*, cup, plate, table, figurine, horse, pond, house				Sichuan sheng wenwu kaogu yanjiuyuan, Mianyang shi bowuguan and Santai xian wenwu guanli suo 2007
161	Bailinpo M3	Santai								bricks with stripe pattern	Sichuan sheng wenwu kaogu yanjiuyuan, Mianyang shi bowuguan and Santai xian wenwu guanli suo 2007
162	Bailinpo M4	Santai	early Eastern Han	II	pillar		*ding, zeng, pen*, box	chariot fittings			Sichuan sheng wenwu kaogu yanjiuyuan, Mianyang shi bowuguan and Santai xian wenwu guanli suo 2007
163	Bailinpo M5	Santai	late Eastern Han	II	pillar, stove	house-shaped stone coffin	*weng*, figurine, chariot fittings		*wan, guan*, dish	carvings on wall and coffin, bircks with stripe pattern	Sichuan sheng wenwu kaogu yanjiuyuan, Mianyang shi bowuguan and Santai xian wenwu guanli suo 2007

Eastern Han (AD 25-220) Tombs in Sichuan

No.	Name	Place	Date	Type	Furnishings	Burial Instrument	Grave Goods - Pottery	Grave Goods - Bronzes	Grave Goods - Ceramics	Tomb Decoration	Source
164	Fentaizui M1	Santai	late Eastern Han	II	pillar, stove	niche-shaped coffin				carvings on wall	Sichuan sheng wenwu kaogu yanjiuyuan, Mianyang shi bowuguan and Santai xian wenwu guanli suo 2007
165	Hujiawan M1	Santai	early Eastern Han	II	pillar	house-shaped stone coffin	ding, guan, pen, bo, cover	ear cup		carvings on wall	Sichuan sheng wenwu kaogu yanjiuyuan, Mianyang shi bowuguan and Santai xian wenwu guanli suo 2007
166	Liujiayan M1	Santai	late Eastern Han	II	niche, stove	pottery coffin	guan, pan			brick with stripe pattern	Sichuan sheng wenwu kaogu yanjiuyuan, Mianyang shi bowuguan and Santai xian wenwu guanli suo 2007
167	Liujiayan M3	Santai	late Eastern Han	II	niche, stove, stone bed	niche-shaped coffin					Sichuan sheng wenwu kaogu yanjiuyuan, Mianyang shi bowuguan and Santai xian wenwu guanli suo 2007
168	Huangmingyue M1	Santai	late Eastern Han	II	niche, stove	niche-shaped coffin				carvings on wall	Sichuan sheng wenwu kaogu yanjiuyuan, Mianyang shi bowuguan and Santai xian wenwu guanli suo 2007; Zhong Zhi 2008
169	Dongzipai M1	Santai	middle Eastern Han	III	stove	house-shaped stone coffin				carvings on wall and coffin	Sichuan sheng wenwu kaogu yanjiuyuan, Mianyang shi bowuguan and Santai xian wenwu guanli suo 2007
170	Qingshanchang M1	Santai	Eastern Han	II		brick coffin	zhong, fu, zeng, ang, zhan, guan, pan, bo, dou, lamp, house, animal, figurine	ring, weapon, mirror		brick with stripe pattern, carvings on wall	Yang Chonghua 1992
171	Yongandianchang M 1	Santai	Eastern Han			brick coffin	guan, animal, figurine	xi, mirror, hu, bird, money tree			Santai xian wenhuaguan 1976
172	Yuanbaoshan M	Santai	middle or late Eastern Han	II	pillar, stove					carvings on wall	Jing Zhuyou 1997
173	Yuanbaoshan M1	Santai	middle or late Eastern Han	II	pillar, stove					carvings on wall	Jing Zhuyou 1997
174	Shenxiandong M 1	Santai	middle or late Eastern Han	II	niche, pillar	platform	figurine, animal, house, granary, fu, hu, zeng, guan, wan, pan, ink stone	hu, guan, wan	bracelet, hairpin, chopsticks, handle		Jing Zhuyou 1997
175	Shenxiandong M 2	Santai	middle or late Eastern Han	II	niche, pillar	platform					Jing Zhuyou 1997
176	Shufangliang M3	Santai	late Eastern Han	I		wooden coffin on brick platform				brick with stripe pattern	Jing Zhuyou 1997
177	Shufangliang M6	Santai	late Eastern Han	I						carvings on wall	Jing Zhuyou 1997
178	Changliangzi M	Santai	late Eastern Han	I					relics	brick with stripe pattern	Jing Zhuyou 1997
179	Xinde M	Santai	middle Eastern Han	I	niche	platform	figurine, lamp	money tree			Jing Zhuyou 1993

APPENDIX 3

No.	Name	Place	Date	Type	Furnishings	Burial Instrument	Grave Goods Pottery	Bronzes	Ceramics	Tomb Decoration	Source
180	Taliangzi M1	Zhongjiang	middle Eastern Han	II	niche, stove	stone coffin, niche-shaped stone coffin	*guan, weng, zeng, wan, pan,* table, figurine, chicken	nail, money tree, gilded piece		carvings on coffin	Sichuan sheng wenwu kaogu yanjiuyuan, Deyang shi wenwu kaogu yanjiusuo and Zhongjiang xian wenwu baohu guanli suo 2008
181	Taliangzi M2	Zhongjiang	middle Eastern Han	II	niche		*guan, wan,* figurine, horse	relics		carvings on wall	Sichuan sheng wenwu kaogu yanjiuyuan, Deyang shi wenwu kaogu yanjiusuo and Zhongjiang xian wenwu baohu guanli suo 2008
182	Taliangzi M3	Zhongjiang	late Eastern Han	II	basin, niche	house-shaped stone coffin, niche-shaped coffin	*guan, zeng, bo, pan, pen,* cup, *dou,* lamp, figurine	money tree, relics		carvings on wall (featuring coloured mural with ink inscription) and coffin	Sichuan sheng wenwu kaogu yanjiuyuan, Deyang shi wenwu kaogu yanjiusuo and Zhongjiang xian wenwu baohu guanli suo 2008
183	Taliangzi M4	Zhongjiang	middle Eastern Han	II	niche, stove	stone coffin, niche-shaped coffin		relics			Sichuan sheng wenwu kaogu yanjiuyuan, Deyang shi wenwu kaogu yanjiusuo and Zhongjiang xian wenwu baohu guanli suo 2008
184	Taliangzi M5	Zhongjiang	middle Eastern Han	II	stove	niche-shaped coffin		relics			Sichuan sheng wenwu kaogu yanjiuyuan, Deyang shi wenwu kaogu yanjiusuo and Zhongjiang xian wenwu baohu guanli suo 2008
185	Taliangzi M6	Zhongjiang	late Eastern Han	II	niche	niche-shaped coffin	*guan, yu, pan,* cup, figurine	relics		carvings on wall and coffin	Sichuan sheng wenwu kaogu yanjiuyuan, Deyang shi wenwu kaogu yanjiusuo and Zhongjiang xian wenwu baohu guanli suo 2008
186	Taliangzi M7	Zhongjiang	late Eastern Han	II	basin	niche-shaped coffin	*guan, zeng,* paddy field, figurine, animal			carvings on coffin	Sichuan sheng wenwu kaogu yanjiuyuan, Deyang shi wenwu kaogu yanjiusuo and Zhongjiang xian wenwu baohu guanli suo 2008
187	Taliangzi M8	Zhongjiang	late Eastern Han	II		platform	*guan, bo, pan, pen,* figurine, animal, house			carvings on coffin	Sichuan sheng wenwu kaogu yanjiuyuan, Deyang shi wenwu kaogu yanjiusuo and Zhongjiang xian wenwu baohu guanli suo 2008
188	Taliangzi M9	Zhongjiang	late Eastern Han	II	niche						Sichuan sheng wenwu kaogu yanjiuyuan, Deyang shi wenwu kaogu yanjiusuo and Zhongjiang xian wenwu baohu guanli suo 2008
189	Tianpingliangzi M1	Zhongjiang	Eastern Han	II	stove, niche	platform				carvings on platform and wall	Wang Qipeng and Wang Kongzhi 1989
190	Shahe M1	Jiangjin	Eastern Han	I							Huang Zhongyou and Zhang Ronghua 1994

Eastern Han (AD 25-220) Tombs in Sichuan

No.	Name	Place	Date	Type	Furnishings	Burial Instrument	Pottery	Bronzes	Ceramics	Tomb Decoration	Source
191	Shahe M2	Jiangjin	Eastern Han	I							Huang Zhongyou and Zhang Ronghua 1994
192	Shahe M3	Jiangjin	Eastern Han	I						carvings on wall	Huang Zhongyou and Zhang Ronghua 1994
193	Chuanshanpo M5	Suining	Eastern Han	I	drainage	pottery coffin	figurine, dog			brick with stripe pattern	Zhuang Wenbin 1994
194	Chuanshanpo M1	Suining	middle Eastern Han	II			guan, weng, bo, he, fu, he, well, figurine, animal	pen, bo, fu, hook			Zhang Caijun 1983
195	Chuanshanpo M2	Suining	middle Eastern Han	II			bo				Zhang Caijun 1983
196	Bijiashan M2	Suining	middle late Eastern Han	I	drainage						Sichuan sheng bowuguan 1985c
197	Bijiashan M3	Suining	middle late Eastern Han	I	drainage		figurine, chicken, dog, guan, lian, fu, ear cup, lamp, bird,				Sichuan sheng bowuguan 1985c
198	Bijiashan M4	Suining	middle to late Eastern Han	I	drainage		figurine, table				Sichuan sheng bowuguan 1985c
199	Bijiashan M5	Suining	middle to late Eastern Han	I	drainage		figurine, pig, bo				Sichuan sheng bowuguan 1985c
200	Bijiashan M6	Suining	middle to late Eastern Han	I	drainage		guan, well, pottery, spoon	hook			Sichuan sheng bowuguan 1985c
201	Bijiashan M1	Suining	middle to late Eastern Han	I	drainage	brick coffin	figurine, guan, hu, wan, cover			brick with stripe pattern	Sichuan sheng bowuguan 1985c
202	Baozishan M	Xinjin	late Eastern Han	II	drainage, niche	pottery coffin	jian, lei, hu, yong, guan, ding, fu, xi, pen, bo, gang, zeng, yu, wan, ear cup, pan, table, figurine, animal, house, pond, paddy field, well		vessel		Lu Deliang 1958
203	HHM6	Yibin	Eastern Han	III							Sichuan daxue lishi xi qiba ji kaogu shixi dui deng 1984
204	HHM7	Yibin	Eastern Han								Sichuan daxue lishi xi qiba ji kaogu shixi dui deng 1984
205	HHM11	Yibin	Eastern Han			stone coffin				carvings on wall	Sichuan daxue lishi xi qiba ji kaogu shixi dui deng 1984
206	HY I M1	Yibin	Eastern Han		pillar, niche, stove	stone coffin				carvings on wall	Sichuan daxue lishi xi qiba ji kaogu shixi dui deng 1984
207	HZM29	Yibin	Eastern Han								Sichuan daxue lishi xi qiba ji kaogu shixi dui deng 1984
208	HZM34	Yibin	Eastern Han								Sichuan daxue lishi xi qiba ji kaogu shixi dui deng 1984
209	HY I M4	Yibin	Eastern Han	I	niche, stove						Sichuan daxue lishi xi qiba ji kaogu shixi dui deng 1984
210	HY I M23	Yibin	Eastern Han	I	niche, stove		figurine	money tree			Sichuan daxue lishi xi qiba ji kaogu shixi dui deng 1984
211	HZ M29	Yibin	Eastern Han	I	niche, stove	stone coffin					Sichuan daxue lishi xi qiba ji kaogu shixi dui deng 1984
212	HZ M34	Yibin	Eastern Han	I	niche, stove						Sichuan daxue lishi xi qiba ji kaogu shixi dui deng 1984
213	HZ M6	Yibin	Eastern Han	I	niche, stove						Sichuan daxue lishi xi qiba ji kaogu shixi dui deng 1984
214	HZ M5	Yibin	Eastern Han	I	niche, stove	stone coffin, pottery coffin					Sichuan daxue lishi xi qiba ji kaogu shixi dui deng 1984

APPENDIX 3

No.	Name	Place	Date	Type	Furnishings	Burial Instrument	Grave Goods Pottery	Grave Goods Bronzes	Ceramics	Tomb Decoration	Source
215	HZ M9	Yibin	Eastern Han	I	niche, stove						Sichuan daxue lishi xi qiba ji kaogu shixi dui deng 1984
216	HZ M22	Yibin	Eastern Han	I	niche, stove						Sichuan daxue lishi xi qiba ji kaogu shixi dui deng 1984
217	HH M3	Yibin	Eastern Han	I	niche, stove						Sichuan daxue lishi xi qiba ji kaogu shixi dui deng 1984
218	HH M5	Yibin	Eastern Han	I	niche, stove	stone coffin					Sichuan daxue lishi xi qiba ji kaogu shixi dui deng 1984
219	HY M6 II	Yibin	Eastern Han	I	niche, stove						Sichuan daxue lishi xi qiba ji kaogu shixi dui deng 1984
220	93ZWM5	Yibin	early Eastern Han	I	niche	stone coffin	*guan, ding, zeng,* lamp, cover				Wang Chaowei 2003
221	Shanguci M3	Yibin	late Eastern Han	I	stove	platform	figurine, house, chicken				Sichuan sheng bowuguan 1985b
222	Shanguci M2	Yibin	late Eastern Han	I	niche, stove	platform					Sichuan sheng bowuguan 1985b
223	Shanguci M1	Yibin	late Eastern Han	I	drainage, stove, niche	stone coffin	Queen Mother of the West, figurine, house, *wan*	money tree			Sichuan sheng bowuguan 1985b
224	98YHYM1	Yibin	late Eastern Han	I	drainage, stove, niche		*fuzeng,* turtle, dog				Wang Chaowei 2003
225	98YHYM3	Yibin	late Eastern Han	I							Huang Jiaxiang and Wang Chaowei 2003
226	98YHYM5	Yibin	late Eastern Han	I	drainage, niche		*guan, bo, fu, hu,* ear cup, lamp, well, boat, pond, animal, house, figurine	chariot fittings			Huang Jiaxiang and Wang Chaowei 2003
227	98YHYM6	Yibin	late Eastern Han	I	stove		*guan, wan, pen, bo, fu, zeng, pan,* ear cup, cover, stove, animal, house, figurine	ring, applique, measure, chopsticks			Huang Jiaxiang and Wang Chaowei 2003
228	81GM6	Yingjing	early to middle Eastern Han	I	niche	platform	*guan, weng, fu, zeng, wan,* table, *bo,* floodgate, animal, figurine				Sichuan sheng weguanhui 1985
229	81GM7	Yingjing	early to middle Eastern Han	I	niche	platform	*bo, zeng*				Sichuan sheng weguanhui 1985
230	81GM8	Yingjing	early to middle Eastern Han	I	niche	platform	*guan, fu*				Sichuan sheng weguanhui 1985
231	81GM9	Yingjing	early to middle Eastern Han	I	niche, drainage	platform	figurine, chicken, *zeng*			brick with stripe pattern	Sichuan sheng weguanhui 1985
232	81GM10	Yingjing	early to middle Eastern Han	I	niche, drainage	platform	*zeng*				Sichuan sheng weguanhui 1985
233	F. H. YM1	Fuling	late Eastern Han	I	niche		figurine, animal, *wan, pan,* ear cup, cover		*guan, bo*		Hu Changyu and Huang Jiaxiang 1984
234	Jiaoshan M1	Jintang	Eastern Han	I			*guan*	*fu, xi,* bow			Guo Lizhong 1959
235	Jiaoshan M2	Jintang	Eastern Han	I			animal, house, *zhong, guan, bo,* figurine	*dui*			Guo Lizhong 1959
236	Weijiachong M	Neijiang	Eastern Han	I			*guan, bo*			brick with stripe pattern	Guo Lizhong 1959
237	Zhangjiagou M2	Hejiang	Eastern Han	I		stone coffin				carvings on stone coffin	Wang Tingfu and Li Yihong 1995
238	04BQQM1	Baoxing	late Eastern Han	II	stove, niche	platform					Lei Yu 2006
239	Yanting M	Yanting	late Eastern Han	I	niche, platform	stone coffin	lamp, figurine, *guan*	seal, *fu, pan, xi,* hook			Liu Zhiyuan 1974

Eastern Han (AD 25-220) Tombs in Sichuan

No.	Name	Place	Date	Type	Furnishings	Burial Instrument	Grave Goods Pottery	Bronzes	Ceramics	Tomb Decoration	Source
240	99W SM1	Wusheng	Eastern Han	I			figurine, animal, vessel, incense burner, table, paddy field			brick with stripe pattern	Sichuan sheng wenwu kaogu yanjiuyuan, Guang'an shi wenwu guanlisuo, Wusheng xian wenhua tiyuju and Wusheng xian wenwu guanlisuo 2010
241	99W SM2	Wusheng	Eastern Han	I			figurine, animal, vessel, incense burner, table, house, paddy field			brick with stripe pattern	Sichuan sheng wenwu kaogu yanjiuyuan, Guang'an shi wenwu guanlisuo, Wusheng xian wenhua tiyuju and Wusheng xian wenwu guanlisuo 2010
242	99W SM3	Wusheng	Eastern Han	I			vessel			brick with stripe pattern	Sichuan sheng wenwu kaogu yanjiuyuan, Guang'an shi wenwu guanlisuo, Wusheng xian wenhua tiyuju and Wusheng xian wenwu guanlisuo 2010
243	99W SM4	Wusheng	Eastern Han	I			figurine, animal, vessel, paddy field			brick with stripe pattern	Sichuan sheng wenwu kaogu yanjiuyuan, Guang'an shi wenwu guanlisuo, Wusheng xian wenhua tiyuju and Wusheng xian wenwu guanlisuo 2010
244	99W SM5	Wusheng	Eastern Han	I		platform	vessel		*ping*	brick with stripe pattern	Sichuan sheng wenwu kaogu yanjiuyuan, Guang'an shi wenwu guanlisuo, Wusheng xian wenhua tiyuju and Wusheng xian wenwu guanlisuo 2010
245	99W SM6	Wusheng	Eastern Han	I			figurine, animal, vessel, incense burner, house, paddy field			brick with stripe pattern	Sichuan sheng wenwu kaogu yanjiuyuan, Guang'an shi wenwu guanlisuo, Wusheng xian wenhua tiyuju and Wusheng xian wenwu guanlisuo 2010
246	99W SM7	Wusheng	Eastern Han	I	niche					brick with stripe pattern	Sichuan sheng wenwu kaogu yanjiuyuan, Guang'an shi wenwu guanlisuo, Wusheng xian wenhua tiyuju and Wusheng xian wenwu guanlisuo 2010
247	99W SM8	Wusheng	Eastern Han	I			figurine			brick with stripe pattern	Sichuan sheng wenwu kaogu yanjiuyuan, Guang'an shi wenwu guanlisuo, Wusheng xian wenhua tiyuju and Wusheng xian wenwu guanlisuo 2010
248	99W SM9	Wusheng	Eastern Han	I			figurine			brick with stripe pattern	Sichuan sheng wenwu kaogu yanjiuyuan, Guang'an shi wenwu guanlisuo, Wusheng xian wenhua tiyuju and Wusheng xian wenwu guanlisuo 2010
249	99W SM10	Wusheng	Eastern Han	I			figurine, animal, beast, well			brick with stripe pattern	Sichuan sheng wenwu kaogu yanjiuyuan, Guang'an shi wenwu guanlisuo, Wusheng xian wenhua tiyuju and Wusheng xian wenwu guanlisuo 2010

APPENDIX 3

No.	Name	Place	Date	Type	Furnishings	Burial Instrument	Grave Goods Pottery	Grave Goods Bronzes	Grave Goods Ceramics	Tomb Decoration	Source
250	99W SM11	Wusheng	Eastern Han	I						brick with stripe pattern	Sichuan sheng wenwu kaogu yanjiuyuan, Guang'an shi wenwu guanlisuo, Wusheng xian wenhua tiyuju and Wusheng xian wenwu guanlisuo 2010
251	99W SM12	Wusheng	Eastern Han	I			animal, vessel, house, granary		hu	brick with stripe pattern	Sichuan sheng wenwu kaogu yanjiuyuan, Guang'an shi wenwu guanlisuo, Wusheng xian wenhua tiyuju and Wusheng xian wenwu guanlisuo 2010
252	99W SM13	Wusheng	Eastern Han	I			figurine, animal, vessel, table, house, paddy field			brick with stripe pattern	Sichuan sheng wenwu kaogu yanjiuyuan, Guang'an shi wenwu guanlisuo, Wusheng xian wenhua tiyuju and Wusheng xian wenwu guanlisuo 2010
253	99W SM14	Wusheng	Eastern Han	I			animal, vessel			brick with stripe pattern	Sichuan sheng wenwu kaogu yanjiuyuan, Guang'an shi wenwu guanlisuo, Wusheng xian wenhua tiyuju and Wusheng xian wenwu guanlisuo 2010
254	NHYM1	Luzhou	middle or late Eastern Han	I	niche	pottery coffin	figurine, table, vessel	money tree			Sichuan sheng wenwu kaogu yanjiu suo and Luzhou shi bowuguan 2006
255	NHYM2	Luzhou	late Eastern Han	I			vessel, house, figurine	money tree			Sichuan sheng wenwu kaogu yanjiu suo and Luzhou shi bowuguan 2006
256	98JYM1	Jiange	Eastern Han	I	stove	platform					Mo Honggui 2004
257	98JYM2	Jiange	Eastern Han	I		coffin	vessel, figurine				Mo Honggui 2004
258	98JYM3	Jiange	Eastern Han	I	stove	platform					Mo Honggui 2004
259	98JYM4	Jiange	Eastern Han	I	stove	platform					Mo Honggui 2004
260	98JYM5	Jiange	Eastern Han	I							Mo Honggui 2004
261	Qikongzi M1	Neijiang	middle or late Eastern Han	I		stone coffin	chicken, figurine, vessel, house	money tree			Luo Renzhong 1996
262	Qikongzi M2	Neijiang	middle or late Eastern Han	I						pictorial brick	Luo Renzhong 1996
263	Guanshengdian M	Neijiang	middle or late Eastern Han	I		stone coffin	house, vessel, figurine			stone coffin	Lei Jianjin 1992
264	Hongying M2	Neijiang	middle or late Eastern Han	I						brick with stripe pattern	Lei Jianjin and Zeng Jian 1989
265	Hongying M1	Neijiang	middle or late Eastern Han	I	niche, drainage	stone coffin	figurine, vessel, lamp, animal	money tree		stone coffin	Lei Jianjin and Zeng Jian 1989
266	Hualongqiao M	Chongqing	Eastern Han	I			drinking vessel, figurine, animal	money tree, hair pin, applique		brick with stripe pattern	Hu Renchao 1958
267	Nan'an M	Chongqing	middle Eastern Han	II	drainage	platform	incense burner, guan, bo, zeng, table, ear cup, pan, fu, well, house, granary, animal (some are lacquered pottery)	xi, fu			Guo Shude and Wang Xinnan 1987
268	Tujing M15	Zhongxian	Shu Han	II			guan, zeng, bo		dish, wan, guan, hu		Zhang Caijun 1985
269	Tujing M1	Zhongxian	Shu Han	I	niche						Zhang Caijun 1985

Eastern Han (AD 25-220) Tombs in Sichuan

No.	Name	Place	Date	Type	Furnishings	Burial Instrument	Grave Goods Pottery	Grave Goods Bronzes	Grave Goods Ceramics	Tomb Decoration	Source
270	Tujing M2	Zhongxian	Shu Han	I					*wan*, dish, *hu*		Zhang Caijun 1985
271	Tujing M3	Zhongxian	Shu Han	I							Zhang Caijun 1985
272	Tujing M4	Zhongxian	Shu Han	I	drainage						Zhang Caijun 1985
273	Tujing M5	Zhongxian	Shu Han	II	drainage, niche, stove		*guan*, figurine	money tree	*fu, hu, xi, bo*		Zhang Caijun 1985
274	Tujing M6	Zhongxian	Shu Han	II			*guan, fu, zeng, bo*	*wan*, dish, *hu*, *guan*			Zhang Caijun 1985
275	Tujing M7	Zhongxian	Shu Han	II	drainage			money tree, *fu*			Zhang Caijun 1985
276	Tujing M8	Zhongxian	Shu Han	I							Zhang Caijun 1985
277	Tujing M9	Zhongxian	Shu Han	II			*guan*, lamp, house, chicken, figurine, *fu, zeng, pen, wan*		*wan, guan, yu, tan*		Zhang Caijun 1985
278	Tujing M10	Zhongxian	Shu Han	I					*wan*, dish, *hu*	carvings on wall	Zhang Caijun 1985
279	Tujing M11	Zhongxian	Shu Han	II	niche		figurine, dog				Zhang Caijun 1985
280	Tujing M12	Zhongxian	Shu Han	II					*wan*		Zhang Caijun 1985
281	Tujing M13	Zhongxian	Shu Han	II	drainage		*guan*, lamp, well, figurine, *fu, hu, bo*, dish, paddy field, animal	*fu, xi*	*xi*	brick with stripe pattern	Zhang Caijun 1985
282	Tujing M14	Zhongxian	Shu Han	II			*guan*, figurine, paddy field	money tree, *pan, zeng, fu, xi*, chopsticks, horse, figurine, table, ear cup			Zhang Caijun 1985
283	Qigedong M1	Changning	middle Eastern Han	I						carvings on wall	Sichuan daxue lishi xi qiba ji kaogu shixi dui 1985
284	Qigedong M2	Changning	middle Eastern Han	I		stone coffin				carvings on wall	Sichuan daxue lishi xi qiba ji kaogu shixi dui 1985
285	Qigedong M3	Changning	middle Eastern Han	I						carvings on wall	Sichuan daxue lishi xi qiba ji kaogu shixi dui 1985
286	Qigedong M4	Changning	middle Eastern Han	I		stone coffin				carvings on wall and coffin	Sichuan daxue lishi xi qiba ji kaogu shixi dui 1985
287	Qigedong M5	Changning	middle Eastern Han	I						carvings on wall	Sichuan daxue lishi xi qiba ji kaogu shixi dui 1985
288	Qigedong M6	Changning	middle Eastern Han	I		stone coffin				carvings on wall and coffin	Sichuan daxue lishi xi qiba ji kaogu shixi dui 1985
289	Qigedong M7	Changning	middle Eastern Han	I		stone coffin				carvings on wall and coffin	Sichuan daxue lishi xi qiba ji kaogu shixi dui 1985